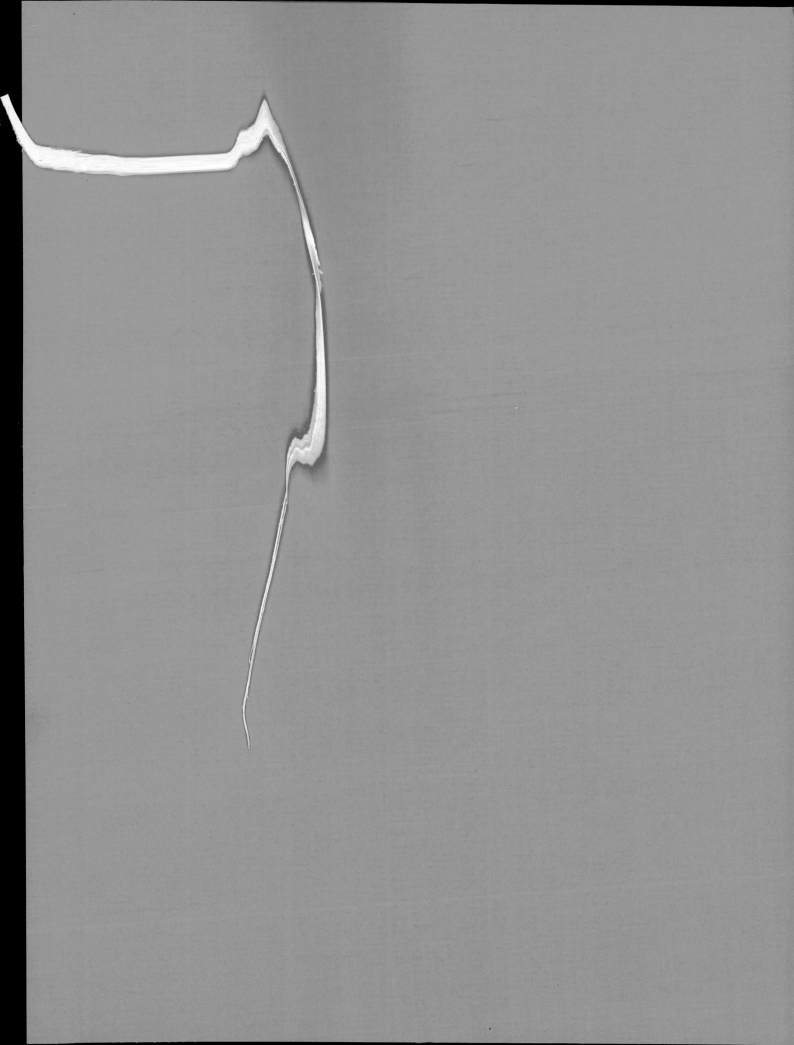

THE COMPLETE BOOK
OF SEWING

The Complete Book of Sewing

LARRY EISINGER: *Consulting Editorial Director*
DOLORES SINI: *Editorial Assistant*

•

LAWRENCE E. MARSH: *Creative Director*
CHARLES A. LEVINE: *Art Editor*

GREYSTONE PRESS • NEW YORK • TORONTO • LONDON

ACKNOWLEDGEMENTS

The publishers wish to thank the following for permission to use certain photographs and written material in this book:

Allied Chemical Corp., American Standard, Bigelow-Sanford, Inc., Bloom-craft, Burlington Industries, Inc., Congoleum Industries, Desley-Edson, Inc., Directional Industries, Inc., General Tire, The House of Kahaner, Monarch Carpet Mills, Royal System, Inc., James Seeman Studios, Inc., Simmons Company, The Singer Company, The Stearns & Foster Company, J. P. Stevens & Co., Inc., 3 M Company, Tile Council of America, Wallcovering Industry Bureau, Waverly Fabrics, Western Wood Products, Westinghouse Electric Corp., Window Shade Manufacturers' Association.

Special thanks to Simplicity Pattern Co., Inc. for all fashion photographs, and to Dan River Inc. for material from "A Dictionary of Textile Terms".

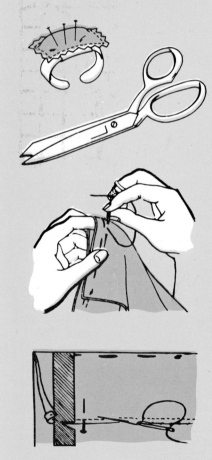

Contents

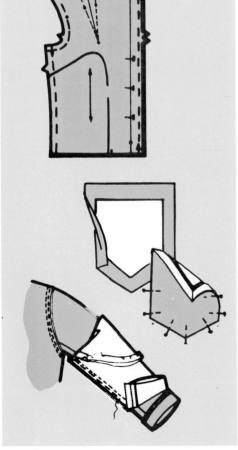

Part IV   SEWING FOR YOUR HOME 191-265

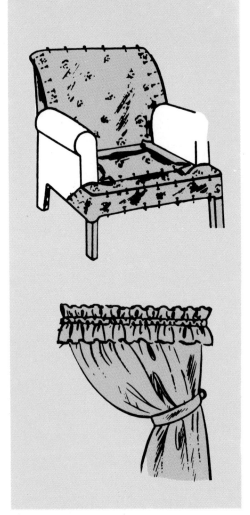

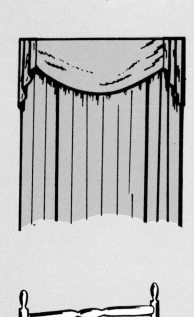

Part I

SEVEN BASIC STEPS TO SEWING SUCCESS

Fitting The Fabric To The Fashion

Above: A softly tailored, ever-so-adaptable costume to make from one of the knitted fabrics or from an equally easy-care woven one.

Opposite: A smashing outfit for parties at home or at friends! Quick-to-sew skirt-pants combination is great in a gorgeous print fabric.

The fabric is one of the most important elements in a garment. Your choice of fabric expresses you—your taste, your style. The way you handle the fabric expresses your skill as a seamstress and your fashion know-how.

Suitability of the fabric to the style of the garment gives your clothes that professional touch. Crisply tailored styles demand firm fabrics to hold shaping and seaming details. Soft, filmy styles need flowing drapable fabrics to form soft pleats and gathers. The most perfectly sewn dress will never look quite right if it is made in the wrong fabric.

How do you know what type of fabric a particular style demands? Looking at well-made clothes in the stores is a good way to tell. Look at the kind of outfit you want to make: what fabric is it made in? Is the fabric firm or soft, heavy or light? Is it lined or underlined to give it extra body?

A quick way to determine the type of fabric a garment requires is to read the list of suggested fabrics on the back of the pattern envelope. If you want to use a fabric other than those suggested, just be sure it is the same weight and approximately the same firmness as the fabrics listed.

With the tremendous use of knits in the past few years, many patterns have been developed especially for knit fabrics; some are even designed for certain types of knits. Be sure to use only the type of knit specified on your pattern. A pattern designed for "sweater knits only" does not have as much ease as one designed for other fabrics. If you try to make this pattern in a double knit, for instance, you would probably find it too tight.

Other pattern clues are the pictures of the garment on the front of the pattern envelope. If a vest is shown in a fake fur, for instance, the guide sheet probably has information for handling this fabric. If one pattern view is illustrated in a plaid, the style is suitable for matching the patterns of a plaid; if no view shows a plaid, you might run into trouble matching at the seams.

In general, when buying your fabric, make a note of its fiber content and any care information given on the fabric bolt. Is the fabric washable? If so, you will want to use washable lining and trimmings. Keep this information together with a swatch of the fabric in a file for future reference. In this way, you can properly care for your finished garment and you will build up a working knowledge of how particular fabrics perform.

Below: A beautifully cut and stitched dress for an afternoon in town or at tea. The gently rolled collar is flattering to all.

KNACKS WITH KNITS

Knits are no longer news; they are a part of the way we live now. Knits offer beautiful styling, color, and pattern along with comfort, easy care, and easy sewing. Since a main advantage of knits is flexibility, linings are almost never needed—you save steps in sewing!

Check the pattern catalogues for styles labeled "suitable for knit fabrics," or "recommended for knits." Other patterns can be used as well. Avoid bias cut styles and circular skirts—these styles tend to stretch out of shape when cut from knit fabrics. Wool and polyester double knits tailor beautifully. You may want to line the jacket of a knit tailored suit with a lightweight knit to keep its flexibility.

Types of Knits: Double knits are perhaps the most popular of all knit fabrics. The right and wrong sides are almost identical, unless of course, a pattern has been woven into one side. Double knits are firm fabrics yet they drape well. They are suitable for dresses, suits, slacks, jackets, even coats.

Single knits such as jersey, tricot, and cire (a wet-look fabric) have a definite right and wrong side. They are lighter in weight and best suited for softly draped or body-hugging styles. Tricot knits are used in lingerie.

Sweater knits are very stretchy and look much like machine-knit sweaters. Use them only with patterns calling for "sweater knits only."

Raschel knits are light, openwork knits that look much like crochet or lace. Unless they are bonded (affixed to another layer of fabric), they have to be lined to avoid the see-through look.

Layout, Cutting, and Marking Knits: If your knit is washable, preshrink it before beginning your layout. Cotton knits have a tendency to shrink; preshrinking eliminates problems later! Polyester double knits often have a finish that adheres to the sewing machine needle and causes skipped stitches. Washing them before cutting helps eliminate this problem. Steam-press wool knits to preshrink them before use.

A regular cutting layout is suitable for knits, if you will take a few precautions. To find the straight grain of a knit, hand baste along one lengthwise rib. Use that basting line as a guide for placing the straight grain of the pattern.

Be careful not to stretch the fabric while pinning your pattern to it. Do not let the end of the fabric hang off the end of the table. Most knits have their greatest stretch in the crosswise direction (at right angles to the selvage edge); for this reason, never lay pattern pieces crosswise on the fabric unless specifically directed to do so. Pieces laid crosswise may stretch out of proportion—your garment may actually get longer if you cut it this way.

Use a sharp bent handle shears to cut out your fabric and cut with long, smooth strokes. Test scraps of your fabric to determine the best method of marking. Most knits can be marked with dressmakers' carbon and a smooth-edged tracing wheel. If the carbon does not show up with light to medium pressure on the tracing wheel, try tailor's tacks, chalk, or pin marking. (See Index.)

Although most knits will not require a lining, interfacing is usually needed for collars, cuffs, neckline areas and front openings. Use a lightweight interfacing so you do not make your fabric too firm. Particularly suitable for interfacing knits are featherweight and lightweight all-bias non-woven interfacings. All-bias means they give in all directions—ideal for flexible knits.

Sewing Knits: Along with the tremendous developments in the production of knits this past decade came the development of polyester thread. This synthetic or synthetic core thread has greater strength than mercerized cotton and therefore is not as likely to break when a seam is stretched.

You can incorporate additional stretch into your seams by using a narrow zigzag stitch, or a special stretch stitch found on some more elaborate sewing machines, or a slightly shorter than average stitch in order to incorporate as much thread as possible into the seams.

Use a ballpoint needle in your sewing machine. Instead of piercing the yarns of the fabric, a ballpoint needle separates them. This prevents damage to the fabric.

A good habit to form before stitching any new fabric is to make a test seam to check tension, pressure, and balance of your machine, as well as pressing techniques. Cut two pieces of fabric about 6 inches by 8 inches and pin them together at each end. Set your machine to the stitch length you plan to use for your garment and thread it with the proper thread. Stitch a plain seam.

Opposite: Now you can sew successfully for the men in your life! This handsome jacket features carefully matched check-plaid fabric.

Examine your seam: the stitches should look alike on both sides. If the top thread is too tight, loosen it by turning the tension dial counterclockwise. If it is too loose, tighten it by turning the tension dial clockwise. (Do not adjust the bobbin tension if you can correct your seam with upper tension adjustments. If bobbin tension adjustments are necessary, consult your sewing machine manual.) If the top layer of fabric comes out longer, your pressure is too tight. Loosen the pressure on the presser foot until a test seam comes out even.

Test press your seam in order to determine the best pressing techniques to use on this fabric. If the seam allowances cause a ridge on the right side, insert strips of brown paper between seam allowance and fabric before pressing.

Do not stitch your garment until you are satisfied with your test seam results. You will save much time and effort later on.

No seam finish is needed for most knits, since they do not ravel. If the seam allowances on lightweight knits roll, stitch again ⅛ inch from the first row of stitches and trim the seam allowance next to the second row.

Finishing Touches for Knits: Allow knit garments to hang for 24 hours before hemming. If the fabric is going to hang down, it will happen in these 24 hours and you won't have to rehem the skirt later.

An invisible hem for knits is a catch-stitched hem. Pin up hem and trim to an even depth. Make a row of machine basting ¼ inch from the edge; then zigzag or edge stitch the edge of the hem. Pull up the line of basting so the hem fits the skirt. Turn back the hem on the basting line and, working from left to right, point your needle from right to left and take a small stitch in the garment, a small stitch in the hem, and so on. Press hem lightly. Your stitches are hidden under the hem; no ridge shows through on the right side of the garment.

Lace seam binding is also suitable for use with knits; just keep your hemming stitches rather loose so they will give.

Knits take beautifully to decorative topstitching. Use silk buttonhole twist for the upper thread and a machine basting stitch. For washable fabrics, use either one or two threads of the type stitched into the seams.

Stretchable trims are needed for knit fabrics. You can buy polyester knit trimming by the yard. Never use a firmly woven trim placed across a knit garment—this would inhibit its stretch.

WORKING WITH BONDED AND LAMINATED FABRICS

Bonded fabrics have a lining fabric fused to the wrong side; usually the lining is a lightweight tricot knit. The fashion fabric may be a knit, a woven, or a lace. Laminated fabrics are fused to a thin layer of foam, adding extra warmth to your garment. Both bondeds and laminates are slightly firmer and bulkier than the fashion fabric alone; be sure your pattern can take this extra firmness. Simple styles with few seams are the most successful with bonded and laminated fabrics.

Layout, Cutting, and Marking Bonded and Laminated Fabrics: Check carefully for straight grain before buying these fabrics as they cannot be straightened. Consider the grain of the fashion fabric when laying out your pattern pieces. Fold the fabric right side out so that the fashion fabric grain is visible. To avoid unnecessary seams, cut facings in one with the garment wherever possible.

When working with a laminated fabric, it is easiest to cut a single thickness, right side up. (The fabric backing tends to stick to itself when folded together.) Be certain when you cut out a pattern piece the second time that you flip over the pattern, making sure you cut a right and a left side.

Although dressmakers' carbon and tracing wheel may work on some bonded fabric, tailor's tacks or pin marking work best and won't mar the fabric.

You won't need a lining or underlining with a bonded fabric, but for appearance sake, you may want to line a jacket or vest to be worn open. Laminated backings tend to adhere to other fabrics, so you may want to line clothes made with these fabrics to avoid their clinging to your undergarments. Use an interfacing as usual if the backing does not offer enough support.

Sewing Bonded and Laminated Fabrics: Make a test seam before stitching on bonded fabrics; two layers of bonded wool, for instance, are considerably thicker than two layers of unbonded wool and will require different stitch length, tension, and pressure.

When stitching a laminated fabric foam side out, place a piece of tissue paper between the fabric and the machine and another piece between fabric and presser foot to help the fabric glide under the machine. Simply tear away the tissue paper after stitching. Since laminated fabrics are difficult to press, topstitch seams open to keep them flat and form a decorative effect.

If fabric is particularly bulky, slash darts almost to the point after stitching. Separate the face fabric from the laminated backing and very carefully trim away the backing close to the line of stitching.

If self-fabric would create too heavy a facing, use a lining fabric for the facing or finish edges with decorative braid.

Finishing Touches for Bonded and Laminated Fabrics: Make a catch-stitched hem or use seam binding for your bonded fabrics. Catch only the backing fabric with your stitches. Make a catch-stitched hem for laminated fabrics, too, but catch both the backing and the face fabric with your stitches—the foam alone is not strong enough to support a hem. Another appropriate hem finish for laminates is a row of machine topstitching about ½ inch from the folded edge. This is an attractive and suitable hem finish for garments which you don't plan to alter—removing such a line of machine stitching might very well leave stitch holes.

Press your bonded fabric with a heat setting suitable for the outer fabric, first testing a scrap to be sure the two layers will not separate with heat. Laminated fabrics generally require only finger pressing—high heat may melt the backing.

QUILTED FABRICS

Ever-popular for loungewear, quilted fabrics have made the fashion scene for long skirts, vests, and sportswear. With quilteds, the fabric itself is exciting enough; choose simple styles and avoid added bulk.

Layout, Cutting, and Marking: Quilted fabrics are three layers—the face fabric, the backing, and the filling. Some are thicker than others, depending upon the amount of filling and the degree of quilting. For a bulky quilted fabric, lay out pattern pieces on a single layer of fabric. Remember to flip the pattern piece the second time you cut it, to assure a right and a left side for each piece.

Tailor's tacks, chalk, or pin marking are most successful for quilted fabrics. The simpler the style of the garment, the less marking you'll need.

Since quilteds have a lot of body and are already neatly backed, interfacing and linings are generally not needed.

Sewing Quilted Fabrics: Don't forget to make a test seam to determine how to handle the bulk of a quilted fabric. Edge stitch or zigzag all seam allowances to prevent the filling from coming out. Slash darts and press open to reduce bulk.

Finishing Quilted Fabrics: A word about closures is in order when working on quilteds. Make only machine-worked buttonholes; bound buttonholes are not suitable because the filling would come out of the patch and the fabric is too bulky. Stitch all zippers by machine, not by hand; hand stitching might not penetrate through all the layers and is not strong enough to hold in a zipper on a bulky quilted fabric.

Use seam binding or stretch lace to finish the raw edge of the hem. Catch hemming stitches to backing fabric only.

Do not flatten quilted fabrics as you press. Press lightly to open seams only.

EASY-CARE DURABLE PRESS

Fabrics labeled durable press are most often a blend of cotton and dacron polyester. Their biggest advantage is easy care and a wrinkle-free appearance. However, these very qualities may present some problems in sewing.

Durable press fabrics cannot be straightened, so be sure plaids, checks, and other crosswise designs are at right angles to the lengthwise grain before you buy.

Because seams or folds in the design are difficult to press in, choose simple, uncluttered styles to stitch in durable press fabrics. Pleats *can* be pressed in if need be, but they will not be heat-set as on ready-to-wear garments. If your outfit calls for pleats, try topstitching them in position.

Layout, Cutting, and Marking Durable Press: If you cannot press out the center fold from the fabric, plan a layout that will avoid it. Try folding the two selvage edges towards the center. This will give you two folded edges on which to position pattern pieces to be cut double. Cut facings in one with the garment wherever possible. Place pins in the seam allowances only, since pin marks may remain.

Test first, but a tracing wheel and dressmakers' carbon usually works on durable press fabrics. Be certain that the tracing wheel does not leave permanent grooves in the fabric. When in doubt, chalk mark the fabric.

Sewing Durable Press: Be certain to preshrink all linings and notions used with durable press; durable press does not shrink, but the notions might!

The main stitching problem with durable press is puckering seams. Be sure to make a test seam to select stitch length, machine tension, balance, and pressure. Use the small hole throat plate. (Zigzag machines have a wide hole throat plate to accommodate the side-to-side action of the needle when zigzagging, but these machines can be fitted with a small hole plate for straight stitching.) Stitch at an even speed with loose tension, keeping fabric taut as you stitch.

The greatest pucker problem occurs on lengthwise seams, so look for styles with seams on a slight bias such as A-line skirts. Darts on a slight bias are also easier to stitch. Avoid lengthwise darts on dress front or back; side seam darts are much more successful.

Finishing Touches for Durable Press: Use a lapped application for zippers wherever possible, since topstitching on durable press causes puckering. Hand-picked zippers are also possible on durable press; be sure to ease the zipper into the placket.

Seam allowances are not apt to ravel, but if you want to finish the seams, try pinking them so that you do as little stitching as possible on this fabric.

Make a catch-stitched hem or use seam binding or stretch lace to finish the edge. Do not turn under the hem edge—this would cause a visible ridge on the right side.

Once you are satisfied with the fit and finish of your durable press garment, do the final pressing with a hot steam iron. To keep your durable press looking new as long as possible, wash it frequently; soil build-up is difficult to see and heavily soiled articles are difficult to clean. Wash by machine at a permanent press setting. If your washer is not so equipped, wash in warm water with a cold rinse. Tumble dry and remove immediately from the dryer—heat causes wrinkles to set.

HANDLING LEATHER, SUEDE, AND VINYL

Leathers and suedes are not truly fabrics—they are neither woven nor knit. They are the treated skins of animals and are sold by the skin. For that reason, bring your pattern pieces with you when purchasing leather so you can lay the pieces on the skins to determine how many skins are needed.

Vinyls, because they are man-made, can be produced in widths and lengths just like any other bolt of fabric. You can purchase vinyl by the yard.

All three of these "fabrics" may be handled in a similar manner unless otherwise indicated. Select patterns that specify use with leather or vinyl, if possible. Avoid gathers, pleats, easing, and difficult fitting. For leather or suede garments, choose patterns with several small pieces rather than a few large ones in order to make the best use of each skin.

Layout, Cutting, and Marking Leather, Suede, and Vinyl: Position all pattern pieces on the skins with the tops pointing towards the top of the skin. The grain of leather runs lengthwise along the backbone of the animal. The nap on suede should run down. Run your hand over the skin; suede feels smooth in the direction of the nap.

For all three fabrics, place pins in the seam allowances

only. Pin holes are permanent. You can also use paper clips or weights to hold the pattern in place while you cut.

Lay out pieces on a single layer of leather, suede, or vinyl. Be sure to flip the pattern pieces as you cut each one again, so that you end up with a right and a left side.

Cut facings which will not show from lining fabrics. Front facings on a coat or vest may have to be cut from self-fabric if the garment is to be worn open. Another possibility is to eliminate facings altogether by lining to the edge.

Chalk marking is the most successful for vinyl. Tracing wheel or pins would mar the surface. On leather, you can use a ballpoint pen to mark the wrong side of the skin.

Plan to line leather and suede to prevent the nap or color from discoloring your other clothing. Vinyl may or may not be lined depending upon the weight and body of the fabric. Since hand sewing is most difficult on these fabrics, put in the lining by machine.

Use durable press interfacing fabrics with leather, suede, and vinyl since these "fabrics" cannot be ironed. Lining for vinyl should be of a dark color since vinyl cannot be dry cleaned or tossed in the washer.

Sewing Leather, Suede, and Vinyl: You can buy three-cornered leather needles for both machine and hand sewing for use on these fabrics. The three-cornered point pierces the skins much more easily than a conventional needle.

Use paper clips to hold layers of the fabric together while stitching, or put pins in the seam allowances only. Stitch slowly and carefully with a fairly large stitch. (You cannot rip seams because holes will remain, so if in doubt about the fit, make a muslin garment first.)

Vinyl has a tendency to stick to the machine while you sew. To prevent this, encase the seam in tissue paper and stitch over paper and vinyl. Tear away tissue after stitching the seam.

Seams cannot be pressed flat. Plan to single or double topstitch seams to keep them flat; this makes a nice decorative finish. To single topstitch, push both seam allowances to one side and stitch from the right side from ⅛ inch to ½ inch from the seam line. To double topstitch, spread seam open and stitch from the right side the same distance from either side of the seam line.

If topstitching is not appropriate for your garment or for certain of its seams, you can keep seams flat by gluing them in place. Use rubber cement or fabric glue. Topstitch or glue darts, too.

Use cellophane tape to hold pockets or flaps in place as you stitch. Do not stitch over the tape, but pull it up as you come to it.

Tips on Finishing Leather, Suede, and Vinyl: Bound buttonholes work beautifully on these fabrics, but machine-made ones are possible, too, if you use a long stitch and go only once around the area. Buttons and loops are popular closures for leather, vinyl, or suede.

Don't plan to hand sew your hem; this is not a successful finish for these fabrics. Instead, topstitch about ½" from

Opposite: A floor-length robe to sew from pre-quilted fabric—lush and lovely dressing for a winter's night by the fireside.

the edge, or glue the hem in place. For a novelty effect on leather or suede, cut the skirt to desired length and "fringe" the edges.

HANDLING PILE FABRICS

Soft, plush, or fuzzy pile fabrics make popular additions to our wardrobes. They range from casual corduroy to elegant velvet. They all have one thing in common: an extra set of yarns that are looped when woven and then clipped to give a third dimension. When buying a pile fabric, always buy the amount listed in the "with nap" column on the pattern envelope.

Layout, Cutting, and Marking Pile Fabrics: Pattern pieces must be laid out on pile fabrics along the lengthwise grain with all the tops pointing in the same direction. That is what is meant by a "with nap" layout on the guidesheet. The direction of the nap affects the color of the fabric as well as the feel. When the nap runs down, the color is shinier and smoother. With the nap running up, the same fabric has a richer color but a rougher feel as you run your hand down its length. Cut velvets with the nap running up to achieve the richest color. To make corduroys more durable in children's playclothes or jeans, cut it with the nap running down.

Velvet mars easily and ripped seams would be permanent lines. To avoid this problem make all possible fitting adjustments before you lay out the pattern.

Match ribs in wide wale corduroy as if they were stripes. Cut facings from lining material if you wish to avoid bulk.

Pin within the seam allowance on velvet; pin marks are likely to remain. Or, use long, fine needles instead of pins.

Mark velvets with tailor's tacks using silk thread. Corduroy and velveteen can be marked with mercerized thread and tailor's tacks.

Interface as usual with an appropriate weight interfacing fabric. Since these pile fabrics are usually firm, underlining or lining may not be needed; it's a matter of taste.

Sewing Pile Fabrics: Silk thread is excellent for stitching velvet since it leaves no marks, but velvet can be successfully sewn with polyester or mercerized cotton thread. Test a scrap to be sure. Stitch with a looser than usual presser foot pressure so that you do not flatten the pile.

Test your pressing techniques before you stitch the actual garment. If you have a needle board, press pile fabrics face down over the needles. If you don't own a needle board, an alternate method is to press with the pile face down over several terry towels. Steam-press, never resting the iron on the fabric.

Bind, overcast, or zigzag the seam allowances on all pile fabrics—pile tends to fall off from a cut edge and the lint is quite messy.

Fine Finishes for Pile Fabrics: The most professional-looking zippers in pile fabrics are hand-picked. Machine topstitching mars the pile. If you must stitch by machine, use one of the new invisible zippers, following the instructions that come with the zipper.

Machine-made buttonholes are fine for corduroy, especially on children's clothes, but bound buttonholes give a much richer, more professional look to velvets. If you want to make bound buttonholes on pile fabrics, try cutting the patch on the bias. Always make a test buttonhole first to get the feel and to be sure you like the finished effect.

Hem edges must be finished just as seam allowances to avoid the pile's shedding. A neat hem for a pile fabric is a completely bound edge (use purchased bias tape) and a catch-stitched hem.

Care of Pile Fabrics: If your velvet dress is wrinkled from hanging or wearing, instead of steam-pressing with an iron, hang it in a steaming bathroom for about an hour. Remove the garment, but do not handle until it is completely dry. The steam makes the pile stand up and the wrinkles are gone!

THE FABULOUS FAKES

Fake furs are much like pile fabrics, but with a very long pile. They are curly, straight, shaggy, fluffy—they imitate nearly every animal in the jungle as well as some out of fairy tales.

When shopping for a fake fur, follow the "with nap" yardages. Select a very simple style with as few seams as possible. An open-front sleeveless vest is a good first project for fake fur.

Layout, Cutting, and Marking Fake Fur: Cut facings in one with the garment wherever possible, or eliminate facings and line to the edge. If the center back seam is parallel to the straight grain, you can eliminate it by placing the seam line on the fold of the fabric.

Place pattern pieces on the wrong side of a single layer of fabric, pile running down. Cut the backing only, not the fur, using sharp shears or a razor blade.

Tailor's tacks or chalk marking should be used on fake furs. A tracing wheel would not penetrate.

Sewing Fake Furs: Stitch seams in the direction of the pile, then use a needle to pull out the pile that catches in the seams.

Plain seams may be used on flat fake furs. Test on a scrap to see if the seam allowance lies flat. It may be necessary to shear away the pile from the seam allowance. If the seams still do not lie flat, catch-stitch them to the backing. Fake furs cannot be pressed to make seams lie flat.

Double stitched seams may be preferable. Make another test to see which you prefer on your fabric. To double stitch, make a plain seam, shear the pile from the seam allowances, then stitch again ¼ inch from the first stitching. Trim seam allowances close to second row of stitching.

Slash open darts and shear pile as for seams. Catch-stitch to backing to hold open.

Fake Fur Finishes: The most successful closures on fake furs are frogs, loops and buttons, buckles, buttons and chain, covered snaps, large hooks and eyes (furrier hooks), or Velcro tape. With all of these closures to choose from, it shouldn't be hard to stay away from zippers and buttonholes which do not work well on the fabulous fakes.

To hem a short, smooth fake fur, finish the edge and catch-stitch hem to backing only. For very hairy furs, trim hem allowance to 1 inch. Stitch wide hem facing or a strip of lining fabric to the hem, right sides together. Turn up both the hem facing and the fur and catch-stitch the edge of

the fur to the fabric backing. Then, slip-stitch the hem facing to the fabric backing. This double hem is strong and flat.

DELICATE LACES AND SHEERS

Lace makes its own details, so choose a pattern accordingly. Make use of the filmy softness of sheers with gathers and folds. Both these fabrics are see-through and therefore may be handled in a similar fashion.

Layout, Cutting, and Marking Laces and Sheers: Place the pattern pieces on lace to take greatest advantage of the motifs; lace has no grain line. The corded or "bumpy" side is the right side of the lace. Fold fabric, wrong sides together, matching motifs. If you intend to use the edge of a motif as the hemline, be sure to cut your pattern off at the hemline and place the pattern edge along one motif on the lace. Trim the lace very carefully between motifs at the hem to achieve a neat finish.

Lay out sheers as you would any other fabric, being careful not to let the fabric slip as you work. Pinning sheers to the cutting board prevents slippage while cutting.

Use *only* tailor's tacks to mark laces and sheers. Dressmakers' carbon or chalk will show through to the right side.

Plan to underline or line at least the bodice and skirt of lace and sheer garments; sleeves are attractive unlined. If desired, you can make a special slip to wear under a lace or sheer dress instead of lining it. For pieces that are underlined, mark construction details on underlining only.

Sewing Laces and Sheers: Make a test seam, including underlining you are using, to see if the seam allowances are visible from the right side. A good, inconspicuous seam is double or triple stitched, with each row of stitching ⅛ inch to ¼ inch away from the first. Trim away seam allowance next to last row of stitching. Double stitch and trim darts in the same way.

A French seam is effective with sheers. Stitch once, wrong sides together, trim seam allowance, turn and stitch right sides together, catching first seam allowances in the second seam.

Finishes for Laces and Sheers: Hand-pick all zippers. Machine or hand-worked buttonholes are fine for laces and sheers, but make a test one first to check your results. Interface the buttonhole area with sheer fabric or net. To leave lace motifs undisturbed, use tiny covered snaps instead of buttons and buttonholes. Try buttons and loops of satin for a delicate closure on a sheer dress.

If you are using a lace motif at the edge of your garment, you have no hem to sew. If not, face the edge of the hem with a tulle strip, instead of having a deep lace hem. This preserves the sheerness of the lace.

Opposite: Gold brocade edged with richly "bejewelled" trim for the most glamorous evening gown imaginable—and you can sew it!

Opposite: The once-in-a-lifetime dress you have dreamed about! Pure elegance, for the most important gala evening of your life.

For sheer fabrics, make either a narrow rolled hem or a very deep double hem. Rolled hems are most successful on circular skirts. For straight edge hems, a deep double hem helps the skirt hang better.

LOVELY LUXURY FABRICS

Who doesn't, at one time or another, love the luxury of silk, satin, crepe, brocade, metallic, or the new Qiana? Besides being elegant, dressy, and "special," most of these fabrics have one of two things in common: a slippery feel or ravel-prone seams.

Take full advantage of the drapable qualities of silk, satin, crepe, and Qiana by selecting fluid folds, gentle gathers, bias cuts, and cowl necklines. Use brocades and metallics for more tailored lines with few seaming details.

Layout, Cutting, and Marking Luxury Fabrics: Follow a regular cutting layout, but pin slippery fabrics to the cutting board. If pins leave holes in a test swatch, pin only in the seam allowances. Do not let crepe hang over the edge of the table or it will stretch.

Pretest dressmakers' carbon and tracing wheel if you intend to use that method. Luxury fabrics mar easily; tailor's tacks are safest to use.

Use lightweight, silky underlinings to protect luxury fabrics from overhandling. For a truly luxurious finish, use a separate lining, in addition to an underlining. A separate lining is advisable on metallics and brocades with metallic threads in order to protect against scratchy seam allowances.

Sewing Luxury Fabrics: You must pretest each luxury fabric you work with to determine the most successful stitch length and machine tension, balance, and pressure. It is also a good habit to pretest pressing techniques at this time. Begin with a low (synthetic) steam setting—many luxury fabrics may be damaged by high heat.

To protect your fabric from the feed dog of the machine and prevent it from catching in the hole of the throat plate, encase the entire seam in tissue paper, or stitch over tissue paper. Tear away tissue after stitching.

Hand baste all slippery fabrics before machine stitching. Finish seams by zigzagging, hand overcasting, or turning and stitching.

Fine Finishes for Luxury Fabrics: Hand-picked zippers maintain that luxury look; so too, do bound buttonholes, if the fabric is not too bulky. Pretest bound or hand-made buttonholes on a scrap before making them on your garment.

For all luxury fabrics, a catch-stitched hem makes a neat and inconspicuous finish. You may want to add stretch lace for a pretty touch as well as an edge finish. Do not press the hem edge hard—a slightly rounded look is much more appropriate.

Check the fabric bolt for information on care of luxury fabrics. Most are not washable. The exception is Qiana, a new nylon-like fabric. If you sew with Qiana, make sure linings and notions are also washable.

Press luxury fabrics with a low heat setting. Qiana, again, is the exception. Press it with a low wool setting and stretch the seam slightly as you press to avoid seam puckering.

Please turn the page for more photographs of fabrics and suggestions for their use.

A Sampler Of Fine Fabrics

THE development of new fabric fibers and manufacturing processes—together with the mushrooming of well-stocked retail fabric shops—has resulted in a fantastic growth of interest in home sewing. Where once our mothers and grandmothers were limited to choosing among perhaps two gingham checks and three percale prints, we today are offered a multitude of weaves, knits, fibers, and colors! Ours is not the dreary task of finding something that will merely "do", but the delicious dilemma of deciding which of a dozen fabrics we like best! On these pages we show but a small sampling of the many styles, colors, and weights available, along with suggestions for their possible use. Let them be your inspiration when you sew for yourself, your family, or your home.

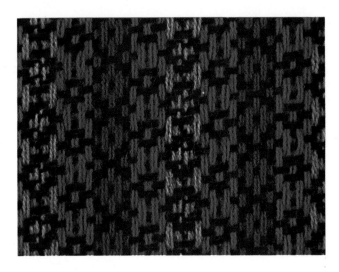

Luxurious mini-geometrics to stripe a soft suit.

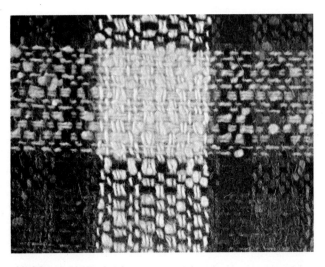

Nubby muted plaid—a natural for a smart ensemble.

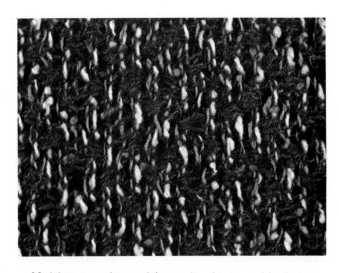

Multi-textured tweed for a city dress and jacket.

Herringbone weave is subtly, softly slimming.

Airy woven star check for a lightweight topper.

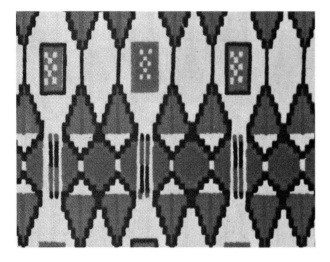

Aztec motifs in earth colors for summer skimmer.

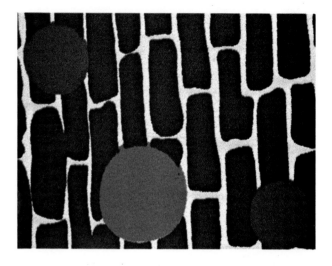

Bubbles float against bricks—good for soft pleats.

Crisp, wrinkle-free fabric for all-season travels.

Easy to cut and match pattern in lightweight fabric.

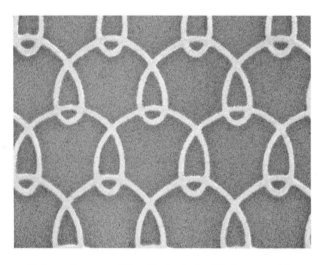

Make a dress and line its jacket with loopy print.

Free, splashy print needs no pattern matching.

Cheerful ''applique'' floral print fools the eye.

Stylized garden to grow on a floor-length skirt.

Freeform flowers in close colors for a blonde.

Scatter pattern is great for gathers, soft pleats.

Polka dots and posies to perk a weary wardrobe.

Field of fresh daisies flatters the full figure.

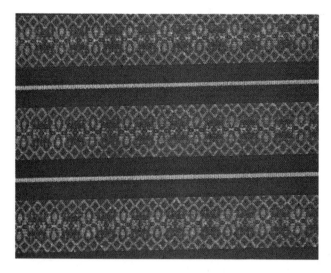

Multi-width stripes add height to long leg pants.

Diagonally shifted stripes—a jacket for the pants.

Jacquard and chalk stripes—a pretty peasant look.

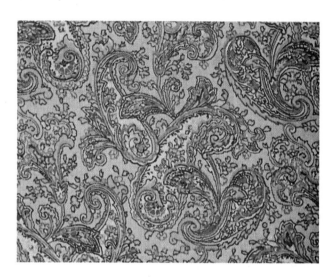

Delicate paisley is soft, feminine, Victorian.

Color-powered adaptation of classic paisley print.

Strong, bold print for a swoopy skirt or pajamas.

Choosing And Using The Proper Tools

*T***he** *best tools produce the best results no matter what the craft. Sewing is no exception. You will save money in the long run when you sew, so it pays to buy the best tools you can afford. Some tools are absolute necessities; others make sewing easier but are not essential. Do not try to own one of every sewing gadget on the market or you will have clutter rather than more efficient sewing equipment. Each seamstress must decide for herself what is essential and what is not, depending on the type and amount of sewing she does.*

Keep all of your sewing tools in the same place, whether you have a separate sewing room or just a few shelves for storage. Having everything handy when you need it saves time and energy and makes for more efficient work habits.

Sewing tools can be grouped according to the various steps in making a garment. We do so here to make for easier use of this list.

CUTTING AND MARKING

Bent Handle Dressmaker's Shears (7 inch to 9 inch, depending upon what size feels most comfortable) are of prime importance. Left-handed shears are available and do make cutting less awkward for left-handed sewers. Bent handle shears make cutting more accurate because they rest along the cutting surface as you cut. They have one round ring for the thumb and a long one for the first two or three fingers, to allow a firm grip. Buy the best shears you can afford. Poorly made shears will snag and chew your fabric. Care for your shears by placing a drop of oil at the joint about once a month. Keep them clean and lint free.

Trimming scissors are straight and have identical rings for the handle. A pair 3 inches to 6 inches long with sharp point should be kept near the machine for trimming seams and clipping threads.

Pinking shears are useful in finishing seams so they do not ravel. Although there are other ways to finish seams, pinking is fast, easy, and economical, and appropriate for many types of fabric. (They are not to be used to cut out the fabric pieces.)

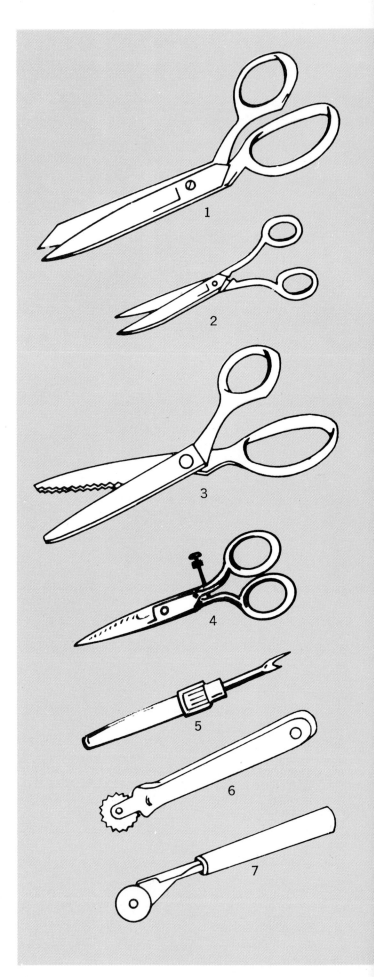

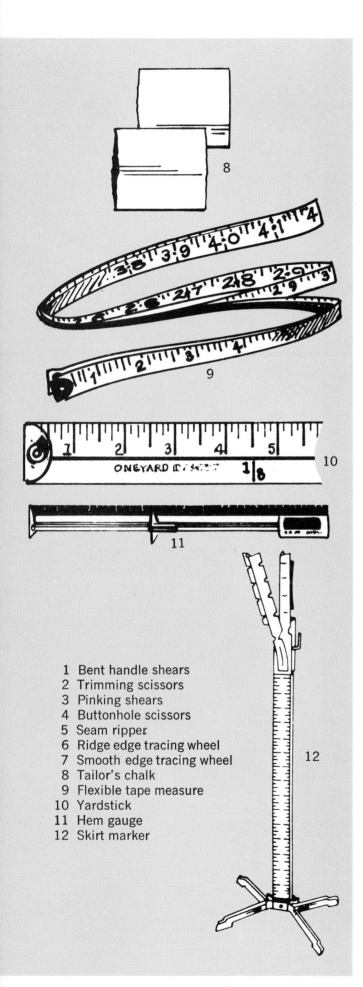

1. Bent handle shears
2. Trimming scissors
3. Pinking shears
4. Buttonhole scissors
5. Seam ripper
6. Ridge edge tracing wheel
7. Smooth edge tracing wheel
8. Tailor's chalk
9. Flexible tape measure
10. Yardstick
11. Hem gauge
12. Skirt marker

Buttonhole scissors are specially made scissors for cutting open buttonholes. They assure accurate measurement for each buttonhole and are adjustable. They are very useful if you make many garments with machine-made buttonholes.

A seam ripper is a must for every sewer. The size of a fountain pen, it has a two-pronged fork-like top with a razor edge between the prongs. The longer prong is inserted under the stitch and the razor edge cuts the thread.

A tracing wheel is a small gadget that looks like a pizza pie cutter. Its function is to aid in transferring pattern markings to fabric. It is used with dressmaker's carbon paper. Two types of tracing wheels are available; one has tiny ridges and produces a dotted line, the other is smooth and produces a straight line. The latter tends to keep tissue pattern intact longer.

Dressmaker's carbon paper is used to transfer pattern markings to fabric. One side of the paper has a waxy finish and is placed face down on the fabric. The pressure of the tracing wheel marks the fabric. Dressmaker's carbon is available in many colors. Always use the lightest color possible so markings will not show through on the right side but will be visible on the wrong side.

Cardboard is a good item to keep near your marking tools. Placed between the fabric and table top, it prevents the tracing wheel from marring the cutting surface.

A cutting board made of heavy cardboard and marked into 1 inch boxes is a great help in laying out and cutting fabric. Fabric can be pinned to the board and it folds up for easy storage. It protects table top from scissor and pin marks.

Tailor's chalk is used to mark wool and other heavy fabrics that can't be marked with the tracing wheel method. It is a quick way to mark fitting alterations on your garment.

MEASURING

A 60 inch Flexible Tape Measure is used to take body measurements when purchasing and fitting your pattern. One that is reversible is easiest to use.

A 12 inch ruler aids in marking straight lines when transferring pattern marking to fabric.

A yardstick is needed when measurements larger than 12 inches must be taken. It is useful when measuring the placement of the pattern grain line on the fabric.

A hem gauge, usually 6 inch, is one of the handiest tools you can own. It has a little movable arrow that aids in marking the depth of hems, facings, ruffles, the distance between buttonholes, and many other measuring tasks.

A skirt marker measures the distance of your hem to the floor and helps assure even hemlines. One type uses pins and requires a partner's assistance. Another type uses powdered chalk and can be operated alone.

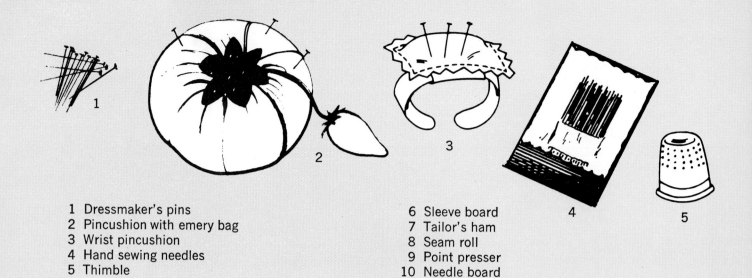

1 Dressmaker's pins
2 Pincushion with emery bag
3 Wrist pincushion
4 Hand sewing needles
5 Thimble

6 Sleeve board
7 Tailor's ham
8 Seam roll
9 Point presser
10 Needle board

SEWING

Dressmaker's pins are an absolute necessity for anyone who sews; have plenty of them. Choose fine sharp pins so you do not mar your fabric.

Pin cushions keep pins handy while you work and reduce the hazards from having loose pins lying around. Have one that attaches to your wrist, another that you attach to the head of your machine with a strip of elastic, to hold pins as you sew.

Hand sewing needles are available in a wide variety of sizes and several types. Check the needle and thread size chart. Many home sewers prefer to do hand sewing with crewel needles rather than sharps. Crewels have long eyes and are easier to thread than the small-eyed sharps.

Machine needles are available in several sizes depending upon the type of fabric used. Ballpoint needles (not available in every size) are for use with knit fabrics. They separate the threads of the fabric rather than piercing them and prevent snagging and skipping stitches.

A thimble is practical for hand sewing. Although it may seem awkward to handle at first, properly fitted it will save your fingers much wear and tear. Find one that comfortably fits the middle finger of your sewing hand, not so tight that it cuts off circulation, but not so loose that it falls off while you work.

An emery bag is useful for cleaning needles and pins. One is often attached, in the form of a "strawberry", to a standard pin cushion.

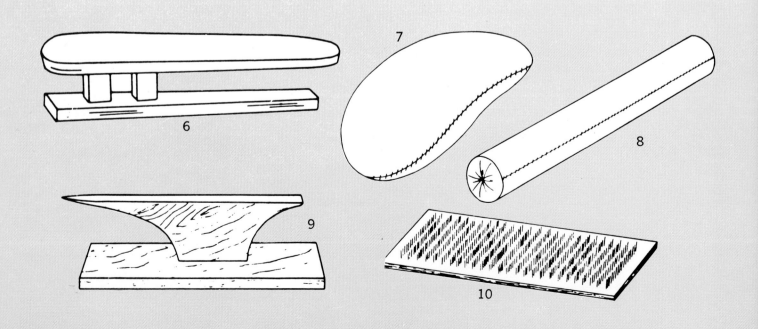

Thread will be an important part of your sewing basket, but do not stock up all at once. Buy your thread to match your fabric, or one shade darker if necessary. Use *mercerized cotton* thread for all cotton fabric. *Polyester core thread* is stronger and stretches somewhat and is therefore ideal for use on knits and synthetic fabrics. It can be used on cottons and all other fabric, too. Many home sewers prefer it to mercerized cotton because of its extra strength. *Buttonhole twist* is ideal for decorative topstitching on all fabrics that will be dry cleaned. It is not washable (it is made of silk) and therefore should not be used on washable fabrics.

As you accumulate thread from all of your sewing projects, you will have many contrasting colors to be used for basting. It is a good idea, if you are making something of velvet or velveteen, to purchase a spool of *nylon or silk thread* in a contrasting color to use for basting, as these pile fabrics mar easily when cotton or polyester thread is used.

Bee's wax is used to strengthen thread to be used for hand sewing an area of stress. The thread is passed over the wax to coat it and is thereby made stronger for sewing on buttons and the like.

PRESSING

Every good seamstress presses as she sews. Keep your pressing equipment near your other sewing tools.

An ironing board is a must. One that adjusts to different heights is comfortable to work at while you stand or sit. Make sure it is well padded.

A steam iron is needed for pressing open seams as you work as well as pressing the finished garment. Invest in a good one, since it can be used for the family ironing, too.

A sleeve board is a miniature ironing board used for pressing sleeves and other hard to reach areas. It, too, should be well padded.

A tailor's ham is a firmly stuffed ham-shaped cushion covered on one side with muslin and the other with wool. It is used to press areas that have fullness such as darts, side seams at the hipline, etc. Place wool fabrics face down on the wool-covered side, other fabrics on the muslin-covered side.

A seam roll is used to press open seams where a sharp line is not desirable or the seam is not otherwise accessible such as the seam on a finished sleeve. It is shaped like an overstuffed sausage and may be covered in muslin on one side and wool on the other, like the tailor's ham.

A point presser is particularly useful in turning collars, facings, and corners where a sharp pointed edge is desired.

A needle board is used to press velvet and other pile fabrics to avoid matting the pile. It looks like a heavy piece of cloth with many tiny needles sticking up. The fabric is placed pile side down on the board and steam is allowed to penetrate it.

Press cloths protect your fabric as you press. Muslin makes a good all-purpose press cloth. Self-fabric is good for wool and pile fabrics.

NOTIONS

It is a good idea to have on hand several of the notions that are frequently used on garments but require no color matching.

Snaps come in a variety of sizes in black or silver. Those with a hole in the center are easiest to apply.

Hooks and eyes also come in a variety of sizes in black or silver. The large flat hooks and eyes usually used on men's trousers are now sold for use on skirt and slacks waistbands and do a better job in those areas than do ordinary hooks and eyes.

Elastic comes in a variety of widths and types. If you plan to make several garments with elasticized waistbands, buy several yards of ¾-inch or 1-inch elastic. It is available in white, black, and pink.

MISCELLANEOUS

A full-length mirror is a must for anyone who sews. It enables you to study your own figure when deciding on a style and is invaluable in fitting your garment as you sew.

A dress form is handy for use in fitting your garment but is not as accurate as a personal fitting on your own body. If you decide to buy one, look for one of the newer types that adjusts to your body not just to your numerical measurements. This can be accomplished by fitting a muslin form to your body and then slipping it over a foam rubber form, or by using a bendable wire mesh cage that fits to your body and then locks in place. Both these types can be adjusted for use with other members of the family, too.

Your sewing machine is perhaps most important of all your sewing tools. It will probably be the most costly. The best machine available need not be the most expensive. Pay only for quality and ease of use, not for gadgets you will not use often enough to make them pay off. A machine that sews forward, reverse and zigzag should be adequate for all your sewing needs, no matter how advanced you become. The zigzag feature is particularly useful in finishing seams, sewing knit fabrics, and creating decorative effects. It is possible to make perfectly acceptable buttonholes using the zigzag machine. However, if you cannot afford a zigzag model, almost all of the techniques described in this book can be done on a forward and reverse machine.

Take good care of your machine. Read the instruction manual not only when you get it but also periodically after that, to take the most advantage of your machine's features.

Many attachments are available for sewing machines. Only you can decide which would be valuable to you. The most common attachment is the zipper foot. It is inexpensive (it is included in the price of many new machines) and invaluable in putting in neat and accurate zippers by machine.

Know Your Stitches

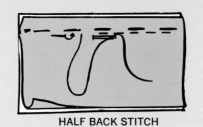

HALF BACK STITCH

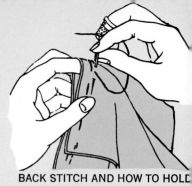

BACK STITCH AND HOW TO HOLD

HOW TO KNOT A THREAD

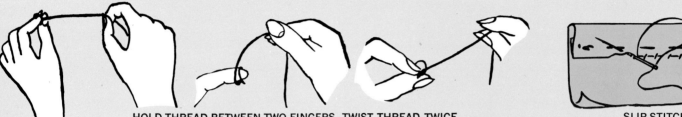

HOLD THREAD BETWEEN TWO FINGERS, TWIST THREAD TWICE
AROUND FINGER, PULL THREAD BETWEEN THUMB AND FOREFINGER.

SLIP-STITCH

*B*eginners *will find this section invaluable, and even those who have some experience in sewing will find here valuable hints for saving time, for doing things more easily and accurately. Here you will find the answers to questions which have puzzled you. The fundamentals of sewing are the foundation upon which successful garments are built. With a sound knowledge of these, sewing is easy; and things you have thought too difficult for you will turn out to be fun to make.*

First select your needle and thread. A finer needle than usual can often be used for the thread, and will help in making small, close stitches. For general sewing an average-sized needle makes for greater speed. Some people prefer a small-eyed needle, others a long or crewel-eyed one. It is important that each stitch be spaced evenly apart.

For information about a specific stitch, consult the index. Better progress is made by learning only the stitches needed for the garment upon which you are working instead of trying to learn all the stitches before beginning to sew.

Knotting a Thread: Twist the end of the thread twice around the first finger of your hand, and with your thumb roll it off the finger. Pull the thread down between thumb and finger, and at the end will be a small knot. Knotted threads are used to prevent the stitches from pulling out as you work. In fine sewing, where knots are considered bad form, take two stitches, one over the other, at the beginning of your work to hold the thread.

Use a Thimble: Women who say they sew without a thimble usually do little sewing. Although it may seem awkward until you get used to it, learn to use a thimble when you sew.

Ending a Thread: When you come to the end of a seam or the thread, it must be secured so it will not pull out as the garment is fitted or worn. Either take three little stitches one over another and break off the thread, or run the needle through the last three or four stitches, then cut the end of the thread. When making gathers, do not secure the thread and cut it; instead, put a pin at the end of the gathers and twist the thread around the pin. This will hold your thread until you can draw it and adjust the gathers. Then secure the thread or make a small knot in the end and cut the thread.

USEFUL STITCHES

Each stitch performs a definite function, and the choice of stitch to use depends upon the purpose for which it is intended. The seams which hold garments together demand *secure* sewing, such as the *back stitch* or *combination stitch*. The hem of a skirt or sleeve is kept in place with *hemming stitches* or *slip stitching*. For quick seaming in light-weight fabrics use *running stitches* or a combination of *running* and *back stitches*. *Running stitch* is also used for gathering. Take tiny stitches or long ones, depending upon the effect desired. *Overcasting stitches* prevent the edges of fabrics from raveling.

Back Stitch: Fasten the thread and take one stitch in the material, *working toward you*. Then pass the needle back in the fabric to the beginning of the last stitch and bring it out a stitch ahead. As you work, you continue to take each stitch backward in order to strengthen the line of sewing.

Half Back Stitch: Make a long stitch and then take a stitch back placing the needle in the material halfway between the beginning and end of the last stitch; bring it out two stitches ahead. Hold the material as for a back stitch.

Overcasting: There are two kinds of overcasting: the loose quick overcasting used on seam edges, and the closer overcasting used on straight edges. The close overhanding used in piecing is another version of the second type. The

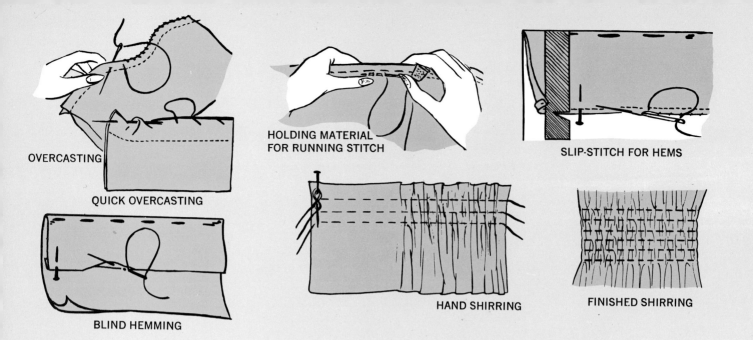

OVERCASTING

QUICK OVERCASTING

HOLDING MATERIAL FOR RUNNING STITCH

SLIP-STITCH FOR HEMS

BLIND HEMMING

HAND SHIRRING

FINISHED SHIRRING

stitches are the same in both kinds. Bring the needle up at one end of the work and take a stitch from behind the edge, passing the needle forward through the fabric. A single edge or two or more edges can be overcast together. For quick overcasting, take several stitches before pulling the full length of the remaining thread through.

Hem Stitches: To prepare a hem, turn the material over ½ inch, then turn it again the size of the hem desired. The first folded edge is held to the fabric with hem stitches. First take a stitch through the garment material and then catch the needle through the folded edge of the hem. Pull the thread. This is not the hemming used for skirts (*see below*). It is more suitable for narrow hems on collars and sleeves.

Slip Stitch for Skirt Hems: Turn the hem as directed above. Take a tiny stitch in the garment, as small as possible. Pass the needle through the turned edge (about ¼ inch), then take another tiny stitch in the garment.

Blind Hemming: These stitches are like hemming stitches, except that they are farther apart and the needle is placed on a slant. Take up only one thread of the garment and make a big stitch in the folded edge of the hem.

Running Stitch: Hold the work horizontal between your hands and run the needle in and out of the fabric. These stitches can be very small or large; small for holding a seam or the final stitching of an edge; large for holding a band that will be later caught in a hem.

Fastening Stitches: It is often necessary to join a band, a fastening or an end securely to a garment. These stitches must be large enough to take a secure hold around the joining. At each corner make it doubly secure by taking stitches over and over in the same place; then rework the edge for extra security. When a fastening is placed where it will not be covered the same security is necessary, but the stitches must be concealed under the edge of the fabric.

Combination Stitch: This hand stitching replaces machine stitching and strengthens the seam. Begin with two running stitches and then take a back stitch. Repeat this for the length of the seam. The stitches must be close, fine, and even. When the fabric is light-weight more running stitches can be placed between the back-stitches.

Gathering Stitches: Stitches for gathers are exactly like running stitches. When a good deal of fullness has to be gathered close, make the stitches long and even and pull the material along so the stitches are spaced evenly.

Hand Shirring: To shirr by hand place rows of gathers one after the other. When a curved edge is shaped with gathers—at the top of a sleeve, for instance—one row of gathers helps to hold the sleeve in shape as you work. When ruffles are made, at least two rows of gathers are necessary; and when gathers are a trimming feature, you need three or more rows.

LEARNING TO STITCH BY MACHINE

It is easy to learn to make a line of stitching true and straight with a machine. Train yourself to watch the distance between the edge of the fabric and the foot of the machine. When you can keep an even seam line with a gauge without basting the seam allowance, the next step is to learn to do outside (or top) stitching for trimming. In this case let the foot of the machine follow a seam line or a turned edge. When the side of the machine foot parallels a straight seam or edge, your stitching *must* be straight. Any number of rows of stitching can be made the same way. The spacing between these rows can be varied by using the stitching gauge attachment. Practice stitching the outside edges of pockets and collars in a true straight line. Practice turning sharp uniform corners so they all have the same angle or curve.

What Seams Best

*T***he** *seam is the foundation of all sewing, and success in making seams is the backbone of successful sewing. Seams fall into two general classifications:* Inconspicuous seams, *which allow the fabric to drape freely as though there were no seam; and* decorative seams, *which emphasize the construction and form part of the trimming. Under each of these classifications there are several types of seam, for use with different materials and for different purposes.*

SUCCESSFUL SEAMS

In making long seams always work on a table. Lay one piece of fabric out smoothly, then carefully smooth the second piece on top of it so that the edges are even. Never pull the edge. Baste the seam with the fabric *flat on the table.* Do not put your finger under the edge of the material or raise it up from the table; instead, put your left hand flat on top of the material and hold it as you pin or baste. For short seams work in your lap. Seams can be sewn by machine or by hand using back stitches or running stitches. The size of machine stitch should be adjusted to suit the material.

Seam Allowances: Accuracy is an essential of good dressmaking. A single pattern may call for different seam allowances for the various seams. Observe these carefully and follow directions. Or, if you have some reason to allow a wider seam as you cut—for instance, if your material ravels—remember to keep this same width constant as you baste.

HOW TO BASTE

Bastings are simply temporary joinings. They hold the pieces of fabric together for fitting, they hold seams together while you stitch. Some bastings merely hold a fabric in place for the time being and are ripped out without stitching. Pleats, for instance, are basted during fitting, but are not permanently stitched.

To baste you will need an extra-long needle of medium size. Fabrics which mark easily, such as velvet, should be basted with sewing silk of a contrasting color. Basting stitches in silk should be very small, while firm woolens need stitches nearly an inch long. Loose woolens take two sizes of stitches—a 1-inch stitch alternating with a ½-inch stitch. If the woolen is basted with silk, the basting may be left in when the garment is pressed. This is not true of cotton thread.

When the thread runs out in the middle of a seam, do not fasten the end, but let it hang free and start the new thread back about 2½ inches. Be sure you begin at the top and baste to the end; don't leave the seam ends open.

BASTING SEAMS

Before you begin basting make sure that the pattern notches and the seam lines meet exactly. No seams should be joined so that one edge extends beyond the other, or is longer or shorter than its partner. Keep your work flat on the table and take care not to pull or stretch the edges as you put the seams together. Put the pins in at right angles to the seam, pushing them in lightly from the edges. This will make a straight line guide for your basting—an even basting line is a great help when you stitch—and also keeps the pins from pricking your fingers as you sew.

If you are working on slippery rayon, place the pins

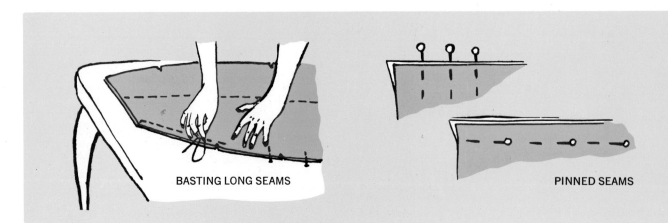

BASTING LONG SEAMS

PINNED SEAMS

Whether you are making a
simple dress to wear to luncheon
in town, or a gown to wear to
an important evening party, you
will need to plan the seams—
whether to emphasize line with
top stitching or other decoration,
or strive for a ''seamless'' look.

closer together. In taffeta use needles instead of pins, for it marks very easily.

To make sure your basting is even, use a gauge until your eye is trained to do it without the aid of a measure.

TYPES OF BASTING

There are several different types of basting stitch, and each has its proper use.

Even Basting: This basting is used to hold seams together. Pass the needle over and under the fabric with equal spacing. The stitches are longer than a running stitch.

Uneven Basting: This is used for a guide line to mark the center front or center back of a garment. Take a small stitch, and space the stitches far apart, so that most of the thread shows on the outside of the fabric.

Dressmaker's Basting: Take two short stitches, followed by one large one. Dressmaker's basting holds a fabric even more firmly than even basting.

PINNING SEAMS

Many good sewers stitch a pinned seam, allowing the foot of the sewing machine to push the material. This method is particularly good in joining two biases in a seam or in stitching velvet or any other napped or heavy fabric.

When a seam is pinned for stitching, the pins should be placed close together and set in from the edge so they can be removed as you stitch. This is particularly important when heavy fabric is to be stitched. For complete success remove the seam pins for 2 inches and let the machine push the excess fullness.

A seam may be stitched by hand or by machine, but always *the stitching must be strong and even.*

INCONSPICUOUS SEAMS

Plain Seam: The type of seam most often used for dresses, coat linings, blouses, and skirts made from fabrics that do not ravel, is the plain seam. The two edges of the fabric are simply pinned or basted together and then stitched.

If the seam is to be pressed open, set the machine for a close stitch; if it is to be pressed all to one side, use a looser stitch. If the seam is sewn by hand, backstitch it or combine running stitch and backstitch. Remove the bastings before pressing.

Puckered seams are caused by the fabric being strained or stretched. They cannot be pressed out. They must be ripped and the fabric allowed to fall into natural folds and then rejoined. When seams are laid flat on a table and basted strain seldom occurs.

Bias Seam: When the edges joined in a seam are cut on the bias, baste a piece of paper in with the two edges of fabric. After the seam is stitched, tear away the paper.

Seam for Transparent Fabrics: Hemstitching makes a neat finish for seams in dresses, collars, and cuffs made from transparent fabrics. Make a plain seam, then stitch the seam a little inside of the finished line and hemstitch. Cut off the raw edge close to the edge of the hemstitching, or cut through the center of it. (This is called *picot.*) If it is a bias seam, baste a piece of paper in with the seam before it is hemstitched. It is important that you do this when working on chiffon, lace, or voile, for it keeps the material from tightening.

Gathers, Darts, or Tucked Edges at Seam: To keep gathers in place and evenly spaced, several rows of gathering should be made, and at least one row must extend below the seam. Darts and tucks must be pressed flat or to one side before the seam is joined. First place the plain edge down flat and the gathered or tucked edge on top. Baste carefully before stitching, and always stitch with the gathers or tucks on top. These seams are always pressed to one side.

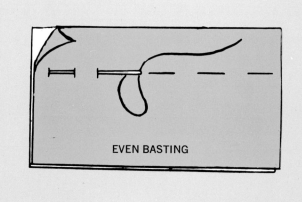

EVEN BASTING

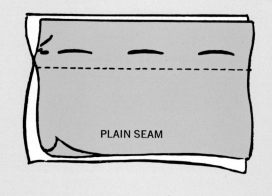

PLAIN SEAM

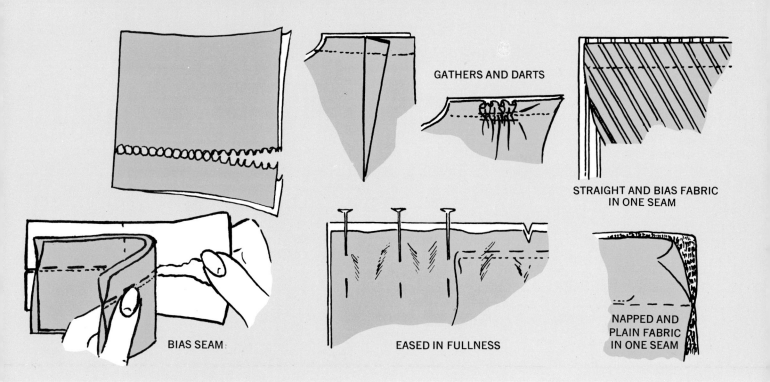

GATHERS AND DARTS

STRAIGHT AND BIAS FABRIC IN ONE SEAM

BIAS SEAM

EASED IN FULLNESS

NAPPED AND PLAIN FABRIC IN ONE SEAM

Napped Fabrics in Seam: When a napped fabric is joined to a plain fabric, use a loose stitching. This applies also to joining two napped fabrics, as in a velvet dress.

Seam with One Straight Edge and One Bias: Always lay the bias edge on top of the straight edge and be careful not to draw the bias edge out of shape as you work. Pin it at frequent intervals to hold it while you baste, or baste it with paper for stitching.

Eased-in Fullness: Often in fitting a curve, fullness has to be eased in. The fabric of one edge of the seam is longer than the other. The longer edge should be placed on top of the shorter one. Hold the edges together with pins, pushing a little extra fullness into the space between each pin. These seams must be basted.

Curved Seam: The fabric must be slashed frequently along a curved seam to allow it to curve in or out as desired.

Whipped Seam: Whipped seams are used in piecing, when the fabric is not wide enough to cut the full sweep required by the pattern. For an inconspicuous joining, the grain of the fabric must be just alike at both edges. Turn the edges and overcast them together. The stitches must be close enough to hold the fabric firm and even, but the thread must not be pulled too tightly. The same seam is used to piece together two selvedge edges.

Joined Seam: When two seams cross, the important things are to keep the joining flat and not to add bulk. The seam in each piece should be stitched and pressed open before the two are joined. Clip away the edge of the seam which is to lie under the top seam.

SEAM FINISHES

Overcast Seam: To prevent raveling in dress fabrics of rayon, silk, or wool, the seams should be overcast—both edges together or each edge separately as preferred. Take up about ⅛ inch of material and take care not to draw the thread too tight.

Pinked Seam: Pinking is an excellent way to finish seams in taffeta and firmly woven fabrics of wool, silk, rayon, or velvet. For speed, use pinking shears or a pinking machine, otherwise fold the edge and snip it with a small scissors all the way along.

Stitched-Edge Seam: This is a popular finish for silk, rayon, or dress-weight woolens and the heavier cottons. After the plain seam is stitched, turn under the raw edge of each side and stitch as close to the edge as possible. Press the seam open.

Seam with Edges Stitched Together: This finish is used on outer garments of light-weight fabrics. The quick way to do it is to turn the raw edges of the seam with the point of an iron. Be careful to turn it under evenly. Then stitch the edges together. This seam is pressed to one side.

Welt Seam: For coats and other sturdy garments stitch a plain seam. Trim ⅛ inch off one edge, put two edges together, and baste flat. Turn the garment right side out and stitch on the outside about ¼ inch from the seam line. For a double welt seam, make two stitchings.

Flat Felled Seam: This is a popular seam in men's shirts, uniforms, and pajamas. First stitch a regular seam, with the raw edges on the *outside of the garment*. Trim off one edge of the seam to within ¼ inch of the seam line. Turn under the raw edge of the other side ⅛ inch and pull it flat over the short side. Hem by hand or machine to the garment so the seam lies flat.

Covered Seam: The covered seam is excellent for clothes which are washed frequently. Baste as for a plain seam. Trim off one edge to within ⅛ inch of the basting. Turn the longer edge over the short one—raw edge turned under—and stitch on the basting line.

Tucked Seam: Baste in a plain seam and press the edges to one side. Turn the garment right side out and form a narrow tuck. Stitch the tuck on the seam line.

Outside Stitched Seam: This makes an easy seam finish for heavy cotton or light-weight wool materials. Stitch the seam and press it open. Turn to the wrong side of the garment and finish the edges of the seam by turning the raw edges under and stitch as close to the edge as possible. Then turn again to the right side of the garment and make a row of stitching parallel to the seam. Sometimes two rows are made, one on each side of the seam for trimming.

Taped Seam: In woolen garments where a bias edge is likely to shrink or stretch, purchase preshrunk tailor's cotton tape. Baste the tape to the seam line after the seam is basted, then stitch through the center of the tape.

Bound Seam: In unlined coats or jackets made of wool or heavy cotton, bound seams are important. The binding may be a true bias you cut yourself, or you can buy a bias binding; straight binding can be used only when the edges of the seam are straight. Stitch a plain seam and press it open. Bind each edge with the bias binding, stitching as close to the edge as possible in the first stitching.

Strengthened Seam: Stitch a seam and press both edges to one side. Then stitch again, through seam and garment, as close to the seam line as possible. This second stitching will show on the right side of the garment. This is a seam often used in tailored clothes and sturdy cotton garments. It is also very useful in joining a transparent fabric—neck edge, yoke, et cetera—to a non-transparent fabric. Fold both sides of the seam *away from the transparent material* and stitch on the non-transparent fabric. This keeps the seam from showing through.

LINGERIE SEAMS

French Seam: This dainty seam can be made by hand, or the first stitching can be made by machine and then hemmed by hand. Use it on children's dresses, and sheer blouses of cotton, linen, silk, or rayon. It should never be used for bias seams. Baste a seam on the *right side* of the garment with small stitches. Stitch it as close to the edge as possible. (If you are a beginner, stitch back a little from the edge, then cut off the edge close to the stitching.) Turn the garment to the wrong side and baste the seam so the edge is even. Stitch on the seam allowance. No threads should show on the right side. French seams are pressed on the wrong side.

Hand-Hemmed Welt Seam: Stitch the seam on the wrong side of the garment. Cut away one side of the seam edge, turn under the other edge, and hem it flat to the garment.

Rolled Seam: The rolled seam is used in fine sewing, where bands of embroidery are joined to the garment with *entre deux*, or in joinings where no seam should be visible through transparent fabrics. To make a rolled seam, join the seam with fine running stitches or machine stitches. Cut off half the seam allowance on one edge and roll the other edge between the thumb and first finger. Overcast this rolled edge close to the seam stitching.

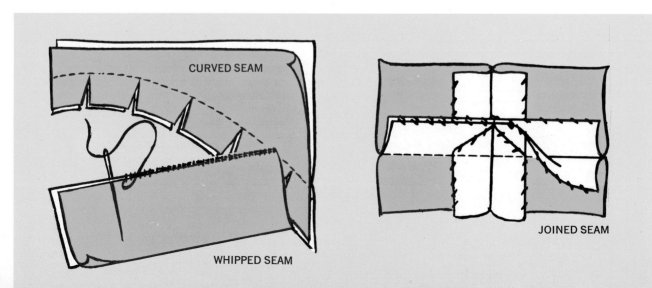

CURVED SEAM

WHIPPED SEAM

JOINED SEAM

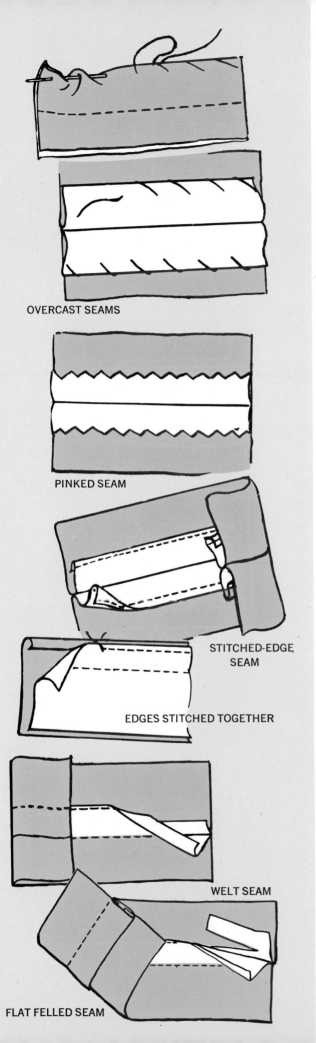

OVERCAST SEAMS

PINKED SEAM

STITCHED-EDGE SEAM

EDGES STITCHED TOGETHER

WELT SEAM

FLAT FELLED SEAM

DECORATIVE SEAMS

Slot Seam: The slot seam is a decorative seam for tailored clothes. Cut a straight strip of the fabric twice the seam allowance and the length of the seam. Run a guide basting through the center. Press back the seam allowance of the garment and place it over the fabric strip with the edges meeting. Baste the edges down. When both edges of the seam have been basted to the fabric strip, the pressed edges of the garment should meet at the guide basting. The stitching is done on the outside of the garment. Stitch down each side about ⅛ inch back from each edge.

Strap Seam: This is a seam used on many unlined coats and jackets. Make a plain seam with the raw edges on the *right side* of the garment. Trim off the edges to ¼ inch and press them open. Cut a bias strip of the garment fabric to be placed over the seam, and turn the edges of the strip with a hot iron. Be sure that the edges of the bias are turned straight and true. Place the strip over the seam and baste it in place. Stitch as close to each edge as possible.

Lapped Seam: The lapped seam is made on the right side and is excellent for joining yokes when the stitching is used as a decorative finish. Fold back the seam allowance of one piece of the fabric and press with an iron, making the fold even and sharp. Place this pressed edge over the flat edge of the other piece of fabric along the line of the seam allowance. Baste the fabrics together and stitch. This stitching may be close to the edge, or back from the edge, depending upon the effect desired. It may be stitched once, or several rows of stitching may be used for decoration.

· **Seams for Set-in Inserts:** Inserts of lace, embroidery, *entre deux*, or self-fabric trimming bands often have a seaming allowance. Place the trimming wrong side up and lay the edge of it on the garment *at the garment seam allowance.* The two sides of these seams are often very unequal. Baste the edges into a seam close to the trimming edge and stitch. Join the opposite side of the insert in the same way. In the case of *entre deux* and lace inserts, the edge of the seam is cut away and closely overcast; in other inserts the seam is pressed away from the trimming and stitched as close as possible to the seam edge of the trimming.

When the lace or *entre deux* has no seam allowance, baste its finished edge to the garment's seam-line and cut away half the seam allowance from the garment edge, then roll the remaining seam allowance and overcast it, taking the stitches through the lace or trimming.

Inserts: Inserts in a garment are placed on the right side of the fabric and pinned in position. Hem each edge of lace, or insert to the fabric by hand or by machine. Turn to the opposite side and cut through the center of the fabric covered by the insert. Press back the fabric edges and stitch down as described above or roll them by hand.

Piped Seam: A piping is stitched between the seams and serves to introduce a contrasting color or to provide a trimming emphasis in self-color. Prepared bias folds can be purchased, or you can make your own by cutting a true bias an inch wide and any length desired. Fold the bias strip lengthwise and press the fold.

Lay one section of the fabric flat on a table, lay the piping over it, and baste. Then lay the second section of fabric, with seam edges matching, so that the piping is between both fabrics, and baste again. Turn over to the right side and be sure that the piping is straight and the right width. Do not stitch until the basting shows just the effect you want. You can stitch on either the right or the wrong side.

Sometimes two colors are piped into the seam for trimming. To do this, place one binding over the other and proceed as directed above.

Corded Seam: Cut a true bias binding the length desired and baste it over a cable cord. Insert between seam edges as directed for a piped seam. For best results, a corded seam must be stitched by machine with a zipper or cording foot. Ready-made covered cord can be bought.

Upholsterers' Seam: This seam gives the effect of a corded seam and is often used in slip covers. To make it, follow directions for the French seam, only reverse the process so that the final covered seam is on the outside instead of the inside. The last stitching is made one-fourth inch from the edge, and it is not necessary to enclose the raveled edges on the inside, as in underwear seams.

TURNING CORNERS IN A SEAM

Sometimes it is necessary to turn corners in a seam, particularly in upholstery. For good results the corners must be as true and even as the straight edges. First decide whether the corners are to be rounded or square.

Rounded Corners: To keep rounded corners uniform, cut a cardboard pattern the shape desired and outline this curve on every flat piece where a corner seam will come. Trim the corners to this shape, allowing for the seam. Join the seam, then snip the curved seam before turning it. On the right side the edge must be true and even. Beginners will baste this edge carefully; experienced workers will press the edge with a hot iron and stitch it, keeping an even seam with the foot of the machine.

Square Corners: These must be watched carefully. Allow a little extra material at the point of each corner. Turn to the right side and check the evenness of each corner before you stitch.

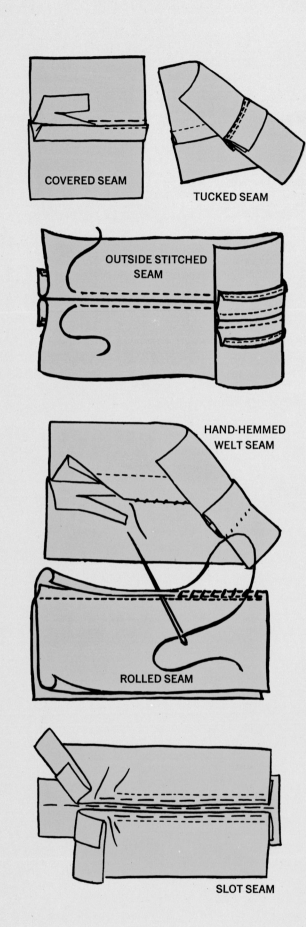

COVERED SEAM

TUCKED SEAM

OUTSIDE STITCHED SEAM

HAND-HEMMED WELT SEAM

ROLLED SEAM

SLOT SEAM

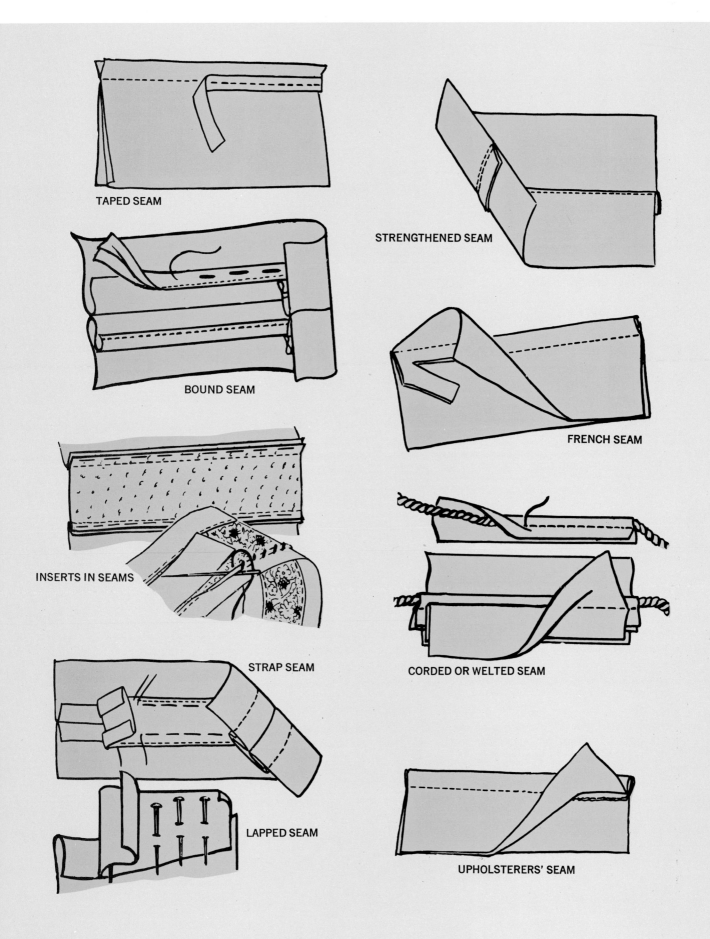

TAPED SEAM

STRENGTHENED SEAM

BOUND SEAM

FRENCH SEAM

INSERTS IN SEAMS

STRAP SEAM

CORDED OR WELTED SEAM

LAPPED SEAM

UPHOLSTERERS' SEAM

43

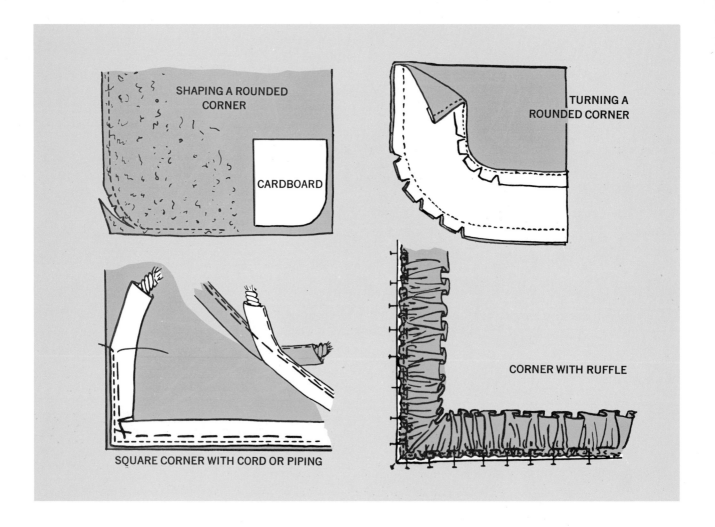

SHAPING A ROUNDED CORNER

CARDBOARD

TURNING A ROUNDED CORNER

SQUARE CORNER WITH CORD OR PIPING

CORNER WITH RUFFLE

With Cord or Piping: Baste the piping or cord to one edge, shaping it square and true at the corner and holding it with a little cross stitch. Baste with careful attention to true square lines. Then you can place the second piece of fabric over this edge and stitch it, assured that your corners are true. If the cord or piping has to be pieced, always piece it on a straight edge, never in a corner. To piece cord or piping, cross the two ends, keeping as straight a line as possible.

Corners with a Bias: Turning corners with a bias is a simple matter because the material adjusts to curves. Take advantage of this and plan a slightly rounded point at the corner. Baste the material, then turn to the right side and make sure you have not stretched the material so tightly that it draws.

Corners with a Ruffle: Test the effect you want by laying the work flat and pinning the ruffle to the edge of the material so that it lies flat. This will show you how much fullness to add at the corner as you turn. Be careful of the corner as you baste, as you must make a true turn.

Edge Finishes: Hems, Facings, Bindings

One *of the most important techniques in sewing lies in the finishing of edges. It should be remembered that some finishes are purely functional, while others add to the appearance of the finished work. In home sewing, edges are generally straight; but in garments the edges which have to be finished are more likely to be curved or shaped. The first and most widely used finish for an edge is the hem; after that come facings, bands and bindings.*

SUCCESSFUL EDGES

It is important that all edges in a garment be considered in their relation to the completed article. There are two important classifications: inconspicuous edges, and decorative edges. Once the style of a finish is decided upon, examine the fabric grain. Be sure to apply straight fabric finishes to straight edges, and bias finishes to curves.

To make a hem, turn your material to the wrong side and fold over the raw edge about ¼ inch; turn over a second fold to the measure of the finished hem. Hem the fabric to the left side of the garment by hand or machine. A measuring gauge is essential to insure an even hem.

HAND HEMS

Hand hems are a feature of fine apparel because they hang more gracefully and are less conspicuous than machine hems. The usual stitch used for hemming is called a felling stitch, and is made as follows:

Fasten the end of the material to something firm you can hold across your knees, or on a table. Sew your hem from right to left and work towards you, taking a tiny stitch in the garment and a tiny stitch in the folded edge of the hem. Train yourself to catch only a thread or two of fabric on the garment side. Some garments require fine, close stitches; but most hems are made with a quicker, slanting stitch.

Blind Hem: Blind hems are used when you wish a hem to be invisible on the right side of the material. Fine matching thread is important. Use a felling stitch. Space the stitches ⅜ inch apart and do not take up more than one thread of the garment fabric with each stitch. On the folded edge of the hem, take a stitch about ⅛ inch deep.

Slip-stitched Hem: This hem is used for facings and for hemming the linings in coats and dresses. It is invisible on both sides. With a thread exactly matching the fabric, take a stitch in the garment, picking up only one thread (in woolens this stitch does not pass entirely through—it only catches the top of the threads). Then pass the needle through the under side of the folded edge and slip it along inside the fold until you are ready to make the next stitch in the garment. The stitches should be about ¼ inch apart, and the thread should not be drawn too tight.

Lingerie Hems: They are usually narrow and on luxurious lingerie made by hand, even though the first turned edge of the hem may be stitched by machine. To do this turn the edge ¼ inch and stitch it. Now measure a hem 1 or 1½ inches wide and hem it by hand. When the edge is short the width of the hem may be very narrow.

Shell Hem: This hem is also used in making lingerie. Baste a narrow hem (about ½ inch). With matching thread take three overcast stitches across the hem—pull tightly— then hem the edge for ½ inch and take overcasting stitches once more across the edge.

Hand-Rolled Hem: This important feature of fine needlework is adaptable to any soft or sheer fabric and can be used on both bias and straight edges. It is particularly recommended for all scarves and neckwear. Use a fine needle and thread. Roll the edge of the fabric between your first finger and your thumb (moistening the fingers will help). Hem this roll with fine, even felling stitches.

Circular Hem: In hemming flared skirts, first baste the finished edge line of the skirt, then control the extra fullness

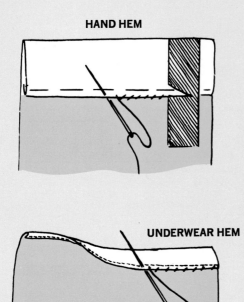

HAND HEM

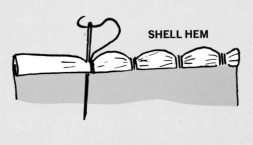

SHELL HEM

SLIPSTITCH FOR HEMS

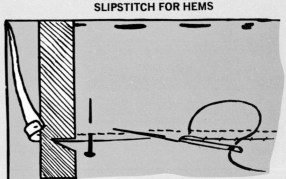

UNDERWEAR HEM

at the edge. There are two ways of doing this. (1) You can turn the edge ½ inch and gather it, then turn the hem and lay it flat, hemming it flat to the garment. Or (2) gather the edge without turning it, and finish with a bias tape; then fold and secure it to the garment on the wrong side.

Hemming Curved Edges: The safe rule is to make a very narrow hem—½ inch or less is often enough. Where the decorative effect calls for a larger hem make it the size that looks best and follow the directions for a circular hem. When the skirt edge is very full, circular stitched hems 1 inch wide are effective. Rolled hems are best for transparent fabrics.

Turned Picot Edge: This makes a lovely finish for straight or curved edges in transparent collars and cuffs. Hemstitch the edge by machine, then cut the hemstitching in half with a sharp pointed scissors. Turn this edge once, as little as you possibly can, and hem it. When a selvage edge is to be hemmed, it can be turned the same way.

Hem in a Pleated Skirt: First rip the bastings that hold the pleats at the lower edge so the hem can be turned flat and finished before the pleats are pressed. If the skirt is curved or circular, lay the extra material in small darts on the wrong side of the hem edge before turning.

Taped Hem: In hemming heavier woolens, omit the first turning in of the raw edge. Instead, place a seam binding flat on the right side of the raw edge the full length of the hem. Hold it in place with fine running stitches or machine stitching; then hem it flat to the garment on the wrong side.

Catch-Stitched Hem: In coats and jackets (made of heavy fabric) that are lined, the hem is turned once and the raw edge of the fabric is catch-stitched to the garment. This edge is later covered by the lining.

Napery Hem: On damask linen, first turn the raw edge under about ⅛ inch, then fold the hem—about ¼ inch. Then fold the hem back on the right side of the material so you can hold the edges to be joined as you would for overcasting. Overcast the edge, taking tiny stitches close together across the edge of the work. The thread must be fine, and the stitches should run with the grain. The hem does not show on either side.

MACHINE HEMS

In sturdy cotton garments for men, women, and children, and in most sewing for the home, hems are usually stitched by machine. Prepare the hem as directed for hand hemming and baste it. Run the machine stitching as close to the edge as possible.

Stitched-Band Hem: In tailored garments or in wide circular skirts made of opaque fabric, a narrow hem finished with five or six rows of machine stitching *evenly spaced* makes a very attractive finish. Omit the first turn and overcast the raw edge.

Hem for Ruffles: Hems that run into big yardage are finished with amazing speed if you use the adjustable

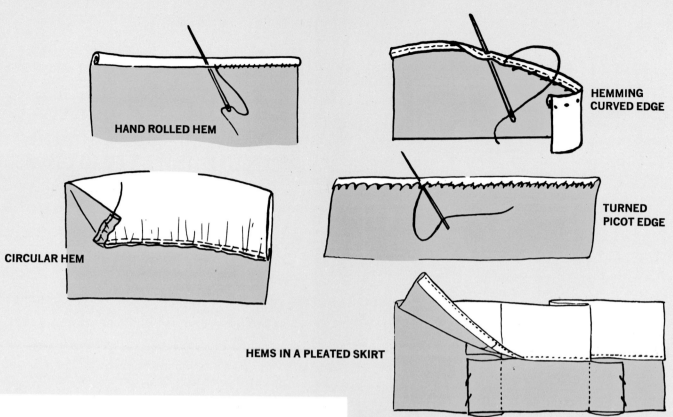

HAND ROLLED HEM

HEMMING CURVED EDGE

CIRCULAR HEM

TURNED PICOT EDGE

HEMS IN A PLEATED SKIRT

hemmer on your machine. This attachment can be used for many types of narrow hems, especially long hems on straight edges.

Faced Hem: Garment edges which do not permit a hem without becoming too short should be faced. Cut the facing band the desired width of the hem and the necessary length. Stitch a seam holding the right side of the band to the right side of the garment. When you turn a faced hem to the wrong side, do not fold in the seam; instead, turn ½ inch or more of the garment fabric in the hem so that the facing will not show. Finish as for regular hem.

DECORATIVE HEMS

Right-Side-Out Hem: Sometimes decorative hems are made by turning the hem up on the right side of the garment (the seams must, of course, be reversed in the hem section). These hems are often bound in contrasting color or finished with piping or corded. Sometimes they are shaped into scallops, points, or squared outlines. They should be used only in reversible fabrics, such as crepe-backed satin, or in fabrics which are the same on both sides. They are not successful when the fabric is ugly on the wrong side or when the garment is so curved that the fullness must be gathered or laid in darts.

Applied Hem or Double Bindings: These hems are an important decorative feature of bedspreads and curtains; they are also used in peasant-type dresses and sometimes in

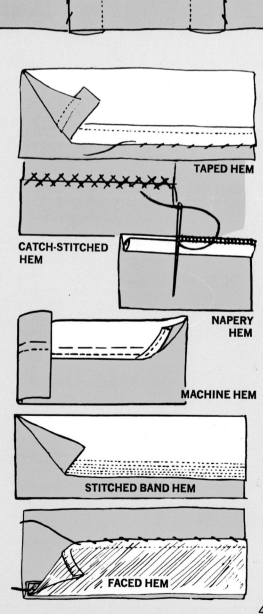

TAPED HEM

CATCH-STITCHED HEM

NAPERY HEM

MACHINE HEM

STITCHED BAND HEM

FACED HEM

47

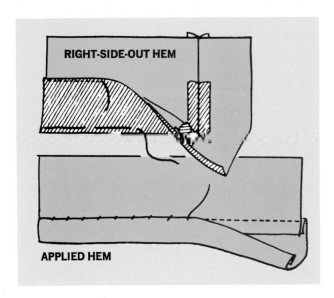

RIGHT-SIDE-OUT HEM

APPLIED HEM

Straight Extension Facing: Cut your fabric twice the width of the facing and the desired length, with seam allowance. Fold it and baste the folded edge. To attach it, place the facing on the right side of the garment and seam the lower edge to the garment edge. Then turn the facing to the wrong side of the garment and hem the other edge on the seam.

Extension facings are often used in waists and plackets to hold buttons or snap fasteners. Make them as directed above, or, for greater strength, cut the facing three times as wide as the finished band. This gives three thicknesses of fabric to hold buttons.

Double Facings: Double facings serve to extend an edge, fill in a neckline, or lengthen a skirt with an added band. Apply the fold under a turned edge, stitching them together; or under a finished edge so the fold can be basted to the garment ½ inch back from the edge; or turn the edges of the fold so they are finished and can be stitched on top of the garment edge.

Facing Scallops: Outline the scallops on the article to be finished, using a cup or other object of desired size. This marking should be done with chalk on the wrong side of the fabric. Cut a bias facing 2 inches wider than the depth of the scallop and the length desired. Lay it right side up on the table and lay the scalloped edge over it with the right side down. Baste the fabric to the facing, following the outline of the scallops, then stitch on this line. Now cut away excess fabric from the edge, following the scallops, leaving a ¼ inch seam allowance. Notch this seam allowance along the curves before you turn the facing. The edge of the scallops should be carefully basted and pressed. Then the edge of the facing can be hemmed above the scallops.

End Finish for Band Facing: When the end of the band is not included in a seam, it can be finished in any of the following ways: (1) Turn in the end and hem it to the garment; this stitching will show on the right side. (2) Roll the end in a self-hem; this stitching will not show on the right side. (3) When facing and garment edges meet, turn both edges so they face each other and slip-stitch them together. (4) When a band finishes with the edge of the garment and is included in a seam or collar joining, baste the three edges together before stitching the seam.

Applied Trimming Band: When trimming bands are narrow, it saves time to cut a cardboard the width of the band without seam allowance, then put this cardboard over the fabric and press the seam allowance over the cardboard so it makes a sharp, clear edge. Apply the band to the garment and baste the edges for stitching.

Band with Pointed End: When the end of a trimming band is pointed or curved, the cardboard used for pressing the sharp edge can be shaped and the end pressed sharply. Cut away all extra material from this end except the seam allowance before you apply it. When a band is stitched to a garment so the shaped end hangs free, allow a double thickness at the end of the band or else face the point or curve.

sport clothes. Girls' dresses of organdy can employ decorative hems, and sometimes they are used on play clothes of chambray, percale, and sturdy cotton. This decorative hem is always *in a contrasting color*. It is cut on a true bias, which is then folded in half. Apply it to the edge of the skirt or bedspread by placing one edge of the binding on the right side of the fabric edge and stitching a seam that leaves one edge of the binding free. Turn to the wrong side of the garment and hem the free edge of the binding on the seam edge.

Stitched Applied Hem Extension: A hem extension may be added to lengthen a woolen garment, especially if the skirt is not too wide. Cut the binding so that it can be applied double as directed above; or cut it in the size of the finished binding and line it with a thinner fabric *also cut on the bias*. Apply it as directed above, then cover it with rows of machine stitching.

STRAIGHT FACINGS AND TRIMMING BANDS

Straight Facing: Straight facings are used to turn an edge smoothly when it is not possible to spare fabric for a hem. They can be turned as facings on the wrong side or as trimming bands on the right side. When the facing is to be turned on the wrong side, apply your straight strip of fabric *on the right side of the garment*. Join the edges of the garment and the band in a seam. Then turn the band to the wrong side of the garment, taking care that the seamed edge is basted and the fabric lies flat and smooth. Turn the edge of the band and hem it to the garment or stitch it in place.

To finish a trimming band on the right side of the garment, reverse the instructions given above and stitch the facing band to the wrong side of the garment first.

Scalloped hems are made by facing the lower edge with bias strips. Use either the same color and fabric as the garment, or try a contrasting color or unexpected texture — satin facing on a dress-weight crepe, perhaps.

When a band, belt, or scarf ends in a point, stitch across the band in a pointed line before turning and cut away the extra material, snipping the corner.

Mitered Corner: When a straight band turns a square corner, fit the edges of the band to the fabric so the corner is square and even. Lay the excess fullness at the corner in a fold and stitch it so the line of stitching extends straight across the corner. Cut away this excess fabric and press the seam open. Turn the band so it lies flat on the fabric, and so the corner is sharp, square, and smooth.

When a band is applied to a deep point, the edges are stitched in an even seam. Lay the fabric flat and pin the mitered corner so the line of pins extends straight through the corner. Cut away the extra material and seam the corner. Snip the seam allowance at the point and turn the band to the right side. This will make the band lie flat.

Banding a Square Neck: The band can be turned to the right side or applied as a facing. A straight band is stitched to the neckline with edges of band and garment meeting. Place it carefully so the outside edge lies flat and the excess fullness at the mitered corners is pinned for cutting. Before cutting it away, stitch across this excess material from corner to corner. Cut away the extra material. Press the short seam and turn the outer edge of the binding, then cut into the corner beside this new mitered seam. Stitch the band to the garment taking a ⅝ inch seam and turning sharp corners. Clip into the corners; grade the seams. Turn band to inside, baste close to folded edge, and press in place.

FACINGS

A facing is a piece of fabric applied to a garment edge and turned to form a neat edge finish. Some facings are cut in one with the garment; others are applied separately. Facings are most often cut on the same grain as the edge they will finish, but sometimes a facing will be cut on the bias for a special effect.

Applying a Shaped Facing: Most printed patterns include facing pieces if there are edges to be faced. The facing is the same shape as the edge to which it is applied and it is cut on the same grain of the fabric. The following steps apply to neckline, armhole, and any other shaped facing.

Stay-stitch curved edges of garment and facing if fabric is loosely woven or stretchy.

Join shoulder (or underarm) seams of garment and facing; press open. Finish unnotched edge of facing by turning under and stitching, pinking, machine zigzagging, or hand overcasting.

Right sides together, pin facing to garment matching seams and notches. Stitch on the seam line. Grade the seam allowance by trimming the seam allowance nearest the garment to about ⅜ inch; trim the facing seam allowance to about ¼ inch. Clip the seam allowance at intervals along the curved edges. Press seam toward facing.

To understitch the facing and thereby prevent its rolling out, stitch from the right side through facing and seam allowance close to the seam line.

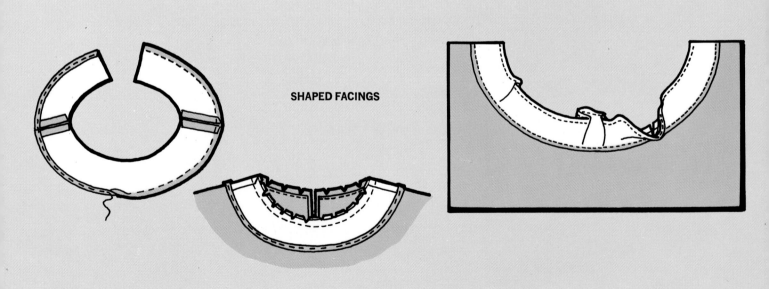

SHAPED FACINGS

50

Turn facing to inside, baste, and press in place. Slip-stitch the facing to the garment at the shoulder (or underarm) seam allowances only.

Facing Cut in One With the Garment: This type of facing is often found at the front edge of a coat or jacket. Its use eliminates a seam in bulky fabric. The facing part is folded back against the fabric, right sides together. The neckline is stitched on the seam line and the facing is turned right side out. Facings cut in one are not usually understitched.

Neckline and Armhole Facing Cut in One Piece: When the neckline and armhole facings would overlap at the shoulder if cut and applied separately, the designer often cuts these two facings as one.

Stay-stitch and finish unnotched edge of facing as usual. Do not join garment or facing at shoulder or underarm seams.

Right sides together, pin facing to front, matching notches. Stitch neck and armhole edges. Grade seam allowances. Clip curves. Press facing to inside.

Prepare back in same manner. To join shoulder seams, with right sides together stitch back of garment to front of garment at shoulders being careful not to catch in the facing. Trim seams. Slip the seam allowances under the facing. Slip-stitch shoulder edges of facing together.

To stitch side seams, open out facings at armhole edges. Stitch front to back at side seams from lower edge to edge of facing. Press facings to inside. Slip-stitch facings to side seam allowances only.

BIAS FACINGS

A bias facing must always be cut on the true bias. A true bias is the diagonal of a square. If you fold the straight grain of the material parallel to the cross grain, the folded edge is the true bias. Cut across this edge, using a measure. Even though cutting on "a near bias" would save material, it must never be done, because the facing would not lie smoothly.

Piecing Bias Facing: The ends of the bias facing must be joined with matching grain. The seam is usually diagonal.

Apply Bias Facing: Place the facing on the right side of the garment and join the edges of facing and garment. Stitch the seam, cut away surplus, and turn the facing to the wrong side, taking care that the edge is smooth and even. Smooth the facing flat on the material and hem it to the garment, turning in the edge ½ inch.

Facing Rounded Corners: A bias facing makes a smoother rounded corner than hemming. First shape the corner, then place the facing on the edge and around the corner, stretching it a little at the curved edge. Pin or baste carefully before sewing. It should be flat and smooth.

BINDING EDGES

Whether bindings are purchased or homemade, always bear in mind that *straight bindings* must be applied only to *straight edges*. Bias bindings are necessary for curved edges. Note that binding covers both sides of an edge, as contrasted with facing, which can be seen only on one side.

Applying Straight Binding: Cut a narrow strip of material on the straight or use a purchased binding. To apply it, fold the binding in half the long way and press. Slip the edge of the fabric to be bound between the two halves of the pressed binding and stitch as close to the edge of the binding as possible. This is the simplest way to apply a binding and popular with most home sewers, but it is likely to pull out with frequent washings.

To make the binding more secure, stitch the edge to be bound by machine.

To make a binding secure to withstand constant washing, use the following method: Place the binding on the wrong side of the material, matching the edge to the edge of the fabric. Stitch these edges together ¼ inch back. Then turn the binding to the right side and hem it flat. It can be hemmed on the seam edge to make a true binding, or it can be pulled up as far as possible on the fabric and hemmed there to make a wider trimming. Bias bindings with folded edges, sold by the yard, are applied the same way.

Binding a Square Corner: In the first stitching continue the binding around the corner as you make your seam. Trim the seam close to the stitching at the corner. When you turn the edge and baste it, make the binding form a tiny inverted pleat at the corner so that the edge lies flat and square. This is called a mitered corner.

Braid Binding: There are several widths of flat trimming braid which can be used for binding. The wider widths are creased through the center and basted to the edge so that the binding is deep enough to hold firm when stitched. Narrower braids are applied to simulate binding, as follows: Stitch the braid at the edge and on the wrong side of the fabric, then turn the edge to the right side and hem the braid down.

Bias Binding: On the household cottons, aprons, house dresses, children's dresses, and so forth, use a folded bias binding purchased at the store or cut your own. Turn both edges and fold the binding through the center. Apply it to curved edges on garments, slip covers, et cetera, as directed for straight binding.

Single Bias Binding: Rayon crepe dresses or underwear can be bound with self-fabric or contrasting fabric, often from scraps left after cutting the garment. Be sure the binding is a true bias, not a near bias. If you are careful to match the grain, the binding can be pieced any number of

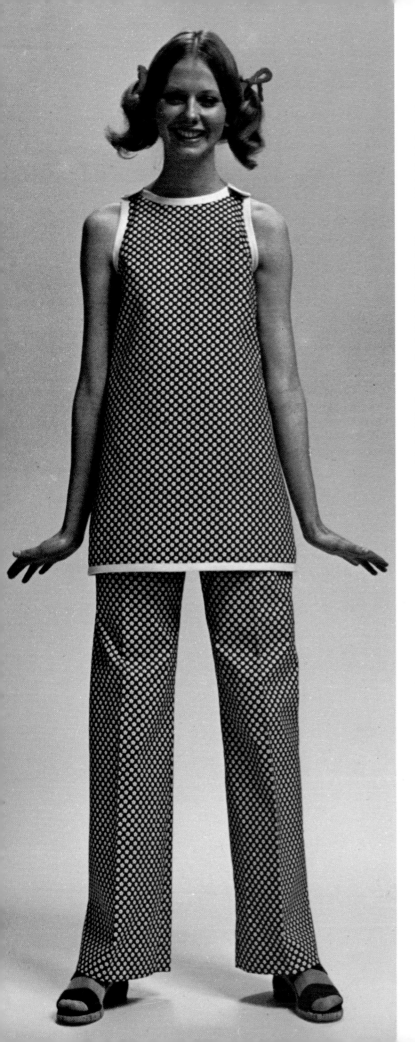

times. To apply it, lay it on the right side of the garment with edges matching and stitch by hand or machine. Turn it carefully; first turn the seam of the binding then turn the binding in half and turn the edge under. This is not difficult if you work on an ironing borad and turn the edges with the point of an iron. Hand-hem the binding to the seam so that no stitching shows on the right side.

Double Bias or French Binding: This makes a good finish for transparent fabrics, sheer underwear, fine cottons. Cut a true bias ¾ inch wide and the length desired. Fold the bias in half lengthwise and baste or press the folded edges. Place the binding on the right side of the garment with the unfinished edges paralleling the edge of the garment. Join the edges in a narrow seam run by hand or stitched on the machine, then turn the folded edge of the binding to the wrong side and hem it by hand to the stitched seam. *No stitches should show on the right side.*

Binding Stitched with a Seam: Pin or baste the seam and place the straight or bias binding over the seam, stitching so that the edges of the fabric and one edge of the binding are caught in the seam. Fold the opposite edge of the binding and turn back so that it lies flat on the garment. Hem it down by hand or machine.

Match bias binding to one of the colors of the garment fabric for a neat touch on sportswear.

The Shape-Makers: Darts, Tucks, Pleats

he group included in this chapter—darts, tucks, and pleats—has many uses both in dressmaking and in sewing for the home. Their function is to control fullness and to add to decoration. Darts, which shape the garment, are functional; pleats and tucks are both functional and decorative.

DARTS

Darts are used to curve a straight fabric to the molded lines of the body. They fit out fullness in a smooth line. Because of this, it is usually better to place several short darts one after the other than to fit out the same amount of fullness in one long dart.

A dart is wide at one end and gradually tapers to nothing at the other end. You will find darts indicated with perforations in your pattern. To make a dart, lay the pattern on your fabric, mark the perforations, and fold the fabric so that the two outer perforations lie exactly on top of one another. Crease the fabric from the overlapping point to the perforation that marks the end of the dart. Then make a running stitch by hand or machine from the perforations at the edge to the perforations at the end of the dart.

FITTING DARTS

Plain Darts: The plain darts which shape the underarm or hip line of a garment are marked on each pattern. If you are not using a pattern, pin extra fullness into darts. Dart stitching should be shaped to a point in a long, gradual line, so as to leave no awkward bulge at the end. Stitch the darts and press them before joining the seam. In heavy material the dart is cut down the center and pressed open; in light material it is pressed to one side or pressed flat.

Shoulder Darts: A dart can be used at the shoulder, running down from the shoulder seam. Shoulder darts can follow the armhole line, placed 1½ inches from the armhole, or be placed over the fullest point of the bust. Slanted darts are sometimes stitched on the right side of the garment as a decoration.

Neckline Darts: Many women find a neckline more becoming if darts are fitted in the back of the neck. This keeps the collar from standing out or away from the neckline. Two darts are often enough; sometimes four or more are necessary.

Darts for Sleeve Control: At the elbow of long tight sleeves, darts are used to curve the fabric. A long fitted

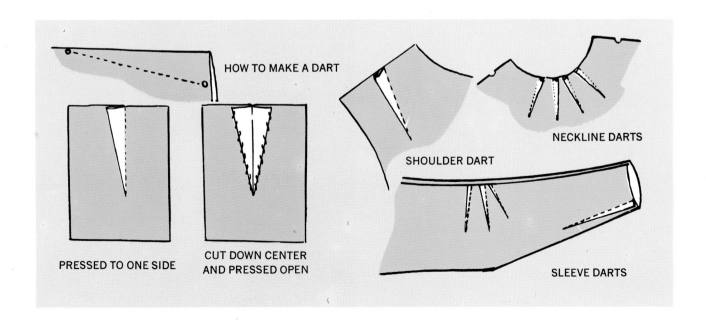

HOW TO MAKE A DART

PRESSED TO ONE SIDE

CUT DOWN CENTER AND PRESSED OPEN

SHOULDER DART

NECKLINE DARTS

SLEEVE DARTS

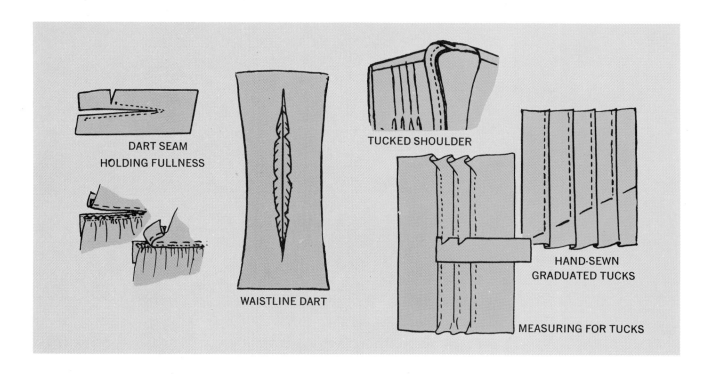

DART SEAM
HOLDING FULLNESS

WAISTLINE DART

TUCKED SHOULDER

HAND-SEWN
GRADUATED TUCKS

MEASURING FOR TUCKS

sleeve should never be made without darts or fullness to ease the elbow.

Darts for Waistline Control: Darts are often placed above the beltline to create a high-waisted fitting or to control fullness in one spot. In princess lines, or in separate blouses, darts are often used to shape the garment to fit closer to the waistline. To make these body darts fold the fabric on a straight line and mark the widest section of the dart. Shape the dart into points at both ends. For the best effect, darts so used should be long. As in other instances of fullness control, several shallow darts are better than one large one.

HAND AND MACHINE-MADE TUCKS

In making pleats and tucks it saves time to work on an ironing board and press the sharp edges before the pleat or tuck is basted. The *second pressing*, which completes the pleat or tuck, should not be done until after it is basted, fitted, and stitched.

Tucks Controlling Fullness: In soft materials, tucks control fullness and take the place of darts. These are marked in the pattern or must be planned to give fullness where it is needed. A large tuck at the shoulder line is sometimes used to cover the shoulder seam. Again, a group of small tucks, or a continued row of shallow tucks, adds fullness. Long tucks between inserts of lace are used in fine underwear, neckwear, and blouses; they should be made by hand.

Measuring for Tucks: Every tuck in a group must be exactly the same width, and the space between tucks must be carefully measured.

When tucks are made by hand, use the marking on the pattern or cut a measuring gauge. Take a straight piece of cardboard and notch it (1) the depth of the finished tuck; (2) the distance between the tucks, measured from one stitched line to the next; and (3) the length of the tuck. When the rows are graduated, instead of using this third measure, baste a line on the garment indicating where the tucks should end.

Hand-Sewn Tucks: Fold the edge for the tuck, then sew it with a running stitch, using fine thread and a fine needle. Measure as you work. Tie your threads securely and cut them close—no knots must show. Never use a draw thread to make a tuck; the tuck would not wear.

Machine-Made Tucks: In making tucks with a machine attachment use the 1/4 inch or 1 inch cleat provided for the purpose. Set this attachment, and it will space the tucks.

Pin Tucks: These are used as decoration on very sheer fabrics. Stitch the tuck by hand very close to the folded edge, so close you cannot measure it. Use the measure for spacing and for length of the tuck.

When the tucks vary in length, mark the variations on the material by running a diagonal basting thread where you want the tucks to end.

Hand-Corded Tucks: Mark the edge of each tuck with a basting so it will be straight and even. Encase the cord in the tuck as you stitch it.

Machine-Corded Tucks: Mark the position of the tucks and baste a tuck encasing a cord. Stitch close to the cord, using the cording or zipper foot. If the edges are not covered by a seam, turn the cord to the wrong side and fasten each end down securely. If you unwind the end a little, it will make less bulk. Never cut off the cording flush with the end of the tuck; it would fray. If the side edge is finished before

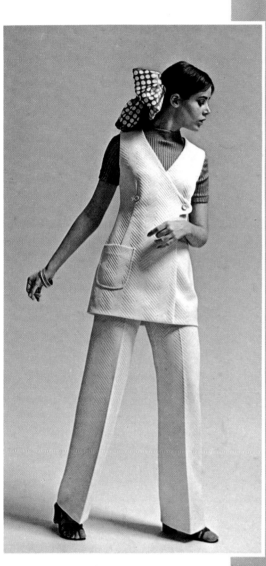

Diagonal darts at the waistline
and armholes lightly shape
the pantsuit's tunic top.

Deep pleats dramatize the skirt
of a tab-trimmed day dress.
See its party version, page 50.

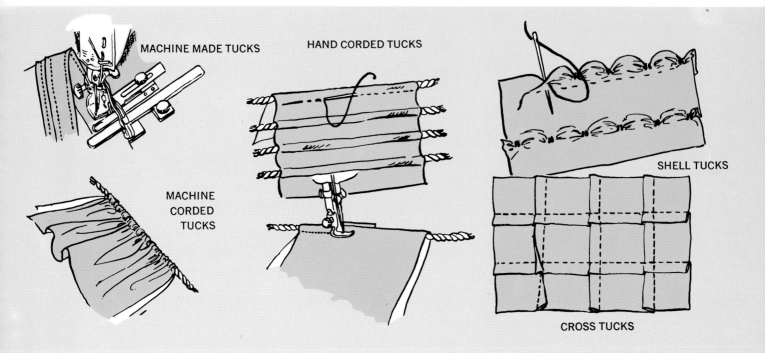

MACHINE MADE TUCKS

HAND CORDED TUCKS

MACHINE CORDED TUCKS

SHELL TUCKS

CROSS TUCKS

you cord the tuck, first finish the end of the cord by unraveling it a little, turning it back, and overcasting it several times. Then overcast it securely to the side edge before you start to run the tuck. The opposite end of the cord must be finished and overcast firmly in place before the tuck is finished. This makes a beautiful finish on the ends of a scarf.

Shell Tucks: First measure for the shells. The gauge should be cut so the shell is about twice as long as the tuck is deep. Mark with a pencil dot. Then make two overcasting stitches across the tuck to hold the shell. Run thread to the next dot and make another overcasting stitch.

Crossed Tucks: Crossed tucks are sometimes used for decoration on yokes or all over blouses made of transparent fabrics. Space the tucks as desired. Mark the measures carefully and make the horizontal tucks all the way across. Press them flat before measuring and tucking the vertical tucks.

Tucks Covering Seams: In skirts and blouses, in curtains and slipcovers, a tuck may be made directly over a seam to hide the joining. Make this tuck the desired width, and stitch the tuck in with the seam stitching.

Circular Tucks: These tucks must be marked carefully *to indicate both edges.* When you join the markings, lay the fullness of the under tuck, spacing it between pins, before basting or stitching the tuck.

GARMENT PLEATS

Although they are called by different names to describe their particular use, there are really two important types of pleats . . . the *side pleat* and the *box pleat.* When a box pleat is made wrong side out it is called an *inverted pleat.* When it is short and inserted in the lower edge of a skirt it is

called a *kick pleat.* A *knife pleat* is simply the description of a pleat with a very firmly pressed edge. Pleats are spaced across the fabric, or in small groups, and are usually folded to a full depth.

Whatever the type of pleating, first seam the sections of the garment and press the seam open. If you are using a pattern, you will find that the size and spacing of the pleat is marked. Carefully reproduce these marks on the material with tailor's tacks, chalk, or a running wheel. If you are not using a pattern, decide upon the size of the pleats and space them evenly. To insure a sharp edge, many people cut a piece of cardboard the length of the pleat and press the edge of the pleat over the cardboard. If you do this, *use a press cloth.*

Straight Pleats: When a skirt or dress is hung from a yoke, or when a pleated flounce is used, a straight piece of fabric can be pressed into straight pleats. (Note particularly whether your pleats are shaped at the waistline.) In straight pleating the fabric is set just the same at the top and the bottom. This can be a box pleat, a side pleat, or an inverted pleat.

Side Pleats: Side pleats are arranged on each side of a center panel, if they are to go all around a skirt. The pleats may be shallow or deep, depending upon the amount of fullness desired in the skirt. They fold away from the center. They can be fitted over the hips by making them deeper at the waistline.

Box Pleats: Box pleats are used in skirts, shirts, and in decorative flounces for bedspreads, slip covers, and so forth. They are used in clusters too; and we often see a box pleat forming a panel. Use the spacing marked on your pattern, or decide on the size and spacing suited to your need and cut a gauge. Mark the folding line with chalk, using a yardstick. Indicate by a basting thread the line to which this folded edge will be stitched. Decide on the top and bottom finish before you fold or press the pleats. A full box pleat is folded under so that the under edges meet;

56

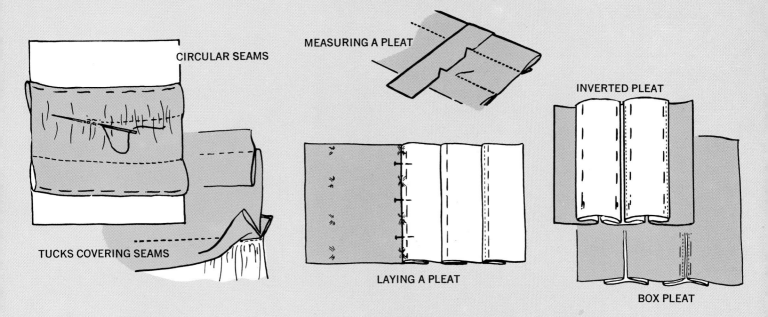

CIRCULAR SEAMS

TUCKS COVERING SEAMS

MEASURING A PLEAT

INVERTED PLEAT

LAYING A PLEAT

BOX PLEAT

shallow box pleats that save material are made with a shallow fold.

Inverted Pleats: These are simply box pleats turned wrong side out. They are often used in the front and back seams of skirts, and the "action back" featured in sport shirts is made of one or two inverted pleats set below a yoke.

Kick Pleats: The extension for these pleats is cut in one piece with the skirt seam. This is a very important construction when pleats are used in transparent material. Stitch the seams and fold the pleat to one side; then stitch across the top of the pleat. This is the only stitch line that shows on the front of the garment and it keeps the pleat from sagging. Turn the hem after the pleat is stitched; cut through the seam above the hem so that the work lies smooth.

Set-In Kick Pleats: Often a feature of pattern construction, these pleats help widen a too-narrow skirt. Fold the seam back and plan your pleat, fitting a stay in place or cutting a stay to suit your needs. This pleat is made like a box pleat with a pointed top. Stitch the seams, press the pleat, and stitch the point carefully with one or more rows of stitching.

Contrasting Color in Pleats: Novelty pleats are made with striped fabrics pleated so that one color does not show until the pleat opens. This can be done with any pleated skirt pattern *with deep full pleats*. Simply insert stripes of the contrasting color in the exact width of the underfold of your pleats. Unless you have the great patience to insert the many stripes necessary for side pleats, it is better to use this effect in box pleats or inverted pleats.

Permanent (Stitched) Creased Pleats: With thread which exactly matches the material, stitch as close to the folded edge of the pleat as possible; stitch the inside folds

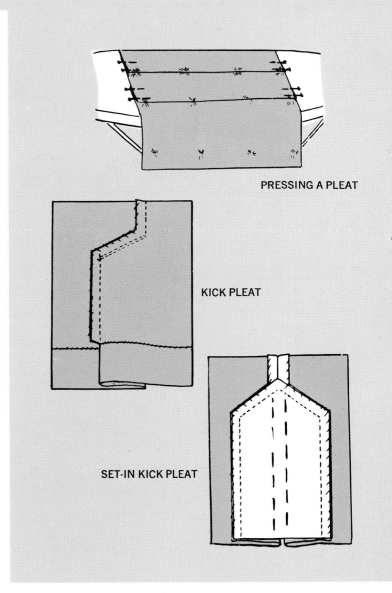

PRESSING A PLEAT

KICK PLEAT

SET-IN KICK PLEAT

Far left: Polka dots and pearls, plus neat little sleeves, make a party-perfect outfit for a full-hipped figure.

Near left: Properly placed pleats—as here, below a hip length tunic—flatter a less-than-perfect hipline.

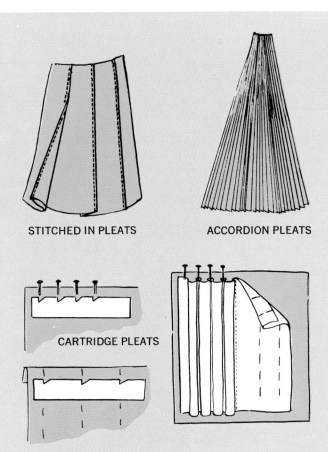

STITCHED IN PLEATS   ACCORDION PLEATS

SET IN GODET   CARTRIDGE PLEATS

the same way. This is very useful in wash garments or to save time by not having to re-press pleats.

Unpressed Pleats: In soft garments, fullness is often laid and allowed to fall as it will. *Do not press the pleat edge* in this case. Mark your pattern, fold your pleats, and baste them flat all the way down. After the garment has been fitted, release the basting and press the lower edge as if it were gathered instead of pleated.

Accordion Pleats: Accordion pleats are pressed in by steam, and pleating them is a skilled art. You simply finish off the lower edge of the necessary yardage of material and take it to the pleater. To compute the yardage, decide on the finished size, then multiply that figure by three. Many skilled artisans nowadays can offer you sectional group pleating and circular pleating. Ask them for directions on how to prepare your material.

Pleated Circular Skirts: Circular skirts with pleats are usually cut in many gores, often twelve, one for each pleat. Seams must be placed at the edge of an under pleat. The outside of each pleat is pressed sharply on an edge like a man's trousers.

Pleated Circular Inserts: These can be set into a seam or spaced like a panel in the front of a skirt. When the insert extends the whole length of the skirt, lay the pleats so they are broader at the hem and narrower at the waist. Space them so they meet at the center. The pleats can be broad or narrow. The edge of the insert can be (1) joined in the seam;

(2) extended back of the seam for extra fullness; or (3) extended over the front of the garment to form a panel in addition to the pleated insert.

Cartridge Pleats: A trimming band of cartridge pleats is often used in garments. The pleated section is straight and is applied to another piece of fabric. Decide on the size of the pleats and then cut a gauge to measure (1) for marking the finished size of the pleat on the under fabric; and (2) for marking the finished spacing of the pleat on the top fabric. Lay the fabrics together with the line of markings matching so the pleats stand out. Then you can stitch all the way down between each pleat, or only part way down so that the end of the pleat falls clear. Do not press cartridge pleats.

GODETS

Godets are circular inserts set into a slash or a seam. They can extend the full length of the skirt or curtain, or they can be shortened to any desired length. Some godets are shallow, others are very broad, at the lower edge. When the godet is a feature of fashion, your pattern will indicate the size and fullness. When you use it in remaking something or in home decoration, you must decide for yourself how much fullness you need. The top of the godet can be rounded or pointed.

To set a godet in a slash or seam, work from the lower edge to the point and shape the point carefully. There should be no wrinkle on the right side. After the seam is stitched, finish the hem.

Frills
And
Flounces

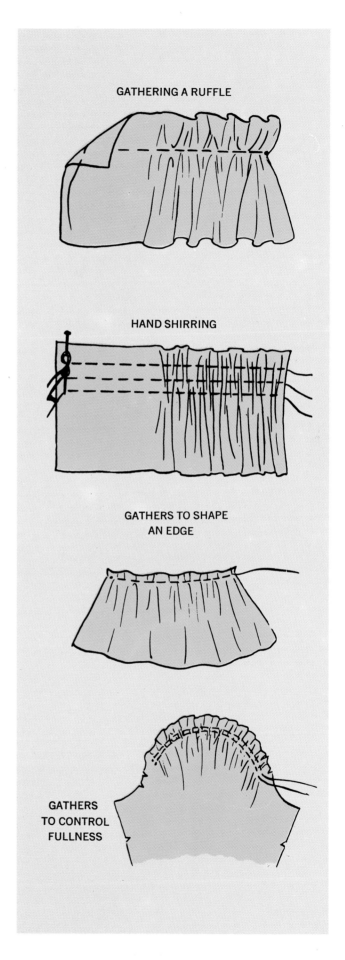

Gathers *are used to give fullness to garments or to shape an edge to a curve. Anyone who sews must learn how to draw fabric together in soft fullness, in gathers and shirrings, and how to make ruffles of every type.*

Ruffles are gathered strips used as a trimming and are best made of soft fabrics or crisp, stiff ones. (Fullness in heavy or stiff fabrics is best laid in pleats or darts.) The amount of fullness is important: soft fabrics can be gathered more closely, giving greater fullness; but when the gathers are spaced, it will sometimes prove wiser to take out a little fullness by shortening the length of the ruffle. If a ruffle wilts, don't add extra fullness, but try binding the edge with ribbon or a double bias of self-fabric. Ruffles can be of any desired width, but the use for which the ruffle is intended will determine whether you (1) gather a single edge—to bind or set into a seam; (2) turn the edge to hem down; or (3) turn the edge to form a heading.

GATHERING

Hand Gathers: Use the coarsest thread a fine needle will hold and always knot the thread. Use a running stitch, and be sure that the stitching is straight. Sometimes it is necessary to use a close stitch for fine gathers in light-weight fabric. A longer stitch is suitable for heavier material. *Successive rows of gathers should always be done with the same stitch spacing.* Many people like to mark the rows for gathering to insure accuracy. Pull the fabric back on the thread as you work. The gathers can be closely or widely spaced depending upon the fullness desired. As each row of gathers is finished, fasten the end of the thread around a pin.

Above: A flirty, be-ruffled young dress wears its heart on its sleeve!

Right: Drawstring-tied split skirt tops a puff-sleeved romper— fun for a teenager!

Vari-colored gingham panels are gathered to make this story-book skirt, its demure little sunbonnet, and a drawstring pouch.

Hand Shirring: Shirring is several rows of gathers in a soft fabric evenly spaced. Shirred effects sometimes form deep yokes, and again are used in allover fullness construction.

Gathers that Shape an Edge: To shape an edge use one row of gathers.

Gathers to Control Fullness: Use two rows of gathers at the top of sleeves, in shoulder lines and other seam construction.

Gathers in Ruffles: To draw fullness into a given measure use at least two and preferably four rows of gathers.

Gathers in Shirring: Use fine thread and make row after row of gathers. You will need ten to twelve rows.

Setting Gathers: After the stitching has been completed, the gathers must be spaced to fall smoothly. Our grandmothers stroked the fabric with the point of the needle, but this too often cuts or damages a rayon or a delicate weave. A safer way is to twist the thread around the needle and pull the material into place.

A Stay under Gathers: When many rows of shirring are used at the neckline or waistline of a garment, or in the heading of a curtain or flounce, a stay is placed under the gathers to hold the shirring in place, to prevent the threads from breaking, and to prevent the shirring from stretching in wear. The stay is generally a piece of thin fabric cut on the straight of the goods. (If you are working with transparent material use a piece of self-fabric.) Turn the ends in and hem it under the gathers.

Estimating Fullness: In flounces or ruffles where the gathered edge is very long, it will save time to space the fabric before you gather it. Between two pins space the fabric fullness on a section of the edge and decide how much fullness you would like. Mark this point with a pin on both fabric edges. Professionals cut a gauge or mark a tape measure and place pins at stated intervals on both the gathered and the ungathered edge. When the edge is gathered the pins are matched, and the fullness will then be evenly spaced.

Machine Shirring: Make three or four rows of machine stitching across the fabric, setting the machine for a basting stitch. Leave the threads on the ends of each row long enough to get hold of. Take hold of the bobbin thread of all

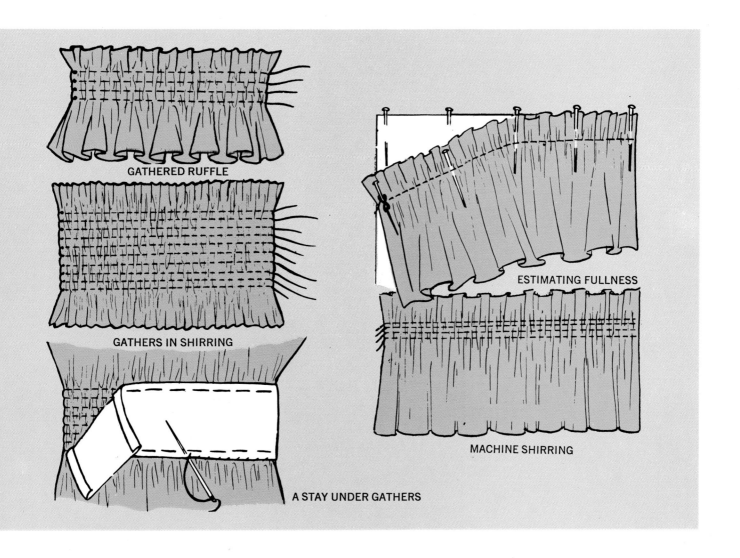

GATHERED RUFFLE

GATHERS IN SHIRRING

A STAY UNDER GATHERS

ESTIMATING FULLNESS

MACHINE SHIRRING

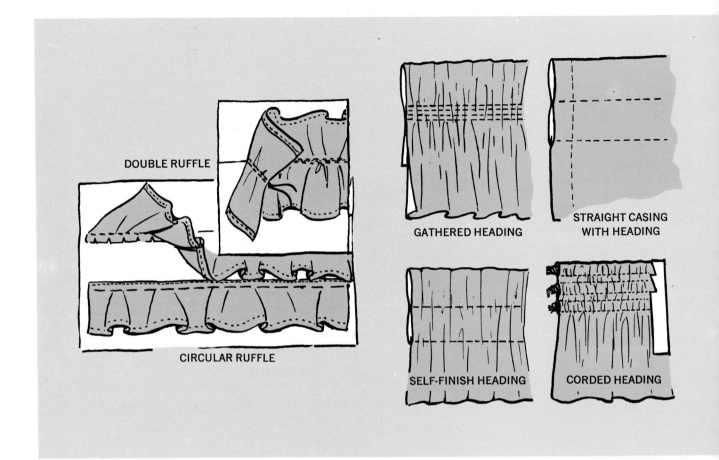

DOUBLE RUFFLE

CIRCULAR RUFFLE

GATHERED HEADING

STRAIGHT CASING WITH HEADING

SELF-FINISH HEADING

CORDED HEADING

the rows together and pull the material on the thread. Machine shirring saves time and insures even stitches.

Machine Ruffling: The ruffling attachment of your machine will save time for you when you plan ruffled curtains or other long yardages. Always test the fullness of the ruffle on a scrap of material before you begin to work. Finish the edges of the material before ruffling. Your machine also includes a gathering foot which will save you time.

Double Ruffle: Finish both edges of the ruffle and gather it through the center, using two or four rows of gathers. A band or ribbon can be stitched through the center of this type of ruffle or it can be applied to the material with a stitching down the center.

Circular Ruffle: Many pattern constructions specify circular ruffles. You can cut them yourself in either of two ways: (1) a true bias or (2) a shaped circle. It is wise to test the shaped circle in tissue paper before cutting your fabric. In joining circular ruffles to a fabric edge, turn a seam and snip it occasionally so it will lay flat. This seam can be stitched under the ruffle, or the ruffle can be basted in place and stitched on top.

HEADINGS

A heading is that part of a ruffle above the gathers, or the fold of the fabric which appears above the casing—as at the top of a curtain.

Gathered Heading: Decide on the width of your heading and turn the edge down far enough to include the heading and the rows of gathers. Run several rows of gathers across this turned fabric by hand or machine.

Straight Heading with Casing: Decide on the width of your heading and casing, and turn the edge as directed above. Run two rows of stitching across this turned edge, far enough apart so the pole or rod can be inserted in the space between.

Self-Finished Heading: Turn the top edge of the ruffle or curtain and hem before gathering or stitching. If this finish is used on a window curtain, allow enough space for the rod between the rows of stitching.

Corded Heading: Turn the edge and stitch it, allowing enough material to cover the cord. If a double or triple cord is desired, turn the edge deep enough to include two or three cords. Stitch on both sides of each successive cord, using a gauge to space them evenly.

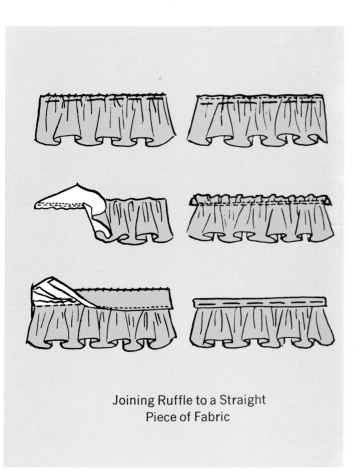

Joining Ruffle to a Straight
Piece of Fabric

JOINING RUFFLES TO A
STRAIGHT PIECE OF FABRIC

The top edge of the ruffle can be turned before gathering; after gathering, it is basted on the fabric. This edge can be hemmed by hand or top-stitched by machine.

An unturned edge of the fabric can be gathered. This type of ruffle is joined with an under-stitching.

A ruffle can be turned in a deep hem and the gathering placed at the edge of the turn. When a ruffle is joined at this gathered line, the frill at the top is called a heading.

A ruffle can be gathered without turning the edge and joined with a bias stitched to the fabric with the ruffle.

The edge of the ruffle can be bound before it is joined. Gather the ruffle without turning the edge, then bind the edge. It can then be basted into place.

Ruffles spell romance! Here they edge graceful sleeves, the hem of the ankle-length skirt, and repeat in the lace peeking out below the hem!

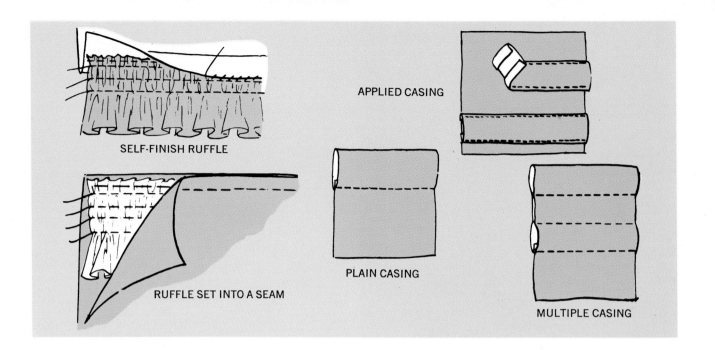

SELF-FINISH RUFFLE

RUFFLE SET INTO A SEAM

APPLIED CASING

PLAIN CASING

MULTIPLE CASING

TYPES OF RUFFLES

Edging Ruffle: Ruffles used for edging collars, sleeves, the bottoms of skirts, and curtains should be carefully spaced, allowing extra fullness in turning corners *so the ruffle will lie flat.* The seam should be pressed away from the ruffled edge, and the seam finish is important. It can be stitched down close to the seam stitching with one or several rows of stitching if a band effect is wanted, or the ruffle can be placed below the joining edge to permit turning the plain edge in a binding. This is called a "French seam turn."

Ruffle Set into a Seam: This may be the seam of a garment, or the contrast band joined to a curtain, or the center front of a blouse with a ruffle down both sides. Finish the outside edge of the ruffle and gather the joining edge without turning—two or more rows of gathers are desirable. Lay the ruffle on the right side of the garment, matching the edges, and baste. Now lay the other edge of the garment over the ruffle, with edges meeting, and stitch the seam.

Self-Finished Ruffle: Place the ruffle over the fabric with edges meeting and space the gathers. Stitch the seam, then trim the ruffle close to the stitches and turn the fabric over the line of stitching and stitch it again, applying the ruffle with bias. Place the ruffle over the fabric with seams matching and space the gathers. Place a binding over the gathers and stitch the three edges in a seam. Turn the binding and hem it to the plain fabric above the ruffle.

CASINGS

Casings through which a pole, cord, ribbon, or elastic is to be run are an important feature in controlling fullness. Stitch the casing securely; be sure it is not too wide nor too tight. Finish ends of fabric before making a casing.

Plain Casing: The plain casing is used at the top of short cotton curtains and also to hold elastic at the bottom of a blouse, et cetera. Turn the edge of the curtain or blouse in a hem deep enough to let the curtain rod or elastic slip through easily. Finish the ends of the casing by turning the edge under and stitching it down. Finally, stitch down the hem of the casing.

Casing with Heading: A heading is a double ruffle above a casing and is used in curtains or garments. Turn a hem deep enough to include both casing and heading and stitch the edge. Next make a second row of stitching that will leave space for a curtain rod or elastic.

Multiple Casing: Plan carefully so you know how deep to make each casing and how much space you want between them. Either turn a wide hem and stitch on the markings, or turn the top edge into the first casing and apply a straight band across the fabric to make the others.

Applied Casing: When the casing does not come at the edge, cut a straight or curved band of fabric in the desired width, allowing for seams. Turn the edges under and stitch the band at both edges.

Part II

SEWING FINE FASHION

Choosing The Right Clothes

*E**ach** season as the fashions change you may be faced with a dilemma: How can I wear what's right for me and still dress fashionably?*

Fashions change in four basic ways. Learning to recognize these changes may help you choose what's best for you.

Silhouette: Change in the basic outline of the figure is the most dramatic change that can occur. For several years fashions were unfitted—the sack and A-line dresses of the sixties. A major change in fashion silhouette occurred when women began wearing the fitted and clingy clothes of the seventies.

Color: Popular colors often change from season to season, from year to year. Actually, red may be popular every year but it may be a blue red one year, an orange red the next, and so on. No woman wants to shop for a new dress and find only dresses in the colors she already has in her closet!

Fabric or Texture: Some seasons smooth and shiny fabrics are fashion news, other seasons offer nubby tweeds. Fabric texture adds considerable variety to our wardrobes. A dress of last year's silhouette or color might look very new in another fabric.

Detail: Although detail is often a relatively minor change, it can make a season's clothes look new. Buttons

Three quick ways to give the look of today to yesterday's wardrobe. At left, change a basic sweater-and-skirt silhouette by belting the waistline. Above, add a fashionable yet inexpensive piece of costume jewelry. Right, try a new, daring combination of patterns and textures.

Below: Light colors have high visibility—they will add to your size!

Above: Avoid wide, contrasting belts if you are not tall and slim.

Opposite: Choose a skirt length to suit your age, figure, and activity.

may become very important one season, pockets the next.

How will you know what is in fashion each season? Shopping can help tremendously. Window shopping is the quickest way to get an overall picture. Large department stores select fashion news to display in their windows. Study the clothes and analyze which of the four aspects are different from last season's or last year's clothes. Shop in the better department stores for *ideas*. These stores are among the first to feature new trends. Once you know what is fashion news, you can buy your clothes anywhere or—better still—make them yourself.

If you can't or won't leave home to get the fashion picture, look through fashion magazines. Keep in mind however, that the clothes shown in high fashion magazines are often the extremes of fashion. Try to determine what is different about the clothes—the silhouette, color, fabric, or detail—and you will get the fashion story.

Even store advertisements in the newspaper or the flyers sent with your charge account bills will give you an idea of what's new in fashion. Keep your eyes open.

Must you incorporate all of these changes into your wardrobe in order to appear fashionably dressed? The answer is *no!* For one thing, all four changes do not necessarily occur in all the clothes from one season to the next. And even if they do, you can choose clothes with the aspects of change that are most becoming to you. For example, if a fitted silhouette does nothing for you, don't wear it. Keep on wearing the silhouette that you find most flattering, but update your clothes by wearing the latest shade of red or a dress with a large collar if that is in fashion. You will look more attractive by dressing appropriately for your face and figure than by wearing all the latest aspects of the season's fashion.

When you sew you have a distinct advantage. You can produce a dress with the most flattering silhouette, in your favorite shade, in the most appropriate fabric, and with just the right details for you!

The first step and the most important one in achieving your goal of dressing right for you is knowing *you*—your good and bad features and your likes and dislikes.

First, examine your silhouette. Check yourself in a full length mirror wearing your most revealing outfit—a bathing suit or leotard and tights, perhaps. Your silhouette is the outline of your figure; it is what you would see if you were featured as a dark shadow against a light background. Your silhouette shows how tall or short you are, how wide or narrow, how curvy or straight. Make a mental note of what your silhouette looks like. *You* must decide what effects you want to achieve. Then, if you follow these basic rules, your clothes can help you appear more like your ideal figure.

Straight outlines add height. They carry the eye upward. Straight slim skirts elongate the figure.

Boxy outlines or wide hems add width to the figure. Full sleeves or allover ruffles add fullness to your silhouette. The eye is carried across at the point of fullness. An outfit with big pockets at the hipline will make the hips look fuller. A large ruffled collar will add width across the top of the figure.

Keep your silhouette balanced. If you are wide at the hip, balance your appearance with top interest. Wear wide draped scarves, wide collars. Skinny fitted tops will only make your hips look wider by contrast. The same rule would apply to broad shoulders: if your hips are narrow, wear hipline interest for balance. Hip belts, pockets, peplums would do the trick.

Next, consider color. The optical illusions of color can affect your silhouette as well as enhance your hair and complexion.

Light colors are more visible than dark colors and therefore make you look larger. Dark colors, with less visibility, make you appear smaller.

Bright colors are more visible than dull colors and reflect more light. Hence, you look larger in a brightly colored dress. Wear dull colors to reduce your apparent size.

Above: Tiny patterns seem to reduce your figure size in general, while top interest carries the eye away from wide hips.

Opposite: Solid color from neckline to floor is proven figure camouflage, as in this well-cut pantsuit.

Continuous color from head to toe will elongate the figure. A solid color dress with matching stockings and shoes will give you a taller appearance. If you wish to appear shorter, wear a top and bottom in different colors to cut your height.

Direct repetition and direct contrast of colors emphasize. If a lovely redhead wishes to emphasize the color of her hair she should wear a rust color that exactly matches her shade of red, or a blue for a direct contrast. Either would play up the color of her hair. Redheads usually do not look well in red because red clashes with their hair. Red hair is really a shade of orange; red and orange are closely related colors. When red and orange are placed next to one another, the red looks redder and the orange, more orange—an unbecoming combination.

Above: Small, overall pattern effectively reduces the apparent overall body size.

Left: Large, bold print seems to add to size, as does the kimono sleeve styling.

Opposite: Subtle stitching seems to slim a pantsuit; scarf draws attention from hips.

"Ladder effect" of the horizontal stripes moves the eye up and down, and so creates an illusion of height in this beach gown.

Another trick to fool the eye is to be found in this long contrasting scarf—its vertical interest makes for greater height.

To lengthen the face and neck area, choose a deeply cut V neckline, and edge it with a ruffle. Long sleeves lengthen arms, too.

Contrasting collar and cuffs calls attention to a pretty face and expressive hands—and away from possible figure faults.

Fashion is fun! Especially when you can make your own clothes, for then you can combine patterns and designs as you wish.

Draw the eye above the waistline with a new-again bare shoulder plaid which shows off a lovely neck or elongates one.

Similarly, when a blond wears bright yellow her hair seems to fade. The pale yellow hair is dull in comparison to the bright yellow dress. A dress in the same pale yellow of her hair would emphasize her blondness as would a purple dress. The purple, being a direct contrast to her hair, would make a blond seem blonder.

The same rules can apply to brunettes when choosing shades of brown and black. Brown hair may be enhanced by a dress in an identical shade of brown, while a darker brown or a black may make the hair look dowdy. Should brunettes never wear brown or black? Not at all! Just remember to wear a bright or light accent color near your face for highlights!

An exciting trick for the blue- or green-eyed girl is to repeat the exact color of her eyes in a garment or accent near the face. Again, direct repetition emphasizes; the identical blue or green lights up her eyes!

Examine fabric and texture. Bulky fabrics will add bulk to your figure; their thickness will actually add inches. Heavy girls should avoid bulky wools and novelty fabrics.

Shiny fabrics will have the same effect as bright colors: they appear to increase your size because they reflect a great deal of light. If you want to look smaller, wear dull-finished fabrics. A matte silk and worsted will look just as elegant as a shiny satin, yet it will give you a slimmer appearance.

When selecting a fabric keep in mind the size of the print or pattern. Small patterns diffuse the outline of the figure and therefore make you look smaller. Large patterns tend to emphasize your size.

If you are choosing a stripe, think twice about the common misconception that vertical stripes always make you look slimmer. Vertical stripes take the shape of their background; they will become long curves on a large curvy woman. Nothing could be more unbecoming! Yet consider the effect of narrow horizontal stripes on the same woman: your eye travels up and down along the "ladder" effect that these stripes create. These horizontal stripes make a heavy woman appear slimmer while the vertical stripes emphasize her bulk.

The distance between stripes and their individual size must be considered when choosing a striped fabric. Very wide or bold colored stripes will add bulk no matter what their direction. Stripes spaced far apart also tend to add width if they are placed vertically; your eye moves across as you look at these stripes.

Pay attention to detail. You can use the details of an outfit to call attention to your best features and minimize your worst ones.

A vertical and contrasting front band on a dress will carry the eye up and down giving you the appearance of height

A simple sleeveless classic can be the basis of a widely varied wardrobe, when you make a collection of collars and belts to accessorize it. An effective, money-saving method of turning one dress into four, suitable for almost every daytime occasion.

For a too long and thin neck,
the turtleneck collar is excellent.

and calling attention away from your width. This is a particularly flattering effect for a short, plump woman. The vertical band may be a piece sewn on purely for decoration, a row of buttons from neckline to hem, a long scarf, or a large contrasting zipper.

Many individual figure problems can be minimized by careful selection of the details of an outfit. Women have a natural fullness at the hips, but many feel that they have been over-endowed. To call attention away from the hipline, place interest high on your outfit. Add neckline interest with collars, scarves, jewelry, contrasting color or pattern at the neckline. Avoid jackets or belts that cut across the hipline.

To fill out too narrow hips, place pockets to add to hipline interest.

Very full sleeves are flattering to too thin arms—and also to too heavy!

Take advantage of a lovely, long neck and wear an elegant stand-up collar. Puffed sleeves widen narrow shoulders beautifully.

If your over-endowment is at the bustline, wear softly draped bodices with just a little fullness. Clingy fabrics outline the large bust. Do not wear very high or very low necklines, but keep detail interest high with collars, jewelry, scarves.

To conceal very narrow hips, wear full skirts or pleated skirts. Hip belts or trims and wide hipline pockets will add width to your hipline.

To add fullness to a small bust, wear bloused bodices, gathers under the bustline. If your waist is small, emphasize it with belts, fitted dresses, and fitted bodices.

If you have a short neck, expose as much neck as possible. The more skin showing at the neck and shoulder area, the longer your neck will appear. Let jewel necklines be the highest necklines you wear. Look for V- or U-necks, collarless dresses, or stand-away collars.

A sleeveless tunic tops a wardrobe-expanding pantsuit; wear it with a variety of shirts, belts.

If your neck is too long and slim, you can shorten it with turtleneck collars, mandarin collars, chokers, dog collars or other high neck interest. Avoid V-neck dresses or other lines that show too much neck.

Arms can be a problem, too. If yours are too heavy, wear long slim sleeves to conceal the fullness. Avoid sleeveless or short sleeved garments that cut across the widest part of the arm.

If your arms are very slender, you can wear very full sleeves, wide cuffs, and high bracelets to add to their fullness.

Once you have analyzed your figure, you should have a good idea of which styles would look best on you. Keep these rules in mind no matter what type of clothes you are looking for. The rules of silhouette, color, fabric, and detail apply to your sportswear as well as your evening clothes, to your loungewear as well as your winter coat.

When you sew you have another point to consider: your sewing abilities. Simplicity is always in fashion. If your abilities are not yet ready for intricate details, keep your clothes simple. Vary the color and the fabric instead of the details. A well-made simple skirt looks much more attractive and is much more flattering than a poorly-made fashionably detailed one. You can always add more detailed clothes to your wardrobe as your sewing skills improve.

Use your sewing skills wisely to increase your wardrobe's versatility. Separates are especially useful. Plan your outfits so that they are interchangeable. Make one jacket that goes with several skirts and slacks. Many patterns feature such "wardrobes" based around a plaid or print and two of its dominant colors. With such a group of items, you will get more mileage from your accessories, too.

Make your dresses versatile as well. Plain dresses are an ideal background for accessories. Consider belts, scarves, and jewelry to change the appearance of a dress. Varying your accessories can make the same dress as appropriate for an afternoon of shopping as for an evening at the theater.

If you don't have time to make all of your clothes, which ones should you make? Sewing can save you money. Consider making the items which will save you the most, if you have the needed skills. For instance, you might save a great deal by making your winter coat, but if you do not yet have the needed tailoring skills you would not produce a garment to be proud of. In that case, buy the coat and make something else, instead.

You will get a better fitting garment if you make it yourself. Consider making the things that you find hardest to buy correctly fitted. If you are hard to fit at hips and waist, you might make all of your skirts and slacks but buy your blouses and tops. Blouses and sweaters don't usually present great fitting problems.

If you know exactly what you want but can't find it ready-made, make it yourself! You can put the elements together and come out with precisely your dream dress. That's when it pays to sew!

Opposite: A perfectly simple, perfectly lovely dress to accessorize as you will to wear everywhere!

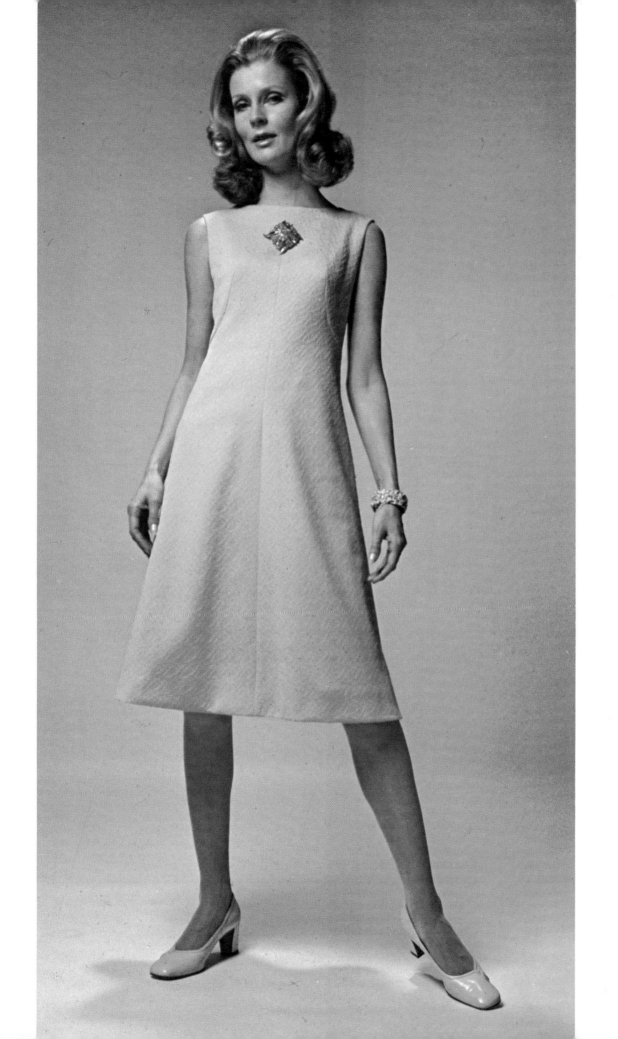

To Frame Your Face: Necklines And Collars

*T*he neckline frames the face, and therefore it must be perfect in all the details of fit, style, and shape. More than anything else, the neck finish shows the difference between skilled dressmaking and amateur sewing. Proportion is the secret of a becoming neckline, and each style must be adjusted to the individual. After you have selected the neckline or collar you like, cut it in paper and try it on and decide whether it should be a little lower, or filled in. Should the neck be cut away a little so the collar will be at a more becoming angle? Should the scarf be narrower or wider, the bow larger or smaller?

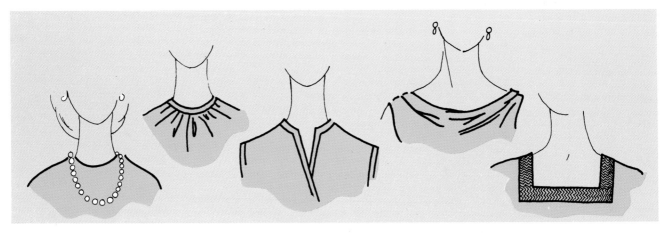

Choose a neckline to frame your face beautifully — your collar can be as important as your coiffure.

TYPES OF NECKLINE

Classic Necklines: This popular neckline finish is particularly adapted to V necks, soft draped necklines, and tailored necklines. To make it, a bias facing of self-fabric or a light-weight lining is stitched to the neckline. It should be cut 2 to 3 inches wide and the length of the neck opening. Place it on the right side of the garment, match the edges, and stitch. Turn the facing to the wrong side, making sure that the edge is smooth and even. Stitch the facing or make an unstitched finish, depending upon the type of garment. In tailored necklines, machine stitching is often a decorative feature of the facing. In soft garments with a draped neckline or a plain neck finish, no stitching should show on the right side of the garment. In jewel necklines, used so successfully as a background for costume jewelry, one line of stitching close to the edge is permissible. It forms a tiny corded effect. This is popular also in surplice necklines.

Bound Necklines: The straight or bias binding can bind the neck all the way around, or it can be extended to form a small bow tie. First bind the neck edge, then turn the edges of a tie and overcast them together; or, if buttons are desired, place them on the edges and hold them with hooks.

Corded Necklines: Turn the round neck of a dress over a cable cord and stitch it close by hand. Then draw the fullness of the cord and adjust the neck to the right proportion. Another kind is made by covering the cord with contrasting fabric. Turn the edges of the neck in and gather it, applying the cord. Still another kind is made by hemming a heavy silk cord to the edge of a soft round neckline which has been turned and gathered. Cording can also be hemmed to the edge of a smooth U-shaped neckline.

Square Necklines: Square necklines are faced with a *straight* facing, which can be applied on the right side and turned back, or applied on the wrong side and turned to

Below: "Keyhole" cutout provides neckline interest in the sleeveless tunic top.

Above: Contrasting collar teams up with cuffs for solid color accents.

Below: An up-dated version of the middy collar makes a fashion splash.

Bow-tied neckline of the polka dotted blouse dresses up the bolero and skirt.

form a decorative band on the right side. A true square neck which is bound or faced depends upon clipping for success. Stitch the band in place, then before you turn it, clip into the seam allowance close to the corner, cutting until you touch the stitching. The corner will lie smoothly when you turn the facing.

Slashed Necklines: This is a popular finish for the straight neck of soft dresses. It gives the appearance of no finish at all. It is also the basic construction feature for necklines which roll back softly from a smooth point without a collar, or with a straight collar worn open, and in middy blouses and pointed collar applications.

The secret of this neckline is to cut deep into the point *after*, not before, the facing is applied. When the lapel is turned to the wrong side, no stitching, wrinkles or dents show. The edge should be cut straight.

Cut a facing of self-material 2 inches wider than you plan to wear the opening turned back. Lay it on the garment *before you slash the front.* Mark the cutting line and outline it in stitching ½ inch back of the line on each side. The stitching can meet in a point at the end of the cutting line, or square corners can be made. Cut the slash along the marked line between the stitching and down into the stitched point, or out into the stitched corners, so that you almost cut the stitching. Turn the facing to the wrong side of the garment and baste the edge for pressing. In a heavy fabric, overcast the raw edge and slip-stitch it to the garment. In a light-weight material, turn the raw edge of the facing under in a narrow hem.

Short Slashed Neck Openings: These can be bound or faced before the collar is attached, as in convertible slashed openings. With this treatment the finished edges meet and can be closed with buttons and loops or decorative hooks and eyes.

Applied Bands in a Short Slash: If the short slash is not wide enough, cut a straight facing for the underedge to hold the buttons. Next prepare the outside trimming band which will hold the buttonholes. This must be cut on the straight of the goods 2 inches longer than the front opening and twice the width of the finished band. Cut a pointed edge. Fold the band with the right side of the fabric on top and stitch the pointed end. Clip the point and turn the band. Press the folded edge and the outside edge. Then join the inside edge of the band to the slash in a seam. Stitch or hem the outside edge of the band to the seam. Continue this stitching around the point and up the folded edge. In these neck joinings the point can be stitched flat to the garment or left separate so that it hangs loose.

Placket Neck Finish: Cut a straight facing twice as long as the slashed opening. Seam it around the opening on the right side. Fold it under on the wrong side of the garment, creasing the facing on one edge flush with the seam, and on the other edge to extend beyond the seam. Hem it on the seam line and tack at the lowest point of the opening to insure a smooth fit.

Timely neckline and collar treatments — soft, feminine, flattering.

Scarf and Bow Necklines: Scarves and bows are applied to necks of almost any shape. The scarf can be self-fabric or contrasting; it can be cut straight and folded double so the ends can be stitched and turned; it can be straight and hemmed or picoted; it can be cut on the bias; it can be made of ribbon or lace. It can be very narrow, or medium width and cut double up to 2½ inches wide; or very wide and cut single. The hems on all scarves should be hand-rolled.

Scarf and Collar Cut in One: These collars are long strips cut on the straight of the goods. Decide on the length and width, include hem allowance, and cut. Sew seams on the open side and one end. Turn to the right side and close the open end with slip stitch. Baste the folded side and press.

Joining a Double Scarf Collar: Try the collar on with the garment and mark the center back of the collar. This is *not* as a rule the center of the scarf. Also mark the point where the collar joins the center front of your dress; then you know how much space to leave open in the center for the collar joining. You are ready then to fold the scarf in half and seam each end, shaping the ends in points or curves as desired. Turn the scarf, baste the folded side to insure an even line, and press it. Join one edge of the open side to the neckline with the center-back marking in place. Seam this edge to the neckline. Turn the opposite edge of the scarf and hem it to the seam, forming a smooth finish for the neckline.

Single-Fabric Scarves: These scarves are hemmed, bound, or finished with a facing of a contrasting color. They are joined to the neck with a bias binding. Unless the scarf is cut double, it is best to face the neckline, then apply the scarf. Joining the scarf only across the back from shoulder to shoulder often gives a more becoming line. This is particularly true of transparent and lace scarves.

Novelty Scarves: Color contrast in scarves and necklines is often a fashion feature. Ribbon can be used in this way by joining it to the back of the neck and overcasting edge to edge—across the back only. Let one color fall freely and tie the other in a bow.

To introduce color in a broad scarf, decide on the length and width so you can cut one half in a contrasting color. The two pieces can be joined in a lengthwise seam or a short seam at the back of the neck. These scarves can be hemmed and draped as single bows or turned double so that the contrasting color looks like a facing.

In a printed dress, a color of the print can be repeated at the neckline in a double collar and scarf by cutting a 2-inch band of the print long enough to go around the neck, then tying it in a bow with long ends. Finish this scarf and attach it to the neck. Then cut a straight piece of contrasting fabric 2 inches wide and about 8 inches shorter than the first scarf. Fold it lengthwise, seam the ends, and turn it. Overcast the opening and baste the band to the neckline *inside the collar band.* When you wear the dress, let the colored ends cross and hang, and tie the self-fabric scarf.

COLLARS

The collars in most dress patterns, and those you will use in remaking dresses, fall into three classes: small round collars, small straight collars, and collars shaped for a V neck.

The collar can be cut from a single fabric or double. Finish the edge with a rolled hem, a binding, a ruffle, or other trimming.

Small Single Collar: These collars are cut round or shaped. The edge must be finished with a hem, a binding, or a small ruffle of self-fabric, lace, or contrasting fabric. Finish the outside edge before joining the collar to the garment.

Small Double Collar: This type of collar is made from either self-fabric or contrasting fabric. The collar pattern is cut out twice. Be sure to include seam allowances. Seam the two collar pieces together with the right sides facing, and clip the seam edge. Turn the collar right side out and baste the edge carefully before pressing. This will help to hold the shape of the collar and make an even edge.

Small Straight Collars: These collars usually are folded through the center, and they fit closely to the throat. Cut a piece of fabric 1 inch longer than the neck size and twice as wide as you want the finished collar to be, including an additional allowance for seams.

Pointed Neckline with Collars: Collars of any shape that fit into a pointed neckline are joined. Collars shaped like the outline of the neck edge lie flat. Collars that roll have a different shape.

The collar is always cut longer than the neck opening. Baste it to the neck edge with a bias binding. Then cross the pointed ends of the collar at the point of the neckline and baste. Cover this point with a stay and outline it with stitching. Now slash the stay into the point almost cutting the stitching. Turn the stay to the wrong side and hem it.

Sailor Collar: Finish the collar single or double and baste it to the neckline. The part of the collar which is joined to the neckline should be slightly longer than the neckline. When sewing in place, remember to join the ends of the collar at the point of the neckline. Finish as for Pointed Neckline.

APPLYING COLLARS TO NECKLINES

Collars which are cut double or are lined can be put on like a wide binding. One edge of the collar is stitched to the neckband, and the other edge is turned and hemmed over the joining. They can also be joined with a bias binding or with a band, or they can be covered by a facing or lining.

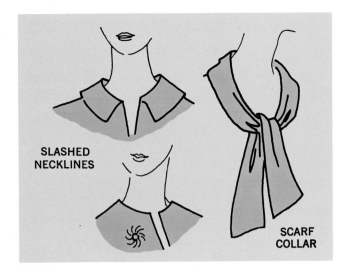

SLASHED NECKLINES

SCARF COLLAR

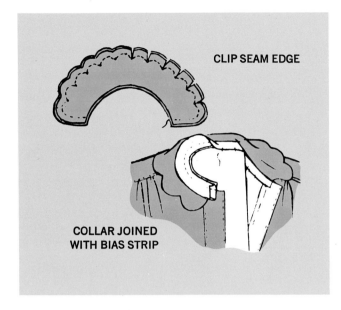

CLIP SEAM EDGE

COLLAR JOINED WITH BIAS STRIP

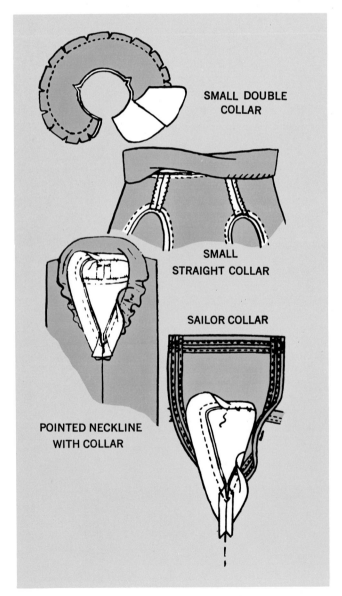

SMALL DOUBLE COLLAR

SMALL STRAIGHT COLLAR

SAILOR COLLAR

POINTED NECKLINE WITH COLLAR

Collar Joined with a Bias: Place the collar on the right side of the garment and baste it to the neckline with edges matching. Include in the basting a ¾-inch bias and stitch the seam. Turn the seam down and hem the bias to the garment. The ends of the bias must be turned in at the neck, hemmed, and finished neatly.

Collar Joined with a Neckband: The neckband is a straight lined piece cut the size of the neck opening. Its function is to raise the collar higher. Cut a lining the same size as the neckband. Seam the neckband to the collar and place the lining over this joining, with seam edges meeting. Finish the ends of the neckband; bind the neckline with the neckband, using a fine hemming or machine stitching. When a collar is applied to a band, the center front of the collar must be centered on the band, not at the edge of the neck opening.

Collar with Facing: Used in coats and button-front garments. Stitch the facing to the front edge of the garment if it is not cut in one piece with the front. Stitch one edge of a double collar to the neckline. Turn the facing and stitch it to the other edge of the collar (on both sides). Press the seams open. Now turn the facing and collar to the right side and press again to form a smooth finish. Hem the collar over the seam line across the back of the neck.

Your Pattern: Choosing and Changing

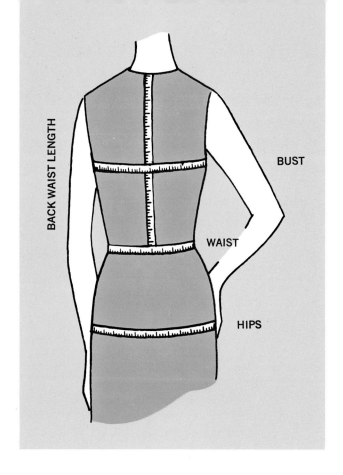

earn to choose your pattern, cut, baste and finish a dress to your exact measurements, so that you need waste no time in ripping, fitting, and fussing with alterations. To do this as professionals do, use the list of professional measurements shown on these pages.

Before you buy a pattern, take the measurements of your figure at the bust, waist, and hips, and also measure your back waist length. To take these measurements accurately, stand straight, with your heels together and your weight on both feet, and measure as follows:

1. Bust: Pass the tape measure around the figure at the fullest part of the bust and close under the arms. Hold the tape snugly, neither too tight or too loose. Keep the tape straight across the back; or if you want to be sure of plenty of ease in the fit of the pattern, raise the tape almost an inch in the center back.

2. Waist: Pass the tape measure around the natural waistline at the smallest part.

3. Hips: Measure at the fullest part, about 7 or 8 inches below the waistline.

4. Back Waist Length: Measure from the prominent bone at the back of the neck to the natural waistline.

When you have taken these measurements, record them on your personal chart on the next page and compare them with the measurement charts which follow; the measurements correspond to the same sizes on all printed patterns. Always buy the pattern which most nearly fits your measurements. But remember, this pattern size has no relation to the size you buy in ready-made dresses.

Choose dress, blouse, jacket, suit, or coat size by the nearest bust measurement. Buy skirt, shorts or slacks patterns by hip and waist measurements. Get the same size in a maternity pattern as you normally buy (by your bust measurement).

Children's patterns are sold by age groups. Compare the child's measurements with those listed on the pattern envelope and buy a pattern for the age group nearest that size.

HOW TO USE YOUR MEASUREMENT CHART

Keep your measurement chart before you as you cut and sew. Check with it often.

Measure the pattern so you will know exactly where to lengthen or shorten it. Make a red ring around any measurements which show that the left and right sides are not alike, then you can cut this difference into the fabric and baste it into the seams.

In cutting a garment with fullness which your measurements do not include, fold the pattern so that the indicated fullness lies flat, then check the measurements and make the adjustments.

When you cut a sleeve, note the dart perforations which mark the elbow. Measure above and below the darts to check the balance of the sleeve.

When you cut a sheer garment, allow a larger margin for ease of fullness. The garment must be looser than your usual measurements. A pattern designed for a sheer garment is cut looser.

Taking Garment Measurements

To cut, baste and finish a garment to your exact measurements it may be easier to take measurements from a dress than from your own person. Select a simple dress that fits well. Lay the dress on a smooth surface and study the diagram and chart. The diagram represents the dress—the numbers indicate the location of the measurements, the arrows are the extremes of each measurement. As you take these measurements, write them on a card.

YOUR PERSONAL MEASUREMENT CHART

	MY MEASUREMENTS	PATTERN MEASURE-MENTS MOST LIKE MINE	ALTERATION NEEDED
Bust			
Waist			
Hips			
Back Waist Length			
Arm Length			

Length Measurements

How to Take Them

1. Center front, from neck to waistline
   Center back, from neck to waistline
2. Right side front, from shoulder seam to waistline
   Right side back, from shoulder seam to waistline
   Left side front, from shoulder seam to waistline
   Left side back, from shoulder seam to waistline
3. Center front, from waistline to hipline
   Center back, from waistline to hipline
4. Center front, from waistline to hem
   Center back, from waistline to hem
5. Right side front from waistline to hem
   Right side back, from waistline to hem
   Left side front, from waistline to hem
   Left side back, from waistline to hem
6. Underarm right side, from armhole to waist
   Underarm, left side, from armhole to waist
7. Side seam, right side, from waistline to hem
   Side seam, left side, from waistline to hem

How to Use Them

Nos. 1, 2, and 3: Use these measurements in cutting to shorten the pieces of your pattern. The side measurements (No. 2) will help you adjust the balance if both sides of your figure are not alike.

In basting, use these measurements to join waist and skirt correctly. Check them with the cross measurements so you will know how to mark your placket and how to adjust the waist fullness without a fitting.

~~~~~~~~~~~~~~~~~~~~

Nos. 4, 5, 6, and 7: These measurements are used in connection with width measurements Nos. 19 and 20 to cut the waist and hipline of the garment exactly. When you baste the garment, use the length measurements to baste a temporary hem at the length most becoming to you. The side measures at the front and back will help you to allow for any irregularities in your figure, so that your skirt will be exactly in balance when you baste it.

Sleeve Measurements

8. Right side shoulder seam to elbow
   Left side shoulder seam to elbow
9. Right side elbow to wrist
   Left side elbow to wrist
10. Underarm seam, right side, armhole to bent elbow
    Underarm seam, left side, armhole to bent elbow
11. Underarm seam, right side, bend of elbow to wrist
    Underarm seam, left side, bend of elbow to wrist
12. Wrist

Nos. 8, 9, 10, 11, and 12: In cutting, you can proportion your sleeves and make any necessary alterations in the pattern by applying these measurements.

Cross Measurements

13. Measure neck in a becoming line

No. 13: Use this measurement when joining a collar, to be sure the neckline of the dress is cut in a becoming line.

14. Shoulder, from neck to armhole
15. Armhole, from shoulder seam to underarm in front
    Armhole, from shoulder seam to underarm in back
16. Front measure, from armhole to armhole
    Back measure, from armhole to armhole

Nos. 14, 15, and 16: Used in setting in a sleeve. No. 14 shows your exact shoulder line, and No. 15 shows a comfortable sleeve depth to be used when you set in the sleeve. No. 16 will give you the amount of material you need, front and back, so the sleeves will not tear out.

17. Bust measure, from underarm to underarm
    Back measure, from underarm to underarm
18. Front waist measure, from side seam to side seam
    Back waist measure, from side seam to side seam
19. Front hip measure, from side seam to side seam
    Back hip measure, from side seam to side seam

Nos. 17, 18, and 19: No. 17 separates the bust measure so you know how much width you need in back, compared to the front. Measure your pattern and balance this width as needed. This measure, combined with No. 18, helps you decide how much, if any, fullness should be fitted out at the side seam. No. 18 also makes it possible to fit the top of the skirt to your exact waist measurements. You can measure across the front and back of the garment and baste the placket line without a fitting. Nos. 18 and 19 can be used together to shape the top of the skirt across the hips. Increase or decrease the size of the pattern according to your measurements when you cut; use them to baste the side seams of the skirt

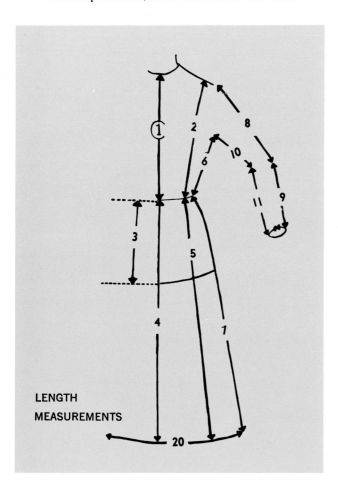

LENGTH
MEASUREMENTS

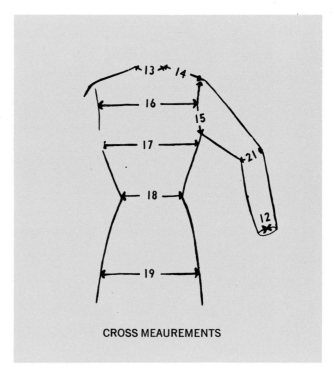

CROSS MEAUREMENTS

STANDARD PATTERN MEASUREMENT CHARTS

MISSES'

SIZE	6	8	10	12	14	16	18	20
Bust	30½	31½	32½	34	36	38	40	42
Waist	22	23	24	25½	27	29	31	33
Hip	32½	33½	34½	36	38	40	42	44
Back Waist Length	15½	15¾	16	16¼	16½	16¾	17	17¼

MISS PETITE

SIZE	6mp	8mp	10mp	12mp	14mp	16mp
Bust	30½	31½	32½	34	36	38
Waist	22½	23½	24½	26	27½	29½
Hip	32½	33½	34½	36	38	40
Back Waist Length	14½	14¾	15	15¼	15½	15¾

WOMEN'S

SIZE	38	40	42	44	46	48	50
Bust	42	44	46	48	50	52	54
Waist	34	36	38	40½	43	45½	48
Hip	44	46	48	50	52	54	56
Back Waist Length	17¼	17⅜	17½	17⅝	17¾	17⅞	18

HALF-SIZE

SIZE	10½	12½	14½	16½	18½	20½	22½	24½
Bust	33	35	37	39	41	43	45	47
Waist	26	28	30	32	34	36½	39	41½
Hip	35	37	39	41	43	45½	48	50½
Back Waist Length	15	15¼	15½	15¾	15⅞	16	16⅛	16¼

JUNIOR

SIZE	5	7	9	11	13	15
Bust	30	31	32	33½	35	37
Waist	21½	22½	23½	24½	26	28
Hip	32	33	34	35½	37	39
Back Waist Length	15	15¼	15½	15¾	16	16¼

JUNIOR PETITE

SIZE	3jp	5jp	7jp	9jp	11jp	13jp
Bust	30½	31	32	33	34	35
Waist	22	22½	23½	24½	25½	26½
Hip	31½	32	33	34	35	36
Back Waist Length	14	14¼	14½	14¾	15	15¼

YOUNG JUNIOR/TEEN

SIZE	5/6	7/8	9/10	11/12	13/14	15/16
Bust	28	29	30½	32	33½	35
Waist	22	23	24	25	26	27
Hip	31	32	33½	35	36½	38
Back Waist Length	13½	14	14½	15	15⅜	15¾

GIRLS'

SIZE	7	8	10	12	14
Breast	26	27	28½	30	32
Waist	23	23½	24½	25½	26½
Hip	27	28	30	32	34
Back Waist Length	11½	12	12¾	13½	14¼

CHUBBIE

SIZE	8½c	10½c	12½c	14½c
Breast	30	31½	33	34½
Waist	28	29	30	31
Hip	33	34½	36	37½
Back Waist Length	12½	13¼	14	14¾

CHILDREN'S

SIZE	1	2	3	4	5	6	6x
Breast	20	21	22	23	24	25	25½
Waist	19½	20	20½	21	21½	22	22½
Finished Dress Length	17	18	19	20	22	24	25

TODDLERS'

SIZE	½	1	2	3	4
Breast	19	20	21	22	23
Waist	19	19½	20	20½	21
Finished Dress Length	14	15	16	17	18

TEEN-BOYS

SIZE	7	8	10	12	14	16	18	20
Chest	26	27	28	30	32	33½	35	36½
Waist	23	24	25	26	27	28	29	30
Neck	11¾	12	12½	13	13½	14	14½	15

MEN

SIZE		S		M		L		XL
	34	36	38	40	42	44	46	48
Chest	34	36	38	40	42	44	46	48
Waist	28	30	32	34	36	39	42	44
Neck	14	14½	15	15½	16	16½	17	17½

Adjust Before You Cut

*M**ost** clothes and patterns are designed and sized to fit what is called the "average figure." But a government survey of women in all parts of the country showed that only 50 per cent could wear any version of commercial sizes and appear well fitted! Half the women in the country, then, have to alter their patterns if they make their clothes, and also their ready-made garments. Learning how to make adjustments in the pattern is essential for many women if they are to be well fitted. Often simple adjustments are all that are necessary, but even those required for the "problem figure" are not too difficult. If you will make adjustments in the pattern before you cut, only minor ones will be necessary later, and much of the ripping out and altering which spoil the fun of sewing will be avoided.*

The varied fitting needs of different types of figures are simplified and presented here in two prefitting methods.

Often a simple alteration in the paper pattern saves hours of adjustment after the dress is cut. Many figures need only the adjustment of length; others need to shorten the proportions of a garment. By testing a pattern before you cut, you can adjust width as well as length and so make it wider or narrower across the back, front, or hips. You can also alter one side of the garment only and so make allowances for irregularities in your figure.

ADJUSTING THE PATTERN

The method used for simple adjustments of length and width is to fit the paper pattern before you lay out and cut the fabric.

For more complex fitting problems it is best to cut the pattern in inexpensive unbleached muslin and make fitting adjustments on this fabric. Since paper does not drape the same way as fabric, you cannot get a truly accurate fit with a tissue pattern. Once the muslin has been fitted to your figure, you can use it as a pattern to cut your fabric or you can transfer all the alterations to your tissue pattern and use that.

You may not have to make a new muslin for every garment. The alterations for one dress may be the same ones needed for another dress. Compare the style lines to be sure. If you are hard to fit, it is a good idea to make a muslin for a dress, one for a skirt, one for slacks and then use these to help fit other patterns you want to use.

To Fit the Pattern: Pin all the sections of the front and back that will be seamed together. Include yokes, pleats, and inserts. Join the waist and skirt and the shoulders. Do not pin the underarm. Do not pin the sleeve. Stand in front of a mirror and slip the pattern on. Bear in mind that paper and fabric have different textures. Paper will stand out from your figure where the woven material will hang softly.

Mark your alterations with tailor's chalk. Pencil will tear the paper.

LENGTH ADJUSTMENTS

To Lengthen a Skirt: When you lengthen a pattern you want to keep the line and proportions of the pattern the same. Most patterns have double horizontal lines for you to use in lengthening. To lengthen a skirt 1'', cut the pattern apart on this lengthening and shortening line. Spread the pattern pieces apart 1'' and insert tissue paper between the pieces. Tape the tissue paper in place, being certain that the pattern pieces remain 1'' apart. Redraw necessary seam and construction lines.

To Lengthen a Dress, you must decide which of two lengthening and shortening lines to use. Compare your back waist length to the back waist length listed for your size on the back of the pattern envelope. If your own measurement is longer, you need to lengthen the dress at the bodice lengthening and shortening line. Compare the finished skirt length given on the pattern to the finished length you want. If your measurement is longer, you need to lengthen the skirt part of the pattern. It is possible that you may need to lengthen a dress both at the bodice and at the skirt. Keep in mind that any alteration in bodice length will affect the finished length of the entire dress, so make sure to alter the bodice first.

To Lengthen a Sleeve Pattern, have someone measure your arm to decide whether the extra length is needed from shoulder to elbow or from elbow to wrist and use the appropriate lengthening and shortening line.

If a pattern does not have a lengthening and shortening line, this means that the proportion of the pattern will remain the same no matter where you add the extra inches. You just add the additional length to the lower edge of the pattern piece. This will be the case with circular skirts; when you add inches to a circular hem the fullness is increased in proportion to the length.

To Shorten a Pattern: Use the lengthening and shortening line as described for lengthening a pattern. Draw a line parallel to the lengthening and shortening line, spacing it the amount you wish to shorten the pattern. Crease the pattern along the lengthening and shortening line; bring up the crease you made to meet this horizontal line. Pin the tuck in place. Redraw seam lines if necessary.

Extending a Skirt to the Floor: Decide on the additional length required and divide this amount in three. Split your skirt pattern in two places and separate each part one-third the additional length needed. Add the third extension to the lower edge. This increases the length without increasing the fullness. If you want to make the skirt fuller, extend the garment mostly at the lower edge.

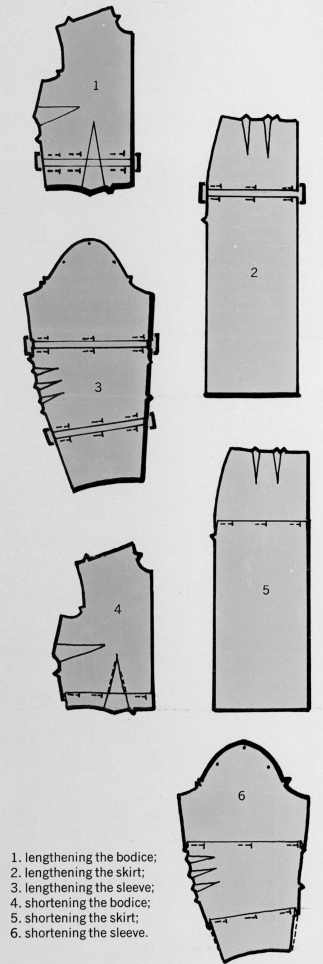

1. lengthening the bodice;
2. lengthening the skirt;
3. lengthening the sleeve;
4. shortening the bodice;
5. shortening the skirt;
6. shortening the sleeve.

97

SHOULDER ADJUSTMENTS

Sloping Shoulders: On the bodice front pattern, mark the amount that must be removed from the shoulder seam at the armhole edge of that seam. Draw a new shoulder seam from the neck edge to the armhole edge. Make the same alteration on the bodice back pattern. Lower the underarm seam the same amount that you removed from the shoulder seam in order to maintain the original shape of the armhole.

Round Shoulders: Slash the pattern back about 4 inches from the neckline from the center back to the armhole seam. Spread the slash apart, adding the necessary amount at the center back and tapering the slash to the armhole seam. Tape or pin a piece of tissue underneath to fill the gap. Redraw necessary seam lines. Use the pattern as a guide in redrawing the original neck and shoulder lines.

Narrow Shoulders: Draw a vertical line halfway between the neck edge and the shoulder seam as far down as the armhole notch. Slash the pattern on this line and overlap the edges at the shoulder seam, removing the necessary amount. Pin or tape in position. Redraw the shoulder line from the neck edge to the armhole edge. Make this alteration on the pattern front and back.

Square Shoulders: Insert tissue paper under pattern and pin in place. At the armhole edge of the shoulder, measure up the amount needed to add to the shoulder seam. Draw a line to the neckline. Redraw the armhole raising it the amount that the shoulder was raised. Make these alterations on the bodice front and back.

BODY ADJUSTMENTS

Small Bust: Continue the lines from the centers of the

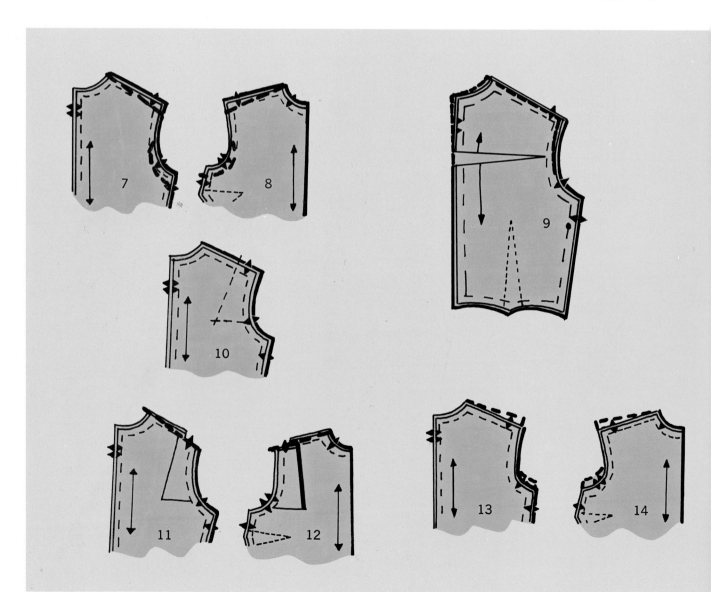

underarm and waistline darts until they meet. This point is the point of the bust. Draw a line from the point of the bust to a point halfway between the neck and shoulder edges. Slash the pattern from the center line of the waistline dart along the drawn vertical line to the shoulder seam. Slash the pattern again through the center line of the underarm dart to the point of the bust. Overlap the edges of the vertical slash, taking out the necessary amount at the bust point. Both darts will be decreased this way. Pin or tape the pattern in place.

Full Bust: Slash your pattern as directed for the small bust. Spread the pattern apart on the vertical slash at the bust point, increasing the desired amount. This will increase both darts. Insert tissue paper under the spread pattern and pin or tape in place. Redraw the tapered ends of the darts.

To Increase or Decrease Hips or Waist: Measure yourself to decide exactly how much to add or subtract to your pattern. (Remember to allow for ease of fit.) Divide the amount by four and add or subtract that amount to each side seam on pattern front and back. Taper the pattern as necessary to change either the hips or the waist if both areas do not need alteration.

SLEEVE ADJUSTMENTS

Heavy Arms: Slash your sleeve pattern vertically from the center mark at the top of the sleeve cap to the lower edge. Spread pattern the needed amount; insert tissue paper and pin or tape in place. To assure that the sleeve will fit the armhole, add half the amount you added to the sleeve to both the front and back at the side seams, tapering to nothing at the waistline.

Thin Arms: Take a tuck down the center of the sleeve from cap to wrist edge. Pin or tape in place. Take out half that amount from both the front and back side seams, tapering to nothing at the waistline.

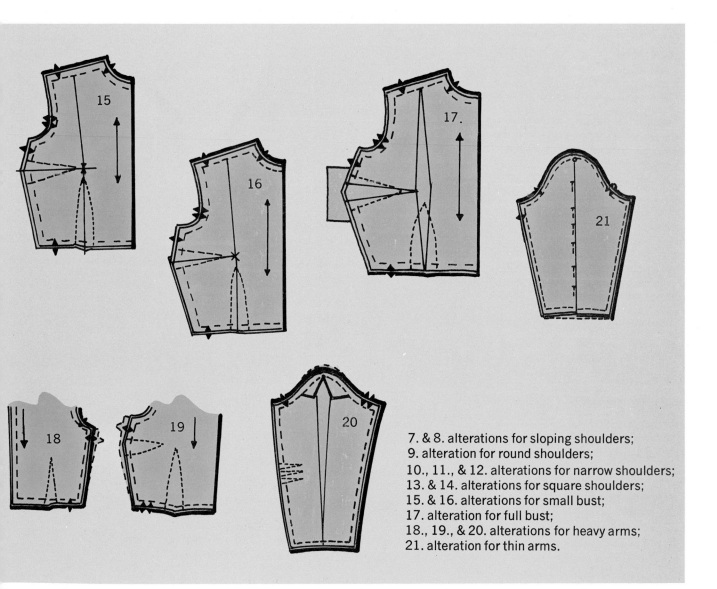

7. & 8. alterations for sloping shoulders;
9. alteration for round shoulders;
10., 11., & 12. alterations for narrow shoulders;
13. & 14. alterations for square shoulders;
15. & 16. alterations for small bust;
17. alteration for full bust;
18., 19., & 20. alterations for heavy arms;
21. alteration for thin arms.

PROBLEM FIGURES

Large Abdomen: Measure your front waistline from underarm to underarm; divide by two. Pin in the waistline darts on the pattern bodice taking in only half as much as the pattern indicates. Measure the pattern waistline from center front to the side seam line. The difference between this measurement and half your own front waistline measurement (as determined above) is the additional amount needed at the pattern waistline.

Slash the front bodice pattern vertically through the center of the waistline dart to the shoulder seam line.

About 3 inches above the waistline, slash bodice horizontally from center front to side seam line.

Slash the front skirt pattern through the center front to within ⅝ inch of lower edge. Slash skirt horizontally about 3 inches below waistline as you did the bodice.

Insert tissue paper under skirt pattern and under bodice pattern, maintaining straight lines for center front.

On both the bodice and skirt, spread the horizontal slashes one half the amount needed at the waistline. Pin pattern to tissue paper.

Spread the lower part of the skirt vertical slash and the upper part of the bodice vertical slash the same amount as for the horizontal slashes, tapering to nothing at lower edge and shoulder seam. Pin pattern to tissue paper.

At the point where the horizontal and vertical slashes meet, spread the vertical slashes the same amount as before, tapering to nothing at side seams. Pin pattern to tissue paper.

To draw a new waistline dart, begin at the point of the original dart and draw a line to the waistline through the center of the slash. Draw the slanted lines from the point of the dart to the waistline so that the new dart will be the same width as half the original dart.

Correct the side seam lines to maintain original shape.

Sway Back: Slash the pattern about 3½'' below the waistline from center back to side seam line. Overlap the edges of the slash, removing the necessary amount; pin or tape in place. Redraw the center back line straight, restoring the original grain line. This reduces the back waistline measurement, which is usually needed with a sway back. If you need the full waist measurement, increase the side seam the same amount that was removed from the center back, tapering from the waist to the hip.

SHORT-WAISTED FIGURES

A garment can be shortened above the waistline by following the directions for shortening a pattern. But this merely emphasizes a short-waisted figure instead of flattering it. A better plan is to have the beltline below your natural waistline, which gives a more balanced line to the garment as a whole. Use a narrow, inconspicuous belt.

If you have a large figure and are short-waisted only in the back, use a slanted fitting line at the waist, shorter in the back and dipping in the front. This line can be emphasized with embroidery or with a narrow set-in belt. Avoid straight fitted belts and never use a buckle except at the center back.

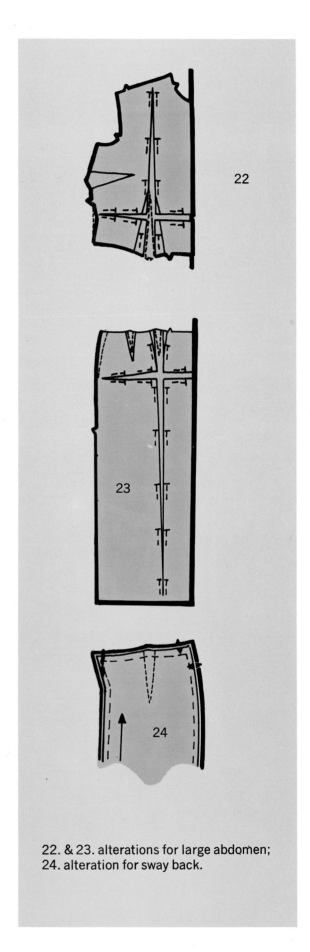

22. & 23. alterations for large abdomen;
24. alteration for sway back.

An empire-waisted A-line tunic worn over pants is flattering to most figures. It draws attention away from natural waist and has an easy fit over hipline. When fitting a pattern such as this one, be sure the empire waistline falls in a comfortable position.

Gathers at neckline and sleeves make this an easy overblouse to fit. Make length and width adjustments on pants before layout. Minor tapering can be done at a later fitting.

102

FITTING PANTS

Buy your pants pattern by the hip measurement since that is the hardest area to fit. Measure your waistline, hips and length.

An additional measurement must be taken to fit pants: the crotch length. Tie a string around your waist to mark your natural waistline. Sit absolutely erect in a straight back chair. Measure (with the help of a friend) from the string at your waist to the chair seat. This is your crotch length.

If your pattern does not have a horizontal crotch line already marked on it, draw one as follows: Find the widest point of the crotch; draw a horizontal line from that point to the side seam, making sure your line is at right angles to the grain line. The distance from this line to the pattern waistline should measure the same as your crotch length plus ¾'' for ease. If it does not, lengthen or shorten the pattern along the lengthening and shortening line as described for skirts and dresses.

Next, adjust the length of the pattern piece if it is different from the length you need. Keep in mind that an adjustment in the crotch length will change the length of the original pattern piece, so measure only after altering the crotch length.

After making all the adjustments in length, make the adjustments in width. If the pattern is too big, take a vertical tuck in the pattern parallel to the grain line. Position the tuck so as to avoid the darts.

If the pattern is too small, slash it vertically parallel to the grain line, again avoiding the darts. Insert tissue paper; pin or tape in place.

To alter the waistline, take in or let out each dart no more than ¼''. If this is not sufficient, add or subtract at each side seam one fourth the additional amount needed. Taper to the hipline.

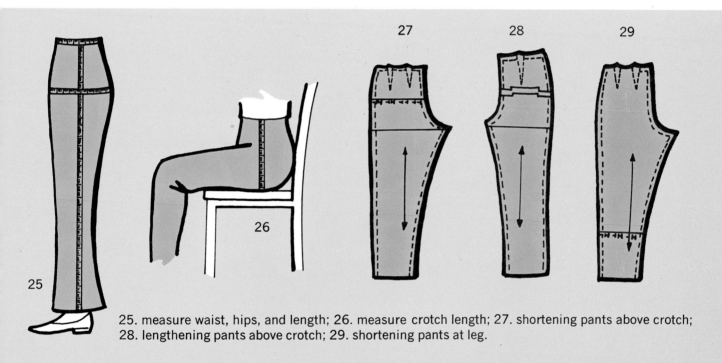

25. measure waist, hips, and length; 26. measure crotch length; 27. shortening pants above crotch; 28. lengthening pants above crotch; 29. shortening pants at leg.

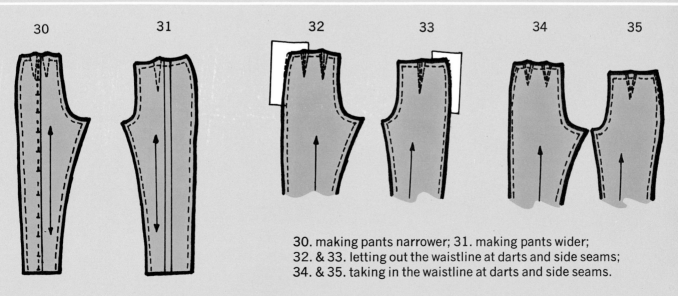

30. making pants narrower; 31. making pants wider;
32. & 33. letting out the waistline at darts and side seams;
34. & 35. taking in the waistline at darts and side seams.

For heavy legs, add to the inside leg seams.

For slim legs, decrease the inside leg seams on the pattern or pin-fit the slacks later.

For a sway back or a large abdomen, alter pants the same way you would alter a skirt, as described above.

If a large derriere is your problem, there are several ways to alter your slacks. It is best to make a muslin on which to test these alterations. Make the back darts longer and deeper. Add to the side seams at the waistline the amount lost by making the darts deeper. If additional fullness is needed, add to the inside leg seam on the back pattern only.

If a flat derriere is your problem, slash the back pattern across from center back to side seam about 3½ inches below waistline. Overlap the slash lines removing the necessary amount. Redraw the center back seam line. Make the darts shallower to give less fullness across the back; decrease the **waistline** at the side seams. Stitch the dart nearest the center back about 1½ inch longer than the other dart to give a smoother fit. Decrease the inside leg seam of the back at the crotch to remove extra fullness below the hip, if needed.

To taper the legs, at the first fitting, taper the same amount on the inside and outside leg seams. Do not try to remove all the fullness from the side seams.

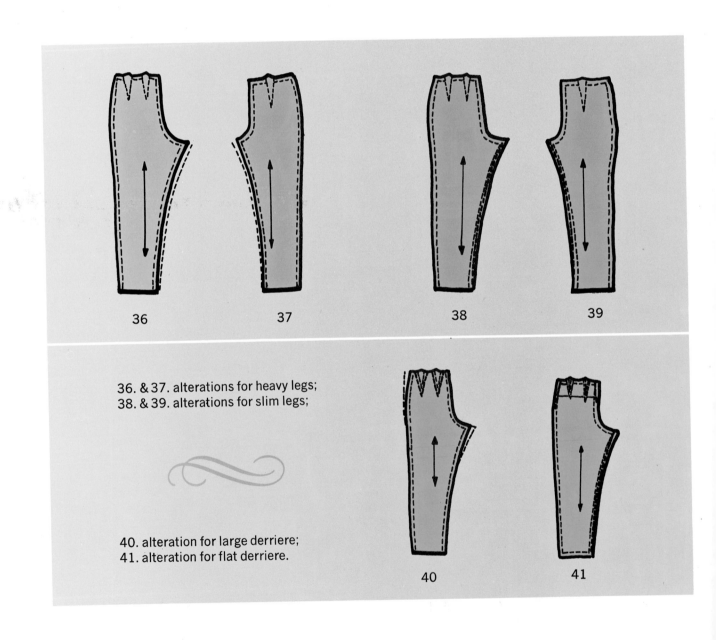

36

37

38

39

36. & 37. alterations for heavy legs;
38. & 39. alterations for slim legs;

40. alteration for large derriere;
41. alteration for flat derriere.

40

41

Marking
And Cutting

atterns include cutting diagrams and instruction sheets for your guidance, so before you start to cut, study your pattern thoroughly. Be familiar with the details of construction and know which pieces are to be cut double. Know which pieces should be laid lengthwise on the fabric. Naturally, you have already checked the pattern and made any necessary alterations.

PREPARATIONS FOR CUTTING

Assemble everything you need, including threaded needles for basting and marking, plenty of pins, and sharp cutting shears. If possible, plan to do your cutting when you are alone and not likely to be disturbed. Cutting needs complete concentration. In planning your time, allow enough to pin the garment together as you cut. This "work-as-you-go" practice is a time-saver in the end because it is easier to put the garment together while the details of the pattern instructions are fresh in your mind.

Cutting Tables: The table on which you cut should be large. Professionals insist on one which provides plenty of space, a hard surface, and a straight edge for testing the straight of the goods. If the table is so small that the pattern pieces slide off, cut on the floor instead.

THE FABRIC

Before you pin the pattern to the fabric for cutting, press out all wrinkles, but leave the center fold. The uncut edge of the fabric must be straight. If the uncut edge is crooked, straighten it.

To Straighten the Edge: Most fabrics can be straightened by drawing out a cross thread and cutting along the line of the thread. In corded and napped fabrics, lay a ruler across the edge and mark a straight line with chalk. In muslins and many cottons, the fabric can be torn for a straight edge.

Holes or Imperfections: If your fabric has any holes or flaws in it, mark them plainly with pins so you can cut around them.

The Right Side: If the fabric has a right and wrong side, be sure to mark the right side with pins so that you can distinguish it easily.

To Fold the Fabric: When you make a fold in the fabric for cutting, the fold must lie exactly on the straight of the goods, or along the lengthwise threads. If the fold is crooked, these lengthwise, or warp, threads—which are the strongest threads in the fabric—will not hang straight, and the garment will never fit. If a sleeve pattern is not placed on the grain of the fabric as marked, the sleeve will always twist.

HANDLING SPECIAL FABRICS

Some fabrics require special handling in making a garment. Here are a few tips—consult the Index for specific fabrics.

Napped or Pile Fabrics: In cutting napped or pile fabrics, be careful to lay out the pattern so that the top section of each piece points in the same direction; the "rough" way as contrasted with the "smooth"—so that the nap will be all one way when the garment is finished. Velvet, velveteen, corduroy, fleece and synthetic fur-like pile are popular napped fabrics. Flannel and wool broadcloth also have a nap. The word "nap" on a pattern means any one-way fabric.

Sheen Fabrics: Such sheen fabrics as satin should also be cut with the pattern pieces laid so the top sections all point one way. Otherwise different sections will catch the light differently.

Fur Fabrics: Such fabrics should be laid out like one-way fabrics, with the tops of all pointing in one direction. If the fur is very heavy, it will be easier to cut it out with a razor than with shears and not so many hairs will be cut.

Knitted and Stretch Fabrics: Knits have a grain which is different from woven fabrics. Knitted fabrics should be folded carefully and the pattern pieces laid along a lengthwise rib. More pins are needed to pin the pattern to the fabric. The pins also should be placed quite close to each other on stretch fabrics, and care must be taken not to stretch the fabric while pinning.

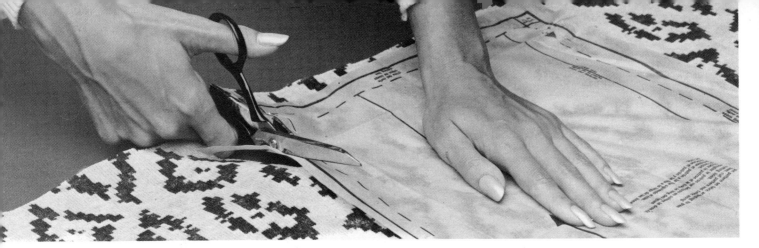

By gliding your left hand along the fabric as you cut, you can prevent pattern and fabric slippage.

Laminated Fabrics: Such fabrics have an insulated backing of chemical foam. Place the pattern on the *right* side of the fabric. Tailor's tacks must be used for marking construction symbols because the foam will not hold tracing wheel marks.

THE CUTTING ROUTINE

Smooth the fabric on the table, right side up, and straighten the edges. Lay the first piece of the pattern on the fabric as directed in the cutting chart and pin it firmly to the fabric so it will not shift as you cut. Place the other pieces in the same way. The wisest course is to follow the cutting chart with the pattern, because experts have worked out the directions for the most economical way to cut the fabric. There are several such charts with each pattern, according to the width of the fabric, the size and style of the garment. Draw a circle around the chart that applies to your selected version of the pattern; then study the chart carefully to be sure you understand the illustrated instructions.

When you put a pattern piece down on the fabric, smooth out pattern and fabric and pin them together. Insert the pins from the top without slipping your hand underneath the fabric. Put pins closer together along curved edges. If you want wider seams than the pattern allows, or if your material ravels easily, add 1 inch extra on straight seams, such as underarm seams, and ¾ inch extra on curved seams, such as at the neck. Stitch on original seam line.

To Cut: With long, sharp scissors cut a clean, straight edge. Cut with a long, steady motion to keep the edge of the seam clean, and slide the scissors along so that you do not lift the fabric more than the space necessary for one blade of the scissors underneath. It will help to put one hand on the material opposite the scissors and keep the scissors constantly on the table. Shears are invaluable because of the bow handles into which you can put two fingers; this gives you greater leverage.

The thick blade should be above the material, the pointed blade underneath it. Cut with the middle of the blades, and remember that short snips will make an untidy edge which you will have to even later. Make sure you cut parallel to the edge of the pattern. If your scissors snip inside the edge,

you tighten your pattern or narrow your seams. If you run a basting thread down the center front of the waist and skirt, it will help you later in placing yokes, pockets, and belts, and in fitting.

PLAIDS AND FIGURED MATERIALS

The cutting measurements in your pattern and the cutting diagram in your pattern, as well as your pattern's fabric measurements, are designed and tested for plain fabrics or those with a small or medium print.

A fabric with a stripe, a plaid, a large spaced print, or a print with a distinct up-and-down pattern, requires special treatment in laying out and cutting. Not only does it require more material to cut these fabrics—you must expect to waste a little fabric when you want to match plaids, stripes, or prints exactly—but also it requires a more careful choice of pattern. When a pattern envelope illustrates a plaid or a matched stripe, you will find instructions in the pattern for carrying out this idea; but patterns that do not illustrate the matched stripe which you want to develop should be analyzed very carefully.

Cutting Plaids: Textiles are printed and woven in classic and decorative plaids which fall into three main categories: (1) a small plaid repeated often; (2) a medium plaid repeated every ¼ yard; (3) a large plaid repeated every ½ yard. The repetition of a printed design does not refer to a single line of plaid; for often several lines in several colors make one complete pattern, which is then repeated over and over again. To estimate the extra yardage, remember that ¼ yard of additional material is required for a design which repeats often, and that when a long space occurs between each repeat, you must allow extra material equivalent to two or three repeats. When you first begin to work with plaids, you will be wise to select a simple pattern with only a few pieces. It can have a two- or four-gore skirt, or it can have pleats. Lay all the material out so you can plot the matching of the plaid in the most becoming manner.

First, place the pattern pieces on the fabric, all running in one direction, and then decide where you want the design of the material to fall on the garment. It is advisable to center the plaid between the shoulders and extend a straight line of plaids down to the hemline on the skirt. You must carefully adjust the pieces of pattern on the fabric so that the notches are each placed on exactly the same position in the repeated design so that when joined they will show a smooth continuation of the design. It is particularly important that the plaids should match on the crosswise pieces which meet at the armhole and where the seams are to be formed on the skirt.

Pay particular attention to the sleeves. The plaid must match the rest of the garment if a satisfactory effect is to be achieved. Note the notches on the sleeve pattern and place the plaid so that the same line of the design meets these notches exactly as the plaid meets the notches in the armholes. Cut the front and back gores of the skirt first, and

Tiny checks and plaids like this classic ever-popular gingham check need not be matched when laying out the fabric. Just be certain that the pattern is placed on the straight grain and you're all set!

A bias treatment produces an attractive plaid design. When selecting fabric, choose an even plaid. When selecting pattern, look for one with a bias version sketched on the pattern envelope.

To find the crosswise grain of your fabric, carefully draw out one thread and cut along the line.

Plan the placement of large motifs carefully to center your design and make the best use of your fabric. Matching patterns is not possible here because the repeat of the pattern is so large.

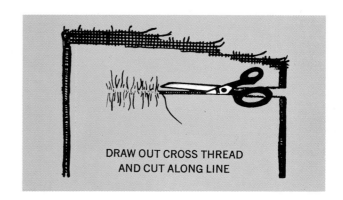

DRAW OUT CROSS THREAD
AND CUT ALONG LINE

More gingham for a crisp summer look! Note the chevron effect at the center front seam on the skirt achieved by the shape of the skirt pattern rather than a bias layout. The rest is straight.

take just as much care in cutting the side gores, so that the pattern matches at the seams. It helps to place an arrow on the notches and put these arrows directly opposite the spot in the design you want placed at that point. This will bring the plaid into harmony at all seam joinings.

Pleated Plaid Skirts: Whenever a pleat is made in a plaid, it must be spaced for the plaid, not the pattern. In other words, you must space the pleat to the plaid so the same line of design comes at the edge of each pleat. If your garment has a few pleats, or a kick pleat, first try out the pleat in the plaid. When you are satisfied with the effect, pin the pleats into the pattern and baste the pleats into the material; cut the pleated section by the pattern as if the pleats were not called for at all. Do this first before you cut the rest of the garment.

Large Checks: When the check in the design is larger than ½ inch, it must be cut so the checks match at the seams. You require only ⅛ yard more material to do this because the design repeats frequently. Make an arrow opposite the notches which must be matched and place corresponding notches on exactly the same line of the check design.

Large-Spaced Prints: These prints must be cut carefully (1) so the center of the design is in the center front and center back of the garment; (2) so the design is placed in a flattering position where it is not cut off suddenly, thus emphasizing a figure defect. To see where the prints fall in the most becoming way, stand in front of a mirror with the fabric loosely draped around you. Avoid having a large motif centered over the bust or stomach or at the neck. To save using a great deal of extra material, choose a very simple fabric construction and fit the pattern carefully before cutting. Study the repeat of the print, and you will see that when a design is repeated often, you need allow only one or two extra repeats of the print. When a design is spaced wide apart you will require more material—the equivalent of three repeats of the print. In cutting fabrics with large-spaced prints, it is not as important to match the print on the side seam as it is to center it in a flattering position in relation to the garment construction.

Up-and-Down Prints: Prints which cannot be turned upside down must be cut so that all the pieces of the pattern

point in the same direction. When the design is small no extra material is required; but when it has a wide-spaced repeat that must be centered in the garment construction, you will require extra yardage—equivalent to two repeats of the design.

Stripes: Stripes which run up and down—especially a wide-striped fabric—must be analyzed carefully. There are simple stripes, all alike and spaced evenly; complex stripes of different widths, spacings, and color (which constitute a design repeat); blended stripes, indefinite and often wide; and simple designs which give a striped effect. If you understand exactly how to go about cutting these lovely materials, you will be proud of the garments you make.

Be sure to select a simple pattern with straight lines. Center the stripe in the front and back of all pieces. In cutting, the stripe should be centered the full length of the sleeve, and any yoke effect should be cut to correspond with the sleeve stripe.

When stripes are cut for decorative trimming bands of self-fabric, you can use any simple house-dress or shirtwaist dress pattern, apron pattern, straight-line dress for girls, tailored shirt type for men, women, boys, or girls. After you have selected your pattern style, make a little diagram (place tissue paper over the picture of the pattern) and mark how you are going to arrange your stripes. Sometimes a dress is cut with stripes running lengthwise; and the pockets, collar, front closing band, and band at the hem are cut crosswise. In other dresses or apron effects, a short sleeve and yoke will be cut crosswise. No matter what effect you desire, it is easy to achieve if you have a little diagram in front of you so that when you lay the pattern on the fabric you know just how to place the trimming touches in relation to the stripe.

Stripes which meet diagonally must be cut with the aid of special pattern directions, and you will be wise to look for a pattern envelope that is illustrated in this way. The skirt should have four gores; the waist should have a seam at the center front and center back. It can be a slip-on or a button-front. For true success, the stripe must have a straight line that is definite and can be controlled to run lengthwise on the fabric or across. If you have a four-gored skirt pattern that does not include this cutting information, place it on the stripe as shown in the diagram here. The notches that meet must be placed on the exact line in the stripe (1); each skirt gore is cut twice (2). In the second cutting you must turn it to face in exactly the opposite direction.

Basting Matching Fabrics: Join the seam on the right side of the material. Turn one edge at the seam allowance and place it over the opposite edge so the seam allowances meet. First pin the edge so the pattern exactly matches, then baste on the right side of the material. Slip-stitch the edges together, taking long stitches through the folded edge and small stitches through the flat fabric. You can then turn your work to the wrong side and lay out the seam for stitching.

Who said plaids can't be romantic? Share your plaid know-how with your guy! Match the plaid at the side seam for his slacks. Place the dominant line down the center front for your dress.

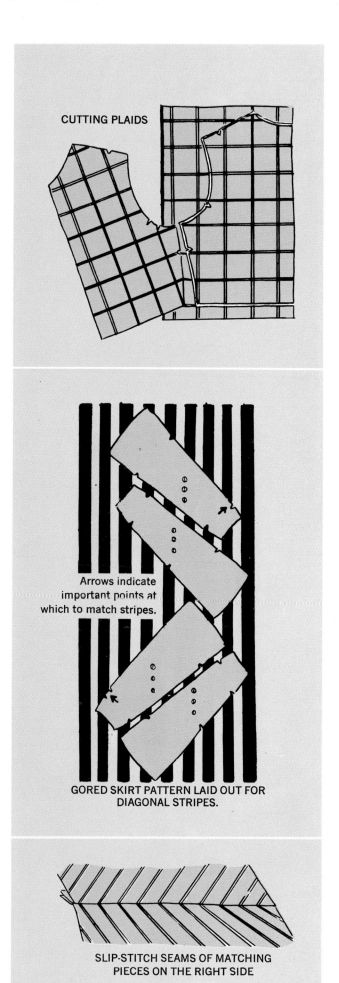

CUTTING PLAIDS

Arrows indicate important points at which to match stripes.

GORED SKIRT PATTERN LAID OUT FOR DIAGONAL STRIPES.

SLIP-STITCH SEAMS OF MATCHING PIECES ON THE RIGHT SIDE

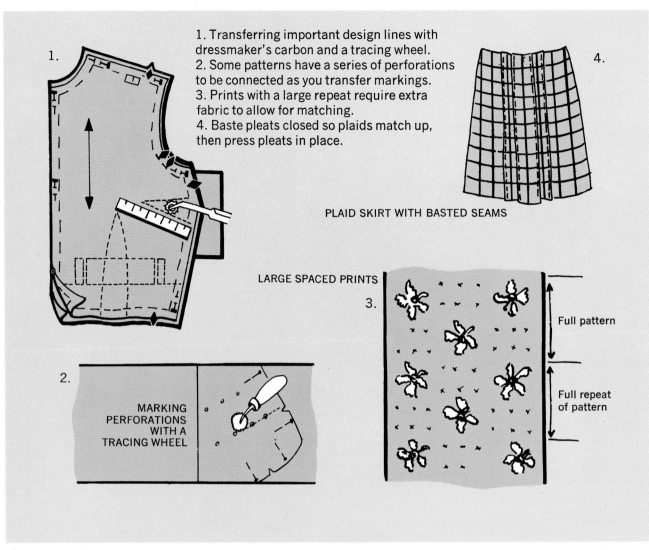

1. Transferring important design lines with dressmaker's carbon and a tracing wheel.
2. Some patterns have a series of perforations to be connected as you transfer markings.
3. Prints with a large repeat require extra fabric to allow for matching.
4. Baste pleats closed so plaids match up, then press pleats in place.

PLAID SKIRT WITH BASTED SEAMS

LARGE SPACED PRINTS

MARKING PERFORATIONS WITH A TRACING WHEEL

Full pattern

Full repeat of pattern

Careful attention to detail in marking and placement of pattern on fabric aids in achieving the professional results you want. Plan before you lay out, recheck before you cut, mark carefully, baste as needed.

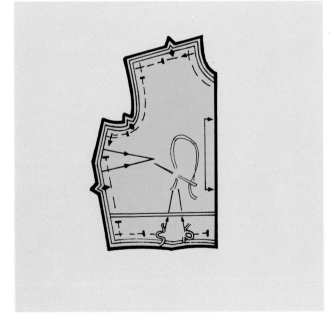

PATTERN MARKINGS

What They Mean: The edge of each pattern piece is marked with notches, which show where each piece is to be joined. The dots, lines, arrows and triangles indicate cutting lines, seam allowance, darts, buttonholes and other construction details. Few patterns are perforated today; most of them use printed lines to indicate the placing of pockets and pleats.

Transferring Pattern Markings: After cutting, all the pattern markings must be transferred to the fabric to assure proper placement of seams, darts, and details. The exceptions are the cutting lines and fold lines which have already been used during layout and cutting, and the grain line which was used to place the pattern piece accurately along one thread of the fabric. You must transfer seam lines, darts, center front and back lines if they are not placed on the fold, buttonhole and button placement lines, pocket placement, inside fold lines, all dots, and any other details

marked on the pattern to be used while stitching the garment.

Tracing wheel and dressmaker's carbon is the easiest method to use on most fabrics, but does not work on heavy fabrics or sheers.

Choose the lightest possible color carbon paper so that your markings will not show through on the right side. Test first on a scrap of the same fabric.

If your fabric was cut double, right sides together, with two pieces of carbon you can mark both pieces at once. Place one piece, waxy side down, between the pattern and the top layer of fabric. Place another piece, waxy side up, under the bottom layer of fabric. Place cardboard underneath to protect the table top. The important point to remember is to keep the waxy side of the carbon against the *wrong* side of the fabric. As you work you may have to remove pins to insert the carbon, but replace them as you complete an area so that the pattern does not slip off the fabric.

Run the tracing wheel along the lines of the pattern to be transferred. Use a ruler to assure straight lines. Mark dots

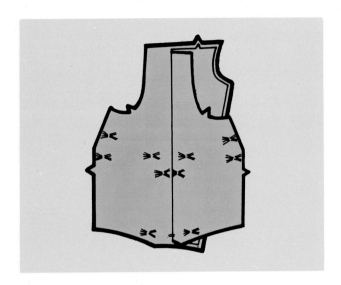
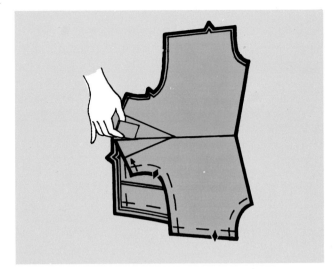

Above, right: Pins and chalk are used to mark fabric.

with an X. Place a short straight line across the point of darts.

Tailor's tacks are suitable for use on any fabric. This is the best method to use on heavy woolens and tweeds. Use a contrasting color embroidery floss since it is not as slippery as other threads.

With double thread take a small stitch through pattern and fabric at the point to be marked; leave a long thread end. Take another stitch in the same place, leaving a thread loop. Cut thread, leaving a long thread end.

Repeat the process at all points to be marked. Mark straight lines at 2-inch intervals. Mark curved lines at closer intervals. When all tailor's tacks have been made on one pattern piece, cut through the top loops and remove the pattern. Carefully separate the fabric layers and clip the threads between them leaving thread tufts on both pieces of fabric.

When construction is complete, threads can easily be pulled out.

Pin and chalk marking is suitable for all fabrics that will take tailor's chalk marking but not dressmaker's carbon marking. Place the pins through the pattern and the fabric on all the symbols to be marked, pin points upward. Carefully lift off the necessary part of the pattern and fold it back. With tailor's chalk or chalk pencil, mark the position of the pins. Then turn the fabric over and mark the position of the pins on the underside. If desired, markings can be connected with straight chalk lines to indicate straight lines on the pattern.

Thread marking is necessary for some details in addition to any other type of marking used. When the center front or center back is cut on the fold, baste a line down the center front or back before removing the pattern and unfolding the fabric. This line is needed for fittings later on.

Placement of buttonholes and pockets must be marked on the right side. This, too, is done by basting. With a contrasting color, hand baste exactly on the placement lines already marked on the wrong side of the fabric.

It's Best
To Baste

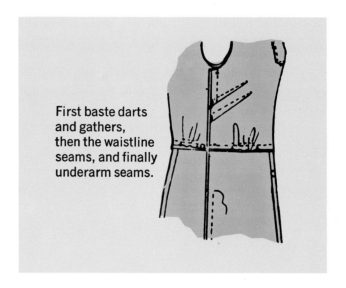

First baste darts and gathers, then the waistline seams, and finally underarm seams.

A garment may fit badly for any of a number of reasons, most of which can be avoided by checking your measurements with the pattern and making your alterations in the pattern before you cut. But even if you do alter the pattern first, you may find a few adjustments to be made at the first fitting, because different fabrics react differently, and a garment fits well only when it hangs well on the figure, without bulkiness caused by too much fullness or wrinkles caused by tightness. Fit your basted dress and examine it carefully, slowly revolving in front of a long mirror. The discussion of professional points in this chapter will help you decide what is wrong, if anything, and how to remedy it.

ORDER OF BASTING

When you start to baste your garment, first look to see how your pattern controls the curved lines. This means you first prepare and then carefully pin in the darts, tucks, or gathers, then baste them.

Next, look over your garment construction for small pieces, such as yokes and insets, then note whether it has pleats or straight facings. If there is a yoke, it must be basted on, and the pleats or facings, too.

After the smaller pieces have been disposed of, join the shoulder seams. Begin at the neck end of the seam and work toward the armhole.

Next come the long side seams under the arms. Begin at the armhole and work down to the waist.

After the side seams, baste the long seam in the skirt. Start at the waist and work down to the hem.

If the garment is in two pieces—other than one with a gathered skirt, in which the skirt seams and underarm seams are not meant to match—join it at the waistline before basting the seams under the arms. Place two pins in the center front and center back of the waistline on both waist

and skirt. Slip the waist inside the skirt, with both on the wrong side. The fronts and backs should be facing and the waist edges together. Pin the two center backs and center fronts together, then pin the side seams. With the seam thus pinned in the four most important points, space out the fullness evenly as you pin the seam along its entire length. This seam must be strongly basted because it has to hold the weight of the skirt. Use dressmaker's basting.

Finally, turn the dress right side out. Unless one shoulder is higher than the other, only one sleeve need be basted in for the first fitting. Pin and baste any darts or other shapings and put in any gathers at the wrist or the top of the sleeve. To join the sleeve seam, pin the top together and then the wrist. Work from both points toward the middle so that you can lay with tucks or gathers the fullness you need for elbow action. Remember that gathered parts of seams need small, strong stitches.

To baste the sleeve into the armhole, begin at the top of the sleeve and work around to the underarm seam. Here again, it is important to see that the notches are exactly matched. When the notches on the top of the sleeve and the armhole are matched, they will show you exactly where the sleeve seam will come. Smooth out evenly on both sides of the shoulder seam any fullness you find across the top. Shape this fullness to the curve of the armhole.

Collars and cuffs and belts should be basted when cut and stitched when you are stitching the rest. This plan makes the construction of the garment go smoothly and take up less time.

REMOVING BASTINGS

As you stitch the seams, remove the bastings. Professionals stitch just inside the seam line to avoid stitching over the basting line, which makes the basting threads much harder to get out. Train yourself to baste a little closer to the edge of the fabric than your actual stitching will be in the finished seam line. When you fit your garment, notice whether the seams should be stitched a little farther in from the basting to make the garment fit tighter, or a little farther out to make it looser, or just right. When you remove the bastings, never pull a long thread—it may punch little holes in the fabric or stretch a bias. Cut the stitches every 3 inches and pull the short threads gently.

SIDE-SEAM ADJUSTMENTS

Look first at the long lines, the up and down of the figure, on all garments. *The side seam must hang straight.* Not just when you straighten yourself or when you tug it into place, but naturally, so that it falls immediately into a straight line after every movement you make.

If the side seam shoots forward instead of hanging straight down, pin a tuck across the back of the garment at the waistline. Make the tuck big enough to make the side seam hang straight. If it shoots backward, make a tuck in the front at the waistline. This tuck can either be placed near a joining so you can rip the seam out and change the line, doing away with the extra fabric in the tuck, or it can be a small dart laid in an inconspicuous place.

Front and Back Lines: Front and back lines must be straight. Unless the style of the garment calls for an exception to the rule, the straight grain of the material must be held in the center front and center back. It does not matter whether the fabric hangs smoothly, is folded in an edge, or is cut in two or more pieces—it will hold its shape only if the lengthwise threads of the fabric hang straight. Home sewers often neglect to run the basting threads to mark the straight of the goods when they cut a garment; but without this marking it is very easy to pull the garment out of shape without realizing it. Always run a basting line down the center of the dress before you cut.

Horizontal Lines: Unless the style demands an exception to the rule, always watch any line which crosses the garment. This includes the hems of skirts, coats, and jackets; the stitched lines which join a garment at the waist or which join a flounce or yoke; and the cross grain of the sleeves. You will save yourself time if you check these lines before you stitch, to make sure they are true. Then look to the shoulder seams, armholes, neckline, and sleeves to be sure they fit and are in balance.

Underarm Seams: When a garment seems loose, bulky, or too full, the most natural adjustment is to pin in a wider seam under the arm. The seams on both sides should be equal. If you take up fullness by making a wider seam on one side only, the garment will be thrown off balance. This underarm adjustment is made on the right side of the material; then take off the garment, loosen the pins, and replace them in one side of the line which you pinned, taking care to put them back exactly where they were each time. Turn the garment to the wrong side and baste the seams on the pin line.

If the garment is tight or seems to draw, you can rip the underarm seam and let out as much material as is possible.

If this is not enough to relieve the strain, set in a piece of the same fabric under the arm. This can be a straight strip, the size of the piece depending on the amount of extra room you need, and should extend from the underarm to the waist. If, however, you do not need as much room at the top or at the waist, this piece can taper to nothing at either end.

WAISTLINE AND HIPS

Look to see if the garment is too loose or too tight at any point. If the skirt and waist are too full, take them in at the side seam. To do this, the dress should be on the right side and the seam should be equal on both sides of the figure. First pinch it in at both sides with your hand to gauge the amount, then pin this amount, beginning at the waistline. Pin this seam from the waist over the hips (do not pull the skirt too tightly). When you have extended the line over the hips, look at your skirt and decide which would look better: (1) making the skirt narrower by extending the alteration from the hips to the hem; or (2) making the alteration come gradually to the original seam.

When a garment is too tight, open the seam. If you cannot let it out, place a trimming band in the seam.

In making skirt adjustments, remember that too tight a garment makes a woman look uncomfortably larger. Bear in mind, too, that opaque, heavier fabrics are fitted closer than sheer, soft, or transparent fabrics. A semifitted waistline is often important in achieving closefitting effects because it straightens the figure. When a garment has many up and down seams, a good fitter makes her alteration in full consideration of the garment cutting—sometimes it is best to take in or let out the side seam; again it is best to take a little out of each seam.

SHOULDER SEAMS

Few people have even shoulders, and adjustments needed in one armhole will differ from the adjustments needed in the other. Sometimes an armhole can be adjusted in the back only or in the front only; but it is preferable to balance the front and back by making a deeper shoulder seam to raise the dress at the shoulder, or by opening the shoulder seam and letting the armhole down.

A good fitter watches the fall of the fabric both at the armhole and across the waist or coat and works for a smooth effect which makes the bustline flatter.

SLEEVES

When a figure is rounded, full at the back, in fitting the sleeve take the precaution to take a narrower seam than the usual ⅝ inch in the top of the sleeve.

When the sleeve draws so that it must be cut away under the arm, clip both the underarm of the sleeve and the underarm of the waist, with short cutting slashes. Continue to do this until the sleeve hangs straight, then rebaste the seam of the sleeve at this lower line. When a sleeve is too short across the top for a very large arm, it forms a diagonal wrinkle from the underarm to the top of the sleeve in both the front and the back. Rip the sleeve from the armhole across the top only. Sometimes letting out a seam will permit the seam to hang straight; sometimes it is necessary to cut away some material at the underarm and make a new seam.

A sleeve which is too long on the top will form wrinkles at the back of the arm. Often this extra length can be fitted out by ripping the armhole and taking up an extra seam on the sleeve edge only.

When sleeve fitting is a problem, it helps to turn the armhole seam and baste it without setting in the sleeve. Pin this seam over the top of the sleeve, inserting the pins from the seam so they can be easily adjusted. Now fit the garment and observe the crosswise line of the fabric. Does the straight grain of the fabric follow a straight line in the sleeve? If not, balance the sleeve at once by taking up a larger seam at the armhole on whichever side of the sleeve the straight line curves away from. You will know how much to take up if you watch the line of the fabric grain take its correct position. It must hang straight. Turn the seam lines toward the sleeve.

If this fitting thus corrects the twisted sleeve, baste it carefully on the wrong side. If the sleeve continues to twist, it may need to be shifted in the armhole. Sometimes a sleeve is shifted to the back, so that the notches do not match. If the sleeve needs turning toward the front of the garment, you make this adjustment in the same way.

After a sleeve has been adjusted, the new seam line must be basted. Before stitching this seam, try the garment on for a test fitting.

Once you have raised or lowered the shoulder seam so that your garment hangs smoothly, you must consider the joining of the sleeve at the armhole. Does it follow the curved line at the end of the shoulder? This is the most becoming angle for sleeves. If you have it placed too far to the back, there will be a bulge at the back of the sleeve top. If it is too far to the front, a similar bulge at the top will appear on the sleeve front. Either way it will be necessary to take out the sleeve and reset it properly.

When the sleeves slip off the shoulder, the sleeve must be moved closer to the neckline or a dart or a few tucks taken across the shoulder. Usually a shoulder seam should be on top of the shoulder from the neck out to the shoulder edge.

Check elbow room and be sure the sleeve is placed so that the fullness adjusts easily when the elbow is bent. Sleeves that tear out at the elbow are often the result of bad fitting, permitting the elbow fullness to be below or above the point where it should be. It may be necessary to shorten the sleeve above or below the elbow. To do this, pin the necessary adjustment in the sleeve and test it, checking the joining of the sleeve in the armhole, the hang of the sleeve, and the correct length of the sleeve.

NECKLINES

There are two important considerations in fitting a neckline. Does it lie smooth? Is it becoming? Careful adjustments must be made to get what professionals consider becoming proportions of the neckline. Is it too high? Is it too low? Will the collar or scarf adjust at the desired angle? Try the effect very carefully. Only when every angle of the neckline has been checked can necessary adjustments be made. When a neckline looks too high and seems to call for adjustment, never cut away on the figure what you think is right. Instead, outline with pins the shape you think would be becoming. Snip your material a little at frequent intervals so you can constantly check as you turn the edge back. Whenever an edge is shaped in this way, lay it on the other edge and make both sides alike. Mark with accurate basting, and try on the garment to verify the alteration.

Collars: If you alter your neckline, your collar must be changed. When a neckline is enlarged, add half the extra space on either side of the back so that the shaping is not lost.

Waistlines, Skirts, Hems

*I*n *a typical one-piece dress, skirt and waist are joined with a seam at the waistline. The dress can be worn with a separate belt, or the joining can be beltless and decorated with embroidery or stitching. Other styles feature a set-in belt, which is a band stitched between waist seam and skirt seam. Dresses with waist and skirt cut in one can be fitted smoothly in princess lines, or fitted loosely and drawn in at the waist with a separate belt or left beltless.*

When skirt and waist are separate, the top of the skirt can be finished with a binding, a belt fitted inside so it does not show, a stitched-on fabric belt, or a separate belt.

An inner belt is sometimes added to hold the waist firm. One way to join the inner belt is to seam the waist and skirt first, then insert the belt, basting it to seam.

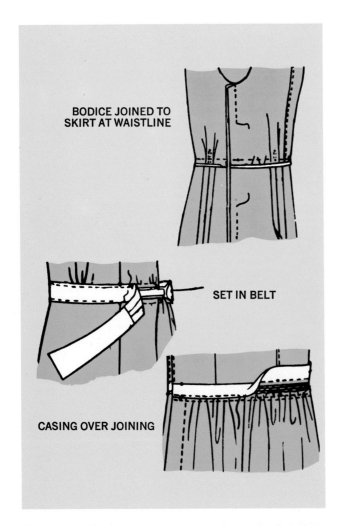

BODICE JOINED TO SKIRT AT WAISTLINE

SET IN BELT

CASING OVER JOINING

Joined with a Seam: The seam joining at the waistline of a one-piece dress may have fullness, or it may have double seams running into it. First press all the seams. Clip the ends at the top of each seam on the skirt and turn the top-edge seam allowance with an iron. Make sure the lower edge of the waist is fitted and that the fullness laid in gathers or darts is exactly where it is needed to flatter your figure. Decide on the length of waist and amount of fullness before you make the joining permanent.

With Set-In Belt: An extra wide beltline on a dress is often a cleverly set-in band, which is sometimes edged with cording which makes it look exactly like a separate belt.

When bands in contrasting colors are part of the styling, the pieces must either be cut according to a pattern or joined before the fabric is cut. As many as three colors may be grouped together, or the belting band can be outlined with a separating color. In either case, all the pieces are joined with seams; and those seams must, of course, be extremely accurate. So, unless you are an expert stitcher, be very careful to measure the seam allowance constantly as you baste. Bands of self-fabric, either straight or shaped to a point in the center of the bustline, are often used in gathered circular or gored skirts.

Slenderizing Waistlines: Princess dresses are fitted with waist darts, or the dress is shaped to the waistline by the seams. The more darts you use, the shorter each dart will be and the smoother the fitting line. Princess dresses should not be too tightly fitted.

Never fit a separate beltline so tightly that the flesh bulges around the belt.

Drawstring Beltlines: When the dress is fitted with scant fullness, a becoming style is to have the belt run through a casing stitched to the dress. This style should not be used on straight-line dresses.

WHEN YOU MAKE A SKIRT

Skirts can be finished to wear over a blouse with a separate belt; under a blouse so the belt does not show; or with a self-fabric belt stitched to the top and worn outside.

Inner Belting: If you want your skirt to extend above the normal waistline, you must fit in an inside belt of stiff belting which is sold by the yard at notion counters. Turn in the ends of this inner belt and attach hooks and eyes placed close together. Turn the skirt edge over this belt and hold it in place with catch stitches so no stitching shows on the outside. Or, if you prefer, turn and press the skirt edge, and stitch it to the belting so that it extends a little above the edge of the belting.

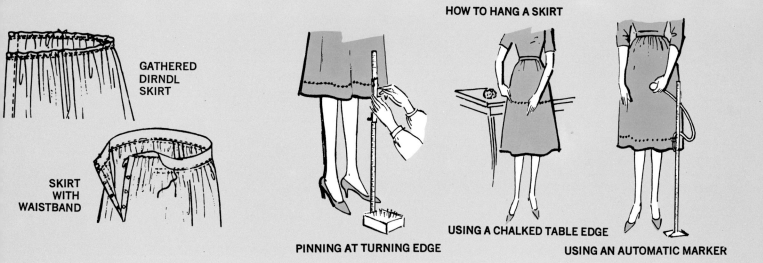

GATHERED
DIRNDL
SKIRT

SKIRT
WITH
WAISTBAND

PINNING AT TURNING EDGE

USING A CHALKED TABLE EDGE

USING AN AUTOMATIC MARKER

When a skirt is raised 2½ or 3 inches by means of an inner belting, the side seams must be fitted smoothly after the belting is in place. Such skirts are often worn with a narrow leather belt which holds the waist firmly in place.

If a wide belting is not available in your stores, cut a straight strip of buckram and fit it with darts so that it is wide at the top and curves into your natural waistline. Bone it at intervals so it will stay in place and bind the top and bottom with a strip of fabric so the buckram won't cut into you. Fit it snugly and close it with hooks and eyes close together.

Pleated Skirts: Pleats can be spaced across the front, on each seam, or in all-around effects; they can be deep pleats, shallow pleats, or unpressed pleats.

After you have decided upon the type of skirt, choose the kind of pleat you want—side pleat, box pleat, inverted pleat, and so forth. Begin by marking the center front and center back; next mark the pleats, using a gauge. Next hold the pleats into the waistline with a straight belt. Now you are ready to fit.

Turn the hem and decide how far down from the waist you want the pleats held by stitching. When the pleats have been stitched and the hem finished and pressed, press the pleats. Some sewers baste the pleats flat all the way down; but this makes it difficult to fit and adjust the skirt. A better way is to press in the folded crease, then lay and baste the pleats only half-way from the waist. This makes it easier to judge the fullness in turning the hem and deciding the length for the pleat stitching.

Shallow pleats, turning only 1 inch of fabric, should be permanently stitched, or they will be difficult to care for. To do this, lay the pleat and stitch it below the hipline. Continue the stitching *on the creased edge only* to the hem. Stitch the creased edge at the back of the pleat. A pleat stitched in this way is easy to press and holds the line of the crease.

When a kick pleat is inserted in the front or back of a dress, first join the piecing for the kick pleat and then join the seam above the pleat. In making a kick pleat without a pattern, it is easier to mark the center of the garment, then lay a box pleat the full length of the skirt. Then decide how deep you want the kick pleat and stitch across the fabric, bringing the stitched line to a point at the center of the pleat. Continue the stitching on both sides of the front, holding the pleat 5 inches below the point. Fasten the threads securely.

Cut away the excess material above the stitching and press the pleats. These edges can be permanently creased by making a stitching as close to the edge as possible.

Gathered Skirts: Straight lengths of fabric simply hemmed and gathered like the peasant skirts of Europe are a feature of the popular dirndls.

The width of the skirt must be decided on the basis of the fabric. Only a very soft fabric is effective in a full gathered skirt. Heavier fabrics can be shaped and then gathered. Most women find this kind of skirt more becoming than a straight gathered skirt.

Skirts with Yokes: Skirts set on yokes or on a band belt, or featuring a pocket cut in one with the garment, should have the yokeline stitched and pressed before the long seams of the garment are joined. Don't be afraid of fashion details like side pockets cut into the skirt below the waistline. The pocket is adjusted first, seamed to the right side, then turned. Then seam the opposite side of the pocket to the yoke and join the yoke to the skirt panel. At this point you are ready to baste the long seams.

If your hips are full, avoid the straight-backed skirt. The skirt will look straight but give a more flattering line if you add a little fullness.

HOW TO HANG A SKIRT

When the garment has been fitted and joined at the waist, you are ready to mark and make the correct hem line, which is commonly called ''hanging the skirt.'' Slip on the skirt and look at yourself in a long mirror. Consider the length of the skirt in relation both to current fashion and to your figure proportions. Then have someone measure from the floor with a yardstick and with chalk mark the skirt at the correct height for the turning edge. Be sure you wear the same style of shoe during this fitting that you intend to wear when the garment is finished. A variation in the height of your heels can make a great deal of difference.

How to Even Your Own Hemline: If a helper is not available, you can even your own hemline by standing beside a table and placing a row of pins around the skirt or chalking a line wherever the table touches you as you turn. The table must be low enough so that the mark comes below

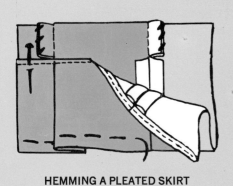

HEMMING A PLEATED SKIRT

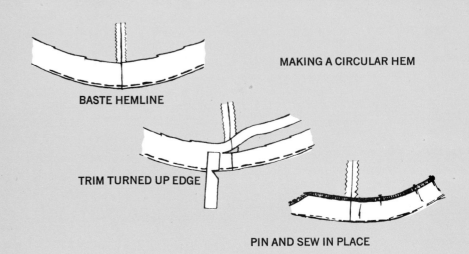

BASTE HEMLINE

TRIM TURNED UP EDGE

MAKING A CIRCULAR HEM

PIN AND SEW IN PLACE

the hip line. Measure from this mark to the hem of the skirt; and a uniform measurement from your chalkline or pin line to the hem, all the way around, will insure a straight skirt hanging at an even distance from the floor. Another way of using a table as a skirt marker, is to chalk the edge of the table. Then as you gradually turn, the chalk will be transferred to the skirt in a regular line. You must have a straight-edged table to do this; a rounded edge will give you a chalk line too broad to be accurate.

You can also hang a skirt with an automatic skirt marker. This ingenious device consists of a square base holding an upright piece of wood which has attached to it a sliding container holding powdered chalk. The container can be raised or lowered on the upright to the proper height for the hem line. To the container is fastened a tube and rubber ball. Place the skirt marker on the floor beside you, adjust it to the proper height, and press the bulb. This squirts a little chalk on your garment. Turn around, keeping close to the marker, and continue to press the bulb. On removing the garment, mark the chalk lines with a basting thread.

Professionals measure for the width of the hem with a gauge, making the edge even to correspond with either the usual 2½- or 3-inch hem or using the narrowest place in the hem as a universal measure. Before turning the hem, they finish the edge with seam binding, with a stitched turn, or with a turn. Once the edge is finished, the skirt can be turned at the basting. Smooth the edge over the skirt so it lies flat and hold it in place with pins or bastings. You are ready to hem the skirt by hand or machine. (See Index.) Press the hem both before and after stitching to insure perfect smoothness.

Hanging a Circular Skirt: When the style feature of your garment is a full circular skirt, join the seams, make the waist, and join the waist to the skirt before adjusting the hem. The garment should then hang on a clothes hanger for at least two days so the fabric can stretch normally.

Even the hem of the skirt and mark it carefully. Then measure for the hem turning—1 inch is ample. The top edge of your hem must be turned and held in place with a gathering thread so that the extra fullness can be laid flat. In circular skirts of woolen fabrics, a one-stitched hem is sufficient. The top edge is not finished and is not turned. In transparent fabrics the edges of circular skirts are often hemstitched by machine. (Cut the hemstitching in half and turn the edge in a tiny hem.)

ALTERING SKIRTS

When you shorten a skirt, take accurate measurements and allow for the edge to be turned and finished. Be careful not to make too deep a hem, as it detracts from the graceful swing of a skirt. Usually 3 inches are allowed in hems. When you lengthen a skirt you may find the edge is so uneven that you cannot turn an even hem, or you haven't enough material to turn any hem. If either is the case, remember that the hemline can be faced with a lining fabric cut on the bias. Stitch the bias facing to the right side of the skirt a little below the line marked for turning. Turn the hem and baste the edge carefully, making sure that the garment fabric turns up a little under the skirt so the facing will not show.

If the center back of the skirt is too long and sags at the back and behind the knees, remove the skirt at the waistline and lift it, starting at the *center* back and working out toward the side seams until it hangs straight.

If wrinkles form across the middle of the skirt because the center front is too long, it, too, should be lifted and treated the same way in the front.

Tips For Tailoring

*O***nce** *you have mastered and feel comfortable with the sewing techniques involved in dressmaking, you are ready to begin tailoring. Tailoring is a much more exact process than dressmaking; additional techniques are used to produce quality effects.*

Tailoring is a process of molding a garment to a desired shape. This molding is achieved by the use of interfacings, hand work, and steam-pressing. Be certain to fit your garment to your own body as you work. Do not be afraid to make any adjustments that will allow your garment a better fit. Once a tailored garment is completely shaped, major fitting alterations are not possible without destroying the shaping.

SELECTING PATTERN AND MATERIALS

For your first tailoring project, select a coat or a suit with simple lines. Since collar and lapels require a great deal of shaping, you might want to make a jacket with only a simple collar at first. Wool is the ideal fabric for tailoring because it is so "moldable" with a steam iron. You must use your steam iron constantly, pressing every seam, every step of the way. Wool can be stretched and shrunk as desired to shape your garment. Choose a medium weight wool, preferably with a pattern that does not require matching. Save the very heavy coating fabrics until you are more experienced. (Heavy fabrics tend to slip under the sewing machine, making it difficult to have ends come out even when stitching.)

Interfacing is used in areas of a garment that require shaping, firmness, stability, or crispness. Interfacing prevents the fashion fabric from stretching out of shape at critical areas. Hair canvas is the ideal interfacing for tailoring wool garments. It is available in many weights. You must choose an interfacing that is compatible in weight with your fashion fabric.

Finely tailored garments are always lined to hide inner construction, make them easier to slip on and off, and to give a neatly finished appearance to the interior. Choose a lining that will withstand the stress and strain given to a coat when it is put on and taken off. Your lining should be durable, dry-cleanable, color-fast to perspiration, opaque to prevent inner construction showing through, as well as color coordinated with your fashion fabric. Do not skimp on the lining fabric—this is an important part of your tailored garment.

Interlining is often used in winter-weight tailored garments to provide extra warmth. It is most successful when put in separately from the lining—this requires an extra step in your work. Choose a soft, light-weight wool or a warm cotton flannel. If you wish to have the extra warmth without the extra work, choose a lining/interlining combination and insert it just like a lining. Such combination fabrics are available as wool-backed satin, aluminum-backed fabric, and fabric with laminated backing.

Since you have already mastered the various steps in dressmaking, or can refer to them elsewhere in this book (see Index), the remainder of this section will deal, for the most part, with the aspects of tailoring that differ from dressmaking. Follow your pattern guidesheet for instructions on cutting, marking, and stitching your garment. Use this chapter as an additional guide to tailoring, or when your guidesheet fails to detail certain information. Be certain to steam-press as you go.

TO INTERFACE A TAILORED GARMENT

If separate interfacing pieces are included with your pattern, cut interfacing from those pieces. If not, cut interfacing as follows:

- Cut front interfacing from front facing pattern ½ inch wider than the facing at the unnotched edge, minus the hem allowance.
- Mark the center front line and the buttonhole locations on the front interfacing.
- Cut the back neck interfacing from the back neck facing pattern, cutting it ½ inch wider on the unnotched edge.
- Cut the collar interfacing from the under-collar pattern.
- Cut bias strips of interfacing for the lower and sleeve edges 1 inch wider than the width of the hems and as long as the edge to be interfaced, allowing for a ¼ inch overlap. (Note: If piecing is necessary, overlap bias strips ½ inch on the straight grain.)
- On a garment with front facing cut in one with the front, if a separate interfacing pattern has not been included, cut interfacing from the pattern front section. Cut from the fold line on the pattern to the outer edge of the facing plus ½ inch. Cut it the full length of the front facing minus hem allowance.
- If you wish your interfacing to extend over more of the garment for additional body and support, you can make an interfacing pattern from the garment front and back pattern pieces following the diagrams and measurements as shown. Mark darts, seams, center lines, and buttonhole locations on the interfacing.

Preparing the Interfacing:
- Cut along one slanted stitching line of each dart. Lap the

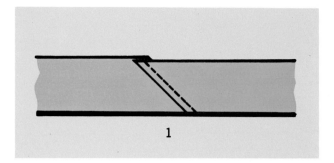

1

1. When joining bias strips of interfacing, overlap them ½″ on the straight grain.

2. and 3. For additional body and support, extend the front and back interfacings as shown; cut interfacing 3″ down from the armhole seam.

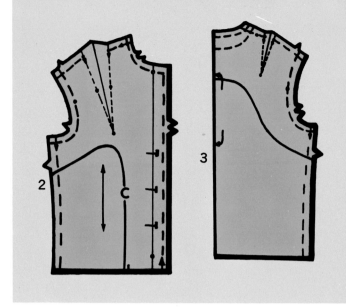

dart so that the cut stitching line and the marked stitching line meet. Pin in place.

- Stitch darts ¼ inch from the cut edge, tapering to the point. Trim cut edges of interfacing close to stitching. Reinforce the darts by stitching several times across the points. This method results in eliminating as much bulk as possible from the interfacing in these areas.

Joining Interfacing

Join the interfacing to the garment after the front of the coat or jacket has been stitched.

For a coat or jacket with plain, unturned closing:
- Trim all outer corners of the interfacing to reduce bulk.
- Pin the interfacing to the wrong side of the garment front, matching edges, notches, and center front lines.
- Machine or hand stitch the interfacing to the front along neck and armhole seam lines and ½ inch from cut edge along front and shoulder. **Optional:** Baste the center of straight seam binding or twill tape over the front seam line to keep edge from stretching.
- Trim interfacing close to the line of stitching to reduce bulk.
- Hand baste along the center front line through garment and interfacing. Baste-mark the location of buttonholes.
- Tack inner edges of interfacing in place with long basting stitches or by catch-stitching.

For a coat or jacket with lapels that must be pad-stitched:
- Proceed as above to pin interfacing to wrong side of garment front and to mark.
- Rather than machine stitching, hand baste (with diagonal basting) the interfacing to the garment at the neckline and shoulder.
- If the roll line is not indicated on your pattern, mark one as follows. Baste front to back of garment at shoulder seams; baste collar to neck edge. Try on garment, lap centers, pin in place, allowing collar and lapels to fall naturally. Mark the roll line of the collar and lapels with pins; remove garment and baste-mark along pin lines. Pull out the basting holding garment sections together.
- Pad-stitch the lapels from roll line to front seam. Hold the lapel over your hand to maintain the shape it will

take when completed. Take a stitch through the interfacing and fabric, taking up only one thread of fabric and having stitch at right angles to the roll line. Take next stitch ¼ inch away. On the next row, repeat process working in opposite direction. This method produces a diagonal stitch on the upper side and a short straight stitch on the underside (the pad-stitching is invisible on the right side of the garment). Work parallel rows of pad-stitching from the roll line to the front seam line, having rows about ½ inch apart.

- Stay the front edge of the garment by trimming off the seam allowance of the interfacing and sewing tape over the front seam line from the neck seam line to the lower edge of the interfacing.

For a coat or jacket with front facing cut in one with the front:
- Clip the neckline seam and the lower edge along the fold line.
- Make a slight crease on this fold line by turning facing to inside and pressing lightly.
- Open facing out flat, pin interfacing to wrong side of front along the crease. Attach interfacing to the crease line with long basting stitches or catch-stitches.
- Attach inner edge of interfacing to garment with long basting stitches or catch-stitches.

Once the interfacing has been joined to the garment front by one of these methods, make bound-buttonholes in the garment front.

TO TAILOR A COLLAR

Used with the lapels described above, the notched collar requires the most preparation. In the pattern, two separate pieces are usually provided for this collar: the under-collar and the upper collar, the latter being slightly larger to prevent the seam line from rolling outward.
- Join the center seam of the under-collar; trim seam and press open.
- Join the interfacing (cut from the under-collar sections) with a lapped seam to reduce bulk; trim seam allowances close to stitching. Trim outside corners diagonally to reduce bulk. Pin interfacing to under-collar.

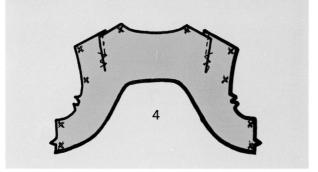

4. To sew darts in interfacing, cut along one slanted line, lap so that stitching lines meet, stitch ¼″ from seam line.

5. Machine or hand-baste interfacing to the jacket front. Baste-mark buttonholes.

6. Catch-stitch inner edges of interfacing.

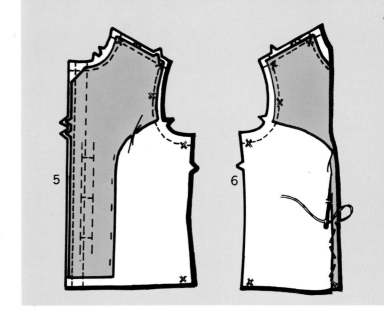

- Pad-stitch the under-collar by hand or by machine. Proceed by hand as follows: Determine the roll line of the collar and hand pad-stitch from the roll line to the neck seam line, holding the collar over your hand to shape it as it will be in the completed garment. Pad-stitch one half of the collar at a time. Then, either lightly pad-stitch the rest of the collar (from roll line to outer seam line), or machine-stitch the under-collar and interfacing ½ inch from all edges and trim interfacing close to stitching.

  By machine, working one half of the under-collar at a time and beginning at center back of the neck edge on the interfaced under-collar, machine stitch on the straight grain of the fabric from a to b, from b to c, from c to d. Begin again at e, stitch from e to f, f to g, and from g to d, following diagram.

  An alternate machine method is to machine stitch along the roll line of the collar and then make parallel rows of stitching ½ inch apart to neckline seam. Then, stitch the interfacing to the under-collar ½ inch from all edges and trim the interfacing close to stitching to reduce bulk.

- Join front and back of garment at shoulder and side seams and join the pad-stitched under-collar following pattern guidesheet.

TO ATTACH A COLLAR AND FACINGS

- Join front and back facings following instructions on pattern guidesheet. Right sides together, pin upper collar to facings matching center back lines and notches; stitch. Clip curves and press seam open.
- Right sides together, pin the upper collar and the front facing to the garment and the under-collar, matching center backs, notches, and neckline seams. The upper collar and facing should be larger than the under-collar and garment; do not trim but ease in place to fit.
- For a jacket, stitch across the facing at the lower edge and along the entire seam line (front of jacket, outer edge of collar) and across the lower edge of the facing on the opposite side. For a coat, stitch as above, but do not stitch across the lower edge of the facing.
- Press seams open.

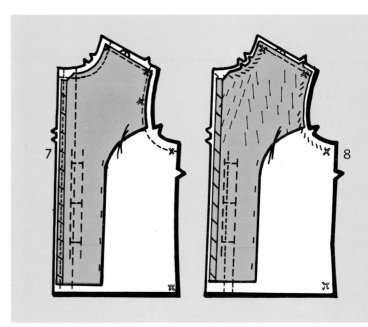

7. To keep front edge from stretching, baste the center of a piece of twill tape over the center front seam.

8. For a jacket with lapels, diagonally hand baste interfacing to garment. Pad-stitch heavily over lapel area, lightly over remainder of top section.

9. Work pad-stitching in parallel rows as shown below; the smaller the stitch, the heavier the padding.

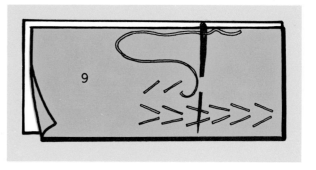

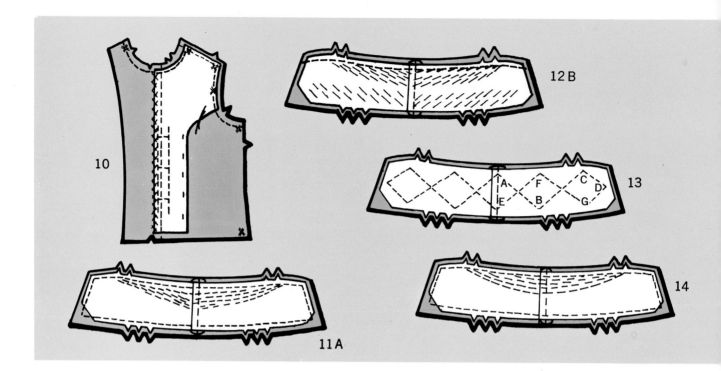

- Turn collar right side out; turn facing to inside. Roll the collar seam towards the under-collar and the lapel seam towards the garment as you press them in place. Hand or machine stitch back neckline seams together.
- Fold the lapels to the outside of the garment on the roll line. Pin in place. Catch-stitch facings to interfacing.

Facing Cut With Fronts

- If facing is cut in one with the front, the procedure is slightly different. Join the upper and under-collars, right sides together, matching centers; stitch on outer edge only. Press seam open.
- Clip neckline curve on the garment. Right sides together, pin the under-collar to the garment neckline; stitch. Press seams open.
- Join front facings to back facings at shoulder seams. Clip facing at neckline curve. right sides together, pin the upper collar to the seam line of the neckline facing; stitch. Press seams open.
- Right sides together, stitch upper collar to under-collar at the open ends. Press seams open.
- Turn collar right side out; turn facing to inside. Hand or machine stitch back neckline seam allowances together. Proceed as above to attach facing to interfacing.

- Prepare sleeve in the same manner as you would in dressmaking: stitch and press dart, ease-stitch top of sleeve.
- Pin interfacing to lower edge of sleeve with lower edge of interfacing ½ inch below hem line; baste in place along both long edges with long basting stitches.
- Stitch sleeve seam; trim edges of interfacing close to stitching.
- Turn up lower edge on hem line; press in place. Tack hem to interfacing with long basting stitches.

- Set sleeve into armhole as in dressmaking, matching shoulder seam to large dot at top of sleeve cap and matching notches and medium dots.
- Pull up machine basting until sleeve fits armhole, distributing ease evenly. Baste securely.
- Place the sleeve cap over the end of a sleeve board, wrong side up. Steam the cap to shrink out any fullness.
- Stitch the sleeve into the armhole. Steam-shrink again, if needed.

- Opening out the facing as needed, pin the interfacing strip to the lower edge of the garment with its lower edge ½ inch below the hem line, lapping the ends over the front interfacing. Baste in place along both long edges with long basting stitches.
- Turn up the hem along the hem line, at the same time turning in the front facings.
- Pink the upper edge of the hem or finish by stitching one edge of bias tape over the raw edge.
- Tack the hem to the interfacing with long running stitches.

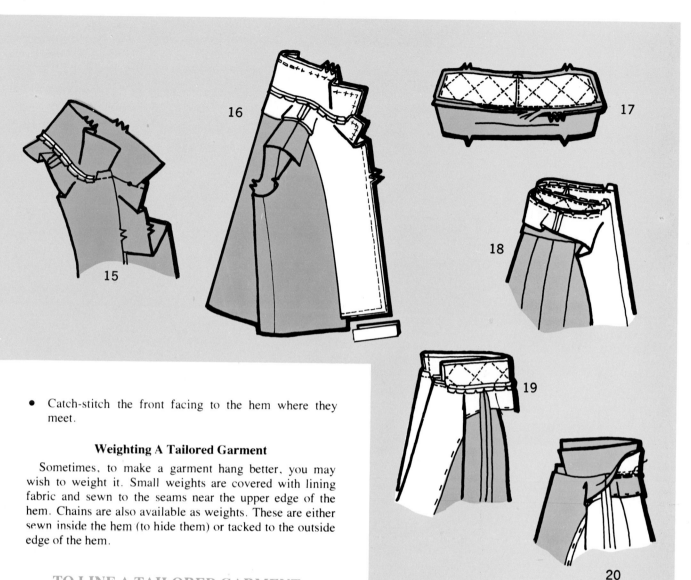

- Catch-stitch the front facing to the hem where they meet.

Weighting A Tailored Garment

Sometimes, to make a garment hang better, you may wish to weight it. Small weights are covered with lining fabric and sewn to the seams near the upper edge of the hem. Chains are also available as weights. These are either sewn inside the hem (to hide them) or tacked to the outside edge of the hem.

TO LINE A TAILORED GARMENT

- If you altered the pattern, make the same alterations on the lining pattern before you cut.
- Cut out the lining allowing a pleat in the center back. (The lining pattern will direct you to do this.)
- Before opening out the back lining, baste together along the fold line of the pattern, forming the back pleat. Machine stitch vertically along the basting for about 2 inches at neckline and hemline. Press pleat to one side. Or, from the right side, after pressing pleat to one side, catch-stitch it for about 2 inches at neck, waist, and hem. (Note: Omit stitching at hemline of coats.)
- Stitch front shoulder darts only about half way down, leaving them loose from the middle to the point so they form tucks.
- Stitch the waistline darts, if any, but clip them at the waistline before pressing towards the center; this will make them lie flat.
- Assemble the lining pieces as you did the garment pieces, but do not set in sleeves.

10. On a facing cut in one with front, catch-stitch interfacing to center front line.
11. and 12. Hand pad-stitch under-collar heavily from roll line to neck seam, then (a) machine stitch under-collar and interfacing ½" from outer edges, or (b) lightly pad-stitch remainder of collar.
13. and 14. To pad-stitch by one of these machine methods, see instructions on page 1 23
15. Joining upper collar and facings.
16. Attaching upper collar and facings to under-collar and jacket.
17. If facing is cut in one with front, join under-collar and upper collar as shown.
18. Stitch under-collar to jacket at neckline, stitch shoulder seams of facing.
19. Join ends of collar and under-collar.
20. Turn upper collar and facing to inside; sew neckline seams together.

Inserting the Lining

- Turn under slightly less than the seam allowance along front, neck, and lower edges; baste and press in place.
- Wrong side of lining to wrong side of garment, pin the lining into the garment, matching center back of garment to center back pleat. Match the side seams at the armholes.
- Turn the lining fronts back to expose the side seams of garment and lining. Tack the lining side seams to the garment side seams from about 2 inches below the armhole to about 3 inches above the hem. This keeps the lining from shifting as you move.
- Complete pinning the lining into the garment, lapping it over the front and neckline facings. Baste in place. Baste the lining to the garment at armhole seam allowances.
- With matching thread, slip-stitch the lining to the garment along front and neckline edges.
- If you are making a jacket, attach the lining to the hem allowing a horizontal pleat to form. This pleat will prevent the lining from pulling as you wear the garment.
- If you are making a coat, leave the lining loose at the hemline. Turn up lining hem so that lining is about 1 inch shorter than the coat. Attach lining to the coat at side seams with long French tacks.
- Stitch the sleeve seams as you did for the garment. Ease-stitch the sleeve cap and turn it under on the seam line.
- Turn both the garment and the lining sleeve inside out. Match the seams and tack together with long, loose basting stitches from about 2 inches below armhole to 3 inches above lower edge.
- Put your hand inside the lining from the top of the sleeve, take hold of both the garment sleeve and the lining sleeve and pull them through the lining. (Although this sounds confusing, it works—absolutely!)
- Lap the sleeve lining over the armhole seam allowance of the garment; pull up ease-stitching to fit, pin and baste in place. Slip-stitch the lining into the armhole.
- Finish the lower edge of the sleeve as you finished the lower edge of the jacket.

TO INTERLINE A COAT

- If you have chosen to make a separate interlining rather than use a backed lining fabric, cut your interlining from the lining pattern pieces. Do not allow a back pleat in the interlining. Cut the interlining the length of the lining, minus the lining hem allowance.
- Stitch the darts in the interlining the same way you

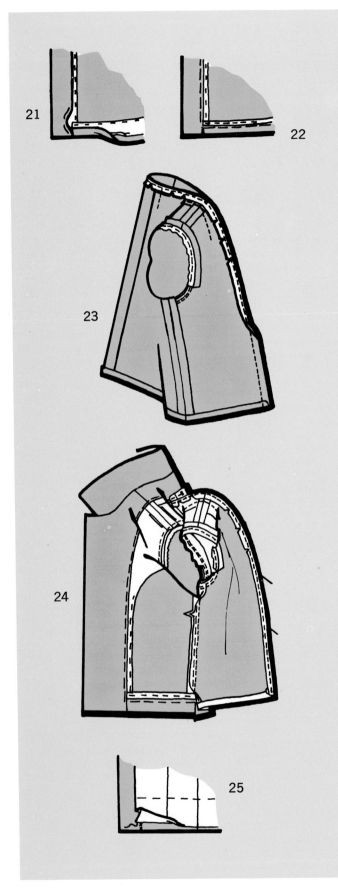

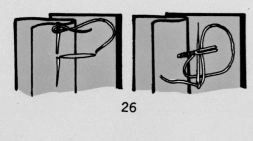

26

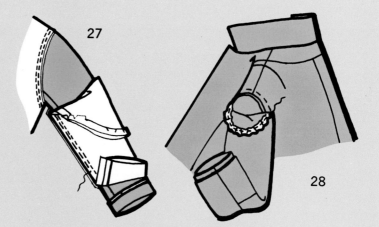

27

28

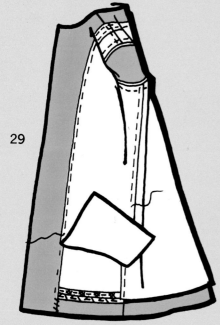

29

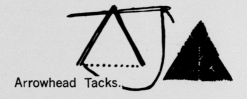

Arrowhead Tacks.

31

Crows Foot Tacks.

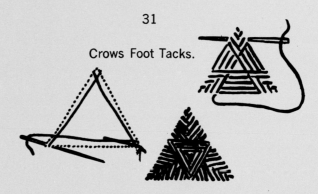

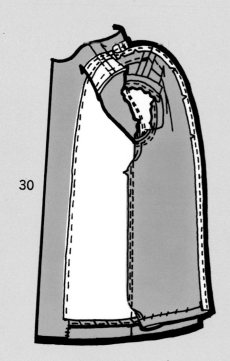

30

21. Interface the hem of a jacket. 22. Neat finish for a jacket hem. 23. Assemble the lining minus the sleeves. 24. Slip lining over jacket; baste at side seams. 25. Pleat forms at jacket hem for wearing ease.

26. Make French tacks to hold lining to coat at side seams. Take several loose stitches between lining and coat fabrics; work blanket stitch over the threads.

27. Baste lining to jacket sleeve before turning. 28. Turn under cap seam allowance before stitching cap. 29. Attaching interlining to avoid bulk. 30. Placing coat lining over interlining. 31. Making decorative arrowhead and crows foot tacks.

stitched interfacing darts—by lapping them to avoid bulk.

- Lap the front seam allowance over the back seam allowance at the side seam; stitch.
- Seam the shoulders in the same way.
- Pin the interlining to the wrong side of the coat, matching center backs, side seams at underarms, and shoulder seams.
- Turn back the front of the interlining and tack interlining to garment at the side seams, as described for linings, above.
- Baste interlining to garment at armhole seam allowances.
- Trim about ¼ inch from front and neck edges of the interlining and lap interlining about ⅜ inch over the front and neck facings; pin and hand stitch in place with running stitches.
- Attach the sleeve interlining to the lining sleeve; then treat the sleeve lining as usual.
- Insert coat lining as described above, being sure to cover the edges of the interlining when stitching in the lining.

ADDITIONAL FINISHING DETAILS

Crow's Foot: At the end of pockets or darts in tailored garments a crow's foot is sometimes used. Mark the shape of the crow's foot with basting, then bring a needle threaded with button hole twist or embroidery floss, through the left lower corner up to the top corner taking a small stitch from *right* to *left*. Bring needle down to right lower corner again taking another small stitch (this time from *left* to *right*) and continue on to starting point taking small stitch (*left* to *right*). Continue up to top point again and thus outline the crow's foot with row after row of thread, each row close to the next.

Arrowhead Tacks: Mark the shape of the tack. Use a needle threaded with buttonhole twist or embroidery floss. Bring the thread through the left lower corner up to the top corner taking a small stitch from *right* to *left*. Pass the needle to the right lower corner and insert it bringing it out close to the starting point. Continue working around so that each thread lies close to the last.

All About Sleeves

he line of the sleeve and armhole is the most difficult line to cut in any garment because it must curve to fit a circle around the fall of the shoulder and also allow for the movement of the arm. A long sleeve must fit at three angles: the shoulder, where the sleeve is joined to the garment in the armhole; the elbow, an important point for movement of the arm; and the wrist or cuff.

CUTTING SLEEVES AND ARMHOLES

Here, for ready reference is a list of "Do's" and "Don't's" in cutting sleeves.

DO note pattern marks for the straight of the goods.

DON'T lay the sleeve pattern on the fabric carelessly. If the sleeve shifts even a little off grain, it will always twist in wear.

DO prefit the pattern for the sleeve before you alter the pattern length. Prefitting saves hours of work, and often it permits changes that can never be made in finished garments.

DON'T rush your cutting and expect to make changes later in fitting.

DO outline the sleeve pattern carefully no matter how strange it looks. Each type of sleeve has an individual shaping.

DON'T cut off the top of the sleeve. Never straighten an edge because it looks crooked. Never nip off a corner.

DO outline the armhole of the pattern clearly and carefully.

DON'T skimp in cutting an armhole edge. Never let the pattern shift as you cut.

DO fit the sleeve at the shoulder; first, so the sleeve hangs straight when the arm is down; second, so the armhole seam curves around the tip edge of shoulder.

DON'T fit the sleeve up high on the shoulder to eliminate the soft fold of waist at front and back or your sleeve will tear out.

DO check the sleeve darts at the elbow to control arm activity and allow elbow room where it is needed.

DON'T shorten a sleeve above or below the elbow and forget about moving the elbow darts to the bend of the arm.

DO fit the wrist snugly when the arm is bent. Pin the cuff line and move the arm before deciding on the length of the sleeve.

DON'T fit the sleeve tightly while the arm is hanging straight.

DO make the sleeves fit the curved shape of the armhole. Pin it carefully, then baste it. Fit the sleeves before stitching.

DON'T stitch the sleeves without a fitting.

DO allow enough length in both the underarm length of the sleeve and the underarm length of the dress to permit raising your arms comfortably to your head.

DON'T fit the underarm of a belted dress so tightly you cannot raise your arm without tearing the sleeve at the underarm.

DO change the sleeve when altering a shoulder line to make the armhole larger or smaller, in order to compensate for the changes.

DO recut the armhole (laying the pattern on the armhole and reshaping it) so the sleeve will fit the armhole.

DON'T take up a shoulder seam even a little and think it will not change the sleeve fitting.

DON'T slash the garment under the arm.

TYPES OF SLEEVES

Most garments are made with a set-in sleeve, which means that the seam at the armhole is curved to the shoulder line and there is no extra fullness at the top. The sleeves can be long, three-quarter length, or short; the cuff is usually finished with a binding, a bias of self-fabric, a hem, or a band. The top of the sleeve is fitted with little darts or gathers, or, in the case of tailored worsted garments, with "shrunk out" fullness. Do not be surprised to find sleeves and yoke cut in one.

Puffed Sleeves: Puffed sleeves can be long or short, scanty or very full. They are cut with an extra allowance of fabric, which is gathered across the top in at least two rows of gathers to shape them to the curve of the shoulder. Use two rows of gathers to join the sleeve to the cuff, which can be made of wide or narrow banding *cut straight*. When you make your gathers, wind the end of the gathering thread around a pin so that you can increase the thread length as the sleeve is joined to the dress. The cuff has no opening; it can be decorated with bands of contrasting material or of lace.

Raglan Sleeves: They have a long shaping at the top instead of a curve. Your pattern will give the correct sleeve shape and armhole. Unlike other kinds of sleeve, raglan sleeves are often set into the garment before the underarm seams of the sleeve and blouse are joined. Stitch the seam and press it open. Clip it a little where it curves.

Tailored Sleeves: In some coat constructions and in all mannish tailored garments, the sleeves are cut in two pieces. This is the classic tailored sleeve. Instead of being shaped to the armhole with darts, the fullness is held in with little gathers. In worsteds or woolens, the fullness is shrunk out so that the sleeve fits into the shoulder smoothly without the use of darts or gathers. It is sometimes possible to shrink out the fullness in other fabrics.

How to Shrink Out Fullness: Gather the top of the sleeve on the seam line and gather it again ⅛ inch nearer the edge. Baste the sleeve to the armhole just as you would any sleeve and distribute the gathers evenly. Ease in the fullness for about 2 or 3 inches, with a little more toward the front than the back. Try the sleeve on and make sure it hangs

Above: Deep double ruffles flutter flirtatiously to form novelty sleeves.

Above: Deep four-button cuffs hold the long, full sleeves snugly to the wrist.

Right: The tiniest caps soften the shoulder line on a sleeveless summer dress.

130

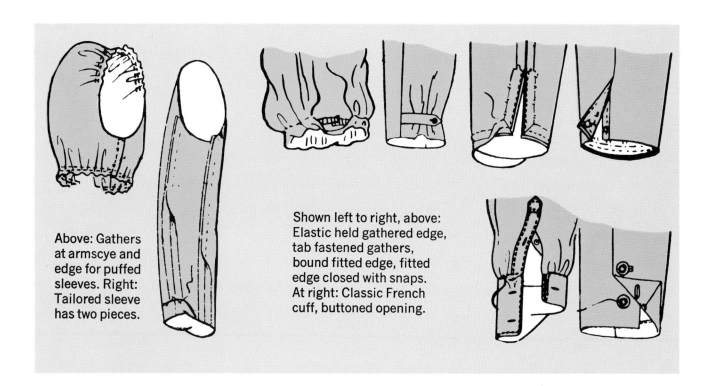

Above: Gathers at armscye and edge for puffed sleeves. Right: Tailored sleeve has two pieces.

Shown left to right, above: Elastic held gathered edge, tab fastened gathers, bound fitted edge, fitted edge closed with snaps. At right: Classic French cuff, buttoned opening.

straight. Stitch the sleeve. To shrink out the fullness, press the top of the sleeve with the gathers on the wrong side using a damp cloth. This will lightly steam the fullness. Turn the garment to the right side and hold your pressing mitt in the cap of the sleeve. Press it with a damp cloth until it looks as though the fullness has disappeared and you have a smoothly rounded shoulder.

Shirt Sleeves: Sleeve and shoulder are joined before either sleeve or underarm of the garment is seamed. When the shoulder seam and yoke are finished, lay your work flat and join the shoulder seam in a flat fell. Join the seams and stitch so that the seam comes on the right side of the garment. Cut away one side of the seam and turn in the opposite edge; stitch it down. Baste this seam on the right side of the garment as close to the edge as possible. Then you are ready to French-seam the sleeve and underarm.

Pressing Sleeve Seams: The seam is usually pressed towards the sleeve and not open.

CUFFS AND SLEEVE EDGES

When you come to finishing the sleeves, there are a number of questions you should take into consideration:

Is it a long sleeve fitted close at the wrist?
Is it a long or short sleeve ending in gathers?
Is it a long sleeve which requires a straight cuff?
Is it a long sleeve that requires a mannish cuff?
Is it a short sleeve with a straight edge?
Is it a short sleeve with a shaped edge?
Is it a wide long sleeve that must be faced?

Sleeve Fitted Close at the Wrist: This kind of sleeve can be stitched wide enough to let your hand slip in and out without an opening. Finish the edge with a binding or narrow hem.

If the sleeve edge is to have an opening, decide whether it will be closed with buttons and loops or with snap fasteners. Finish the edge of the opening and the hem of the sleeve with a seam binding. If it is too narrow, apply an extension facing. When snap fasteners are used, the edges of the opening must lap; with buttons and loops, they must meet.

Gathered Sleeve: Gathered sleeves are usually finished with a narrow band of straight material. The easiest way to apply it is to seam one edge of the band to the gathered sleeve edge, turn, and hem to wrong side. Or simply turn up the lower edge to form a casing and insert elastic to hold sleeve snug.

Straight Cuff: Both straight and gathered sleeves can be finished with straight cuffs. Cut the cuff twice the width desired. If it is to be fastened with a button, finish the ends and turn it. Finish the seam opening of the sleeve like a placket and bind the edge of the sleeve with the cuff. Finally, make the buttonhole and attach the button.

French Cuff: Used in shirts, blouses, and shirtwaist dresses. This cuff looks like a double straight cuff when completed. Cut a fold of straight material twice the desired width (at least 4 inches) and 3 inches wider than your wrist measure. Then proceed as described for straight cuff. Fold back and make marks for 4 small buttonholes through which to slip cuff links.

Fasteners: Frivolous Or Functional

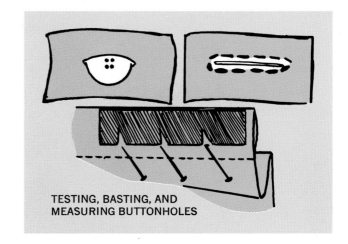

TESTING, BASTING, AND MEASURING BUTTONHOLES

*T**he** closing of a garment may be concealed or emphasized for decoration, depending upon the type of garment and individual taste. In choosing the fasteners it is just as important to understand the uses of the different kinds of fastener as it is to know how to put them on.*

TYPES OF GARMENT CLOSING

Concealed: In concealed garment closings the main purpose is to keep the closing flat and smooth. Suitable fasteners are snap fasteners, hooks and eyes, zippers, or flat buttons. Fly closings require buttonholes which must be cut and finished with buttonhole stitch, never bound.

Tailored: Closings such as these are used in shirts and feature tailored buttons or zippers or hooks and eyes. Buttonholes are cut and finished with buttonhole stitch or bound. In cuffs, link buttons can be made to take the place of cuff links, and they are sometimes used as a novelty closing on sport dresses. Be sure buttons used on wash fabrics are washable.

Soft Dress: Dresses often feature closings with edges that meet instead of overlapping. Close them with a zipper or a small self-fabric button held with a loop, a small pearl, a decorative button, or with hooks and eyes. In many cases hooks catch into flat buttonholed loops instead of metal eyes. This is useful in closings at the back of the neck, at sleeve edges, etc. In garments made of lace, embroidered eyelets are used with hooks, and embroidered loops with buttons.

Decorative: Closings which are emphasized for decoration feature decorative buttons or closures of the same or contrasting color. Bound buttonholes or buttonholes worked with buttonhole stitch may be used as preferred. In all cases these decorative notes should be in keeping with the style of trimming of the garment as a whole. In coats and other tailored garments the buttons are large, decorative, tailored, or novelty. Bound buttonholes or cord loops are used to fasten them.

SEWING ON FASTENERS

An even line and accurate measuring saves much disappointment. Run a straight basting to mark the line where the center of the fastener will be, then mark off with pins where each one will be sewed.

Snap Fasteners: These fasteners are made in matched pairs, and must be put on so they match. Separate them one at a time as you sew them. Place the fastener at the pin, marking correct position, and center it on the basting line. Sew through the four thread holes with over-and-over stitches, and secure the end of the thread before you break it off. Close the joining and place a pin directly opposite, where you will sew on the other half of the fastener. As you go on to sew a second fastener, watch the spacing. If the closing is puckered when you finish, you have been careless in measuring, and the fasteners will have to be removed and sewn on again.

Fashion with a flair! Here, a dramatic
—and beautiful—example of the importance
of choosing a fastener to fit the style.

Hooks and Eyes: Fasten the top of the hook with a loop of thread to the edge of the garment to hold it firmly in place. Then pass the thread to one eyelet and overhand it securely; overhand the second eyelet and then come back to the edge. Be sure the hook is firmly anchored before you fasten and break the thread. Sew the eye on the opposite edge so that when the hook is caught in it, the edges of the garment meet and no fastening shows. When larger eyes are used, they must be sewn on each side of the loop as well as through each eyelet. When the hook and eye are placed back from the edge, the smaller eye is better and should be sewn on first. Then it will be easy to put the hook into the eye and mark the place where the hook should be.

Inner belts at the waistline, and light-weight separate belts which you can make, must be held very securely with hooks and eyes. These beltings are often stiff, and the edge is turned before the hooks and eyes are sewed on. Use heavy cotton or linen thread and pass the needle back and forth in the fabric. (Do not try to take a stitch over the eyelet of the hook.) Be sure the hook is secure at the edge as well as at the eyelets. This kind of fastening needs the larger eye for security; just enough of the eye protrudes over the edge so that the hook can catch in it. Both sides of the eye must be fastened at the edge as well as through the eyelet. On wide belting the top hook can be reversed, so the eye is on the other side.

Flat Buttons: Use a heavy, extra-strong thread, and never sew a button flat to a garment or the stitching will not last. Raise it on a "stem" by placing a pin across the top of the button and catching the pin in your stitches as you bring the thread through from the underside and pass it back from the top. Repeat this operation several times, then make the cross threads. When the button is held securely, pull away the pin and wind your thread around the threads under the button. This stem makes the button easier to manipulate in the buttonhole.

Shank-Stem Buttons: In these buttons the shank takes the place of the stem, and they are sewn flat to the fabric. Round decorative buttons often omit the shank, and it is impossible to use a pin. Allow a leeway in the thread that can be twisted for a stem.

Covered Buttons: Cut a circle of fabric almost twice as wide as the button and gather it near the edge. Place a little cotton over a button mold and secure the fabric in place by drawing the gathering thread. *Be sure it fits tightly.* Secure the end of the thread with many strong stitches. In sewing a covered button to the garment, leave the thread loose and form a stem unless the fabric raises the button enough without it.

Linked Buttons: Cut a cardboard to measure the size of the loop between buttons. Pass buttonhole thread from one button to the other, spacing them the desired distance. Then cover these threads with buttonhole stitch.

Buttons Held with Fabric: In these buttons there must be a large hole. They can be attached for closing or made into linked buttons. Stitch the fabric and turn it; pass it through the button and join it at the back, allowing a little leeway for a stem. Sew this joined stem to the garment. For linked buttons, pass the fabric through two buttons and separate them the desired distance. Turn one end of the fabric and place it over the other end, fastening it neatly and securely. One of the linked buttons should be fastened to the garment on one side so that they won't be lost.

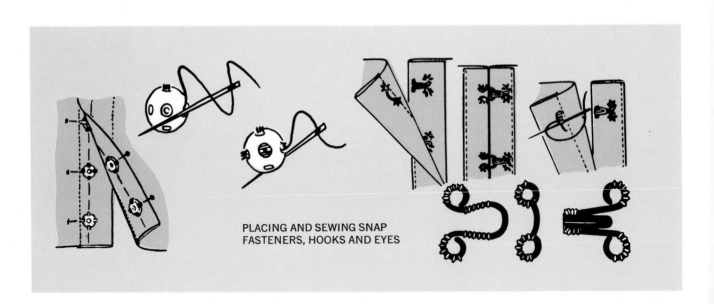

PLACING AND SEWING SNAP
FASTENERS, HOOKS AND EYES

Tailored Buttons: For garments that receive very hard wear, such as overcoats, mackinaws, overalls, or work clothes made of heavy fabrics, tailored buttons are used. To fortify this button, sew a smaller button on the underside of the fabric so the thread passes through both buttons with the fabric between them. Place a pin on top of the big button to make the stem. Twist the thread securely around the stem and fasten it before cutting it off.

Tiny Buttons: These can be placed directly at the edge or back from it. Round ones should be held with buttonhole loops; for flat ones a slash finished with buttonhole stitch is preferable.

BUTTONHOLES

Lay the buttons on the outside of the garment and space them to give the effect you want. The top button should be close enough to the top edge of the collar to make a finished line; but be sure it does not extend beyond the edge. When you have decided the spacing of the buttons, put a pin under each one and verify the measure so that they are evenly spaced. Then cut a gauge wide enough to extend from the edge of the garment to the line where you want to put the button; make a notch where each button comes. Run a basting thread on the underside of the closing where the buttons will be to indicate the center line. Put a pin on the center line to indicate the position of each button. Now you are ready to mark your buttonholes.

Lay the garment flat and place the gauge over it with the edge of the gauge at the edge of the garment. Place a pin in each notch to indicate the center of the buttonhole. On a scrap of material, test for the size of the buttonhole by cutting a slash and trying it over the button. Remember that heavy buttons need a larger buttonhole than thin ones. Cut a gauge with the finished length of the buttonhole and mark the center. Place the center of the gauge over the pins in the garment and baste a line indicating each buttonhole. When the lines have been basted, try on the garment and examine them critically to make sure they are straight and evenly spaced.

Now you are ready to make a buttonhole. It can be finished with buttonhole stitch or bound. In either case, run a basting around each buttonhole to keep the fabric from slipping as you work.

Worked Buttonholes: After your eye is trained you can make the stitches close together and keep them even; but in the beginning it is better to run a basting along each side of the hole to guide you in keeping your stitches the same length. Use a tightly twisted buttonhole thread and work from left to right on the right side of the garment. Cut the buttonhole on the cutting line, beginning at the center and cutting toward each end marking. (If the fabric frays easily, overcast the buttonhole.) Finish with buttonhole stitch as follows: Bring the thread up in one corner and take a stitch through the buttonhole and out at your marked line. The thread must pass under the point of the needle. When you pull your thread up, it will form a little knot at the edge.

Make another stitch close to the last one, and so continue across the buttonhole. Some buttonholes are square at both ends, others round; and still others are square at one end and round at the other.

Tailored Buttonholes: Mark the position before cutting and then punch a hole at one end with a stiletto or the point of a sharp scissors. Overcast this hole fanwise. When you are working through several heavy fabrics, take the precaution of basting the several layers together at the edge before working the buttonhole stitch. In vertical buttonholes it is important to run a stay on each side of the buttonhole before working it.

Eyelets: When a fine cord or tubing is used to lace a closing, punch the hole with point of scissors, overcast, then buttonhole stitch around.

Bound Buttonholes: Do not cut a bound buttonhole until after the binding is in place. (If the hole is cut first by mistake, only an expert can bind it. If you are not an expert, it is better not to use bound buttonholes, but work them in buttonhole stitch instead.)

Separate bindings can be cut, or a binding of one piece can be placed over a row of buttonholes. The binding piece must match the grain of the fabric; it can be either straight fabric or a true bias. Mark the cutting line and the exact size of the buttonhole on both garment and binding. Put the binding on the right side of the garment over the cutting line. Baste it in place, then outline the buttonhole with a little box of running stitches, either by hand or on the machine. Be sure the corners are turned sharply and the lines are even. Beginners should use a gauge to insure accurate lines. Cut the buttonholes, beginning at the center and cutting toward each end. Within ¼ inch of each end,

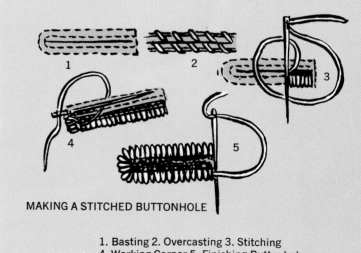

MAKING A STITCHED BUTTONHOLE

1. Basting 2. Overcasting 3. Stitching
4. Working Corner 5. Finishing Buttonhole

stop and slash into each corner. *Be sure this slash extends to the stitching.* If you cut through the stitches, reinforce them with a few overhand stitches; a beginner would be wise to try to making a perfect buttonhole on a discarded scrap of fabric before trying to make it on a garment.

Turn the binding to the wrong side of the garment, through the buttonhole opening, and pull it into shape. Watch the right side while you do this and pull the fabric on the reverse side until you see two even lines on each side of the cut line on the right side. On the wrong side all seams must turn away from the slit. Now bring your needle through from the wrong side at the end of the buttonhole and secure the ends of the binding. Outline the buttonhole on the right side with tiny stitches, taking them in the seam allowance so they do not show. Turn to the wrong side and overcast the edge of the binding.

Bound Buttonholes In a Faced Coat: When a bound buttonhole is made in a coat, it is worked through the outer garment and the interlining. When the facing is applied, a slit is cut opposite each buttonhole; the edges of the slit are turned back and slip-stitched to the stitching on the buttonhole. This makes the buttonhole look finished both front and back. In unlined garments worn closed, the buttonhole can be left unfinished unless you are an expert at details. Only very skillful work can turn this edge and catch it in place without pulling the buttonhole out of shape or showing telltale amateur marks on the front of the garment.

LOOP AND RING FASTENINGS

Button closings are often loops instead of buttonholes. These loops can be threads covered with (1) buttonhole stitch, (2) self-fabric tubing, (3) soft cord covered with self-fabric, or (4) fancy cord bought by the yard. They can be made singly or in a continuous cord.

Lacing on a garment can be inserted through (1) buttonholed slashes, (2) worked eyelets, or (3) metal rings covered with buttonhole stitch.

Buttonholed Loops: Finish the edge of the garment and sew the buttons in place. Mark the spacing for the loops on the opposite edge. Then, with a buttonhole thread that matches the color of the garment, make a loop of four or six strands and cover it with buttonhole stitch.

Self-Fabric Loops: Make a tubing. The size of the tubing depends upon the weight of the fabric, the width of your seam, and whether it is a bias or straight cut. In cloth, tubing is usually cut on the straight. When a very fine tubing is wanted, cut a true bias and stitch it with a very loose machine stitching.

Fold the tubing lengthwise and stitch it. Clip off the seam at one end so the tubing will not be too thick. Then attach it to a cord or bodkin to turn the tubing right side out.

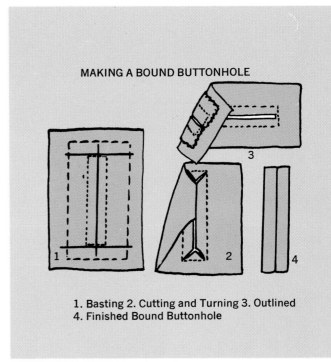

MAKING A BOUND BUTTONHOLE

1. Basting 2. Cutting and Turning 3. Outlined
4. Finished Bound Buttonhole

Corded Tubing Loops: Cut a strip of true bias the length desired and stitch the edges to form a long tube. As you turn this tubing, baste cord and a thin bodkin to the end of the casing. Push the bodkin through the casing, pulling it over the cord.

Decorative Cord Loops: Decorative loop cord comes in several sizes and is purchased by the yard. It can be applied to an edge in a continuous loop fastening, or it can be cut and attached in single loops. Wind a piece of thread around each end of the cord as you cut it to prevent it from raveling and to give a firm foundation for the stitches.

Applying Joined Loops: Fasten one end of the tubing or cord at the edge of the garment. Use a gauge to measure both the spacing on the edge of the garment and the length of each loop. Where the loop is joined to the edge of the garment, overcast securely. When a garment is faced, the loops are applied to the garment and the edge of the facing is turned and applied over the loops. Stitch the edge of the

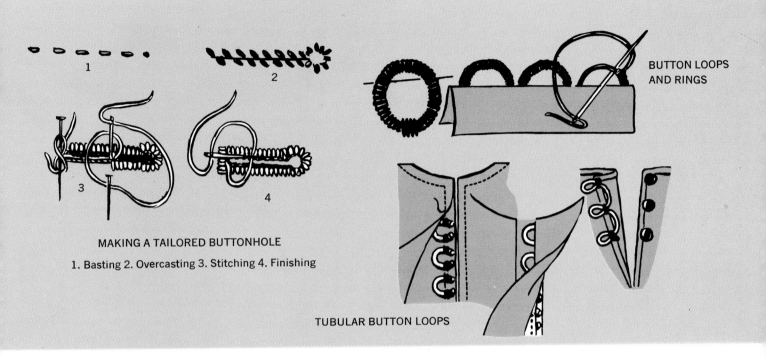

MAKING A TAILORED BUTTONHOLE

1. Basting 2. Overcasting 3. Stitching 4. Finishing

BUTTON LOOPS AND RINGS

TUBULAR BUTTON LOOPS

garment through all the edges so that the stitching holds the loops securely.

Single Loops: Cut the tubing or cord in the lengths desired. Either join the tubing or cord in a circle or apply it in a U-shape. Mark the edge of the garment carefully and pin the loops in place. Stitch on the machine, holding the loops and the edges together.

DECORATIVE CORD FASTENINGS

These fastenings can be made at home very easily. Women to whom a belted garment is not becoming should learn to make interesting closings in striking designs to give variety to the beltline of a coat or dress.

Frogs: Draw the design for your frog closing on a piece of paper and follow this outline with cord you buy by the yard—or, if you prefer, make it of garment fabric tubing as described previously. As you form your design in the cord, join it securely at each crossing, stitching on both sides.

Finish the end at some place in the design where you can sew very securely. Frogs may be single or double. In double frogs, the loop that holds the button goes on only one side.

Cord Motifs: Small or large circles of cord laid close together are easy to make if you cut the size of the circle in crinoline or unbleached muslin. Poke a hole in the center of the fabric circle and push one end of the cord through the hole, fastening it securely on the wrong side. Turn the cord and sew it to the fabric with a slip stitch. The last coil extends beyond the lining. These motifs can be used on each side of a neck closing with a hook and eye beneath them. You can use a row of circles down the center of a garment, or you can put them side by side to decorate a closing. When the circles are made of bias cords of self-fabric, one end can be left free for a tie.

Metal or Bone Rings: Rings—or even a piece of wire twisted into a ring—can be closely covered with blanket stitch, using a coarse embroidery thread. The covered rings can be used on the edge of a garment to hold lacing.

Fasteners: Frivolous
Or Functional

The Technique of Installing Zippers

1. Shown above are a conventional zipper insertion (left) with two lines of stitching and invisible zipper (right) with no lines of stitching visible.

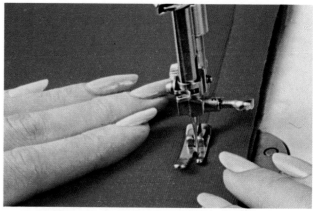

4. Leaving a seam allowance as specified in your pattern, machine baste the opening closed; sew remainder of seam with regular stitch for your fabric.

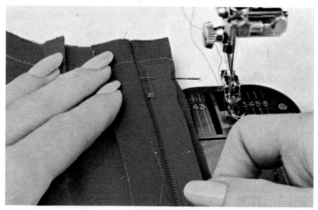

7. Replace presser foot with zipper foot; open zipper. With wrong side up, placket top away from you, keep rest of garment to the left.

Zippers are available in different sizes and lengths and are made with synthetic coils as well as with metal teeth. Before you buy a zipper for a garment, check your pattern envelope for the length needed. Also take your fabric into consideration—synthetic coil zippers are very light and flexible and are especially good for use with sheers and knits.

The color of the zipper you choose should *blend* with the fabric if it cannot be matched. If the zipper is applied correctly, it will be completely covered and, therefore, the exact matching of zipper and fabric is not of prime importance. Remember also, it is essential to have the thread you use match the fabric as closely as possible since it is the thread rather than the zipper tape that will be seen in the finished placket.

APPLYING ZIPPERS

Zipper Set into Slash: A zipper set into a slash or seam can be covered so that the edges of the fabric meet above the zipper; or the metal teeth may show if the fabric edge is turned back enough to show the metal but not the tape. Zippers should be applied with machine stitching whenever possible.

Cut the slash the length of the zipper (the metal, not the tape) with a pointed or squared end. For an open-faced application, in which the metal teeth show, place your garment over the zipper and turn back the edges of the slash so the metal shows but not the tape. Baste them in place and stitch close to the edge on the right side of the garment, outlining the zipper. If the teeth are to be covered, (1) cut two strips of self-fabric the length of the zipper, (2) fold

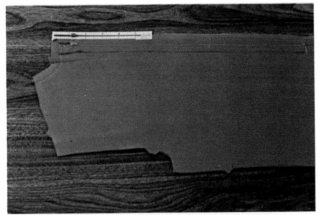

2. First will be demonstrated a centered or slot application of a conventional zipper placed before shoulder and side seams have been stitched.

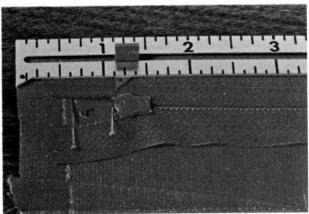

3. The placket opening should equal the length of the zipper measured from the top stop to the bottom stop, plus 1⅛″.

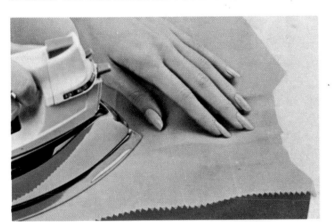

5. Be sure to press seam open—as in other areas of sewing, pressing as you go will result in the saving of time and effort in the long run.

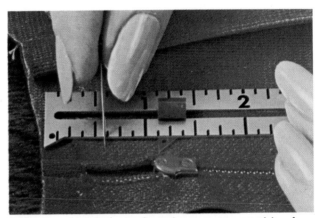

6. Center closed zipper face down on wrong side of garment, with top stop 1⅛″ from cut of neckline. Pin right tape to right seam allowance.

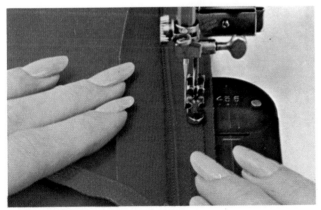

8. Machine baste right hand side of tape to seam allowance. Stitch from top to bottom, following the woven guideline on the tape.

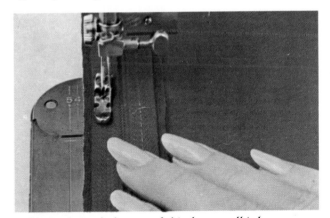

9. Close zipper being careful to keep pull tab up; place left hand side of zipper over left seam allowance, keeping rest of garment to the right.

each lengthwise, (3) press the edge, (4) baste the folds together so the edges touch and place this fold over the zipper on the right side. Now place the slashed garment over the zipper and fold, and turn under the edges of the garment. This will outline a piped effect on the folds under the edge. Baste carefully and stitch close to the edge, with as fine a stitch as possible. Professionals use a cording foot in the machine.

Zipper Set into Seam: Baste the opening and press the edges open. Place the zipper over the seam on the wrong side of the garment and baste it in place. Work flat on an ironing board or table. Turn the tape ends at the top of the zipper under so they catch in the stitching. Stitch the zipper, with stitching as close as possible to the metal teeth and outlining the zipper. Be sure to turn a sharp corner. Remove the basting at the seam.

10. Stitch left hand side of tape to seam allowance, with zipper foot at the left of needle. Zipper is now positioned exactly in center of tape.

11. Spread garment flat, right side up. Starting at top, hand baste through garment, seam allowance and fabric, ¼" from center seam on both sides for guide.

12. Change to proper stitch length. Stitch from top along left of stitching to bottom, pivot, stitch to center seam; work on right hand side in same manner.

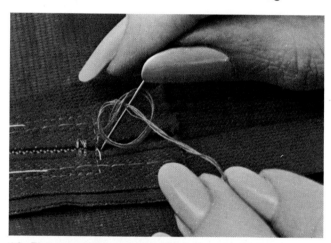

13. Pull threads to wrong side at center seam at bottom of placket; tie them together in a single knot close to fabric, using sewing needle as shown.

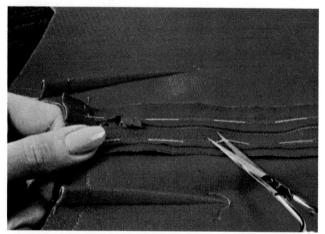

14. Remove hand basting and center seam machine basting. Using a press cloth, press seam open first on wrong side, then on right side.

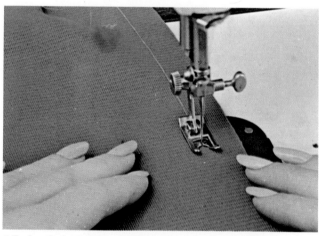

15. Apply invisible zippers only to open seams; stitch only from top to botton. Start by machine basting seam allowances on pieces as guidelines.

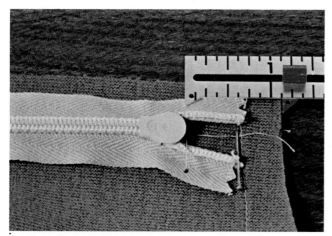

16. On right hand side of garment, right side up, place closed zipper face down 1⅛" from neckline edge; pin left tape to garment just above top stop.

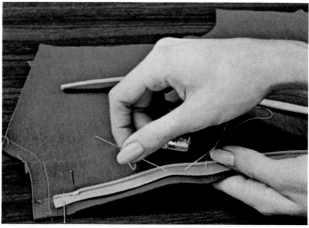

17. Hold pinned end firmly and carefully open zipper all the way; pin tape so coil lies evenly along basted guide; hand baste in place.

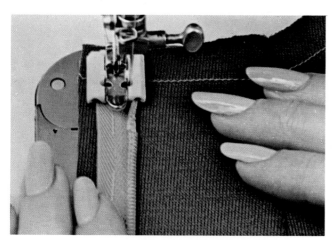

18. Using regular stitch and invisible zipper foot, guide coil into the right hand groove as shown and stitch from top of zipper to bottom.

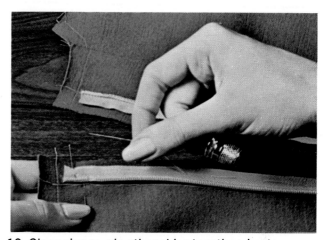

19. Close zipper, pin other sides together, baste, and complete in manner similar to that for right side (coil will be in left hand groove).

20. After finishing stitching and pressing, using zipper foot, fold seam allowance away from garment and stitch to tape along edge on right and left sides.

Zipper in Jacket Closings: Finish the neck and lower edge of the garment. Fit the closing edges carefully, pinning them together on the figure so the garment hangs smooth. Separate the seam, marking it with pins. Take off the garment, baste the front edge together with the seam on the wrong side, and press this basted seam open. This gives an exact, well-fitted edge, and the zipper can now be applied. It must be shorter than the garment. Baste one edge of the zipper tape to one edge of the garment; then baste the opposite edge to the other side. Sew in place as a zipper set into a seam. (A stay may be placed behind the zipper to keep it from catching on clothing.)

Finish With A Flourish:

Dressmaker Details

*T**he** last touches, when the garment is almost ready to wear, can make all the difference in its smooth finish, smart appearance, and usefulness. A little extra time and effort at this point will result in a garment that has a couture look.*

POCKETS

Pockets are easy to make once a few simple rules have been mastered. They are useful, decorative, and give a professional touch.

Types of Pocket: There are four different kinds of pocket: patch pockets, bound pockets, welt pockets, and pockets with a flap. Each of these fundamental types can be cut in many different styles.

Patch Pocket: The secret of success with patch pockets is to have them absolutely true and even, and the best way to do this is to cut the pocket shape in cardboard, omitting seam allowances. Place this cardboard pattern over each of your pocket pieces and press the seam allowances over the edge of the cardboard. This will insure that all pockets are the same size and every edge is true.

Next finish the top edge. In light-weight fabrics, turn the edge and hem it; in heavier fabrics, cover the raw edge with flat seam binding after you have turned the edge, then hem it. Pin the pocket on the garment and check accuracy of placing.

Decide whether the pocket is to be stitched close to the edge or back from it. Pockets stitched close to the edge are finished at the top with one or more rows of machine stitching. When a pocket is stitched back from the edge, the same seam line is followed across the top to complete a decorative detail.

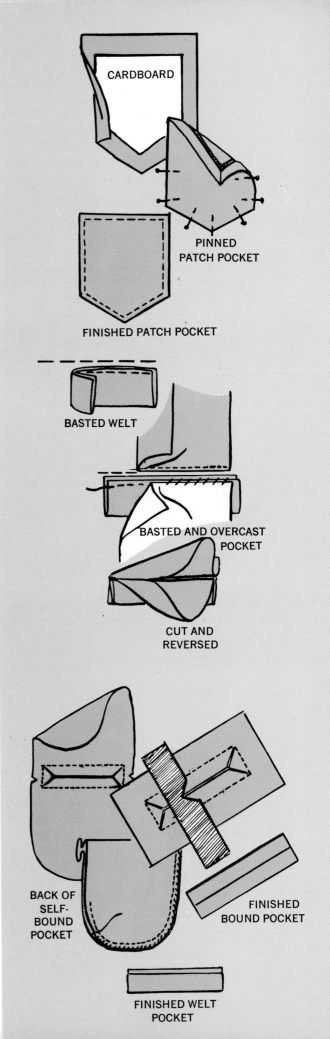

CARDBOARD

PINNED
PATCH POCKET

FINISHED PATCH POCKET

BASTED WELT

BASTED AND OVERCAST
POCKET

CUT AND
REVERSED

BACK OF
SELF-
BOUND
POCKET

FINISHED
BOUND POCKET

FINISHED WELT
POCKET

Left: A sublimely simple tunic tops beautifully fitted pants. Patch pockets made with a cardboard pattern are a perfect finishing touch.

Above: Flapped patch pockets add a fun touch to sportswear. Again, a little extra care in making them results in the extra-special look.

Bound Pocket: There are two ways to make bound pockets: (1) In heavier fabrics self-fabric is used for the binding, and the pocket is made of lining fabric. (2) In light-weight fabrics the pocket is used for the binding, which makes for a great saving in time.

Pockets Bound in Self-Fabric: Mark the pocket opening on both garment and binding. The binding is cut 1 inch longer than the finished pocket and 3 inches wide. The grain of the material should match the garment at the cutting line. If the cutting line of the pocket parallels the cross grain of the material, make the binding on the straight of the goods; if the pocket slants across the grain of the goods, it must be bound with a true bias.

Finishing a Bound Pocket: Place the binding on the right side of the garment with the cut lines matching. Pin it in place and baste it carefully.

Stitch a little box around the cutting line by machine or by hand—the size of the box depends upon the length of the cutting line and the effect desired. For a piped effect, stitch ¼ inch away from the cutting line on both sides. In a heavy fabric, stitch ½ inch from the cutting line. Turn the corners sharply at each end and make the same number of machine stitches down each side. When working by hand, use a gauge and turn the corners carefully, making them firm with extra stitches.

Cut the slash from the center toward each end, and cut into the corners as for bound buttonholes, cutting almost to the stitches at the corners.

Draw the binding piece through the slash to the wrong side of the garment and pull it into straight even lines, watching the effect on the right side as you pull. Keep pulling until the binding looks like two perfectly even rows with squared ends. Fasten the material at each end. This stitch holds the edges of the binding together and is caught firmly in the edge of the pocket slit at this point. When both ends have been stitched, outline the opening by making running stitches in the seam edge, catching the back of the binding with these stitches. This makes the seam lay flat away from the edge.

Join the pocket on the wrong side of the garment. First join a pocket piece to each side of the binding, then smooth the two pieces together and baste them. If the edges are not even, it does not matter—you can shape them alike. Stitch, and overcast the seam.

Welt Pocket: The welt pocket is very easy to make. To prepare the welt, cut a piece of the garment fabric 2½ inches wide on the straight of the goods. Make it 1 inch longer than the length of the pocket. Fold this piece lengthwise and stitch both ends. Clip the corners before turning, to insure square edges. Press with an iron.

Place the welt below the cutting line of the pocket with the raw edges of the welt piece turned up toward the cutting line. The lower pocket piece is placed over the welt. Stitch across the pocket, paralleling the cutting line about ¼ inch back from it.

Cut the pocket, from the center toward the ends, cutting into each corner to the stitching. Turn the pocket pieces to the wrong side of the garment. The welt piece remains on the right side and is turned up to cover the pocket opening. Slip-stitch each end of the welt to the garment. Turn to the wrong side and join the pocket pieces in a seam. The pocket must lie flat. If the pieces are uneven, they should be reshaped.

Flap Pocket: Pockets with flaps are made like welt pockets. Cut the flap any size and shape desired. When it has been seamed and turned, it should be exactly the length of the finished cutting line of the pocket. Baste the flap to the right side of the garment *above* the cutting line and stitch. Cut and turn it like a welt pocket. When the pocket is turned, the flap falls over the cutting line. Sometimes, the ends are finished with tailor's arrows.

TRIMS BY-THE-YARD

The trimmings described here are simply to stimulate your thinking. Trimming details change continually, and you should study trimming types and check them in the fashion news. Watch out for the newest ideas in trimming when you plan your dress. Plan the trimming as an integral part of the garment, not as a last-minute addition.

Trimming Bands: Bands of contrasting fabric or color are often applied on top of the garment fabric and hemmed or stitched on both edges. Other bands are inserted either in a seam joining or on top of the fabric, which is then cut away under it. These decorative touches of color can be used at necklines, in sleeve trimmings, in cuffs, and to form stripes extending the length of the garment.

Slenderizing Trimmings: Contrast trimmings can help slenderize the figure if they add height by following the horizontal lines of the garment. Surplice lines and V necks can be emphasized with narrow or wide bands to add interest to the costume and height to the figure. Here are three specific examples:

1. The surplice waistline of a dress is edged with a narrow fold of white. If it ends at the waistline, it has not accomplished its purpose; but if it is extended to the hem of the dress, the trimming helps to make the figure look more slender.

2. The surplice line from shoulder to hem can be trimmed with two or three flat bands in blending colors. Three shades of light blue on a navy blue dress; or brown, tan, and yellow on a brown dress—these give a smart and slenderizing effect.

3. A slenderizing neckline which dresses up a costume can be developed in lace or in a contrasting color. The neck of the dress is cut in a deep V, filled in with a 1½-inch double fold of color or lace.

Rickrack: A sprightly finish, it is used in contrast on dresses, pinafores and play clothes.

Binding: Used to hold the edges of a dress or jacket firm and trim, when it is used purely functionally it is narrow and made of self fabric. But binding often combines a decorative quality with its functional purpose; then it is in contrast of color or fabric or both.

Fringe: Narrow wool fringe or self-fabric fringe adds a distinctive touch to casual wool dresses or suits. Lustrous silk or rayon fringe is used on more formal daytime and dinner clothes.

Beads, Braids and Bangles: These include the metallics, rhinestones, spangles, jets, and so on. The style dictates the design—it may be a banding, an allover effect, or a small motif.

Narrow soutache braid can be formed into elegant Oriental motifs. First trace the design on your fabric with chalk. Then apply the braid, stitching it through the center. The stitching can be done by hand or by machine. You can buy braided motifs in the stores and apply them to the garment by hemming them in place.

Before starting your work, consider the line of the garment which you will trim. Place the braiding so that it will emphasize the good lines of the design and your figure.

LACE EDGINGS AND INSERTS

Edging for Allover Lace: Allover lace, which is cut like a fabric, must be finished with a very narrow lace edge sold especially for this purpose and called a picot edging. Set the picot edging on the right side of the garment, covering the edge. Attach it with tiny running stitches. Turn to the wrong side and hand-roll the raw edge under the picot.

Allover lace can also be bound when you use a narrow insertion or ribbon beading. Crease the beading down the center and bind the edge of the lace, holding the binding in place with tiny running stitches.

When the edge of the lace is joined to chiffon, the seam can be picoted by machine. When the picoting is cut, the joining appears to be seamless.

When a ruffle of chiffon or lace is joined, make the joining as you would for any ruffle; turn the edge and hem it over the stitching, like a French seam. Never make a flat fell in transparent lace or fabric.

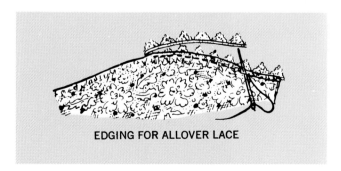

EDGING FOR ALLOVER LACE

Let fringe-by-the-yard be the final touch on a young girl's dress or tunic. Here it emphasizes the pockets and creates a yoke effect.

Another effective use of fringe! Remember it, too, when a skirt needs just a bit more length— fringe is the fashionable way to add it.

Lace Edging: Lace edgings can be wide or narrow; they can be joined to a fabric edge; they can be joined with a beading, (a narrow lace insertion sold by the yard); or they can be joined to a lace insertion. Applying lace should always be considered fine needlework and done by hand. The seams should not show when lace is applied. When the work is done by machine the garment is immediately stamped with the sign of cheap workmanship.

In many of the joinings described here, the lace edging may be applied either straight or gathered. To gather a lace edge, simply pull the thread at the straight edge of the lace until the desired fullness is reached.

To Overhand Lace to a Finished Fabric Hem: Hold the lace toward you and work on the wrong side, use a fine thread, and overcast loosely so that the lace will lie flat.

Lace Edge Joined with Beading: Turn the edge of the fabric at the side of the beading in a tiny rolled hem and whip the hem, catching the lace in each stitch as you hem the beading.

Lace Edge Joined with Raw Edge of Fabric: Baste the lace on the right side of the fabric close to the edge. Turn to the wrong side and roll the edge of the fabric, catching the lace with each stitch in the hem.

Lace Edge Joined with Lace Insertion: With a fine thread overcast the edges together. Do not take too tight a stitch, for a looser stitch more widely spaced will allow the lace to lie flat.

Lace Insertion: Baste the insertion, or the lace motif to be inserted, onto the right side of the fabric and work a satin stitch to cover the joining. If preferred, the lace can be joined to the fabric with a fine running stitch. Turn to the wrong side and cut away the fabric under the lace, leaving ¼ inch for a hand-rolled hem. Catch the lace in each stitch of the hem.

Corners in Lace: You can turn a flat mitered corner in a lace insertion or edging which has a prominent design. Center the design at the corner and cut away the excess material. With a fine thread overcast the lace edges together. The stitches must be so close together that they look like a fine cord.

Invisible Lace Joining: When a joining is necessary in cutting a garment of allover lace, study the pattern, and whenever possible cut your edge following the pattern of the lace and place it so the pattern looks logical in the lace design. Overcast this edge with fine stitches in a thread that matches. In working with very fine lace it will help to baste the work on paper.

MACHINE EMBROIDERY EDGES AND INSERTS

Machine-embroidered trimmings fall into two groups: white embroidery on batiste, organdy, or lawn; and self-colored embroidery on chiffon, crepe, or velvet. Passementeries and prepared trimmings are also part of this group.

Embroidered Insertions: These are often used in soft blouses, and summer dresses, and are often joined to a plain fabric of the same weave. This joining can be a fine French seam or a lace insert.

Embroidered Edging: Embroidered edging is used to finish the edge of an embroidered insert or allover embroidery. A narrow edging is generally used for this purpose.

Heavy narrow embroidered edgings are joined in a straight seam; sheer ones are gathered and joined to a straight fabric.

Wide embroidered edgings are usually gathered before joining to a straight fabric.

Tucked Joining: Turn the edge of the embroidery down, then turn it up. Baste this in place. Then turn in the edge of the fabric twice the size of the desired tuck. Place the stitching edge of the tuck over the edge of the embroidery and stitch as if it were a tuck. Place tucks above and below this joining to conceal it. The embroidered edge may be used as a facing. Turn in the raw edges of the fabric and the garment, and apply one over the other in a flat felled seam.

Passementeries and Prepared Trimmings: This type of trimming, sold by the yard or in motif effects, has finished edges. Some of this work is heavy and is hemmed to fabric to enrich the design; other varieties are fine and sheer and are set into fabric.

Set-in Motifs: Place the design over the fabric and hem the edges with a close stitch. Cut the material away under the motif and overcast the edge.

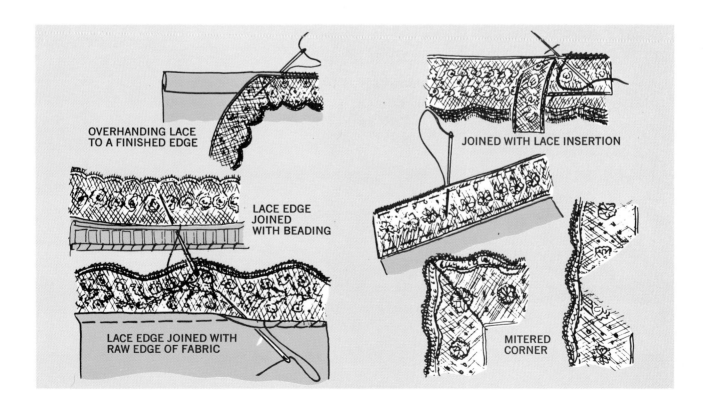

OVERHANDING LACE TO A FINISHED EDGE

LACE EDGE JOINED WITH BEADING

LACE EDGE JOINED WITH RAW EDGE OF FABRIC

JOINED WITH LACE INSERTION

MITERED CORNER

148

Fabulous frostings for fine fashions! Lavish trims for your most luxurious gowns. Use them lightly—underplay them—and you need no other jewels. On the opposite page, pretend jewels and crystal beads are used in pristine white trims; rhinestones, sequins, and metallics are combined in lush color; braids and passementeries are perfect for more subdued elegance. On this page, embroidered applique motifs to add a touch of special femininity. Just stitch them to a collar or pocket perhaps. All, from House of Kahaner.

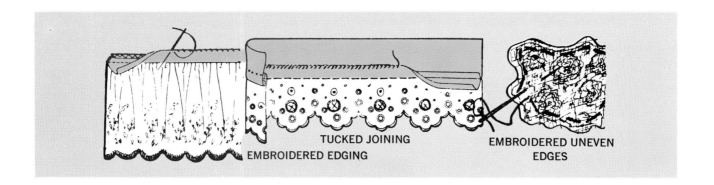

TUCKED JOINING
EMBROIDERED EDGING

EMBROIDERED UNEVEN EDGES

Embroidered Uneven Edges: These are a feature of most passementeries. It is best to apply them by hand, placing them over the fabric and hemming the edge with fine hand stitches.

Allover Embroidery: Allover embroidery is cut like any fabric with a print that must be watched. The edges must be finished with a narrow embroidered edging, applied in a rolled hem.

APPLIQUE

Often a small piece of applique is the trimming of a dress—a white pique flower on a dark dress; three self-color flowers in a group, or one after another to form a band; three or more circles in different colors arranged in a group—these are only a few of the ideas which can be carried out in applique.

Applique Monograms: The simplest type of applique monogram is the block letter. Stamp the initial or outline it on a piece of fabric. Cut it out and baste it on any smooth-textured material. Stitch over the edges of the initial with small zigzag stitches.

Another method is to stamp the initial on a square piece of fabric but do not cut it out. Baste this piece in place then stitch around initial with a straight stitch. Next, make zigzag stitches directly over the stitched outline. Work slowly to insure neat results. Finish by carefully trimming away excess fabric, cutting close to stitches.

Note: Other designs may be appliqued in either of the two ways described, depending on texture of material.

THAT EXPENSIVE LOOK

The trimming details made from self-fabric and the handwork used in trimming touches are the mark of quality that often makes the difference between the expensive and the inexpensive dress. The home sewer who will note these details and add them to a dress will be abundantly repaid for the additional time. These trimming touches give to dresses what is recognized as "that expensive look."

SCALLOPS are a pretty, feminine finish for yokes, necklines, closings, on soft little crepe dresses. Since they represent quite a bit of labor, they give a dress an expensive, custom-made look.

SADDLE-STITCHING is a very smart, and very simple finish for tailored clothes. It can be done in self-color or in definite contrast, white, for instance, on navy. It is used down the fronts of jackets and on lapels, cuffs and yokes of tailored suits, dresses, and coats. Saddle-stitching is done by hand.

TOP-STITCHING is the frank use of stitching on the outside of a dress, suit, or coat to emphasize lines that are important in the design. It is often combined, as in the sketch, with *lapped seams*. Top-stitching is done by machine.

PLEATED EDGINGS are best used on simple dresses. They make them charmingly feminine without being fussy. Either self-fabric or contrast can be used. White, on a dark or print dress, is a perennial favorite.

BOWS

Two-Piece Bows: Cut a piece of material 4 inches wide and 6 inches long—or any size desired for your bow. Cut another piece 3 inches by 3½ inches. Fold both pieces in half and stitch them. Turn these tubes and join the ends of the larger tube; this joining is the center back of the bow. Lay two or three pleats in the center and hold them with a thread. Attach the smaller tubing to the back of the bow and pass it around the center, joining the edge at the back. These little bows can be made of any fabric or ribbon. For extra decoration, make an insert of cotton rickrack braid or gold and silver braid in the center of the bow. The braid must be spaced inside the finished lines. Fold your bow and mark the place for the braid before you stitch it. Lay your fabric out and place the braid before you turn it.

Tied Bows: Bows you tie and apply can be cut from ribbon, lace, or fabric. Transparent fabric is usually cut single and finished with a hand-rolled hem. Dress-weight rayon crepes are cut double, stitched lengthwise, turned and finished at the end, and then tied. In heavier fabrics, bows are often finished with a binding or a narrow facing of ribbon. This adds to the decorative effect without adding to bulk.

In joining these bows sew them securely on the wrong side so they do not rip or slide out of place, and so they cannot pull off in wear. These over-and-over joining stitches should never show.

Bows for Tying: Bows of self-fabric tubing or ribbon can be joined to the garment edge so that the closing is tied together with little bows. To do this, first decide on the size of the bow by testing it with your tape measure for length and width, then cut your fabric twice this width and 1 inch longer. Stitch, shaping one end in a point. Turn to the right side—it can be pressed or it can be top-stitched on both edges—and sew the straight end to the garment edge 1 inch back. When a garment is faced, these stitches will not show. Join the opposite ends of the bow and tie them. When a garment has three or more bows, it saves time to join your fabric in a long tube and cut it into the bow sizes after tubing is turned to the right side.

A swirling flame-like applique pattern makes a simple floor-length skirt the star of the evening party! Keep today's appliques big, bold, and bright for the greatest effect.

Young-in-heart applique trim that really looks good enough to eat! Stitch it on by hand, by machine, or use one of the new ever-so-easy bonding products to apply it with an iron.

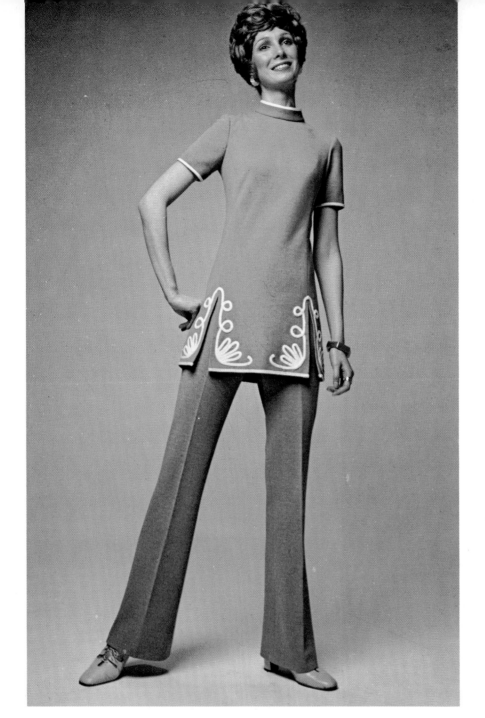

Beautifully executed soutache braid trim transforms a basic tunic-and-pants set into an extra special outfit for extra important events. Just transfer the design to the tunic and sew the braid in place.

SEPARATE BELTS

Soft Fabric Belt: To make a soft fabric belt, cut a straight piece of fabric the desired length and twice the width desired, plus seam allowance. Fold the fabric lengthwise and stitch the edges together with a close-running stitch. Turn the tube of fabric inside out. Most home sewers do not interline fabric belts, but interlining makes a smarter belt. The belt can be 1 inch wide; most are 2 inches. Belts over 3 inches wide are classed as wide belts and must be stiffened.

Stiffened Fabric Belt: To stiffen a fabric belt, either turn the fabric over the stiffening and cover it, or turn the edges of the fabric belt and overcast them to the stiff lining. You can buy belting by the yard and cover it, or cut buckram the size and shape of your pattern and cover that.

Stiffened belts can be finished with both edges straight or pointed or curved; or one end can be shaped and the other straight. They can be exactly the size of your waistline and close with a button, clasp button, or hooks and eyes; or they can be longer and pointed so that one end passes through a buckle or slide.

Part III

FOR YOUR FAMILY AND FRIENDS

Clothes For The Family

Delight *your family with clothes you have made especially for them. All the basic techniques you learned in sewing for yourself apply, whether you are making an infant's layette or a man's smoking jacket.*

INFANTS' CLOTHING

In selecting a pattern for an infant's clothing, the important things to consider are protection, comfort, room for activity, and room for rapid growth. Requirements for protection differ in different climates, and in this respect you should have your doctor's advice.

Approach the making of a layette with a practical and not a sentimental plan. The kind and number of garments is a matter of personal adjustment, but wise mothers plan for very few infants' clothes. Few of them make the gift-type of garments, and those who do usually regret it when their friends begin to send gifts.

When you select your patterns, keep these three things in mind: the garments must be comfortable; they must be easy to launder; they must be easy to slip on and off. Select garments that tie instead of button. Give preference to those that open and close in front, and to raglan sleeves. Resist tiny collars that crumple up, no matter how adorable they are; and resist garments that slip over the head. They are hard to adjust and hard to iron. A christening dress is enough of this type. You can make that as elaborate as your heart desires.

The fabrics must be soft. Fine nainsook, lawn, and batiste, and soft crepes are satisfactory. The soft flannels are made especially for babies. Finish the seams flat or in French seams and hand-roll or bind the edges. Ribbon binding is decorative and can be made into bows, thus serving a double purpose.

CLOTHES FOR THE TODDLER

The baby who is crawling or learning to walk needs special consideration. Plan garments which allow the greatest freedom for reaching, kicking, getting around on hands and knees, and trying out the first steps. They must be long enough, and the neck opening large enough so the garment can be easily slipped on and off. They should be buttoned at the crotch for easy changing. The garments should be made with a little fullness and no frills.

Bind the neck and make the garment in pretty colors which can be washed frequently. Soft, flexible fabrics with a smooth surface which does not pick up dirt should be used. They should be preshrunk and color-fast. All seams should be narrow, flat, and smooth. All neck edges and arm and leg openings must be smoothly finished and easy to iron. All stitching should be secure—the garment will receive hard wear. Buttons and buttonholes must stay fast and keep their shape. Remember, they will have to stand a great deal of buttoning and unbuttoning.

Little dress-up garments in white or colored batiste are made by hand, and the tiny frill on the collar can be lace or a hand-rolled ruffle of the garment fabric. But dresses are a sentimental addition to the toddler's wardrobe, and the time might better be spent on making a coat and an assortment of overalls in progressive sizes.

Opposite: Make pants for the whole family—new patterns and techniques make sewing them as much fun as wearing them! Choose easy-care fabrics.

Above and below: Sewing for your toddlers will result in low-cost clothing, for party or play.

Whether you sew for your children, your husband, or as a special favor for a dear friend, the personal touches express the love in your heart.

CLOTHES FOR THE TOT

Clothes for a child who has learned to walk must have action features—raglan sleeves that permit high reaching, seats with extra length that permit freedom in bending and spread for squatting, shoulder lines with gathers or tucks to add fullness. The garment should fit the child. Little girls' dresses with hems can be adjusted; little boys' suits with trousers buttoned to the waist permit of some adjustment, but they are outgrown more quickly than dresses because of the crotch length.

To encourage self-reliance in the child, fastenings and plackets should be in front within easy reach. Very large or very small buttons, snap fasteners, and hooks and eyes are taboo; they are too difficult for tiny fingers. Little children can easily learn to use a medium-sized round, flat button. It should have a slight groove to keep fingers from slipping off, and it can have a tape adjustment to give the child something to pull. The garment should have as few fastenings as possible.

Dresses should be slipped over the head and fastened at the neck with one button. Boys' suits can be buttoned together and slipped on and off like a one-piece garment with one or two fastenings. Drop seats controlled by a belt which buttons in front are easy for a child to manage.

Children are active and the textiles and workmanship of their clothing should above all be sturdy. Make the armholes extra size, and make sleeves that allow plenty of freedom.

CHILDREN'S COATS

The easiest patterns to adjust for length are those with straight lines. As the child grows and the hem has to be lengthened, there is no telltale beltline to spoil the effect of an otherwise good garment. Many mothers prefer a double-breasted coat for children. They also save a little fabric to make cuffs when the sleeves need lengthening.

Fabrics: Fabrics for children's coats must be durable and colorfast. A "bargain" which fades, shrinks, or wears poorly will not in the end be as economical as a first-quality woolen which lasts several years. Plain-colored fabrics and smooth-surfaced tweeds wear longer than rough tweeds and novelties. But children love bright colors and every child wants at least one plaid coat.

Don't overlook the possibilities of the soft woolens made especially for snow suits, some of which are treated with a water-repellent. These fabrics, however, do not wear well enough to be used for all-purpose coats. Raincoats, lined with wool or unlined, are easy to make; the heavy cotton in close weave, treated to repel water, is easy to manage when you use a straight, simple cutting construction.

Children's Reversible Coats: Select a boys' or girls' coat pattern in a straight-line model, either single- or double-breasted. It will be worn on both sides, and you will work with two fabrics, wool and cotton. Both fabrics should be treated with a water-repellent. Fit the pattern carefully and make the necessary adjustments. Do not use the facing in the pattern; you simply cut two full coats, one from each fabric.

Cut the cotton first and pin it together. Fit it to the child and make any alterations needed. Use this fitted garment for a pattern to cut the wool. Remember that if your wool is a plaid, you must match the pattern of the plaid.

Join the pieces and make two separate coats, one cotton, the other wool. Seam the underarm and shoulder and press the seams open. Turn up the lower edge and hold it with a catch stitch. Make the pockets and sew in the sleeves. Do not join the collar or finish the front edge.

The front edge of the woolen coat must be reinforced with an interfacing of unbleached muslin, adjusted exactly as the pattern directs. Turn the woolen coat wrong side out and have the child stand still while you adjust the cotton one. This must be done on the figure. First pin the shoulder seams and neck edges together, then the underarm seams down to the elbow. Pin the front edges together and test the closing line of the coat, marking it for buttons and buttonholes.

Lay the coat on the table and turn the front edges so they face. Slip-stitch these edges together. Run a machine

stitching at the top of the hemline, through both the woolen and the cotton. The edges will not be joined below the stitching. Stitch the edges of the sleeves together, turning them so they face each other. The edges should meet exactly and be slip-stitched together.

Join the collar as directed for tailored classic coats. (See Index.) Make the buttons and buttonholes so they are finished on both sides. If you are not expert at this, have the tailor do it.

Children's Raincoats: Select any straightline tailored coat and follow the directions in the pattern. The fabric should be a heavy cotton treated with water repellent. These garments have felled stitched seams, and the facings are stitched to the garment. These rows of stitching are part of the trimming and are repeated at the edge of the collar and pockets.

Children's Fitted Coats: Coats in princess lines or with definite waistlines require more tailoring than the straight-line casual coat. They are not difficult to make, however, and amply repay the time spent on them. They are usually made of luxurious fabrics of tweed or plain-colored woolens. Often tailored leggings are made from the same fabric to go with the coat.

Cut the garment from a pattern which has been carefully fitted, and make allowances for growth in your cutting. These coats have separate facings which are applied after the interfacing is adjusted. The pattern directions show you clearly how to make the coat. For lining and interling, see Index.

Extra Heavy Fabrics: For boys' mackinaws and boys' and girls' all-purpose coats, extra heavy fabrics are available. The extra weight of the fabric will not complicate your problems. These coats are cut in straight lines, and all you need do is remember that these fabrics have a pile and must be cut with the top of each piece pointing in the same direction, and that you must adjust the needle, thread, and stitch of your machine. You will need a heavier thread, a coarser needle, and a looser stitch.

These coats are not faced. Instead, the front edge is bound with a straight binding of thin woolen, easy to apply. It must be wide enough to hold the buttonholes comfortably. Make the collar to match the binding. These coats are often lined with the same kind of wool used for the binding. Some textiles are double-faced and need no lining. In that case, make flat stitched seams and bind the armholes.

FOR BOYS AND MEN

Boys' Shirts: Once you learn the simple tricks of constructing a tailored garment, you need not hesitate to make boys' shirts of heavy cotton. It saves time to make several at once, using the same pattern and varying the material. Use any style suited to your purposes and remember that all this work is machine work and not difficult. Most of the seams are stitched on the outside, and the double yokes and facings are simplified. The most important things are accurate turning of edges and corners (use an iron) and straight stitched lines.

Pin the patch pockets in place before you join the garment. Turn the edge of the yoke and pin it in place. Turn the edge of the facing and pin it in place. Put the facing on the sleeve and prepare it for stitching. Now stitch pockets, yoke, facing, and sleeve edge one after the other. Turn all edges for a second stitching except those joined to the garment. Once the shoulders are stitched you can pin the sleeve in place. Turn the facing and pin the collar at the same time. The underarms of sleeves and shirt are stitched in one seam. Do not close this seam until the collar is finished.

Boys' Shorts: Boys' shorts are easy to make if you pin the pieces together as you cut them. The usual difficulty is that the pieces look so much alike it is hard to assemble them if they get separated. Some shorts are finished with a casing and elastic band, others with a fabric belt. When seams are stitched and pressed, hem the edge.

Men's Shirts: Buy a pattern and follow every detail of the tailor's art. Apply the patch pockets correctly—that is, make it first and pin it in place with a tailor's precision. The stitching should be ⅜ inch from the edge all the way around, and the same stitching must continue around the edge of the flap. The flap is closed with a button and buttonhole.

Join the yoke lining to the back, then baste the outside of the yoke to the lining and stitch them all together, on both inside and outside. Join the front at the shoulder, stitching it first to the inside of the yoke, and basting the outside edge of the yoke over this seam. The sleeve is stitched before the underarm is placed. This seam is a flat fell. Stitch it the first time as you would a regular seam, then clip away half of the edge on the armhole side of the shirt. Turn the other seam edge over and stitch it flat to the garment. Now baste the underarms of shirt and sleeve. Before you make the collars and cuffs, consider whether you want to make an extra set now or to lay away enough material to replace them later. The lower edge of the shirt is hemmed. The collar is

Above and opposite: Boys garments often have double yokes, firm bands, patch pockets, and tailored details to provide longer wear.

interlined with unbleached muslin and the interlining is stitched to the collar. The seam is then clipped away close to the stitching and the collar is turned. Baste the inside edge of collar and lining to the neck and stitch the collar in place. Turn in the opposite edge and hem it over the seam. The collar centers at the center front of the garment, and the edges beyond the collar are turned in and slip-stitched.

The cuffs are finished in a classic line with a band. In casual sport shirts make a single cuff. In this type some men prefer a short sleeve finished with a narrow hem.

Make buttonholes by machine.

160

DRESSES, SKIRTS AND JUMPERS

Growing girls need gored or gathered fullness in their skirts, and they like the fitted effect of a basque waist. Edges can be bound or faced.

Pockets always please, and they are useful as well as decorative.

The skirt of a dress cut on the straight can be given variety by turning the hem to the right side of the dress and finishing the top with a contrasting binding. Make a collar to match the binding and repeat the color in the buttons.

Plaids are popular in the schoolgirl's wardrobe. Choose a small plaid and buy an extra ¼ yard of material to allow for matching the pattern. Except for precautions in cutting (see Index), plaid dresses are easy to make and always decorative.

Children's jumpers are often made of corduroy. When you use heavy material, be sure the lines of the pattern are straight and slender or cut circular. This kind of fabric cannot be pleated and should not be gathered. All facings are made of lining material in a matching color. Velveteen is cotton, but it must be steamed like velvet because of the pile, not pressed. When it is used for children, it is wise to select the lighter color tones, because the darker colors mark in wear.

When you sew for girls, encourage them to help you develop individual trimming touches. It will interest them in sewing.

FOR ALL THE FAMILY

All sleeping garments and underwear can be made in two types: plain sturdy garments or fragile, luxurious ones. The fabrics of both kinds should first of all wear well. The advantage of making underwear at home is that it can be made from the kind of material which gives longer wear than that in garments we buy. Be sure to ask for a textile label on the fabric you buy, because fabrics which look very much alike may have very different wearing qualities. Read what the label says about color fastness, preshrinking, tensile strength, fiber quality, and washing directions.

In the selection of both fabric and pattern, consider how the garment is to be washed. If you include underwear in the family washing done in your own machine or by a laundry, don't select a garment which needs hand care; choose a simple pattern construction. If it is to be ironed by hand, select the kind which irons easily, or needs no ironing at all.

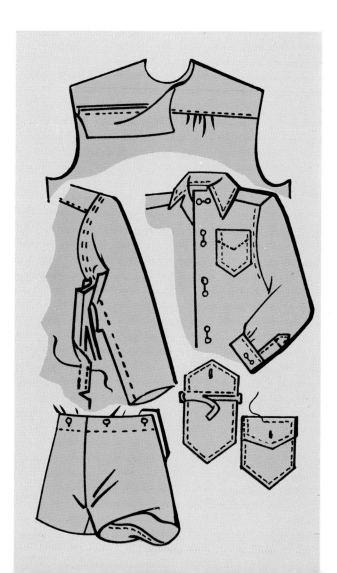

Top stitching secures double yokes, patch pockets, sleeve and shorts details on play clothes for boys.

161

Opposite: Surprise a fortunate friend with a colorful scarf to tie at the throat of her favorite outfit. Or even better, make several so that she can change the look from one wearing to the next.

Below: Make an eye-catching, boldly printed skirt for your best friend's birthday. Choose a pattern with the most fit-adaptability and the least seams and darts, then whip it all into shape in no time.

By the sea, by the sea, by the beautiful sea . . . sew up a nifty nautical playtime outfit for your daughter's summer vacation — it could inspire her to learn to do her own dressmaking!

Pajamas: Pajamas can be one-piece or two-piece, with full-length pants or shortie ones. The pattern companies offer a wide assortment of tailored pajamas for every member of the family. Select pattern and fabric to give you a garment which will be comfortable, serviceable, and attractive. Cotton, nylon, dacron, broadcloth shirtings, cotton mesh, and seersucker are all used for pajamas. (If you choose seersucker, be sure it is fast color and will not shrink.) Winter pajamas for cold climates are made of cotton flannel, flannelette, baby flannel, challis, or cotton novelties.

A two-piece garment with a slip-on top will save much work. One-piece pajamas and coat-front pajamas necessitate buttons and buttonholes. There are no construction problems in pajamas except those for tots, which must be made with a drop seat.

To save time in making sleeping garments for all the family, adopt the assembly-line technique of the factory. Adjust the pattern and assemble all the materials. Cut the garment, pinning it together as you cut it. As you pin, sort out all the "stitch first" pieces and put them in one pile. In your next sewing period do all this preliminary stitching at once, including front-edge bands and facings, pockets, and cuffs (when they are applied flat). Then prepare for the second stitching. Join the shoulder seams, apply the neck bands, and apply the sleeves to the armhole before you stitch the underarm and sleeve seams.

Nightgowns: Nightgowns made of cotton, cotton flannel, orlon, and nylon are cut from patterns especially designed. These garments are simple—speed depends upon planning and assembling the material so that everything is ready to work with. Check your pattern details and decide whether the neck and sleeves will be bound; whether any tape or bias binding is required; whether buttons will be required.

Washable garments need not be dreary. Much can be added by selecting a fabric with a tiny dot, stripe, or flower; by using rickrack braid or bias trimming in contrasting colors; by outlining contrasting yokes and hems (stitched bands). The cotton flannel nightgown can be edged with a little ruffle or heavy lace or hand crochet. The buttons can repeat the color of the trimming.

BATHROBES AND LOUNGING ROBES

Every member of the family needs tailored bathrobes, warm ones for winter, and cool, light ones for summer. For all of them, the keynote should be simplicity and

A monogram—stitched by hand or on your machine, personalizes a gift as well as adds an elegant finishing touch.

usefulness. Choose the patterns with care to give the necessary comfort. In winter a double-breasted bathrobe is an asset; for warmer weather the single-breasted coat type is preferable. Slip-on robes are another possibility and easier to make.

In winter, flannel or a blanket material assures warmth. Remember that a napped fabric gives warmth. Warm robes made from cotton blankets with a thick napped pile will wear through continual washings for four or five years. When warmth is not the prime consideration, tailored bathrobes can be made from corduroy, velveteen, the heavier rayon novelty ribbed fabrics, and the heavier cottons. Mixtures of cotton and rayon are developed in lovely fabrics especially for bathrobes.

Fabrics which will keep you cool in hot weather are found among the cool cottons—lightweight toweling; cotton crepes, printed or plain; seersuckers; and any opaque dress fabric. Cotton meshes which permit quick evaporation are very cool, and residents of the tropics report that fine linen is cool and does not stick.

Men's and Boys' Bathrobes: First adjust your pattern, shortening or lengthening the sleeve, testing the length and width across the back. The robe should fit loosely. Be sure that the robe is ample through the hips and crosses over to give just the protection the wearer likes. Some people like a large overlap, others a small one. Find out whether your men like a notched collar or a rolled collar in contrasting satin. Men have distinct preferences in sleeves—some like a set-in sleeve and others a raglan.

Baste the seams and insert the interfacing, except in cotton fabrics. In heavy woolens, this interfacing must be cut from canvas; in lightweight woolens, it is cut from unbleached muslin. Pin on the pockets and finish and join the collar. When a tailored lapel is used, the collar must be carefully interfaced to hold its shape. A rolled collar requires less tailoring, but it must be interlined with unbleached muslin. Join the sleeves to the armhole. Before stitching, fit the robe for proportions, and at this time turn the lower edge and mark the buttons and buttonholes.

If you are experienced in working with heavy fabrics, make the buttonholes yourself. Otherwise, take them to a tailor. Select the buttons and belt with care. The belt can be self-colored or contrasting, fabric or cord. Many men like a plain bone button in a harmonizing color. Be sure to include slides to hold the belt and a hanger at the back of the neck. These finishing touches should be carefully made and sewn

Women's and Girls' Robes: Use a pattern designed for women and make the robes as described above for men's robes. Make the robe decorative as well as useful. Many are bound with the blanket binding sold in stores. If you prefer, you can use a bias binding of any trimming fabric.

Blanket Bathrobes: In cutting a bathrobe from a bed blanket, lay the pattern so that all the edges touch the binding. When the bottom edge, the sleeves, and the collar are cut this way, the robe is partly finished before you join

A robe can be as simple or as detailed, as tailored or as frilly as the wearer desires —or the occasion permits. Fleeces make cozy cuddle-ups, brocades are for formal hostess attire, while chiffons and sheers are appropriate for more intimate hours.

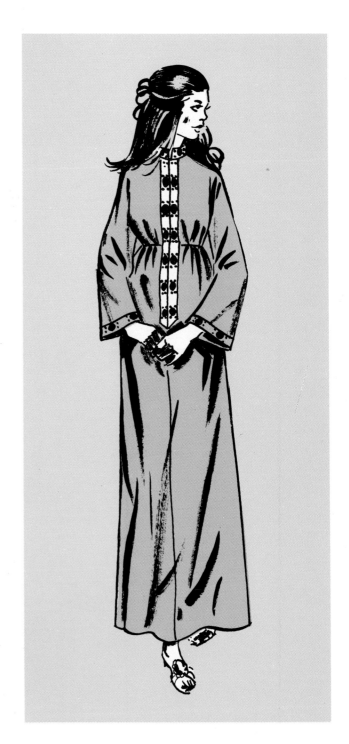

the seams. These robes are not faced; the front edge can be turned in a hem or bound to match the bottom edge, or you can simply use the blanket selvage for the front edge. The seams in these heavy fabrics are overlaid—one edge laid over the other and basted flat without turning. When you stitch both edges, you have a flat seam; it should overlap at least ½ inch. The armholes should be bound.

LUXURY LINGERIE

Fine needlework is the hallmark of luxury lingerie. Its beauty depends upon fine hand finishing; one popular type features edges bound with self-fabric or ribbon. All ruffles should be finished with hand-rolled hems, and lace should be applied with the same kind of hems.

Lace trimmings are important features of luxurious nightgowns, slips, and panties. Women who enjoy handwork can make really beautiful lingerie, and it's not hard to apply lace motifs or sections of lace cut from allover patterns. The better quality of machine embroidery is often used in combination with tucks and lace. For directions for applying these finishes, consult the index.

Teaching Your Daughter To Sew

This chapter is dedicated to all girls—those who love to make things, those who have talent and creative ideas, those who want fashion careers, and those who can't afford frills on their budgets.

If you are already an experienced home sewer, you will take pride and joy in teaching your daughter to sew yourself. If you are a beginner, share with her the fun and satisfaction of learning a new skill.

Home sewing that is fun, based on a streamlined routine, permits girls of any age to make what they like without restraint or tradition and helps bring forth talent. In developing a talent, a girl must not think of sewing. She must think of expressing her ideas. Beginners should not be asked to learn more than to work neatly.

Sewing should be thought of as an art expression. Learn to develop beauty and line in textiles. Rid yourself of the fear of drudgery. Have fun as you sew. Learn about careers that are open to girls who know how to sew. Many of the creative workers of America's great fashion industry —designers of dresses and accessories, writers who describe garments for magazines and newspapers, artists who illustrate for the fashion industry, the highly-paid sales-promotion women and editors of magazines—have said that as girls they sewed with their mothers. The girls who learn how to sew at home and really practice fashion coordinating and the solving of home problems will be best qualified to advance into the splendid positions offered by industry for this talent.

A beginner's first problem is to overcome the false fear that sewing is difficult and to banish the feeling that one cannot sew without learning a long and complex science. The best way to prove that this is wrong is for the girl to make something all alone. It should be a garment she really wants and it should be made in a hurry. When it is finished, she will be proud to wear it.

Girls who make themselves a basic dress, and continually change it with accessories and trimming so that their wardrobe looks five times larger than it really is, are preparing for jobs as fashion co-ordinators—equipping themselves with experience that is needed in all stores in every city.

Too many beginners with artistic talent who set out to take courses tend to believe in nothing but art for art's sake, and make their designs around fairytale dresses. They are so seldom needed that it is pitiful to spend time this way. Instead, they should set out to solve actual problems in the home.

HELPING YOUR DAUGHTER TO SEW

Too often youth is discouraged by Victorian methods. Our daughters live in a machine age and want streamlined speed. To them, samplers and long-drawn-out routines vanished with the horse and buggy.

Sewing, like all other sciences, must be presented in modern dress. When a girl wants to sew, expressing the natural urge to make things, meet this wish with an invitation to have "lots of fun." Lay aside pet traditions and let the girl prove *to herself* that she can sew. Let her make something she will be proud to wear. She will surely make mistakes, but you and she can laugh them off together and learn as she goes. Once the fear of "spoiling something" is proved false, both mother and daughter can progress in one of the happiest bonds—making pretty clothes. Youthful taste is simple, and if the choice is not wise, can be easily guided to something "prettier" that an adult head knows is easier and youth describes as quicker. If, however, a young sewer's heart is set, whatever her choice, let her make it, explaining only that it will take longer—and so prepare her for unusual patience.

The secret of helping a girl to love sewing, or developing a talent, is to concentrate on speed in making the first garment. It must be finished so quickly that she, you, and all are amazed. She must do it all by herself.

If you do not sew, join your daughter and make your first dress with her in a merry class for two. Beginners should choose their own patterns and fabrics. Without any help, they should assemble the trimming and anything else they may need. Make no suggestions that she must learn to hem before she makes a dress.

Remember that the pattern should have as few pieces as possible. This insures speed. Remind her to look for patterns designated "How to Sew" or "Jiffy" or similar names. It is also wise that the fabric be printed so that unskilled stitches are not emphasized. It is important also that the trimming touch be style-right.

Let a super-simple project guarantee success the first-time she sews. Here, the skirt is a breeze to make, the trim can be an expression of her own color and style preferences—let the decision be hers!

Here are two delightful suggestions for choose-it-yourself sewing projects for beginners. A very young lady, left, might like to learn to sew a bibbed skirt like the ones worn by Scandinavian milkmaids. Young teens have a strong fashion sense, and the kicky shorts, below, might well lure them into learning to sew for themselves.

It should be made with no preliminaries and no outside help or assistance. It will be fun for any mother to watch the capable efficiency of her daughter when she examines her first pattern. Our commercial patterns do not need to be explained to modern girls. Just say to your daughter that all the directions are there, and she need only open the package and read the directions. She must circle with a pencil the cutting guide for her size and width of material. It is a good idea to check the pattern before cutting, as sizes differ from those in dresses we buy in the stores. A suitable time should be set for cutting the garment so that you and your daughter can have quiet. Either cut your own dress on another side of the room or sit quietly and do some mending. Your daughter will pin her pattern to the fabric and cut it with quiet determination. Ask that she let you see the pattern when it is all pinned before the actual cutting.

Immediately the dress is cut, it should be pinned together. Here again the girl must be on her own. The picture diagram in the pattern will help her speed things up. Watch her joy as she tries it on.

The seams are stitched, the hem is turned. Even if this is her first hem, no matter; she can do it. Girls are deeply interested in the trimming touches and can make facings, casings that hold ribbon, or wool pompoms, or tiny bows to decorate a dress. They usually have good style-right ideas about trimmings and should be encouraged to develop any idea that is not time-consuming or difficult. Your daughter will appreciate your help in hanging the skirt and in fitting, otherwise let her be an independent artist.

Great emphasis is placed on the fact that the mother is not to help. This is most important in developing confidence and establishing a desire to learn more about sewing.

Once a beginner has made her first dress, she should be encouraged to progress only when she wants to. When the first experience has been quick and a lot of fun, she will want to sew again; but her own timing is the best guide to a happy mother-and-daughter sewing relationship.

SUGGESTED PROGRESSION OF BEGINNER PROJECTS

If your daughter seeks your guidance—but *only* if she does—here are some pointers you could offer:

The first garment should be a one-piece dress cut in 2 or 3 pieces (sleeves cut in one). This slip-on type of dress, made of a printed cotton, a wool jersey, or a spun-rayon that looks like wool, will be easy and quick to make. These fabrics absorb amateur stitches.

The second garment should have a set-in sleeve and a joining at the waistline. It should be made in a textile with a surface interest. Avoid plain-surface crepes or transparent fabrics, satin, and fabrics that are not firm.

The third garment should be a one-piece dress with a jacket—one with the fewest number of pieces. It can be a simple dress with a jacket, a bolero or a vest. It can be made from printed crepe, spun rayon, lightweight wool, or the firmer types of cotton.

The fourth garment should be a coat or a coat-style dress or a smock.

When these four types have been made successfully, the sewer is no longer a beginner and she can choose any garment in the pattern books.

A beginner may prefer to make curtains for her room. Because this work is straight, it is an easy approach to sewing. Many beginners approach sewing by altering or remodeling garments, which quickly encourages them to venture into the making of a new garment of the simpler kind.

Gifts And Accessories

one of the greatest rewards a knowledge of sewing can offer is the ability to make delightful gifts for your family and friends—gifts that will be appreciated far more than a twice-as-costly purchased token would be.

For a fashion-conscious teenager, make a tote and suspenders to match. Sets like this are great money-makers at bazaars!

Next time you sew for yourself, buy some extra fabric and whip up a matching tie for the man in your life. He'll love you for it!

Of course, we are all familiar with the charming gifts for which patterns are available and which are pictured in the pattern catalogs in fabric shops, department stores, and variety stores. In them you will find not only stuffed toys, doll clothes, and art needlework transfers, but also exciting new gifts and accessories—men's neckties, tote bags, "boot" tops, and so on.

Another fine source of things to sew for friends and festivals are the needlework magazines on sale at newsstands and in many supermarkets. They usually contain patterns and directions for items shown on their pages, as well as suggestions for adapting other ideas.

Because this kind of sewing often calls for patterns or specific directions which are too space-consuming to include in this book, we are going to limit our suggestions here to a few gifts and accessories which are comparatively simple. You will, in fact, find scattered throughout these pages things which would be easily adapted to gift making—scarves and bows, for example, are always welcome!

FOR CHILDREN

For the very young, a soft, colorful felt ball is an attractive toy. You will need eight scraps of felt, each about 2½ inches by 9 inches, in a variety of colors, plus two small fifty-cent size circles. Using the pattern here, cut eight pieces, whip-stitch them together two-by-two (leave an opening for stuffing), then stuff as firmly as possible with kapok or cotton batting. Whip-stitch the circles in place to cover the joining of the points, and stitch the opening closed.

FOR MEN

Make covers for his address book and telephone book, his favorite paperback, or a desk dictionary. To determine the amount of fabric needed, measure from front edge of cover, around spine, and to front edge of back cover—then add 4 inches for a 2-inch "pocket" allowance for the front and back covers; for the depth, measure from top to bottom edges on front cover and add ½ inch for ¼-inch seam allowances top and bottom. If you wish, stitch a monogram or applique a bright motif on the front cover.

Finish in one of two methods. For a hidden seam, with right side of cover against book, fold carefully around, tucking ends under front and back covers; pin extensions in place inside the covers. Remove book and stitch extensions against covers, taking slightly less than ¼-inch seams. Turn to right side and trim remaining top and bottom edges as needed. For a stitched seam, proceed as above but place cover wrong side against book; after stitching, do not turn but simply trim edges, with a pinking shears if desired.

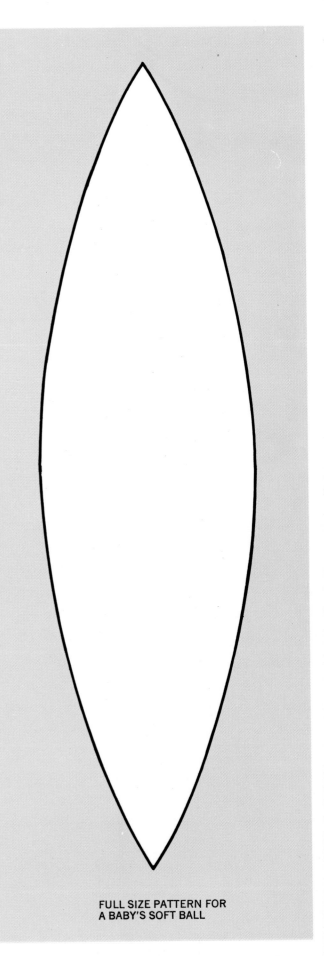

FULL SIZE PATTERN FOR
A BABY'S SOFT BALL

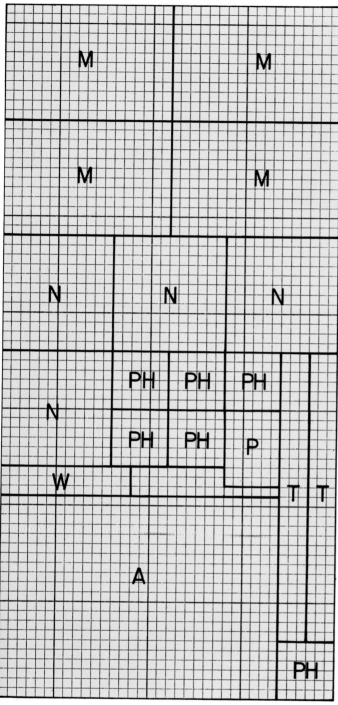

EACH SQUARE = 1"

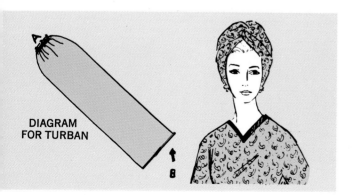

DIAGRAM FOR TURBAN

Make a charming coordinated set containing apron, three potholders, and place mats and napkins for four—a lovely hostess gift, a bazaar best seller, or a delightful shower gift for the bride-to-be.

You will need two yards of 36 inch wide fabric—cheerful gingham or a printed cotton. For trim, one package of doublefold bias tape and five packages of rickrack to match one of the colors of the fabric. Cut the pieces following cutting diagram: Place mats (M on diagram) will be 18 inches by 12 inches, napkins (N) 12 inches square, pot holders (PH) 6 inches square, front of apron (A) 21 inches by 30 inches, waistband (W) 3 inches by 16 inches, pocket (P) 6 inches by 8 inches, and ties (T) 3 inches by 30 inches.

If you wish to monogram, embroider, or applique the set, do so before assembling the pieces. Such trims should be placed on the left edge of the mats, in a corner of the napkins, or centered on the pocket.

To finish the mats and napkins, make a rolled hem around the edges, then stitch rick rack all around, with the points extending beyond the edge. For the pot holders, cut several layers of padding from an old cotton blanket or pieces of flannel, each 6 inches square. Sandwich padding between covers, baste together, and machine quilt following the design of the fabric. Bind edges with bias tape, forming a hanging loop at corner.

To assemble the apron, turn ¼ inch of each edge of waistband to wrong side, fold waistband in half lengthwise, and press. Sew narrow hem along each side (narrow) edge of apron front; turn 1½-inch hem to wrong side of one long edge, press, sew rickrack on right side to hold hem in place. Gather raw edge of front to fit within waistband; sew in place. Hem all but one short edge of each tie, gather raw edge and insert into open sides of waistband; stitch securely. Turn in ½ inch around pocket, press; turn one 6-inch edge 1½ inch to wrong side and finish as for lower edge of front. Sew pocket to front about 4 inches below waistband and 5 inches from right edge (as it is worn). (Delight a left-hander by placing it on the opposite side!)

HATS

With the return of the "lady-like look" to the fashion picture, hats are again important. Here are two to make yourself, of fabrics the same as, or color-coordinated with, your newest dress or ensemble.

Wrap-around Turban: Use soft wool jersey. A yard of 40-inch material will make two turbans. Cut the turban 36-inches long and half the width of the material (20 inches). Fold lengthwise and seam one end. With a series of gathers, gather this seam into a 2½-inch measure. Starting at opposite end, cut along fold for about 24 inches. Place the gathered material at your hairline, center front, and wrap the ends around the head. Tie the turban and make sure you have split it so it ties at the most becoming angle. When the effect is just what you want, hem the unfinished edges.

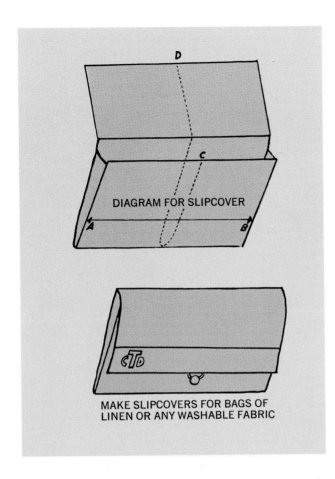

DIAGRAM FOR SLIPCOVER

MAKE SLIPCOVERS FOR BAGS OF
LINEN OR ANY WASHABLE FABRIC

Fabric Covered Hat: Use a new buckram frame or an old one from which the fabric has been removed.

1. Cut a circle of new fabric to fit the top of the crown, allowing about ¼ inch for seam. Baste it to the crown with catch stitches.

2. Cut a strip of fabric on the bias, 1 inch wider than the height of the crown and long enough to go around the crown with ¼-inch seam allowance at each end. Turn one edge of this strip over a narrow cord and baste it. Place this edge over the circle on the edge of the crown; fit it smoothly all around and pin it in place. Then sew it with matching thread just under the cording, using a fine running stitch. Be sure to catch the fabric on the crown with each stitch. Join the ends with a fine slip stitch. Turn the remaining cut edge of the fabric in a hem inside the hat edge and stitch in place.

3. Finish the inside of the hat with a lining. First cut a circle of thin lining fabric about 4 inches in diameter. Put this inside the hat against the top of the crown. Cut a piece of bias fabric wide enough to reach from this circle to the brim edge of the crown, and long enough to fit smoothly around the head size. Allow ¼ inch seam allowance on all sides. Sew the ends of the band together. Then gather one side and sew it to the circle of fabric, distributing the gathers evenly. Drop this lining into the hat, pin it around the brim edge of the crown, and hem it in place about ¼ inch from the edge of the crown.

The hat body is then complete and can be trimmed as desired.

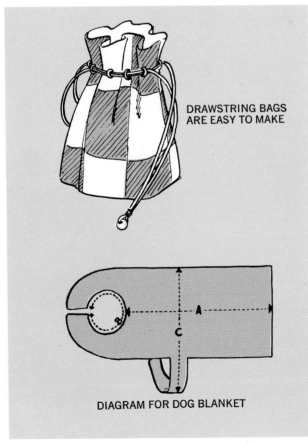

DRAWSTRING BAGS
ARE EASY TO MAKE

DIAGRAM FOR DOG BLANKET

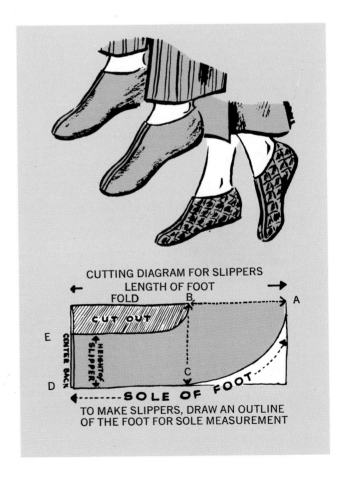

CUTTING DIAGRAM FOR SLIPPERS
LENGTH OF FOOT
FOLD
CUT OUT
HEIGHT OF SLIPPER
CENTER BACK
SOLE OF FOOT
TO MAKE SLIPPERS, DRAW AN OUTLINE
OF THE FOOT FOR SOLE MEASUREMENT

HANDBAGS

Handbags made of fabric require an interlining of hair canvas, non-woven interfacing, or buckram. For the softer bags, hair canvas is suitable; buckram is necessary for shaped styles. Bag slipcovers can be made of washable or decorative fabrics to fit an old bag, preferably a flat envelope shape. Small bags for the country and the small envelope bag attached to the belt are not interlined when made from felt, but they must be interlined if they are made of fabric.

Frame Handbag: Frames of wood, tortoise shell, or metal are sold in the notion departments of many stores. They are finished with the type of ring or eyelet to which a bag can be attached. Notice the difference between this type of frame and the frame in bags you buy. The latter requires a machine for framing.

Make the bag to match or contrast with any coat or dress. The fabric should be heavy enough to hold its shape, and the lining should be sturdy. Follow manufacturer's directions (which come with the frame) for assembling it.

Drawstring Bag: Casual bags can be made of combination fabrics or one fabric; or you can use fabrics or leathers in a patchwork design. Cut two cardboard disks for the base, which is usually 6 to 10 inches. Cut material to cover both the circles, allowing ½ inch for seams. Overcast them together. Cut the bag itself in: (1) the outside fabric, (2) the lining material, and (3) the interlining. All three pieces should be long enough to go around the base with 6 inches additional for fullness. Cut lining and interlining the desired depth, at least 10 inches; the outside fabric should have an additional 3 inches or so to form a double fold for a heading with a casing.

Seam the bag and sew it to the base; insert interlining, then line. Finish with a casing or tiny rings sewn to the outside; run drawstring through. A leather drawstring is suitable for casual, sturdy bags, while velveteen is lovely with dressy fabrics such as silk or velvet.

Handbag Slipcovers: Any envelope bag can be supplied with a slipcover. Examine the shaping on the side of the bag and make a paper pattern of the gusset insert. Cut the pattern in fabric. Measure the bag for your slipcover as follows, allowing ¼-inch seam allowance on all sides: First measure the width from A to B in the diagram; then around the bag from C to D. Cut your fabric in this size plus additional on one end to fit over flap D. Fit this end to the top of the bag while it is on the wrong side. Then fit in the gusset and seam it to the sides of the bag cover. Bind the top of the gusset and the unfinished edge of the cover with self-binding or contrasting color texture. Trim as desired. Tack this edge to the edge of the bag. For a secure closing, sew to the top edge a loop of trimming cord or a fabric-covered cord, and sew a fancy shank button to the lower edge so the loop will catch it.

SLIPPERS

Men's Slippers: Men's slippers can be made from old felt hats, or from scraps of coating, carpet, or drapery. Use a shoe to make the pattern, outlining it on a piece of paper. No seams need be allowed. For the top, measure from the floor at the big toe up the foot as high as the slipper is to extend (A to B on diagram), then at that point measure to the floor on each side (B to C is one-half that measure); measure up from floor at heel to determine height D to E; length will depend upon sole length. Cut the top of the slipper double, by the diagram, fitting it around the sole. All seams are joined on the right side and should first be basted. Then bind them with a strong binding, stitching as close to the edge as possible. Run a binding flat to cover the back seam and bind the top edge.

Women's Slippers: Dainty slippers can be made from any of the fabrics mentioned for men's slippers, or they can be made with quilted tops made from dress fabric in plain colors or prints. (Quilt the fabric before you cut out the slipper. To save work, outline the shape of the slipper top on the lining.)

Children's Slippers: Slippers for children can be made to match their bathrobes, but bathrobe material will not make a suitable sole. Follow the directions above for men's slippers. Use felt, or scraps from an old coat or blanket. Slippers for toddlers and tots should be made of washable material.

DOG COAT

Make a coat for your dog to match your own! Shape the fabric as in diagram. Measure the dog from collar to tail and put the measurement in the center of the diagram, at A. Measure his neck and put this measure at B. Measure around his chest behind his front legs and put this measure at C, adding sufficient length to extend up again to A. Cut a piece of fabric in these measurements. The edge which meets under his chin must be closed with snap fasteners. Attach a buckle where A and C cross and use it to fasten ''belt''. Bind all edges.

Home Cleaning And Pressing

The care of clothing—cleaning and pressing—is a time-consuming item in any household routine. A systematic plan and a little expert knowledge can substantially reduce the number of hours required for this task. This chapter gives suggestions for time-saving schedules for cleaning and pressing, including a check list of common spots and how to treat them.

SPOT CHECK LIST

Kind of Spot	Cleaning Fluid	How to Use It
Fat or grease	Perchlorethylene Tri-chlorethylene	Sponge with perchlorethylene or tri-chlorethylene, and wash as usual.
Candle wax	Perchlorethylene Tri-chlorethylene	Scrape off as much wax as possible. Sponge with a dry-cleaning solvent such as perchlorethylene or tri-chlorethylene.
Fruit stains	Sodium perborate Ammonia water	Wash in usual way. If a stain remains, cover stained area with a sodium perborate bleach. Add a few drops of hot water to make a paste; add a few drops of ammonia. Wait 15–30 minutes, then wash as usual.
Lipstick	Perchlorethylene Tri-chlorethylene Chlorine bleach Perborate bleach	Sponge with perchlorethylene or tri-chlorethylene. Use diluted chlorine bleach if stain lingers in white fabrics; perborate bleach for colored ones.
Ink or ballpoint pen ink	Perchlorethylene Tri-chlorethylene Ammonia water Chlorine bleach Perborate bleach	Sponge with perchlorethylene or tri-chlorethylene. Brush with a detergent paste and ammonia water. Bleach with diluted chlorine bleach if necessary. For colored fabrics, sodium perborate bleach should be used.
Iron or rust	Lemon juice Salt	Apply lemon juice and salt and place in the sun for an hour or so. Rinse well and wash.

Most homemakers know a great deal more about the care of washable garments than about nonwashable ones. Spots on wools, wool blends, silks, and cottons and rayons are a perpetual trial because most people have one home cleaner and one method of cleaning for everything. Anyone who has had a good dress returned from a cleaner with "persistent spots" knows that cleaning troubles are not confined to the home. Dry cleaning is a problem in chemistry, and the only sound approach to it is to follow expert advice and prepare to act quickly. To do this we must have a "quick cleaning kit" and know how to apply the right cleaner at the first appearance of a spot.

SPOT CHECK LIST

Kind of Spot	Cleaning Fluid	How to Use It
Scorch	Chlorine bleach Perborate bleach	Bleach with diluted chlorine bleach, then follow normal washing procedure for whites; perborate bleach and hot water, for colored fabrics.
Paint	Perchlorethylene Tri-chlorethylene	Scrape off fresh paint. Sponge with perchlorethylene or tri-chlorethylene.
Dye and running color	Hydrogen peroxide	Ease with which dye is removed depends upon the nature of the dye. Dye stains in white fabrics can often be removed by soaking in warm or cold water for 10 or 12 hours, and then bleaching in the sun. For white wool or silk, soak in hydrogen peroxide solution, made slightly alkaline with a few drops of ammonia. Rinse thoroughly.
Blood	Water Hydrogen peroxide	Always use cold water first (never soap or warm water). Soak in cold water until the stain is almost gone, then wash with soap and warm water. Delicate fabrics should be sponged with cold or lukewarm water. To remove the last traces, sponge with hydrogen peroxide to which a few drops of ammonia have been added. Heavy material, blankets, mattresses, etc.; make a paste of raw starch and cold water. Apply to the stain and brush off when dry. Repeat.
Egg	Cold water Carbon tetrachloride	Cold water first (no hot water). Washable color-fast material (1) cold water, (2) wash in hot water. Other fabrics: sponge with cold water. Allow stain to dry. Then apply cleaning fluid by the pad method.
Chocolate and cocoa	Carbon tetrachloride Soap and hot water Javelle water Wood alcohol	Washable material: soap and water. On white linen and cotton, when stain remains, use javelle water. For colored material, if dye is fast, soak stained portion in wood alcohol with a few drops of ammonia solution. For non-washable material, use carbon tetrachloride, pad method.

QUICK CLEANING

Government chemists say that spots should be removed while they are still wet, or as soon afterward as possible; and there would be few stubborn spots to cope with if this practice were followed. Too often a spot is set by the wrong treatment, or a garment is pressed without cleaning, for "just one more wear" before it goes to the cleaner.

Spot Removal Kit: You will need two cleaners, an absorbent cleaner and a solvent; also brown paper; a blunt knife; a clothes brush; an assortment of swabs; and a frequent change of pressing pads. Keep all this equipment in a tightly closed box to keep out the dust. Paste the rules for using solvents and abrasives on the lid of the box for ready reference. Always keep the box well supplied with clean pads and swabs.

Absorbent Cleaners: These are cornstarch, chalk, and magnesium. They act like a blotter, absorbing the ingredients of a fresh stain. An absorbent cleaner will not injure fiber or fabric. To use it, place the garment on an ironing board with the right side up. Spread a layer of it on the wet stain and work it into the stain with a blunt knife, taking care not to injure the fabric. As soon as the powder is grimy, brush it off and apply another layer. Repeat the process patiently until the spot is gone. Check your work in a bright light, then brush away every trace of powder with a piece of clean fabric.

If the spot persists, try leaving a layer of the absorbent on it overnight. To speed the action of the absorbent when the spot has a trace of oil or grease, spread a layer of absorbent, put a piece of brown paper over it, and press with a warm iron. Heat is necessary to dissolve the grease before the absorbent can blot it up.

Solvent Cleaners: These include benzine, turpentine, alcohol, and water. They dissolve the spot, and it is important to work on the wrong side of the garment so that the spot is eliminated and not soaked through the fabric. Solvents may be used by the pad method, the bowl method, or immersing the whole garment.

Swabs: The swabs used for applying solvent cleaners should be of the same material as the garment if possible. Rub wool with wool, rayon with rayon, cotton with cotton. Swabs must be cleaned after each use.

Pads: Pads are made from old Turkish towels, absorbent cotton, or white blotting paper, and they must be changed frequently to prevent rings.

Press Cloths: At least three press cloths made of unbleached muslin or old sheets should be included in the spot removal kit.

THE CAUSE OF RINGS

A too-generous application of a solvent forms rings. The solvent must evaporate as you work and never be permitted to run. Another cause is that the garment was soiled before the cleaning was started, so a clean spot forms a ring. Solvents may loosen the fabric finish and flood it to the edge of the damp section, thus forming a ring.

METHODS OF CLEANING

Pad Method: Pads are made from white blotting paper or clean pieces of fabric swabs from a fabric like the garment. They must be spotless, and plentiful, as they are changed frequently. Place the spot face down on a pad and apply the cleaning fluid to the back of the fabric with a swab. Be sure that there is not too much moisture on the swab. There must be enough to penetrate the spotted section only, with no surplus to run. Apply it again and again, changing the pad. When the spot is removed wipe the spot dry with a clean swab and blow on it until it is dry.

Bowl Method: You will need two bowls, a medicine dropper—separate ones for acid and alkali solutions—and a swab and several dry pads. Stretch the fabric over a bowl of lukewarm water, holding it over the bowl with an elastic band. With the dropper put a few drops of the cleaning fluid on the spot. When the spot changes color plunge the material into the bowl of water if it is washable; if it is not, steam it over the spout of a teakettle, with a cloth over the spout.

PRESSING

Pressing must be distinguished from ironing. In ironing, a hot iron is pressed directly on a fabric to smooth the surface, which is sometimes dry, sometimes damp, sometimes wet. In pressing, the iron is not applied directly to the surface of the fabric. A cloth or paper is put over the fabric, and the iron applied to that. A tailor's iron is heavier than the usual household iron and makes a sharper fold in the edges of the fabric. Ironing is used for lightweight fabrics, particularly cottons; pressing is essential for woolens and worsteds, for heavy cottons and blended fabrics which look like wool. They cannot be ironed.

Dry Pressing: Lightweight dress fabrics of rayon, cotton, and silk are pressed dry. The garment is turned to the wrong side and pressed without a press cloth. Set the iron so it will not scorch, and keep it moving so it does not mark the fabric.

When a stubborn crease persists, wipe the fabric with a damp press cloth and press again.

Wet Pressing: To press with a dry iron it is necessary to use a press cloth of lightweight lint-free fabric. Moisten one-half of the press cloth with warm water; fold the dry half inside the wet half and wring, making the whole cloth damp. Apply the iron with very little pressure. A cotton press cloth may still be necessary for some fabrics, especially when pressing on the right side of the garment.

Steam Pressing: With a steam iron many fabrics may be pressed on the wrong side without a press cloth. All lined garments, or those with double collars or facings, must be steam-pressed. Lined garments are pressed on the right side, using two press cloths. Unbleached muslin is used for lightweight garments, but for heavy coats the press cloth should be canvas or wool. The wetter the press cloth, the better the steam, and these garments require a great deal of steaming. The muslin cloth can be soaked and squeezed out so it is wet but does not drip, but the heavier press cloth must be wet with a sponge dipped in water.

Put the wet press cloth over the garment and press it with a hot iron. Keep the iron moving. Press around buttons, not over them. Remove the press cloth and brush the garment. Use a soft brush for woolens and a hard brush for worsteds. This brushing will eliminate the steam and dry the fabric, prevent shine, raise the nap, and prevent sharp marks on the edges of pockets and seams. Then place a dry cloth over the garment and press until it is almost dry. A wool or blended fabric should not be pressed dry, because it makes the fabric shine. Hang up the garment while it is still damp and let it dry in the air. The coat-hanger must be as wide as the shoulders of the garment so it will not sag as it dries.

Professionals first press the sleeves, then begin at the underarm on one side of the garment, working toward the front. Then they turn the garment so the pressed side rests carefully on the table beside the board and press across the back toward the other front edge.

Pressing a Sleeve: When you press on a flat surface, fold the sleeve at the underarm seam. If you want a crease on the outside edge of the sleeve, let the iron reach this edge. Most dress sleeves should not have an outside fold, and in this case the sleeve is pressed so that the iron does not reach the outside edge. When all but the edge has been pressed, the sleeve is laid so the center line lies flat in the center, then the center is pressed. Another method of avoiding an outside fold is using a seam roll to press the sleeve.

The rounded shaping of armhole and shoulder in any garment must be protected in pressing. A tailor's ham, a pressing mitt, or a sleeve board will help. The secret of pressing the armhole joining is to first lay the shoulder flat on the sleeve board and press it with the collar turned out. Never let the iron touch the seam which joins the sleeve to the armhole. When the shoulder has been pressed, place the garment on the sleeve board so that you can press the waist or jacket fabric around the armhole. Do not touch the seam. When this fabric has been pressed, place the top of the sleeve on the broad end of the sleeve board and press the gathers or rounded shaping at the top. The iron comes up to but does not touch the seam. In the making of a garment, this seam joining the sleeve to the armhole is pressed toward the sleeve. To do this, first press the seam firmly; then remove the sharp line by moving the seam back and pressing the sleeve under the seam, removing the press lines from the sleeve.

Removing Shine from Woolens: Worsteds made from long, tightly twisted brushed wool shine most easily. Woolens made from unbrushed wool in a fuzzy fabric seldom shine. To remove shine from top-quality, fast-color worsteds, wipe the fabric lightly with a solution of vinegar, lay a press cloth over it, and steam it. Lift the press cloth and brush the fabric. If you are not sure of your fabric, test this treatment on the inside of the hem only.

If your fabric will not take the vinegar treatment, use the following method: Soak a press cloth; it must be wet but not drip. Hold the iron just above the cloth, so it creats steam but does not press the cloth. Move the iron continually, but very slowly, so that the steam penetrates the fabric, over a section of the garment. When that section has been thoroughly steamed, lift the cloth and brush the fabric. If the shine is not removed, repeat the process. To dry the material, hold the iron close to the dry press cloth so the heat dries the fabric and it seems to have been pressed, even though the iron never touches the fabric.

PRESSING SPECIAL FABRICS

The yarns of pile fabrics should not be flattened in pressing. Lay pile fabric wrong side up over a heavy turkish towel and press lightly. Laminated fabrics need very little pressing. Paper should be slipped under the seam allowance so that the iron will not come in contact with the foam. Knitted fabrics should not be ironed back and forth since this may stretch the fabric out of shape; a gentle stamping motion should be used. Nylons should be pressed on the wrong side with a cool iron or with a steam iron. A low setting should be used when pressing dacron and a press cloth is necessary.

Better Repair For Longer Wear:

Repairing *clothing and linens is an inescapable, and in too many cases, a time-consuming part of the routine of every household. It can save many dollars by prolonging the life of clothing and household linens; and skillful organizing to catch the tear in time saves hours of needless labor. "A stitch in time saves nine" is no idle saying.*

TIME-SAVING PLANS

Your own habits and circumstances will determine the exact details of the plan you work out for mending, but whatever it is, "do it now" should be the keynote. One good way is to watch for tears and missing buttons as you iron and make it an iron-clad rule to mend them before the garments or linens are put away. If you send your washing to the laundry, check each item for rips and tears as you check the laundry list, especially sheets and pillow cases.

The clever mother enlists the children in her mending program. In each bedroom is a pincushion with threaded needles, and each child learns to do a little quick mending—catching together the small rip, sewing on the button hanging by a thread.

APPRAISING YOUR MENDING PROBLEM

There are different kinds of mending appropriate to different cases—quick-stitch mending, tide-over mending, and permanent mending. The last of these can often be decorative mending, in which the mend is concealed by being made to look like part of the trimming. The condition of the garment, of course, will largely determine which kind you use. A well-worn garment, on the last lap of its life, hardly deserves the same careful mending as a perfectly good garment. Hold the fabric to the light and examine it for slippage and small holes, strained seams, and so forth. Such garments merit only quick tide-over mending.

Good Outside Garments: When a perfectly good garment has suffered an accident, the problem of mending it needs careful consideration. It should not look mended; so the problem is, can it be repaired with an inconspicuous mend, or must you resort to decorative mending to disguise the spot? If the latter is the case, the nature of the spot to be covered will determine the kind of thing you can do. Is it a tear, a permanent spot, a burn? Has the fabric slipped and worn at the seams? Is the fabric faded? Has the garment shrunk or been outgrown? At this point mending merges into remodeling or alteration.

Turning Men's Shirt Collars and Cuffs: Before removing the collar, mark the center of both collar and neckband by folding the neckband in half with edges matching. Use pins to do this marking. Then rip the stitches and take off the collar, reverse it, and replace it in the neckband. Pin it in place and check to make sure that the worn edge of the collar faces the right side of the shirt so it will be inside when you fold the collar. Then you are ready to stitch.

Cuffs are ripped and reversed in the same way as collars.

Split Seams: When the stitching of a seam gives way, it is easy enough to restitch it, on the machine if possible. When the fabric splits at the seam, you can overstitch the seam on the right side. Run the first row of stitching as close to the split edge as possible (do not turn the edge under). Then run several rows of stitching close together, stitching through the seam allowance on the wrong side.

There is a difference between a clean tear at the seam and slipping of the fabric at the seam. Seam slippage must be stayed with a band.

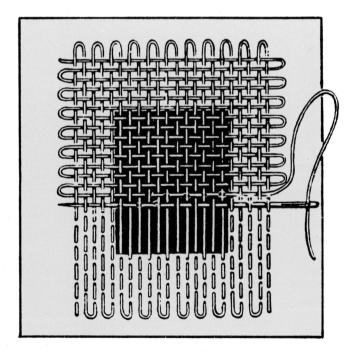

Darn a hole by weaving back and forth, then weave across it at right angles.

DECORATIVE MENDING

Tears and permanent spots can be covered with applique or trimming bands, or, if they come in the right place, turned into a pocket or covered with a pocket.

Mending Gloves: Ripped seams in the fingers should be closely overcast with a cotton thread the exact shade of the glove. Do not take the stitch too close to the edge or it will rip out again.

In mending gloves do not use knots. Allow extra thread and tie in the ends carefully.

Mending Machine-Made Sweaters: Cut a piece from the seam or hem of the sweater and unravel it to use for darning the hole and overcasting the cut edge of the sweater. If the darn shows, make a few embroidery stitches over or around it in a design. Another possibility is to make allover embroidery on the sweater which will cover the darn. This can be scattered sprays of little flowers in lazy-daisy stitch, or the effect can be achieved with applique spots of embroidery or colored felt patches in diamond or heart shapes. If the hole is in the front or side, applique a monogram over it.

When a sweater is torn at the elbow, there is little to be done except make a darn or patch. But you can use one of the decorative patches suggested above and place a matching one somewhere on the body. If the sweater is of good wool, cut off the sleeves and make a sleeveless sweater.

You can finish the lower edge by using some of the yarn you raveled out for darning and overcast the cut edge. Stretch the edge as you work and be sure to catch your needle through every stitch. In a turned band, take care to catch every stitch in the back row as well as the front.

REPAIRING GIRDLES

At the first sign of a rip or tear, mend your girdle promptly. Catch the end of each rubber thread and tie it with cotton thread so it will hold. Then darn these threads down into the seam or whatever part of the girdle ripped. Be careful not to put a needle through the rubber threads. If the tear is on a seam, rebind it with tape or a satin ribbon after mending. If the garter rips on a seam, use an overcasting stitch; it holds better and has some give.

MENDING LINEN

Sheets: Put bands of percale (solid color, or gay print) on a torn hem. Small holes can be darned or covered with appliqued stars or tiny flowers. Large holes must be patched. To overcast a split sheet, join the outside edges and overcast by hand so the seam is flat.

Towels: Torn towels can be cut down to guest size. If the towel is small, applique amusing designs for a patch, such as red lips or a small hand. Towels too badly torn for repair can still give service as washcloths or potholders.

DARNING

The time spent mending socks can be cut down by watching for the thinning-out which precedes a hole. This thin fabric is much easier to darn than a hole. An inside heel guard on the shoe saves socks and is well worth the trouble of having it put in or putting in a ready-made one. If you have an unusually large family to mend for, it will pay you to buy a sock-mending attachment for your sewing machine.

Mend a small corner or triangular tear neatly so that there is no extra bulk.

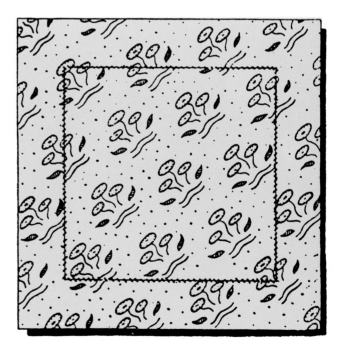

When patching prints, match the pattern of the print as well as the fabric grain.

Darning Small Holes: With the sock right side out, slip a darning egg into place under the hole and draw the sock tight over the egg. Thread a darning needle with cotton or wool the same shade as the sock. Begin ¼ inch above the hole and pass the needle in and out in a weaving motion. The thread line should extend beyond the hole on each side. Draw the thread through—no knot in the end—then run another thread line back the other way, close to the first one. When you pull this second thread, leave a very small loop at the end between the two lines of stitching. Weave back and forth in this manner until you have passed the hole and gone ¼ inch on the other side. Turn and do the same thing at right angles to the first set of threads. When you come to the hole, weave under one thread and over the next, and when you come back, alternate—under when the last thread was over, and vice versa. Fill up the hole with close darning in this manner, and when you finish, the darn should lie flat and smooth like part of the sock. It should not be bulky and thick.

Darning Large Holes: Trim the frayed edges around the hole and cut a piece from a discarded sock to fill it. Catch-stitch the piece in place, then darn back and forth over the catch stitching so there is no seam or bulk at the edge. This is a time-saving way of mending holes, and women who do not like to darn can use it for small holes as well as large ones, or even for thin places.

Darning Garments: A small tear can often be darned inconspicuously if you use a very fine needle threaded with a thread drawn from the fabric. The hem, a seam edge, or the inside of a pocket are good places to draw out self threads. A short thread is best. First catch the edge of the tear with a basting stitch and then darn. In tears the darning is seldom recrossed; you pass the needle in and out, back and forth across the tear. If there is a corner, cross it twice for strength. On plain fabrics the loops at the end of the darning rows *must be even*. They can be shorter on woven fabrics that do not stretch than on knitted fabrics that do stretch.

If the tear is diagonal or across the grain of the goods, work first across the tear, then work lengthwise of it.

A piece of fine net is often placed under a darn to strengthen the thread without adding bulk.

Darns conspicuously placed can be decorated. For suggestions see Decorative Patching below.

PATCHING

If you have no extra material for a patch, see whether you can cut a piece from the hem or an inside facing. If the garment has faded and the patch is bright and new, wash it first and dry it in the sun. There are two kinds of patches, decorative and inconspicuous.

Decorative Patch: The patch need not match and is not cut the size and shape of the hole, but in some decorative shape—diamond, square, heart-shaped, or whatever you wish. Apply it with catch stitch or hem it down on the right side. Making the decorative patch into a pocket can be considered only when the tear is in such a position that the pocket will be right on the garment. Short tears can be made into bound pockets, or patch pockets placed over mended rips. Pockets in flower outlines can be placed over the darned tears in a child's dress.

Overcast Patch: Square the hole and snip the corners. Cut your patch ½ inch longer and wider than the hole and join it with a seam. With matching thread, turn this seam and overcast it closely.

Underarm Patch: When a sleeve tears at the underarm, rip the seam a little way so that a square overcast patch can be set in. Snip the seam of the garment above the patch so it will not draw. When a sleeve and underarm are too tight, a band can be set into the seam from the elbow to the waist, or the band can be shorter and tapered into a point at any part of the seam.

Blanket Patch: Cut the patch larger than the hole and square the hole. Pin the patch under the hole and hem the edge of the hole to it, working from the right side. These stitches appear on the wrong side only. Remember—do not turn the edge of the patch, but finish it by catch-stitching the raw edge down. Some people prefer to catch-stitch both edges, and this is preferable in a very heavy blanket.

Patch in Print Fabrics: Whether the garment is a cotton print, shirting, or rayon print, you must match not only the grain of the fabric, as in all patches, but also the design of the print. Examine the pattern of the print you are using to patch with, and mark with pins the sections which correspond in pattern to the hole in the garment. Allow seams in cutting the patch and place it so that the design matches exactly.

Patches Under Torn-out Buttons: A hole left by a torn-out button or fastening requires a double patch for security. Cut a piece of cotton tape or strong cotton fabric big enough to cover the hole and apply the patch. Then turn to the opposite side and apply a similar patch. Sew the button in place.

Patches Under Torn-out Lingerie Straps: If a shoulder strap tears a hole in the garment or pulls out the finish of the edge, repair it in either of the following ways: (1) If you have fabric left, join a patch and refinish the edge in the shape of the edge of the garment. (2) Cut a band of ribbon 1½ inches long, fold it in half, and bind the edge, then hem the ribbon to the garment. The ribbon should extend to the edge of the garment to replace the fabric torn away, and well below the torn edge to reinforce it.

Restyling And Remodeling

Dressmakers' *tricks of restyling and remodeling can give new life to a worn or outmoded outfit—or to one you are merely tired of. Many home sewers think that remodeling always means completely remaking, but frequently some very simple adjustment will give months of wear to a dress which otherwise would have to be discarded.*

When you begin to remodel any garment, first check these three things: style, fit, and condition of fabric.

Checking Style: Consider the garment in relation to current fashion. Study the new color combinations and observe the new lines and trimmings. Discover what fabrics are being combined and contrasted, and how contrasts are being used. From the clothes in stores, pattern catalogues, and fashion magazines, you can not only check fashion details, but often get a new idea you can adapt. If you need additional material, first look in your scrap box for something you can use. If that fails you, buy a remnant.

Checking Fitting: When a garment is in fashion but looks wrong on you, examine the fitting. A complete refitting often restores a dress to usefulness. Try on the garment and check the lines and proportion.

Checking Fabric: When you are considering remodeling, the condition of the fabric is most important. Naturally, it will not pay you to remodel unless the fabric promises to give additional wear. If the surface is rubbed or faded, can it be dyed or reversed? Are there spots and holes in the fabric? If you decide it will not pay to remodel, cut out whatever material is good and save it for future use in remodeling some other garment.

Dressing up a Plain Dress: When you are tired of a dress, or want to dress it up for a special occasion, an easy way to give it a completely new character is to change the neckline. Insert a yoke of lace or net or a draped color contrast. Or a pretty new collar can perk up a too-familiar dress.

SKIRTS

Adjusting the Hem: Probably the most frequently needed alteration is adjusting the hem of a skirt. First rip out the hem and press it on the wrong side. If it has a binding in good condition, save it for future use. Try on the garment as you would for a new hemline and mark the new hem. Turn the edge carefully and hem it in place.

Removing a Mark: When a mark shows after lengthening a hem, treat it by one of the following methods, depending upon the fabric. If it is wool, steam the fabric with a wet press cloth and a hot iron; then brush, using a soft brush on woolens and a stiff one on heavy worsteds. Washing often removes the mark in cottons. In rayons, steam lightly. If the mark still persists, consider covering it with a line of machine stitching, a band of machine stitching, or rows of ribbon or bias trimming.

Lengthening a Hem: When the skirt is too short to turn a new hem at the length you want, consider not only the possibility of a faced hem, but others as well. Can you use a band at the hemline? Stitched bands are decorative, and so are bands of contrasting fabric set on with scallops or squared outlines. Ruching or ruffles can be added around the bottom of the skirt and repeated at neck and sleeves.

In many garments, skirt length can be added at the waistline. In pleated skirts, consider the addition of a yokeline, in matching material if possible. Another waist adjustment is a set-in wide beltline in contrasting fabric. For a woman's suit, consider the possibility of using the self-fabric belt for a set-in belt on the skirt. This will add 2 inches or more.

Skirt Too Full: When a skirt is too wide through the hipline, fit out the extra fullness at each side seam. Rip the seams and try on the garment, wrong side out, fitting the skirt to your figure. Baste the new seams as soon as you take off the garment. Finish the seam the same way it was originally.

Adjusting a Skirt Seam: When a skirt seam is taken in to fit a smaller waist or hip, the placket must be removed and the seam finished as on a new garment—unless, of course, the adjustment can be made in another seam. Then replace the placket as though in a new garment and sew on the fasteners again. A zipper in a placket must be carefully ripped off and reset. In a buttoned placket, it is sometimes possible to move the buttons and make a deeper lap. But if this cannot be done without hurting the line of the skirt, remove the facing with the buttons and buttonholes and adjust the skirt, then replace the facings neatly so that the edge is like new.

Tight Skirts Stretched in Wear: Bagginess in the front or back of a skirt can be adjusted by raising the skirt at the waistline. Stand in front of a mirror with the skirt on and take a little tuck across the waistline, at center back or center front. When the line of the skirt is straightened and the sag removed, the tuck is deep enough. Rip the waistline and take up this amount of material. Your skirt should hang straight. If it does not, rip the side seams and adjust them too.

Concealing a Worn Spot: When a skirt has a tear or a persistent spot, consider the possibility of turning the skirt so that the bad spot can be covered by a pocket. Make the pocket of self-fabric or contrasting fabric as a decoration. Or cover it with a decorative appliqued patch.

DRESS TOO TIGHT

When the dress is too narrow throughout its entire length, you can set in a panel by slashing the front of the garment from hem to neckline. Adjust it to your figure, pinning a piece of paper into the front to serve as the panel, so that you can decide exactly how wide the panel should be. Keep in mind that no more than 2 or 3 inches in finished width can be allowed in the panel or the side seams will not be placed correctly.

Types of Panel: Panels can be overlaid, or inserted. Overlaid panels are of velveteen, velvet, pique, and other firm fabrics, and they may be buttoned to the dress. They can be straight or shaped. Soft panels of rayon crepe in plain fabrics or prints can be gathered or pleated.

To insert panels, face the garment fronts with the contrasting fabric and then cut a plain or print panel wide enough to join the facing 2 or 3 inches back from the edge. A smart version of this alteration is to use an inverted panel which is like an inverted pleat. This makes the finished garment look like a coat dress. The sides of the dress are

A trio of wardrobe modernizers: (1) A tunic top from a too-short dress; (2) a bolero and skirt converted from a dress with a too-snug bodice—new blouse added; (3) figure-flattering redingote was a tight-skirted dress.

joined to cover the panel at the waistline with a buckle or some other decorative fastening which will cover the space between the two sides. If the dress has a low neckline, matching collar and cuffs are attractive.

Bolero: When the skirt is good and the bodice worn or tight, the skirt can be used as a separate unit and the bodice made into a bolero effect. First separate bodice and skirt, then finish the lower edge of the bodice to form a becoming line. Stitch this turn in a hem. If the dress has a buttoned front, it may make an attractive bolero. If the front is straight across, put a basting down the center front and cut on this line. This edge can be faced. If you have no self-fabric, make a print blouse and use the same print for the facing.

Buttonholes: Worn buttonholes in a dress can sometimes be concealed by adding a band over the buttoned edge in a simulated fly closing. Ribbon can be used or a band of fabric made into a trimming. Center the band over the buttons and hem one edge of it to the garment.

SLEEVE PROBLEMS

Refurbishing Outmoded Sleeves: A ruffle to add to the end of a sleeve can be cut without a pattern. First cut a circle of tissue paper, then shape it into a ruffle and try it on against the sleeve before you cut the fabric. Any lightweight fabric can be used. Make the circle in paper the size of the desired ruffle, and cut a small circular hole in the center, big enough to fit the edge of the sleeve. Finish the ruffle with a hand-rolled hem.

Sleeves Torn at Armholes: Sleeves torn out of the back or front of a dress can be put back in a broad armhole. Select a pattern with a broad armhole, or a different type of armhole, which may mean recutting the shoulder seam. In these adjustments it is wise to use a contrasting fabric—it can be the same color and different texture, or a contrasting color, or a print.

Outline the proposed alteration on the dress with basting or a row of pins. This will help you decide what kind of

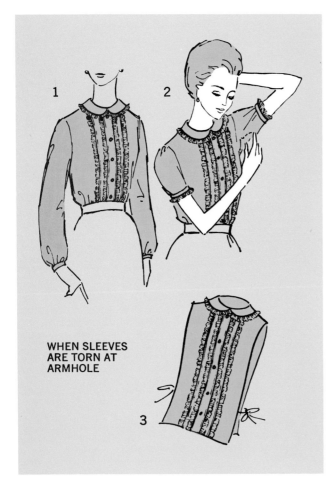

WHEN SLEEVES
ARE TORN AT
ARMHOLE

Add new full sleeves (1), or cut sleeves off (2) and finish the sides for a dickey or vestee.

replacement will be most becoming. If you are inserting a piece without a pattern, measure carefully and cut a paper guide, allowing for seams. Baste the new fabric in place before you cut away the old material underneath.

Sleeves Torn at Underarm: First find out why the underarm tore. Did the fabric tear or split? Is the dress too tight? Is the sleeve too narrow to permit movement? Mending will not overcome the difficulty unless you remove the cause. If the sleeve is too narrow, set in a strip along the entire length. Rip the underarm seam of the sleeve and the blouse; lay the dress fabric over the edge of this new strip of material. The insert should be tapered off, wide in the middle and narrow at the ends.

When you have no matching material, insert a contrasting band from the neck edge to the end of the sleeve. Open the shoulder seam, slash the sleeve, and set in the new band. This will give you extra inches in the neckline and make the blouse a little longer on each side. Stitch very evenly so that the insert looks like a trimming.

Torn Sleeves at Elbow and Underarm: The sleeve can be shortened above the tear and finished with a hem or cuff made from the lower part of the old sleeve. If you want to

keep the long sleeve, you can insert a crosswise band to cover the damage. Decide on the width of the band; you may prefer 2 or 3 narrower bands of different colors, and insert it or sew it on top of the sleeve. Use self-fabric, harmonizing texture or contrasting color repeated in the trimming of the dress. Rip the underarm seam of the sleeve, lay it flat, and apply the band or bands. Shape the ends of the bands to follow the side edges of the sleeves. Baste it in place and try on the sleeve before you stitch it.

RECUTTING A GARMENT

Combining Two Garments: One or more smart new garments can sometimes be made out of several old ones. For instance, a plain woolen dress can be combined with a print or an old crepe dress with a satin, or two plain fabrics that are opaque and harmonize in texture can be combined. Velvet or velveteen can be used as a jacket with a wool or crepe dress.

Making Two New Dresses Out of Three Old Ones: Illustrated here are three garments: a plaid dress with a badly fitting blouse, worn lower sleeves, and a tight hipline, (the skirt is in good condition); an old solid-color dress with worn armholes and sleeves, in which the skirt was too tight and too short; and an outgrown shirtwaist dress with badly fitting waist.

The solid-color dress was used to make a long top for the plaid skirt (thus raising its hipline). A trim was added from the sleeves of the plaid dress to bind the neckline and the armholes. This made one new dress.

The bodice of the shirtwaist dress was ripped off the skirt, and a smart vest added, made out of the plaid bodice. (The plaid bodice was ripped and pressed flat, and a new vest pattern was used.)

A major alternation pays only when the fabric is in good condition. First the garment should be cleaned—washed if possible. If it cannot be washed, remove soiled spots. (See Index).

Ripping: Careful ripping is important. Find a thread in the seam which can be pulled, or clip a thread and pull it out a few stitches at a time until it breaks. Then turn the garment and pull the thread again, and so on until no threads are left in the seams. If you rip with sharp scissors or a razor blade, you may nick the fabric edge. Every piece of the garment must be ripped, and each piece must be pressed. To remove the lines of the old stitching, dampen the edges of the fabric before you press.

Patterns: Select a pattern to help you in recutting all or part of the garment. There are always fashions which adapt themselves to remodeling plans, and frequently you can find one which exactly fits your requirements. Make a little diagram of the pieces of the garment and put the actual measurements of each piece on the diagram. Such a diagram helps in choosing the pattern, for you can compare the cutting diagrams of the patterns with your diagram of what you have to work with.

Fabrics: In pattern books, many garments combine two fabrics. Look for them when you are considering a remake. There may be one which solves your particular problem. When a little extra fabric is needed, consider new material. Sometimes you will have remnants which match or contrast, sometimes you will have material left over from some other dress which can be used. If not, consider using another garment and combining the two.

Fabrics which contrast successfully must be considered for texture interest as well as for color and design. In plain fabrics the choice of a contrasting fabric in either a print or contrasting plain color is simple. Don't overlook the possibilities of texture contrasts by using a shiny-surfaced satin with crepe, or velveteen with wool, or a transparent fabric with a cotton print.

Jumpers: They are easy to make from any kind of dress in which there is enough good fabric. Jumpers can be worn by women and girls of all ages for many different occasions. When made with a long skirt or of a luxurious material, they are suitable for all but the most formal occasions.

How to Cut a Jumper: When the sleeve, underarm, or neck edge of a dress is worn, and the dress is otherwise becoming and in style, cut the armhole in the deep open styling of a jumper. Stand before a mirror and place a row of pins, following the line which seems most becoming. Place another row of pins at the neck edge, outlining a V, an open-front slash, or a deep U. Before you cut, verify these edges. Is the pin line alike on both sides? Is the curve exactly the same on both sides? Are you sure you are not cutting away too much fabric? When all of these questions have been settled, make a basting on the cutting line, placing it far enough outside the pin line to allow for a seam. Make a row of machine stitching on the cutting line and then cut. The edge can be faced or bound.

COTTON GARMENTS

Dresses and Shirts: Good cotton garments with fast color often wear at the underarm and sleeve when the rest of the garment is in good condition. Add a new yoke or sleeve in matching or contrasting colors. If you have a dress which is too tight, insert a band down the front with a tailored finish. If the buttonholes are worn out, cut off this section entirely and put in a new band of fabric and make new buttonholes. If the dress is too short, add a yoke or band to the skirt and use the same fabric to trim the collars and cuffs. When a dress or a man's shirt cannot be mended and there is enough material, combine the two into a new apron, or sunsuits for a child.

Men's and Boys' Shirts: Worn collars should be carefully removed and turned over, then sewn back in the original seam. In the case of small-patterned materials or solid colors, new collars and cuffs can be made. Rip the old ones off entirely, press them flat, and use them as patterns for the new ones, which can often be cut from the tail of the shirt without impairing its usefulness. In a striped shirt it is

When making two new dresses out of three old ones, choose colors and textures that combine properly.

not possible to do this without destroying the shirt; if new collars and cuffs are added, make them of new material which matches the background color of the shirt.

WOOLEN GARMENTS

Remaking woolen garments, especially the heavier fabrics used in coats, is an important economy in the family budget. Sweaters and underwear as well as outer clothing can be remade into attractive garments. The first paper pattern, created by Mrs. Butterick in 1862, was a pattern for remaking men's suits into small boys' trousers. Remodeling father's and older brothers' suits is still a useful practice. Although Mrs. Butterick knew nothing about tailored leggings there is no reason why your children shouldn't have leggings and coat, made from a man's tweed suit. Remodel a man's suit into a woman's suit. The skirt is made from the trousers, and the jacket preserves the most important tailoring details of the coat.

Uses for Old Coats: A coat may have fashionable lines even though the fabric is faded. Examine the wrong side. It may be unfaded and the coat can be turned. At least it can be used to make new garments. If you have a skirt which harmonizes with the coat material, make a jacket.

Shortening a Coat Hem: Rip the lining from the facing on the bottom of the coat, then rip both the hem of the lining and the coat hem. Adjust the correct length for the coat, marking it just as you do in a dress. Mark the new place for the facing, then mark the new line for hem and facing by putting pins in the marked line at right angles to it. Cut it to 1½ or 2 inches, using a measure. Then shrink out any additional fullness. Pink the raw edges, run a machine stitching close to the edge, and catch-stitch it in place; or bind the hem edge. The hem of the lining should be 1 inch shorter than the coat hem.

Shortening Coat Sleeves: Free the lining from the sleeve fabric and lower the hem. Mark the desired length and check for evenness. Baste the turning, then press it. Trim the hem to 2 inches or less; catch-stitch it in place. Baste the lining to the sleeve about ½ inch to 1 inch from the edge of the sleeve and slip-stitch it into place.

Worn Buttonholes: If the buttonholes are worn beyond repair, or if the overlapping edge of the coat is shabby, apply a facing of contrasting fabric or a wide strip of fur, which can be purchased by the yard. A fur strip should be applied with a felling stitch and can be used all the way down the front. Either use braid loops for the buttons, or take off the buttons and use tailor-bound hooks and eyes (large metal fasteners covered with a fine braid which can be purchased at any trimming store) which will not show when the coat is closed.

Worn buttonholes can be rebound with a piece of fabric from the end of the belt or the hem. Undo all the old stitching or binding and proceed as for new buttonholes.

When repair is not possible, you may overcast the opening of the buttonholes so that the garment looks unbroken and put new large buttons—perhaps fur—over each buttonhole. Remove the buttons from the other side of the coat and replace them with tailor-bound hooks and eyes.

Worn Coat Sleeves: A narrow strip of fabric or fur down the entire length of the sleeve and over the shoulder seams to the neckline will disguise a worn spot at the elbow. If a cuff edge or sleeve hem is shabby, it is often possible to rip the edge and bend it back a bit so that no worn edge shows, and slip-stitch it to the lining. When this is not possible, you may be able to salvage material from the skirt hem or pocket to make a false hem or cuff.

Worn Pocket Edges and Flaps: Take off a worn flap and finish the pocket edges without it, or with a strip of fur placed along the lower edge. If you do this, use fur trimming somewhere else in the garment. If a piece of matching material can be salvaged, the pocket can be rebound.

Collars: Collars can be turned by ripping the seam which holds the collar in place. Reverse the collar, turn it over, and replace it. Baste it before sewing and try it on to see that the collar fits properly around the neck. Or a new collar of contrasting material or fur can be sewn on top of the old one; in that case the trimming can be extended down the front edge of the coat.

Lengthening a Coat: If it is not possible to let down the hem, a band of fur can be added to the bottom of the coat. Be sure to line this band. A bit of fur should be placed elsewhere on the coat when the band is used—at the edge of the collar, cuffs, on buttons, or pockets. If the hem can be let down, rip it out, press the fabric, and mark and turn a new hem like the old one.

Mending Coat Lining: A coat lining usually wears out first under the arms. If you have some scraps of lining material or matching fabric, make underarm shields and put them in. The shields should be inserted so that they extend down into the sleeves as well as under the arm. Match the center seams in the shield and armhole and sew the shield flat to the lining.

The sleeve edge and the neckline are other trouble spots. The best way to mend the sleeve edges is to make a neat patch over the lining. At the neck, where a patch might show, use a harmonizing fabric and make a patch which suggests a yoke.

Worn seams can be covered with harmonizing braid.

Men's and Boys' Clothing: Only minor alterations are possible on men's and boys' clothing. Hems may be lowered to within ¼ inch of their full extent and a small piece of matching lining added to join with the old. Remove the line of the old hem by pressing with a damp cloth and hot iron.

TAKING OFF AN ALTERED GARMENT

After the alterations have been pinned, take the garment off carefully so that the pins are not lost. Put it on a table and run a basting thread through the seams. Clip the thread from time to time and separate your seam. There should be little threads marking the seam on both sides. Then turn the garment to the wrong side and straighten out the fitting, which means basting the seams straight, ignoring any little irregularities in the pinned line. In necklines, panels, and so forth, fold the garment to make sure both sides are alike. Alterations on the sides need not be made alike, because most figures are not quite the same and the alterations should be different.

Before you stitch the garment, check your alterations. In quick alterations the old stitched seams remain and the new ones are run up beside them; in good alterations the old seams are ripped, the new ones are stitched, and the excess material is cut away.

Part IV

SEWING FOR YOUR HOME

It Pays To Plan
Know Your Fabrics
Successful Slipcovers
Window Decor
Draperies And Valances
Measuring And Estimating
Making Curtains
Spreads And Covers
Quilts And Quilting
Decor Accessories
Family Fun Rooms

It Pays To Plan

*A **well-planned** room is lovely to enter and pleasant to live in because it is held together—made into a unified whole—by the proper use of color in textiles. With a few yards of carefully chosen fabrics and a little work, any woman can transform a dreary thrown-together room into a place of cheer and beauty. It is simply a question of planning—not money. Whether the whole house needs refurnishing, or only a few replacements are necessary, it costs nothing to consider color and balance in the fabrics.*

Good planning does not depend upon the size of the budget. If the budget is ample, a plan can be put into effect immediately; if it is not, the plan can be extended over a period of time, doing a little at a time. This chapter outlines a simple planning program which can be set into the routine for any room in any home. Curtains, hangings, slipcovers, and cushions can be chosen with forethought according to the rules of proportion and harmony. These supplement redecorating and redoing furniture.

Begin by appraising your own problem. This is easier to do just after you have been away for a time. Come into your house and look at it as critically as though you were a stranger. Make a list of everything you would like to change; then make another list of ideas for making the family more comfortable. Review the lists carefully, scratching out those items which are obviously beyond reason. The result will be a list of pointed suggestions which describe your need and give you a definite objective.

Make another list, of the colors which must remain in the room. Note the colors of the wood in the furniture, the upholstery, the rug, the walls, and the woodwork. List all the colors, no matter how many, and whenever possible pin a little swatch to your list which approximates the color. If the rug or upholstery is multicolored, note both the predominating color and the most important contrasting color.

Don't shop for fabrics at once. Do a little window-shopping and magazine-browsing first. Search for the new ideas in decorating and appraise them in relation to your needs. Put price out of your mind for the moment. When you look at a model room, note what textiles are used and how. Note also how contrasting colors are used. Answer these questions for each display: How often is the print repeated? How often is white or a pale tone introduced? What kind of textile interest or stripe is contrasted to the print? How are trimming touches introduced in slipcovers, bedspreads, curtains, lampshades? What pillow cushions are in the room?

Don't dismiss a model room with the thought, "I can't afford anything like this!" Look at it and glean ideas from it. Look at the length of the curtains and the fullness in them; look at the type of valance and the curtain headings. There is a great difference in the amount of fullness in curtains you can buy and those you can make at home for the same price. One fine decorator advises everyone to buy cheaper fabrics in abundance rather than costly ones.

List the ideas you have gathered together and see how many of them you can use in your room. Perhaps you can rearrange the furniture. You may want to reproportion the windows. You may decide to rearrange the small pieces in new groupings. Forget the things you saw which you can't afford and give your attention to those which cost nothing and those within your means. At this point your decision should be made about the kind of textile to use in decoration—a print, a geometric design, a stripe, a brocade, a textured fabric, or a crisp cotton.

CHOOSING A PREDOMINATING ROOM COLOR

A successful plan based on the colors already in the room can be developed immediately if you know exactly what you want. If not, develop several plans from which later you can choose the one you like best.

Choose a print, stripe, or textured fabric which is correlated with your rug and upholstery for each plan. A print or stripe exactly the color of the rug can often be found; sometimes there are several of them from which to choose. Pin a sample of each to a piece of paper and start a color chart. On each color chart pin a plain-textured fabric which matches the color of the predominating design; then to each pin a white or pale tint matching the background of the prints or stripes.

A tailored treatment for a bedroom-study. Braid-edged bands on the spread, chair seat, window shades, and draperies lend a design accent to an absolutely uncluttered room that a man would especially appreciate.

Left: An unusual piece of furniture or a fine collection of bibelots can be the eye-catching feature around which you plan the room.

Opposite: Well-proportioned valances and draperies can create an elegant background at comparatively little cost when you sew them yourself.

Below: The professional's flair for combining a variety of patterns—florals with plaids, for example—is shown in this exciting contemporary bedroom.

Below: Strong verticals are repeated throughout this modern living room to lead the eye up and lend height.

Five fabulous ways to make your sewing area into a well-designed studio, an integral part of your home's interior design. Whether your overall effect is modern or traditional, your redecorating budget small or large, take a tip from these beautiful examples of how much can be done within a limited area.

Carpet Color	Wall Color	Drapery Color	Dominant Upholstery Color	Secondary Upholstery Color
Beige to Brown	Beige or Ivory	Apricot	Brown	Green
	Blue	Rose	Burgundy	Blue
	Green	Gold or Beige	Cedar	Green
	Peach	Green	Cedar	Gold or Beige
	Rose	Turquoise	Burgundy	Beige
Blue	Beige or Ivory	Rose	Burgundy	Beige
	Blue	Apricot	Brown	Beige
	Apricot	Beige	Cedar	Blue
	Rose	Blue	Violet	Beige
	Grey	Rose	Burgundy	Gold or Beige
Wines	Beige or Ivory	Green	Gold	Wine
	Blue	Oyster	Blue	Gold
	Green	Wine	Gold	Green
	Rose	Turquoise	Gold	Beige
	Grey	Rose	Blue	Violet
Green	Beige or Ivory	Green	Cedar	Beige or Gold
	Green	Apricot	Cedar	Beige or Gold
	Apricot	Beige	Brown	Cedar
	Rose	Green	Violet	Grey
	Grey	Apricot	Green	Gold
Apricot	Beige or Ivory	Green	Brown	Cedar
	Blue	Beige	Cedar	Gold
	Green	Cedar	Green	Beige
	Apricot	Beige	Blue	Gold
	Grey	Apricot	Green	Brown
Rose	Beige or Ivory	Violet	Turquoise	Beige
	Blue	Oyster	Violet	Blue
	Green	Rose	Violet	Gold
	Rose	Blue	Burgundy	Oyster
	Grey	Violet	Turquoise	Oyster
Turquoise	Beige or Ivory	Apricot	Brown	Beige
	Rose	Beige	Violet	Blue
	Apricot	Turquoise	Cedar	Beige
	Turquoise	Gold	Violet	Beige
	Grey	Rose	Burgundy	Beige

Next, choose the second most prominent color in each print or stripe and match this in a plain fabric and pin it to the chart. For a large room look for a stripe and a print in the same colorings which can be combined.

Put each chart in a separate pocket of a shoebag or expanding file folder, and slip into the pockets' pictures clipped from magazines in any detail of room decoration or arrangement which interests you. To each pocket add a sample labeled "accent color," a color to be used in the trimmings of curtains, lampshades, slipcovers; and in such accessories as pictures, table mats, pottery, and ashtrays.

This kind of color plan helps even for simple rooms —kitchen, children's rooms, playroom, et cetera. The assortment of samples helps you to work out more interesting trimmings and details which give your finished product a more professional look.

When you have your working color plan completed, the next step is a practical shopping list. Compare prices and replace samples of color fabrics with a fabric within your price range. When you know exactly the type of curtains and slipcovers you want, you can estimate yardages exactly and thus save money. In deciding on the best styles and types for curtains and slipcovers you must take into consideration the proportions of your room.

Harmonizing Room Proportions: Good proportions are as important to the success of your plan as good colors. It is wise, then, to analyze the proportions of your room before you decide on the proportions of your draperies and curtains.

Make a list of those things which influence proportion. Begin with the measurements of the room, in feet. Note the ceiling—is it high or low? Set down any irregularities, such as a bay window, an alcove, a fireplace. List the doors and draw little plans of the windows without curtains. Make a diagram to show the proportions of the windows in relation to the walls.

Next consider the large pieces of furniture in relation to the room. Can a piano, a bookcase, a secretary, be moved into an alcove? Can the sofa and chairs be grouped for conversation or coziness? Can space be made for a game table in a far corner? These are typical questions to apply to a living room, but they illustrate the point of balance between room and furniture, which must be applied to all the rooms in the house. Once you understand defects in the proportions of room and furniture, you can use textiles to disguise them.

Ceilings: The higher the ceiling, the more formal the room; the lower the ceiling, the more cozy and informal the room. High ceilings make a small room look smaller. To make a high-ceilinged room look less formal, plan tie-back draperies and slipcovers which touch the floor. To make a low-ceilinged room look higher, plan straight-hanging

draperies and make slipcovers as short as possible so that the chair legs show.

Windows: Must they be curtained separately or are they so placed that they can be curtained in a group? Think of windows, not as separate items, but in relation to the room as a whole. Remember short tie-back curtains lend a note of informality to the room; long straight ones, amply full, denote comfort and luxury, while tall slender curtains are formal. Many modern rooms use a textile hanging across the entire side of a room. These wall hangings are plain where they cover the side wall and finished with a heading simulating a drapery and valance where they cross the windows. They hang from ceiling to floor. They can be made in plain homespun, textured rayon, chintz, prints, or any fabric which is not transparent. It is an inexpensive way to add new interest to a room.

Long curtains which sweep the floor for 10 or 12 inches add formality to the room. They can be headed with a valance, a valance board, or a French-pleated heading.

When you have considered the relationship between your windows and the room and furniture, decide upon whether you want long or short, straight or tie-back curtains. Then it is time to decide upon the specific style of your curtains, considering your fabric, the window, and the furnishings.

Room Furnishings: After the window treatment is chosen, consider the other textile furnishings. Slipcovers, bedspreads, dressing-table skirts, and table covers are developed either to repeat the curtain or drapery fabric, or to pick up the contrasting color which breaks the monotony of an all-print room. The style of each furnishing is correlated in type as well as in color. If your room is plain and simple, confine your desire for frills to such little accessories as lampshades and cushions. In your other room furnishings carry out the tailored or luxury theme. Decide upon the type of slipcovers, curtains, or bedspreads suited to your need—pin a picture of each to the color chart.

Odd Pieces of Furniture: When an odd piece of furniture is out of harmony with the room, consider the following remedies: (1) Can it be cut down? If it is too tall, particularly old tables and chests, it is often possible simply to have it cut down lower. (2) Can it be covered with a slipcover? Old-fashioned wooden chairs can be covered with loose slipcovers and so brought into harmony with any room. Sometimes superfluous fancywork has to be cut off the top of the chair. If the woodwork of the chair is attractive, consider a slipcover which will show it. (3) Can it be painted to match the wall color? This is the remedy for mantelpieces and furniture which cannot be covered. Those the same color as the wall are less conspicuous.

Room Accessories: Like dress accessories, room accessories make or break a well-planned effect. This does not imply that your accessories must be radically changed; but it does often mean eliminating and replacing over a period of time.

First decide which of the three policies described here are best suited to you. (1) Correlated accessories, each one carrying out an accent color. (2) The little things you love to have around you correlated with the room furnishings. This includes photographs and all types of knicknacks. They can be framed in groups, placed in wall brackets, and made a definite part of the decoration. (3) The trophy type of room, where the color scheme and plan of decoration is built around the trophies. In this case the trophies must be arranged in the room and listed as room furniture when you make your plans for color, type of curtains, and room furnishings. Children's trophies and current interests should be treated this way. If the child collects photographs, put a bulletin board over his desk to save the wall. Put a sectional bookcase in the children's room and let them display their collections proudly.

Accent Color: All trimming details can be developed in accent colors—pipings, edgings on curtains, tie-backs, and so forth. Lampshades and scrap baskets can be correlated with the room by (1) trimming them with bands or bows made from scraps of your material, or (2) by making your lampshades out of your printed fabrics, or (3) covering scrap baskets with leftover pieces, or (4) developing cushions in an accent color.

CO-ORDINATING YOUR COLOR PLAN

You have selected the predominating colors, added contrasting and accent colors, and made notes of the types of curtains and room furnishings best suited to the proportions of your room. You have various assortments of these colors and types collected with your color plan, and now it is time to review them and test them for practicability.

The first step is to lay out the different types so they are grouped together, and all the groups close enough to compare. Imagine yourself living in each of these rooms or color schemes. Which is the kind of background you would really like to live in?

When you have finally chosen the scheme you like best, it is time to decide how much you can spend and how you can get the best fabric available for what you can afford. If you go shopping with a definite plan for colors and types, you will not be tempted by a bargain unsuited to your room. You will search out a bargain which suits it ideally, because you know exactly what you want. The time spent in making the plan will repay you many times over when you begin to shop.

Know Your Fabrics

Home *sewers naturally put color and decorative value first in choosing a fabric for the home; but the wise woman expects serviceability as well as beauty in every yard of fabric.*

Textile designers supply a group of living room fabrics, printed, striped, and textured, which permit color harmonies in one room without using too much of any one textile. As you search for ideas, look particularly for textiles which harmonize in a single room and notice how textures of different types complement each other. The correct use of the fabric, as well as the correct use of color, has much to do with the success of your room.

Brocades, boucles, matelasse, jacquard weaves, chintzes, and satin contribute richness and elegance to rooms in Sheraton, Queen Anne, Hepplewhite, and Chippendale periods.

Modern rooms call for linens, novelty cottons, taffetas, velvet, and such familiar names as scrim, cotton, and unbleached muslin, all too often ignored.

In Early American rooms, homespun effects with self-patterns woven in designs or stripes, combined with quaint patterned chintzes, are very effective.

Fabrics designed for bedrooms feature small prints, ribbon stripes, and designs totally different from those in living-room prints. Both colors and fabrics help to create the kind of bedroom you want. Early American furniture in the bedroom calls for chintz and muslin, and the frilled white curtain is deeply rooted in this tradition. Feminine bedrooms are full of frills made from taffeta or organdy. Luxurious bedrooms feature satin, chiffon, velvet, and the modern developments in transparent fabrics.

Gingham, calico, voile, and other novelty cottons are used in the kitchen and nursery. Houses built in the Victorian style feature today's version of the lace curtain.

CONSIDERATIONS IN CHOOSING FABRICS

Serviceability: Draperies, curtains and slipcovers can often be made of the same material, such as chintz, cretonne, sateen, velveteen, and corduroy. When you make this combination, be sure to pick a fabric which can withstand wear.

Slipcovers get harder wear and soil more easily than window treatments, and therefore it is well to keep in mind how much the fabric will show dirt. Smooth-surface fabrics will not show soil so quickly. Fabrics with a nap and a soft weave, such as monk's cloth and homespun, gather more dust than do denims, mohairs, and other smooth-surface cottons and nylons.

Women who live in smoky cities should avoid the extremes of pale and dark colors; they should choose clear, intense shades. They should give preference to smooth fabrics which can be dusted or wiped and avoid those which demand brushing. They should avoid fringes and small headings which cannot be dusted.

Above: Three beautiful swatches of the kinds of patterns from which today's home decorators can choose. Remember to check on the availability of the same or coordinated patterns in papers and linens for additional decorating touches.

Opposite: The lesson here is the importance of blending lines—curved ones with angular, straight with softly flowing.

Opposite: Strong patterns can be especially effective in comparatively small areas.
Below: Choose a fantastic fabric for an important window or wall treatment.

Budgetary Considerations: If, when you buy your material, you are cautioned that the one you selected has to be dry-cleaned, stop and consider what that will mean to your budget before you make the final decision. Fortunately the modern trend in fabrics for the home is toward washable materials. But ask your questions about washability carefully. A material colorfast to washing is not always colorfast to sun. You will find your answer on the label or the selvage. If the label says "washable," keep on looking for the comment on sunfastness. Sunfast tests are made for temperate zones. If you live in the tropics, avoid colors unless extra proof of their durability is offered.

When you consider a fabric, decide whether your household routine and your budget can take care of it as it should be taken care of. If it is washable, make sure you have the essentials for washing it correctly. For instance, some fabrics have to be stretched every time they are washed. Have you a stretcher and a place to use it? Or would you rather substitute a fabric which can be washed and then ironed? Many formal overdraperies can be washed; others must be dry-cleaned. Some can be washed only if they are not lined.

If your budget forbids the expense of dry cleaning your draperies, see that the stiffening or buckram in the valance is as washable as the draperies. Be sure that any trimming used on a washable fabric is color-fast and washable.

In analyzing and comparing prices, take into consideration the fabrics which give extra service, such as a permanent starched finish which assures that the curtain will always be fresh and new. Let the developments of modern science save you work; the additional cost is negligible.

Blended Fabrics: Rayons and wool fabrics are labeled by law, and the labels tell of amazing blends: cotton mixed with rayon, rayon mixed with wool, all-nylon, nylon-and-wool and various man-made fibers. Nylon, for example, is created to last. It is naturally tough and pliable, and can take an immense amount of wear and tear. In upholstery fabrics

this extra wear means real value. Normally, moths and other insects will not attack nylon fabrics. Shoppers who buy what look like bargains without inquiring for the facts about wear-ability are the ones who have troubles when their curtains and slipcovers are washed or cleaned. It is impossible to see quality in a fabric; you must read the labels to ascertain the facts about color and shrinkage.

Coated Fabrics: Many fabrics are finished with chemicals and coatings which render service—for instance, giving a starchless crispness to organdy, marquistette, and so on. Because this chemical penetrates the fibers and is as fast as the dye, it stays through the life of the fabric. Always ask whether the coating on a fabric penetrates, or whether it is just on the surface, as in glazed chintz. The first washing of a glazed chintz removes the coating unless the chintz is labeled washable. When the fabric is finished with a chemical, the label tells you how to care for it. Fiberglass is excellent for long-wearing sheer curtains.

Summer Fabrics: For summer months or for life in the tropics, the homemaker should consider linens and cottons for her slipcovers. They look fresh and starched, and they are cool to sit on. Curtains should be functional and shut out the sun. In the tropics, pongee, linen, grass linen, and homespun are used for this purpose. Unbleached muslin can be tailored and arranged to be taken down and sent to the laundry. Transparent fabrics give a cool effect, but they are not actually cool fabrics. Glazed chintzes, cottons, and smooth fabrics are cool when they are selected in cool colors.

Winter Fabrics: Warm fabrics can be elegant or informal. If you change your draperies and slipcovers from summer to winter dress, not only make a change in the color harmony of the room, but also select a fabric which suggests warmth. Napped fabrics, ribbed fabrics, and rough-textured fabrics combine to make a room look warm.

Successful Slipcovers

lipcovers were originally designed for protection, but they are now part of the decorating scheme. They can be used to conceal bad proportions and to modernize a piece of furniture. They should contrast with the rug coloring and harmonize with the color of the room. A good plan is to have one or more slipcovers to match the draperies. If the draperies are print, another slipcover should repeat in plain color one of the colors of the print. With white ruffled curtains, striped and flowered slipcovers can be used. In rooms with colorful wallpaper, slipcovers can be striped or made of textured fabrics in solid color.

This chapter gives complete instructions for making four types of slipcovers: an easy-to-make slipcover, a professional slipcover with tailored boxing, an upholstery slipcover which makes the chair look as though it had been upholstered, and a "petticoat" slipcover.

ORDER OF PROCEDURE

1. Decide on the type of cover you wish to make and list all the style details.
2. Measure the chair and estimate yardage.
3. Plot your fabric or cut a muslin pattern. Cut fabric or pattern on the chair.
4. Fit the cover to the chair, one piece at a time. Cover back and seat first, then front edge below seat and sides.
5. Pin and fit the long seams.
6. Gather and fit all rounded shaped edges and bands.
7. Set trimmings into seams.
8. Pin all joinings.
9. Prepare the skirt or lower banding.
10. Press the skirt and apply it, or join lower banding.
11. Finish side opening and cover cushions.
12. Press slipcover.

CHOOSING THE FABRIC

Select your fabric not only for its beauty but also for its serviceable qualities. Inssist upon preshrunk fabrics, and avoid soft weaves which hold dust. Smooth surfaced fabrics shed dust and stay clean much longer. In very dusty cities, prints are preferable and strong colors give better wear.

Choose firmly-woven fabrics such as glazed chintz, cretonne, mohair, linen, and the sturdy cotton reps. Plain fabrics cut to best advantage, but for allover designs you need allow only ¼ yard more. However, in a fabric with motifs or a repeated design which must be centered on the back of the chair and each arm, you will need at least a yard extra for matching the pattern. When your curtains have a large floral figure in the print, consider making the slipcover of plain fabric in one of the colors of the print, then cutting out a floral print design and appliqueing it to the center back of a chair and the cushions of a couch.

The proportions of a slipcover, except for the length of the flounce, are controlled by the measurements of the chair. You are really putting a new skin on the chair. Decide whether you want a loose or a tight fit; decide upon the length, the type of cover, and the trimming details.

Soften the shape and improve the comfort of a favorite area by using beautiful slipcovers. Here, the charming window shade carries the accent too.

Opposite: Making a slipcover is possible for chairs of almost any shape—though covering a wing chair is not a project for a beginner.

ESTIMATING YARDAGE FOR SLIPCOVERS

Determining the yardage necessary to cover a certain type of chair in a certain width of fabric is very difficult unless you use an accurate measuring chart. The rule is to take the length measurements so that you know how much yardage is required to go over the chair, from the floor in front to the floor in back. When the fabric is wide and the chair small, you can often cover the sides of the chair or cut ruffles or pleats out of the excess fabric from this one length. When the fabric is narrow or the chair large, you must buy twice or three times the length.

Make a list of all the details you will use in your slipcover—including the style of skirt and the trimming. When welting is used in the seams, you must estimate the yardage both of the cord and of the bias strips of self-fabric which will cover the cord.

Remove the cushion from the chair seat when you take your measurements. The estimate for yardage is made the same way, whether you cover a small chair or a large sofa.

Length Measurements: The total of the following measurements is the length of the fabric yardage: (1) front from floor to chair seat; (2) front across chair seat, plus 3 inches; (3) front back from chair seat to top, including width of top; (4) back from top to floor.

Width Measurements: The width measurements are: (5) width across front of chair; (6) width across seat, plus 3 inches; (7) width across back of seat; (8) width across front back of chair; (9) height of arm inside, plus 3 inches; (10) width of arm outside; (11) width of arm inside; (12) length of arm outside to floor; (13) bands around chair.

Consider the longest width measure in relation to the width of the fabric and find out whether the sides can be covered from the extra width of one length of fabric, or whether you must buy an extra length.

Type of Fabric: If the fabric is plain, your final estimate will be the amount you buy; if it is striped, you will need a little extra for centering and matching stripes. Allow at least a yard for this in covering an overstuffed chair. When the fabric has a large floral design which must be centered, see whether you can use the side yardage from these pieces for ruffles or a pleated skirt, or for the bias covering of the welting.

Estimating Welting: First measure the seams which will be welted. This gives the yardage for the cording, but allow ½ yard extra for joinings if the cord is not in one piece. To estimate the amount of fabric needed to cover the cord, figure as follows: From ¾ yard of material, bias strips 1½ inches wide can be cut in these amounts: from 36-inch material 25 yards, from 50-inch material 34 yards.

ESTIMATING YARDAGE FOR SEAT CUSHIONS

Measure the top of the cushion at the widest (14) and narrowest width (15); measure the length (16) of the cushion. Then (17) measure the cushion all around and (18) its depth. Allow 2-inch seams all around.

Decide now whether the bottom of the cushion and the seat of the chair will be covered with the fabric of the slipcover or with an inexpensive lining fabric.

MAKING A SLIPCOVER

Before you cut your fabric, drape it over the chair. Let it lie in front of the chair and pull one end up over the top, across the seat, and down as far as you want the finished cover to go in back. Push the fabric down to the back of the cushion and tuck it into the sides of the chair so you can see the effect. If the design is patterned, center the pattern in both seat cushion and back cover. If it is striped, center the stripe and decide whether you will have the cross sections

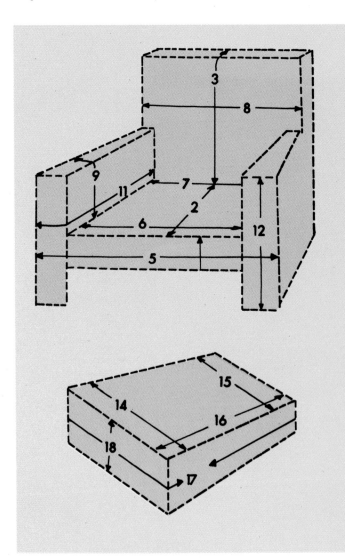

on the arm running parallel to the back or at right angles.

If the seams are to be welted the fabric must be fitted on the *right side*. If they are double stitched upholstery or plain seams the fabric must be fitted on the *wrong side*.

Slipcovers which are frequently removed as you work on the seams, as professionals do, and those made from a tested prefitted pattern, should have the seam lines marked with a colored pencil. Otherwise cut fabric away as you work.

Easy-to-Make Slipcovers: First pin the fabric to the chair around the edges of the back so the pins mark a seam line at the edge, corresponding with the seaming on the chair upholstery. The covering of the back must extend down to the chair seat. Pin it in place. If the cushion is not removable, press the fabric down; if it is removable, take the cushion out. In both cases cut off the fabric at back of the seat. Now cut a piece to fit the seat. Cover the seat of the chair with lining under a removable cushion. This lining is attached to all the edges which go into the seat. It must be smoothly fitted but not strained. It should be faced across

the front edge for 2 or 3 inches of fabric so it does not show when the cushion is in place.

Then analyze the shape of your chair. In some chairs you you can extend a band from the front up the arms, across the arms, up the side of the chair, and across the top. In other chairs the natural seamline is at the far edge of the roll. In these chairs the front is often shaped and must be fitted with a shaped piece. (See "Fitting Details" later in this chapter for hard-to-fit chairs.) Fit the fabric smoothly over the arms, tucking the ends well down into the sides of the chair. Fit the pieces over the arms and join them to the back section so that you can tuck the fabric well into any section of the chair when the seam is pinned. When the seam falls on a hard surface it must be fitted closely. A curved edge often has to be gathered to fit smoothly.

Consider the best place for the opening—either center back or side back—and decide how you will finish the opening, with snap tape, a zipper, or ties. In bedroom chairs, the slipcover can often be fitted without an opening.

Turn to the rear of the chair. Cut the back section. Pin it in place so that it joins the edge of the front section. Once

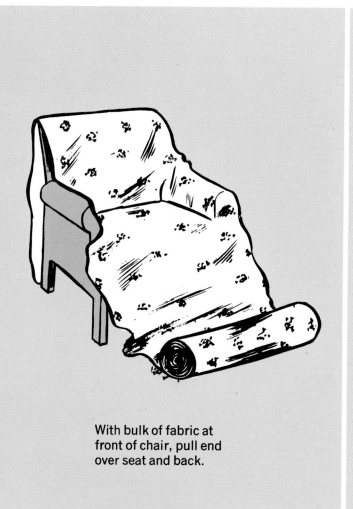

With bulk of fabric at front of chair, pull end over seat and back.

Fit the back with a single piece of fabric.

Leave an opening at the back for snaps or zipper.

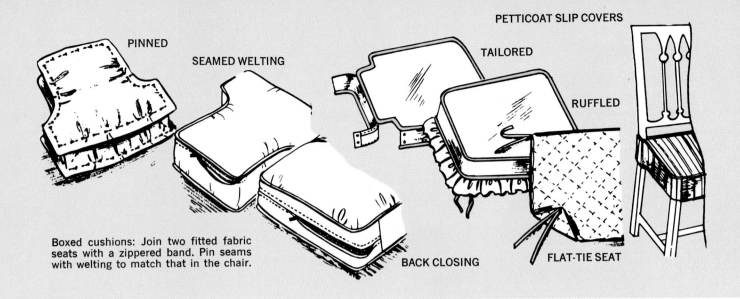

PETTICOAT SLIP COVERS

PINNED

SEAMED WELTING

TAILORED

RUFFLED

BACK CLOSING

FLAT-TIE SEAT

Boxed cushions: Join two fitted fabric seats with a zippered band. Pin seams with welting to match that in the chair.

this seam is pinned, you can cut away the extra fabric on the side of the back section for use in other parts of the chair.

Then fit the fabric across each side of the chair under the arms from the back of the chair to the front. These edges join the back, the end at the roll top of the arms, and the shaped front edge. Often you can cut a strip extending across the front of the chair and across each side, making a boxed effect.

Decide on the length of the skirt, measuring up from the floor and placing a row of pins around the chair. The finished skirt should cover all the upholstery of the chair. Decide on the finished length of the slip cover from the floor and the length of the skirt. Then you are ready to seam your slipcover. Check your seam fitting and prepare to baste seams for stitching or to open them for trimming details such as welting. Do not remove the slipcover from the chair until the trimming is inserted and all seams are basted.

Professional Slipcovers: The boxed slipcover with welt seams and a box-pleated skirt is the most popular cover among professional upholsterers.

First he places his fabric on the chair and sets the design, if any, so that the stripe or pattern is centered. Next he decides on the length of the skirt. He begins by shaping the boxing at the front of the chair, pulling the fabric smoothly over the seat, and pinning the apron, or front banding, in place. This work is done on the right side of the fabric, and every seam is folded ¾ inch so that it can be basted for a welt.

He chalks the line where the seam will be placed, and chalks the outline of the seat and front bands. Then he removes the fabric and places it on the floor. With a yardstick he proves the edges, folding and basting a seam for the welt. He cuts the chair seat, allowing for seams. An allowance must be made at the end of all bands or flaps so they can be given a neat tailored finish when they are joined to the skirt.

Now the upholsterer lays the material he has cut, pinned, and basted on the chair. He measures the inside of the back, from the lowest possible edge where it folds into the chair to the highest point of the back, and chalks the lines. He measures and chalks the width of the back. Then he lays the fabric on the floor again and cuts the back of the chair from his measurements and chalk lines, allowing seams. He turns in the edges and fits the material to the back of the chair, smoothly at all points. Upholsterers always leave generous seam allowances of ¾ inch.

Next he fits the fabric to the arm of the chair and around the wing section, trimming away the excess material but allowing the material to push into the folds, with ¼ inch additional for seams. He pulls the fabric around the end of the chair and marks with chalk the edge where he will join the shaped endpiece. Then he pins a piece in place to cover the end and outlines the edge with chalk. This piece is cut, with a duplicate for the other arm, and both are pinned in place; then he trims away the excess material.

He measures, cuts, and pins a small piece for the chair side, and then prepares the skirt, in equal box pleats all around or in spaced pleats. The pleats at the corners require 4 inches. He hems the edge of the skirt and joins it to the band of the cover with a welt seam.

He fits the back in place, leaving an opening to be finished with snap tape; then he removes all parts of the cover from the fabrics and applies the welt to the seams. The joining seams that tuck in, however, are not welted; they are stitched. Finally he finishes the box cushion, joining the top and bottom sections with a band and finishing the edges with a welting.

Upholstery Slipcovers: Slipcovers which allow parts of the chair to show should look as much as possible like upholstery. This demands upholsterers' or welt seams and a plain boxed skirt. The boxed skirt can be made with a narrow hem or a fringed edge, or it can be cut long enough to turn over the bottom of the chair. Catch-stitch it in place with a heavy thread in this case, or nail it to the wooden frame of the chair on the underneath side. Slipcovers like this should be fitted just like the upholstery they cover and made with very square corners. The seams should be in the same places as those in the upholstery.

Petticoat Slipcovers: These are for dining-room chairs and wooden armchairs. The seat can be covered with a boxed slipcover. Fit the boxing at the front edge of the chair and fit the seat smoothly. At the back corners cut the fabric around the back of the chair, finishing the corners with snap fasteners or ties.

A petticoat cover can be finished with a ruffle, narrow or wide, pleated or gathered; or it can be finished with a hem, a piping, or a welting; or it can be turned over the bottom of the chair and basted in an upholstered effect. All-wood chairs that have outdated proportions can sometimes be covered loosely so the cover holds good lines. In other chairs the arms and back have to be padded. An unbleached muslin is put over the padding before the slipcover is measured and made.

MAKING A SLIPCOVER PATTERN

Some experts hold that you should always make a pattern of unbleached muslin before you cut a slipcover for a difficult chair, yet a pattern is necessary only when you are cutting a very expensive fabric. You then can gain confidence by making a trial cover first, using an inexpensive summer covering.

To make a slipcover for a sofa, work from the center. When the front is covered, do the arms and sides, then the back. Finish cushions in the same style as the sofa.

To make a pattern, follow the directions for either the easy-to-make slipcover or the professional type. When the slipcover is fitted, instead of finishing the seams, mark them carefully with notches and perforations so the pieces can be easily joined. Pencil the seam allowances and press the pattern. Then use it to cut the costly fabric.

SLIPCOVERS FOR SOFAS

The seams of the slipcover will follow the seamlines of the sofa. Work from the top center, covering the top, seat, and band. Then cover the top, seat, and band on each side. When these three sections are fitted into place, join them. The fringe, piping, or welt cord is placed on both edges of the center section, and these are stitched over the side sections. Outline the top edge of the sofa and the line where the seat joins the band, basting the trimming to one section before the next is joined.

Many sofas are so constructed that a band can be run across the top. This makes the work easier, but if it cannot be done, fit the material smoothly over the curve at the top of the sofa and make the seam at the far side of the roll.

When the front of the sofa is covered, you are ready to do the arms and sides. After that, cover the back. The seat cushions must be boxed and the seams finished to correspond with those of the sofa.

For details of fitting and finishing, see the directions for chair slipcovers. You can use either the easy-to-make or the professional routine.

IMPORTANT SLIPCOVER DETAILS

Decide on the details best suited to your type slipcover before you finish it. Allow for seams as you cut the fabric on the chair. For directions for making any seam, see Index. Seams are 1 inch wide until the final fitting, when they are trimmed to ¼ of an inch. Professionals prefer a ¾ inch finished seam so that the upholsterers' method may be used in applying welting.

Slipcover Seams: The seams in a slipcover can be plain or decorative, or both can be used. When both types are used, introduce decorative seams in joinings that show and seam the tucked-in joinings with plain seams.

It is important to decide on the type of seam, as the seam finish dictates whether you fit the chair with the fabric on the right or wrong side.

Right Side Fitting: When you use welted, piped, fringed, or bound seams right-side fitting is necessary.

Wrong Side Fitting: When the seam is finished with an upholsterers' seam or a plain seam, wrong-side fitting is necessary. A slipcover fitted for an upholsterers' seam should be loose enough to allow for the second stitching on the right side. Both these seam treatments are recommended for chintz and other close flowered designs.

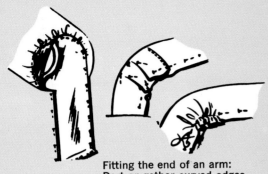

Fitting the end of an arm:
Dart or gather curved edges.

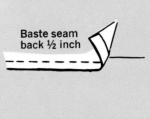

Baste seam
back ½ inch

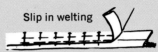

Slip in welting

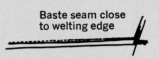

Baste seam close
to welting edge

Outlining
paper
pattern

Fitting to
chair wing

To turn corners
squarely clip the
seam allowance
of welting. To
make a joining,
cross the ends.

Shaping end
around arm

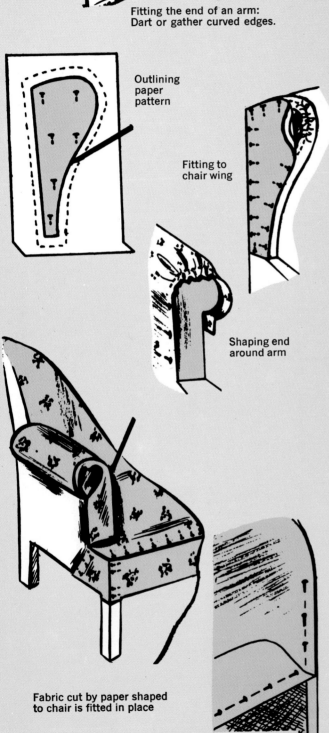

Fabric cut by paper shaped
to chair is fitted in place

Refit all seams
in the slipcover.

Joining a
boxpleated
skirt

Joining a
gathered
skirt

210

FITTING DETAILS

The seams which join the back and arm coverings, and those around the outside edge of the chair, are fitted snugly. The back seams around the cushions are loose. Allow 3 inches on tucked-in seams. Box-spring cushions can be boxed and covered snugly, but down-filled cushions cannot be squeezed. Fit them smoothly and easily. When the slipcover is fitted, check the rounded sections and hold them in with gathers so the seamlines can be joined in a smooth seam. Watch shirred fittings of the arms in front and the rolled sides or the roll in back, or the over-roll of some arms and back constructions in which the plain surface is joined below a deep roll. It is sometimes necessary to introduce darts to fit under heavy overhanging areas.

Shaping Front of Arms: Shaped ends and wings of chairs must be fitted with special attention. To do this place a piece of paper over the shaped edge and outline it with the side edge of a pencil point to get a heavy line. Cut on this pencil line and use it for a pattern in shaping the fabric. Be sure to allow for seams. Baste on the turned edgeline and outline the piece with welting; or, baste the welting to the edge of the fabric while it is on the chair and then add the fitted piece. Be sure the fitted lines fit snugly and are straight and true to the shaping of the chair.

APPLYING WELTING

Beginner's Welted Seam: Fit the section of the chair where welted seams will be used. Pin the welting to the seam, taking care to fit the corners accurately. Baste the welting with long stitches. (Do not remove the slipcover from the chair until it is finished.)

Seams are finished with piping, cording, or a fringe. When the front of the slipcover is finished, pin in the cording or piping before you join the seam, taking care to make the corded corners rounded or squared at exactly the same angle. Baste it as you shape it to the chair. Then fit the joining piece over the welting so the cording is sandwiched into the seam. Baste it close to the edge. All bandings should be edged with the piping or cording on both sides before they are attached. When all seams are basted remove the slipcover from the chair and stitch all seams.

Professional's Method: (You remove the slipcover continually). Cut the seams 1½ inches wide where welting is to be used. Fit the slipcover on the right side. When all the seams are fitted, pin them and remove the slipcover. Working on the right side, with the work flat on a table, carefully baste each seam to be corded ½ inch back from the edge. Slip the welting under the seam edge and pin it evenly. Baste the welting close to the edge. You can then choose between stitching the seam on the right side or turning it to the wrong side. You will need a cording foot on your machine. Be careful that joined seams are trimmed. The straight-line rule holds true here. Often the end of the cord is cut to make the cross seam flat. The drawing shows how to cross the ends of the trimming. Never make this joining at a corner.

SLIPCOVER SKIRTS

Slipcover skirts can be gathered, box-pleated, or a band can be tacked to the bottom like upholstery. If pleats are used, they can be close together, widely spaced, or arranged in clusters.

Before joining a skirt, measure the band at the lower edge of the chair and set the line at which you will join the skirt. Mark it with a row of pins, using a ruler. Measure from the top of the skirt. In some the ruffle shoots out below the chair cushion and no band is in evidence; in others tiers of ruffles start at the cushion.

Full Box-Pleated Skirt: Allow twice the measure of the chair. Hem the lower edge and turn the top in ½ inch. Measure for the pleats, spaced at 2 or 2½ inches. Baste them even, press them, and stitch them down as you stitch the top edge. Baste the welting or trimming to the band at the end of the slipcover, and join the skirt to the lower edge of the band.

Group-Pleated Skirt: Measure around the chair and add to that measure the extra inches needed for the pleats. For example, if you set 6 groups of 5 pleats, multiply the depth of each pleat by total number of pleats and add this amount to the chair measure. Join strips to form this length. Finish top, hem and lay pleats.

Gathered Skirt: Measure the chair and use 1½ times this measure for the gathered flounce. The top of the flounce can be finished over a cord or joined in a welted seam.

Slipcover Closings: Fit the material so carefully that the edges which will be closed are: (1) turned so they meet exactly and (2) finished with a cording or piping or a stitched edge to simulate an upholsterers' seam. Remove the slipcover and lay these edges flat on a table. Baste the narrow snap tape (or zipper) over the unfinished edge of the slipcover and stitch it on both edges with the cording foot. The fabric is turned under and the tape placed over the turned edge. The end of the tape is turned in. Stitch the other edge over the other section of the tape.

Anchoring a Slipcover: The lining is stitched to the seam which joins the skirt. Cut the lining the size of the chair with seam allowance and stitch the seams, leaving openings for the legs. Close one edge with snap fasteners or anchor by ties sewed to each corner and tied around the legs of the chair.

Window Decor

*T**he** use of curtain poles is an important part of the decorator's art. The correct use of curtain poles may make the difference between a well curtained house and one in which the curtains look like "bargain buys".*

When windows are very large, use your ingenuity to curtain them inexpensively, as shown below.

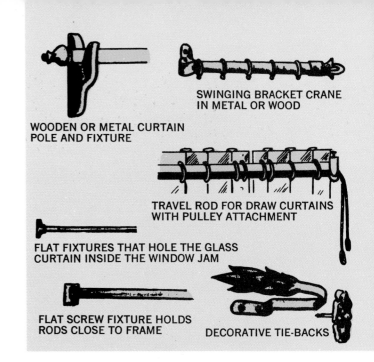

WOODEN OR METAL CURTAIN POLE AND FIXTURE

SWINGING BRACKET CRANE IN METAL OR WOOD

TRAVEL ROD FOR DRAW CURTAINS WITH PULLEY ATTACHMENT

FLAT FIXTURES THAT HOLE THE GLASS CURTAIN INSIDE THE WINDOW JAM

FLAT SCREW FIXTURE HOLDS RODS CLOSE TO FRAME

DECORATIVE TIE-BACKS

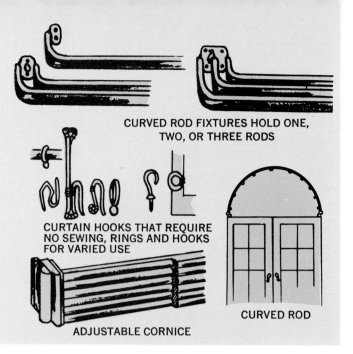

CURVED ROD FIXTURES HOLD ONE, TWO, OR THREE RODS

CURTAIN HOOKS THAT REQUIRE NO SEWING, RINGS AND HOOKS FOR VARIED USE

ADJUSTABLE CORNICE

CURVED ROD

Two tiers of curtains—to open or close as you wish—are topped by a scalloped valance.

Tie-back curtains are not only pretty in a kitchen, but are extremely practical, too.

Correct curtain poles need not entail expense. In fact, studying the type of window treatment in relation to the curtain pole, and so deciding on the type of window to make, often makes it possible to save money. In this chapter are certain types of curtains which look as though an expensive fixture was used; but close examination will show that the hanging on a costly fixture and the hanging on a simple curtain rod entail a different treatment in the making of the curtain. In other words, you can follow the orthodox method, or you can create the same effect more inexpensively. To help you we have detailed illustrations with captions, each explaining the use of the curtain poles. Before making use of this information, you should understand something about the curtain poles which are offered in the stores.

Inexpensive Extension Rods: These rods are sometimes flat, sometimes round, and they are designed to hold light-weight curtains which are not stretched beyond the measure on the inside of the window jamb.

Extension Rods: Many extension rods are especially designed to hold light-weight draperies joined to the outside edge of the window frame. Be sure never to over extend a rod so that it is weak and sags in the center.

Rods Cut to Measure: Both round and flat rods can be cut to the exact measure of your windows. It will repay you to buy a sturdy rod. They are not expensive.

Side Brackets: Side brackets are designed to hold one rod or a group of rods. Some of them are screwed inside the window frame, others flat on the outside of the window frame. The side brackets designed to hold a curtain away from the window frame are an important addition to effective window trimming. In the stores you will find them shaped to carry one curtain rod. Two or three curtain rods can be joined so they are hung one behind another, all held in the same bracket.

Left: Light-as-air glass curtains keep
a summer time interior bright and cool.

Costly Rods: Much beautiful art work has been developed in straight rods and in swinging cranes. They are made particularly for curtains without valances and add an important touch to the final decoration of the room. Sometimes these rods are made of wood and are placed on brackets that permit the pole to extend beyond the bracket. This type is particularly good for portieres and formal cascade draperies, or those hung on rings. The end of the pole is often finished with an elaborate decoration.

Curved Rods: These rods are especially designed to put over windows in place of a high formal valance. They are particularly good to add height to French doors and casement windows.

Traveler Rods Equipped with Pulleys: Rods equipped with pulleys so that a curtain or drapery may be opened and closed are made in many types. In the less costly versions,

Dramatically draped valance and circular cut side panels frame a high, curtained window.

For a touch of Americana, enhance a bay window with coordinated, pole-hung draperies.

rings finished with an eye to which the curtain can be hooked are easy to use. Other rods are so elaborate that the rings do not show, but are covered by decoration.

Cornices: Wooden cornices are often used to cover the tops of curtains or to add height to a short window. They can be treated to match the woodwork of the room.

Tie-Backs: Tie-backs made of metal, composition, or glass are offered in the stores in lovely designs. These can be used to hold back simple or elaborate draperies, or you can buy a small hook and ring to join a fabric tie-back.

Rings and Hooks: Your stores also offer upholsterer's pins which can be hooked into a curtain and need no sewing. They also offer hooks and rings which can be sewn to your curtain. Once you know the style of the curtain and the type of pole suited to your need, you will be ready to choose the best type of ring or pin.

COORDINATING CURTAINS AND RODS

The finish at the top of the curtain should be one suitable for the curtain-rod arrangement you plan to use. Below is a check list of the popular types of curtain, explaining the finish required for each rod arrangement. It tells you just what you need for one rod, two rods, or three rods, and explains the use of a valance board and other fixtures which help to make draperies successful.

RUFFLED TIE-BACKS

Valance and Curtain—One Rod: Gather the top edge of the curtain without turning and seam it to a ¾-inch band of curtain material. Make the valance twice the length of the curtain rod and the depth desired. Finish the lower edge

An unusual window treatment to inspire you to find imaginative solutions to your decor dilemna.

Triple-tiered curtains offer a multiple choice of open-or-closed arrangements in an informal room.

with a narrow hem and turn the heading; stitch the heading hem and gather it. Make another row of gathers 1½ in hes below. Place this valance over the band at the top of the curtain so that the heading can be stitched to the top of the band and the gathered row of the valance to the lower edge of the band.

Valance and Crossed Curtains—Two Rods: Place one curtain over the other, laying them out carefully on the floor. Turn the top edge of both curtains in a casing extending across both curtains and double in the center. Stitch the casing and hang the curtains on the under-rod. Cut the valance in the desired width, allowing for a heading and a casing. Finish the valance and hang it on the top rod. This makes a permanent cross-line when the curtains are hung.

Valance and Crossed Curtains—Three Rods: In this case the top of each curtain is finished with a separate casing, and the valance with a heading and casing. The valance hangs on the top rod, and one curtain on each of the other two rods. The cross-line of the curtains can be adjusted at the window after the curtains are hung.

Crossed Curtains with a Valance Board: The valance is cut double and finished with a ruffle. Then it is carefully fitted around the valance board and held in place with thumbtacks. The curtains can be hung on one or two rods placed close below the valance board.

PINCH-PLEAT CURTAINS

One Rod: They can be finished and hung in any of the following ways: Add an applied casing to the back of the curtain to slip over the rod. Finish the curtains with valance pins, which hook over the rod and pin to the curtain. Finish the curtains with rings and make draw curtains, as follows:

Draw Curtains—One Rod: You will need a round rod and small round rings. Sew a ring to the back of each pleat. Secure a cord four times the width of the window, and fixtures which hold the pole to the window frame with a pulley attachment. Slip the cord through the pulley at A, then through the rings, knotting it to the left ring at the center, as at B, and on through the remaining rings at the left. Bring it through the pulley at C, then back through the rings, knotting it to the right ring at the center as at D Bring it through the pulley at E and put weights at the ends of the cord.

CONTRASTING VALANCE

Two Rods: The valance can be cut 10 inches wide and hemmed, or shaped in a shallow scallop. Turn the top edge so the ruffle at the top of the casing is 3 inches deep and the casing wide enough to go over one rod. Make the valance twice the width of the window in length.

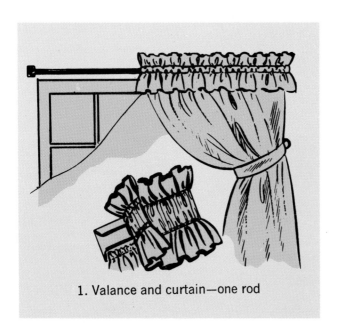

1. Valance and curtain—one rod

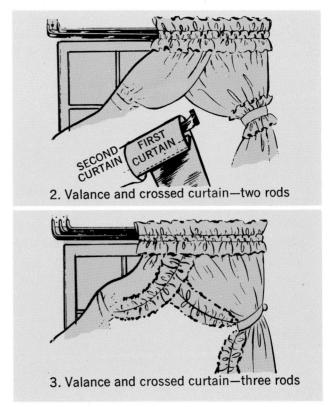

2. Valance and crossed curtain—two rods

3. Valance and crossed curtain—three rods

Band Valance—One Rod: A plain valance with contrasting bands gives the tailored effect of a valance board, but the whole curtain is hung on one rod. The band can be 4 or 6 inches deep when finished, depending upon the size of the window. Cut it double. Prepare the trimming bands of the contrasting fabric and press them into straight folds. The curtain is joined to the end of the valance and must be measured in this length. Gather the curtain and sew it to one edge of the band. Turn the band double and hem the opposite edge over the seam. Measure down 2 inches from top edge and place a trimming band, stitching it at both edges. The top casing is for the rod. Stitch another trimming band at the lower edge of the valance.

CURTAINS FOR A GROUP WINDOW

Long Rod for Draperies; Short Rods for Each Window; Valance Board or Valance Rod: Windows in a group can be curtained as one, and spaced windows can be grouped together and curtained as one. Each window should have a rod for a glass curtain attached inside the window frame close to the pane. A rod extended clear across the window will not be stable enough, because these rods are small. The long rod for the draperies is attached outside the window frame at the extreme edge. When a long rod holds the valance, it is placed just above the drapery rod. A valance board is nailed to the top of the frame.

Three Rods: Place the rods for the glass curtains at each window, attaching them inside the window frame. The gathered or pleated valance can extend over the top of the draperies, or the top of the draperies can be finished like the valance and the valance hung on the rod between the draperies.

Colorful draperies cheer a dining alcove.

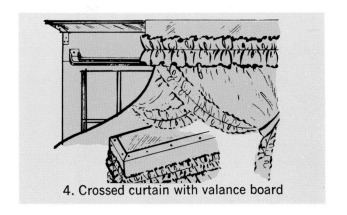

4. Crossed curtain with valance board

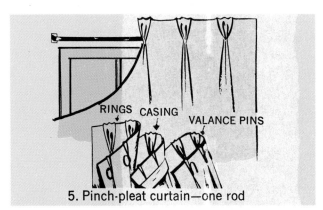

RINGS   CASING   VALANCE PINS

5. Pinch-pleat curtain—one rod

Beautifully tailored draperies are suspended from poles in an elegantly formal room.

FORMAL VALANCE

Valance Board and Two Rods: Adjust the valance board on top of the window or nail a board to the front of the window frame. Adjust the rod for the glass curtains inside the window frame as close to the glass as possible; adjust the rod for the drapery on the outside of the window frame as close to the end as possible—or, if you want to make the window look wider, extend it out over the wall. The glass curtains and draperies are finished with casings. The valance is interlined with buckram. Cut a paper pattern of the valance first, and pin it above the curtains so you can decide the right shape and width for the valance. Then cut the duplicate of the pattern in buckram, and the lining, interlining, and valance fabric.

SWINGING CRANES

Doors or windows which swing out can use this Italian type of window treatment particularly well, but it can be used at any window. The cranes can be very simple or very decorative indeed. A swinging bracket is never combined with a valance, but a panel is often used over the window to add height and dignity. The best curtain for this arrangement is a straight floor-length drape with the fullness laid in pleats. Finish the top with pinch or box pleats and put a drapery pin behind each pleat. You can also make a casing and run the swinging crane right through it.

Patterned panels and solid shades are arranged to heighten and brighten a room in the modern manner.

Pinch pleats across an entire window and wall form an unobtrusive backdrop for a conversation corner.

The windows of your room can be made to look wider, higher, or narrower, depending on the draperies you plan and the placement of the fixtures to hold them.

The first rule is to have the rod as high and as wide as the window frame permits. A window can be made to look wider by extending the rod beyond the window frame so the over-drapery extends over the wall and covers only the frame of the window. Use a fixture on the framework that permits the pole to extend out on the wall, or have a board nailed to the wall on each side of the window and set the fixtures for the pole at the end of the wood. From 4 to 8 inches can be added in this way. Swinging fixtures can be hung outside the window frame, and so not shut out the light. Higher windows can be treated in the same way. Have a side board and a valance board nailed above the window frame and paint it like the woodwork, or nail a strip of molding where you want the curtain pole and attach the fixture for the pole to the molding. The higher pole adjustments are often wide as well as high and this is a good way to cover the fact that windows are uneven. Ignore the top of the windows and set the curtain poles even, then make the curtains to cover the defect.

Group Windows: When two windows can be treated together, it makes a picture in the room. Make a little diagram of the side of the wall, then cover it with tracing paper and sketch some different types to see which one you like. Windows treated as a group often need the glass curtains hung close so they show a sweeping line instead of a separated one. They can then be framed with the overdrapery at each end, or set in between.

Sometimes a piece of furniture can be placed in the center of the window and covered with a new slipcover that helps the effect. Don't forget the possibility of flower boxes or a flower shelf under the window.

In bay, and set-in windows, the window can be brought into the room by extending the treatment across the whole. Often the window can be framed as if it were a cut-out. To do this, have a board nailed to the wall and shape valances over buckram to fit the opening.

Narrow Windows: Arrange the curtain poles so they extend beyond the windows and are attached to the wall, making the window look any width you want. Don't use a bracket which turns; use a pole which rests on a bracket attached to the window frame. The inside edge of the drapery which is to extend over the wall must cover the side hem of the glass curtain. In some windows a pole is hung over the wall and does not extend across the window. With this arrangement the whole side wall of the room and both sides of the window can be covered, and the curtains can be floor-length. Glass curtains cover the window, and flower boxes can be put in front of them and hanging flower pots arranged against them.

Short Windows: Place a valance rod above the window frame so that it extends over the wall. Make the curtains long and put a flower box or shelf under the window.

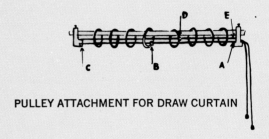

PULLEY ATTACHMENT FOR DRAW CURTAIN

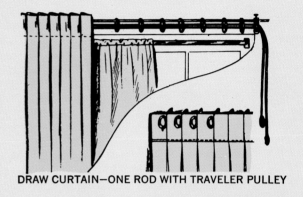

DRAW CURTAIN—ONE ROD WITH TRAVELER PULLEY

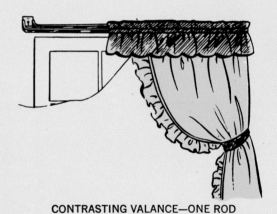

CONTRASTING VALANCE—ONE ROD

BAND VALANCE—ONE ROD

Group window

Place valance board above all windows in the group. Place rod that carries over curtain below valance board. Glass curtains are hung at each window, showing wall space between. When two or more curtains are used, one must be placed forward of the other so they can all hang freely.

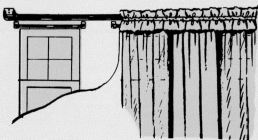

Glass curtain rod hung close to window pane and long rod extending over all windows carries both over-drapery and valance on one rod.

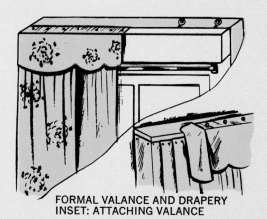

FORMAL VALANCE AND DRAPERY
INSET: ATTACHING VALANCE

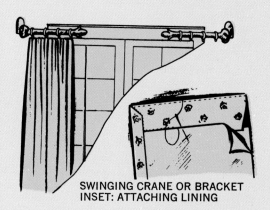

SWINGING CRANE OR BRACKET
INSET: ATTACHING LINING

Blocks of wood placed on each side of curtain pole or valance board to add width.

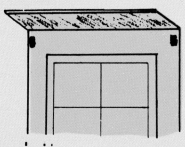

Valance board and curtain rod marking placed to take advantage of full width of window frame.

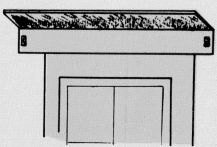

Board is placed above window frame to extend valance higher for taller appearing window.

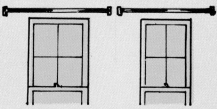

Curtain rods can extend over the wall, above and beyond a window frame.

When windows are uneven, place valance board as for equal sized windows.

Bay window

The rods carrying overdraperies and valances are placed at outside of bay windows. To get the effect of one curtain over the entire window space, the glass curtain poles are placed end to end even if they extend beyond window.

Half curtains are hung with rod attached to outside of window frame.

Dutch curtains are hung on separated rods, placed on the window joint of both top and bottom casements.

Front door curtains should be attached to poles top and bottom.

French doors and windows feature sheer curtains drawn between rods placed at top and bottom of window pane.

Use short draw or tie-string curtains for casement windows that open out.

Small Windows: For very small windows, keep the curtains on the outside of the windows, against the wall. Whenever possible, group two windows as one, with a mirror between them. Sometimes a false window is made around a mirror in order to balance a room.

Bay Windows: Outline the window with a floor-length drapery placed on the outside of the bay. Use a gathered or pleated valance. Fit each window in the bay with a glass curtain hung on a rod inside the window frame. If there is a window seat, cover it with a matching or harmonizing fabric. If the outlining drapery is not used, the glass curtains can be hung on the outside of the window frame and feature a gathered heading, French-pleated heading, or a valance. The curtains should be long and touch one another to give a graceful effect.

Swinging Windows: When the window is hinged in the center so that the top swings in and the bottom out, the curtain must be stretched between two rods, one on the top sash and the other on the bottom.

Front Doors: The window in any door should be paneled with lace or finished with a net curtain stretched between two rods placed at each end of the panel. It is a mistake to hang a loosely gathered curtain at a door. If you want to make the door opaque, use semi-transparent fabric stretched between the two rods.

Vestibules: The outside door of the vestibule in a formal city house is not curtained. The front door and any side windows should be curtained alike. In suburban houses with many windows in the vestibule, they can all be curtained like the door or a novelty fabric can be used, depending upon the type of house.

Sun Porches: The windows of a sun porch may be left uncurtained, or uniform glass curtains used. Sometimes draw curtains are arranged to be pulled over the windows when desired. These curtains are usually floor-length and present a formal and colorful note.

Draperies And Valances

The modern trend, even in formal rooms, is toward simplicity—in choice of textiles, number of curtains to each window, and construction of the curtains.

If you prefer not to use the same fabric for draperies as for slipcovers in the room, choose a fabric that coordinates—either colorwise or pattern. Fullness is most desirable.

In selecting window treatments, consider the window as a whole. The style of the overdrapery, its relation to the room, the lines of the window, the color of the walls, and the glass curtains—all these make up the whole.

When you use glass curtains, the textures of the overdrapery fabric and the curtains must be harmonious as well as the color. Make them of net, scrim, lace, or ninon. Some curtains are made of cotton, others of lustrous blends of cotton and rayon. They are always transparent and delicate in color. In dark rooms, yellow can be used to give warmth only when it harmonizes with the window treatment as a whole. Except in very formal treatments, glass curtains are not used with Venetian blinds. The overdrapery should cover the ends of the blinds.

Problem windows become decorating pluses, as shown below. Let tied-back draperies frame a favorite chest, or a collection of precious objets d'art.

Above: To inspire your decorating imagination are two room settings using draperies effectively—a dramatic bedroom and geometric bath.

SWEEPING OVERDRAPERIES

Satin, velvet, taffeta, or transparent rayon can be used for a beautiful drapery and valance hung over a pole fastened to the window. Use a fabric 50 inches wide for wide windows, 40 inches for narrower ones. You will need twice the finished length, plus 18 inches. Mark the center of the fabric with a long line of basting and drop the fabric over the pole from the back, draping the center and ends of the valance and drapery in folds. Hold the folds in place with pins. This drapery can be basted or pinned in place. When the valance is securely held, adjust the tie-backs at the sides.

For an added note of luxury, the edges can be faced with a contrasting textile in self-color, and the hem can sweep the floor for 10 or 12 inches.

In draping a curtain, fold it back in pleats so the lower part of the outside edge cascades to the floor. The length of the tie-back and the position of the hooks screwed to the window frame govern this proportion. In formal draperies which slant abruptly, a low-placed short tie-back adds to the formality. In informal rooms, the tie-back is placed higher and the drapery allowed to hang more freely. Test out the sweep of the drapery with your tie-back before you finish the hem.

UNLINED DRAPERY

The easy-to-make unlined drapery can be elegant as well as informal, especially if you add the extra fullness which spells the difference between skimpiness and luxury. Full draperies need not be costly, for you can use joined lengths of plain or print fabrics, or make a striped effect by joining harmonizing tones of sateen in 4-inch stripes. Measure and cut the drapery. (See Index).

MACHINE-LINED DRAPERIES

Linings add body and draping qualities to the fabric. The richness of high-ceilinged rooms with formal windows requires draperies with both lining and interlining.

Many lined overdraperies hang straight and are finished with a formal pleated heading. Others are used for valanced windows.

Lining Fabrics: For most draperies use sateen or muslin in a warm rose tan. Remember the lining must be sunfast. Use white if the background of a printed drapery fabric is tinted. Velvet curtains are lined with satin, and some of the French broches are lined with taffeta. Taffeta is lined with a contrasting taffeta or with mull.

Making a Lined Drapery: Place the drapery on the floor, right side up. Place the lining on the drapery, right side down. The lining must be 3 inches shorter than the hem at the lower edge of the drapery, 5 or more inches shorter than the hem at the top, and 4 inches narrower than the width of the drapery. First arrange the lining along one side of the drapery so that the edges of lining and drapery exactly meet. Pin this edge in place with pins running across the selvage edge. Then move the lining so the opposite edge exactly matches the edge of the drapery fabric and pin these

edges together. Stitch the edges on the machine and turn lining and drapery so the seam is inside.

Lay the lined drapery on the floor so the lining is in the center with a 1-inch hem of the drapery fabric on each side. Baste this edge where the lining joins the fabric. Then finish the top of the drapery, sandwiching the stiffening between the hem. Baste the hem; turn the edge of the lining in and baste it over the edge of the stiffened hem. Hold this edge in place with slip stitch.

Turn the side hems at the top over the stiffening, cutting a mitered or slanting corner. Slip-stitch the mitered edge and the edge of the hem as far as the lining.

Top Finishes: The types of top finish for draperies are these: (1) a turned hem which is sewn to rings, (2) a casing with or without heading, or (3) a pleated top in any style of pleat.

Let the drapery hang for two days so the lower edge can be hemmed exactly parallel to the lines of your woodwork. After the fabric has had an opportunity to hang out or stretch, mark this hemline.

Finishing the Lower Hem: First turn the hem and baste the finished edge. Lay it smoothly and draw the lining fabric over it. In this way you can estimate the depth of the hem on both drapery and lining fabric. The edge of the lining should be about 2 inches shorter than the drapery. Baste this edge. Cut off the hem of the drapery so it is 1 inch deeper than the lining. It can be held in place with large catch stitches. Finish the ends of the side hems, turning them over the edge of the drapery hem. Hem them to the end and slip-stitch the open edges which meet. The lining can then be slip-stitched over the hem of the drapery.

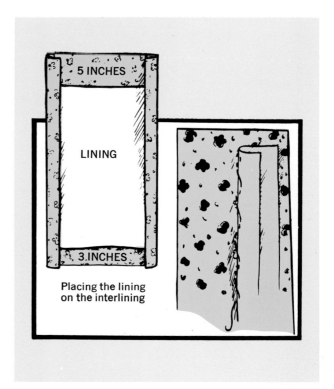

Placing the lining on the interlining

Baste the interlining or heaving lining fabric to the drapery with long invisible tacking stitches.

INTERLINED DRAPERIES

Few draperies today are interlined, but if your drapery will serve you better in excluding light, or if the interlining will add to the richness of the draped line, do not hesitate to use it.

Draperies are interlined with canton flannel, which is much narrower than the usual drapery fabric. The interlining is cut in the exact size of the lining. It is wise to seam the strips of flannel together before cutting, so they can be cut in the correct length and width. These joining seams should be laid flat, one over the other, and stitched on each edge so they will show no mark.

Place the interlining over the drapery fabric so the center of the drapery and the center of the interlining follow the same grain line. Fold the interlining back and tack it to the drapery, following the fold line. The stitches should be spaced far apart, passing long threads from one stitch to the next. When the drapery is very wide, use several rows of tacking to keep it firmly in place. Do not finish the edges of the interlining, but lay drapery and interlining flat and finish the side hems and the top edge of the drapery.

When the stiffening band has been basted in place and the hem turned and basted, the side seams of the drapery should be turned so they extend over both stiffening and interlining. Hold them in place with broad catch stitches spaced far apart.

Turn the edges of the lining fabric and stitch them. Then place the lining on the drapery so that it covers the side hems and top hem. At the opposite end it will be much shorter than the drapery fabric. Pin this lining in place on all edges except the lower and slip-stitch it to the drapery.

POINTS TO REMEMBER ABOUT DRAPERIES

Cutting: Never try to cut draperies on a small table. Working on the floor, as professional upholsterers do in the homes of customers, insures an accuracy difficult to match any other way.

Side Hems: The side hem of the drapery must be basted first. Cut off all the selvage to make your work easier. Turn the edges ¼ inch and stitch on the machine. Press the edge, and then it is ready to turn in a hem. It is very important that all hems be turned on the grain of the fabric, and that all seams and hems be pinned and basted in order to avoid the "drawn" seams which so often mark the work of amateurs. Do not baste the side seam at the top and bottom edge of the drapery until the top and bottom hems are adjusted.

When the seams have been basted flat, stitch them and press them. Then you are ready to finish the top.

Stiffening a Top Hem: To make this stiffening, cut a band from 4 to 6 inches deep and as long as the width of the curtain minus the hem allowance. In other words, it should extend to the point where the side hems turn. In a well-made drape the stiffening never extends into the side hems. Lay the top of the drape flat and pin the canvas 1 inch below the top edge. Turn the 1-inch edge over the canvas and baste it. Turn the side hems over the ends of the canvas. Then turn the canvas top down over the curtain to form the top hem. To eliminate bulk, clip away the excess material at the ends of the side hems. Turn the side hem over the top hem and stitch in place through the two thicknesses of material and the canvas. The long hem across the top of the drape is usually basted and not stitched; the pleats or other finishes put on later hold it in place.

French Pleats and Box Pleats: For direction in measuring and making pleats, see Index.

Cartridge Pleats: Finish the drapery before inserting this type of pleat. Be sure to use a stiff buckram. Mark the distances on the top edge so that you provide 4 inches between the pleats and 4 inches for each pleat. Also mark the length of the pleats—usually about 3 to 6 inches long.

To hold this space, catch the top edge of the drapery for the first pleat, beginning about 3 inches from the edge. Catch the other pleats all the way across the top; then lay each pleat and stitch. Before you do this, press the fabric, and be careful not to crease the pleats in stitching. They bulge out from the front of the drapery and are never pressed.

Pipe Organ Pleats: These are like cartridge pleats, but they are filled with padding so they cannot be crushed flat. They are usually placed close together, and they are more appropriate for formal draperies in a modern room where the ceiling is high and no valance is used.

These pleats are usually longer, extending about 6 inches into the curtain. You must decide upon the size and length of the pleats before you cut the padding. Cut a buckram piece the length and width of the pleat and fill it with a roll of cotton. Stitch the buckram around the edge of the cotton. When you stitch your pleats, insert a buckram roll in each one.

Finishing the Lower Edge: Window frames are not always true, so it is a good plan to hang your draperies before finishing the lower edge. Let a heavy or stretchy fabric hang for two days before you mark the hemline. If the hemline is not on the grain of the fabric ignore the grain and follow the line of the floor or window sill. If the window is off balance, the drape should be made to look true.

The hem at the lower edge extends the full width of the fabric and is turned up over the side hems. Measure the hem, lay it flat, and trim it off. Turn in the edge ¼ inch. Slip-stitch this edge to the drapery and slip-stitch up both ends of the hem or miter the corners.

DRAPERY VALANCES

A valance is the decorative strip of fabric stretched across the top of the window. It serves to hide curtain fixtures, to link up two or more windows into one unit, or as a connection between separate draperies. Valances can be French-pleated; they can be draped. They can be made in cascades or on buckram foundations. The buckram valance is sometimes straight, but more often it is shaped—divided into three scallops, one over each drapery and one over the center space. This formal scalloped effect can be arranged in a straight row of scallops; or a scallop can be arranged on either side as a heading for the draperies, and the space in

The beauty of soft satin is dramatized in a valance and drapery cut in one piece.

between made into a deeper scallop or a high arch. Sometimes formal draperies have a pleated section set in at either side of the center motif or across the center.

Draped valances can be hung on a curtain pole with brackets which extend a little beyond the window frame. Pleated, ruffled, and scalloped valances can be hung on a rod which extends beyond the rod holding the curtain. Squared formal valances are tacked to a valance board.

When an overdrapery and a glass curtain are used, choose a plain tailored valance or a pleated one, either continuous pleats or spaced groups of pleats. Or, if you prefer, have a wider valance shaped to complement the drapery.

Valances are hung on a straight rod, a curved rod, or a valance board. They are always interlined and often wide. Always allow 4 inches at the end of the valance to turn around the corner of the rod or board so the valance hugs the wall on the sides. This is called "the return."

The graceful formal valance repeats wall covering, window shade and drapery motifs in this dining room.

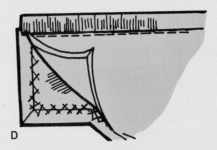

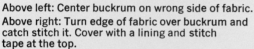

Above left: Center buckrum on wrong side of fabric.
Above right: Turn edge of fabric over buckrum and catch stitch it. Cover with a lining and stitch tape at the top.
Right: Attach valance to valance board.

FORMAL VALANCES

If you want a formal valance, you will need a valance board fitted to your window. Some are shelves which hold the top of the buckram-lined valance away from the curtains; others are boards nailed above the window. Draped valances need not necessarily have a board, but decorators feel that a more flattering draped line is achieved when the drapery is held away from the curtain by a board or rod. Valance boards are usually the exact width of the window frame and 4 inches wide, unless you want an extended board. The valance can be tacked to the top of the board or attached to a buttoned tape tacked to the board. In this case, the valance buttons in place and is easy to remove. The ends of the valance are tacked to the window trim.

Formal Buckram Valance: Choose a shaped straight-line valance. It is always attached with tacks to the valance board. It is lined with heavy buckram and should be interlined with canton flannel as well. Its size and shape are a matter of artistic proportion.

Make a valance out of wrapping paper first and place it over the curtains to try out: (1) the width of the valance, (2) the relation of its shape to the proportions of the drapery, and (3) its relation to the proportions of the room. The corner turn is important. Be sure to allow the 4 inches to meet the wall.

When the size, shape, and proportions of the valance are all decided, use your paper pattern to cut both lining and the buckram with no seam allowance. Cut the outside fabric and the canton flannel interlining by the same pattern, allowing for seams. When the outside fabric has a design, take care to center this design in relation to both the shaping of the valance and the spotting of the design in the curtains.

Place the canton flannel interlining over the buckram, and the outside fabric over that. Turn the edges of the interlining and the outside fabric over the buckram and hold them in place with catch stitches. Use a large needle and coarse thread and make big stitches. Miter the corners carefully. Then turn in the edge of the lining and slip-stitch it over this seam. Strong cotton tape is stitched to the top edge of the valance, and this tape edge is nailed to the valance board.

Draped Valance on a Pole: This formal valance is one long straight length of a soft fabric like satin, rayon crepe, or taffeta. Use the full 36-inch width. Cut it the length of the window, plus 20 inches. Finish the edges, press the valance, and hang it over the window on a long wooden pole, arranging the soft drapes with pins. This is an easy drapery to take down and keep clean.

Draped Valance with Cascade: Make a paper pattern and set it above your draperies to test the proportions. To make a cascade with a draped section through the center, cut a pattern in muslin like Diagram A. The side cascade turns the corner of the valance board and joins the front drapery 4 inches from the corner.

The Valance: Cut a piece of muslin the length of the valance board and as deep as you want the valance. Fold the muslin in half and measure in 3 inches from the outside edge (X in Diagram A). From X cut to Y as shown by the dotted line. This line can slant slightly or as much as you wish, depending on the effect you desire.

Then cut a curved line from Y to Z (the center bottom of the valance). Unfold the muslin and divide into three units as shown by numbers 1, 2, 3, on Diagram B. At each of these points make a deep tuck. Pull them so they form a drapery and pin them to the valance board.

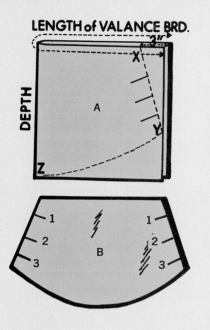

Cascade valance with pleated side drapery and gathered glass curtains.

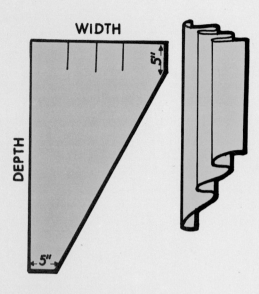

Above: Diagram for a draped valance. Planning the shape (A) and making for drape (B).

Diagram for cutting and pleating side cascade.

The Cascade: Make a muslin pattern before cutting the fabric. Unless your ceilings are very high, the side length of the cascade should be about 30 inches and should measure about 18 inches across the top. In this way a pair of cascades can be cut from ½ yard of 40-inch material. Measure down 5 inches from the top edge and 5 inches from the lower edge, and draw a diagonal line (Diagram C).

Then pleat the fabric in three large pleats, including all but 4 inches at one end. This 4 inches extends around the corner of the valance board and permits the drapery to hang close to the wall. Baste the pleats across the top and try your cascade at the window. The end should exactly match the end of the drapery section, and the edge should cascade in ripples.

When you have tested the patterns for both valance and cascade, cut your fabric.

Finishing: The edges can be hemmed or finished with a trimming. Choose a contrasting band of fabric, a band of ribbon, a fringe, a pleated edge, or a ball trimming. Apply the trimming, then press the fabric.

TIE-BACKS FOR DRAPERIES

Fabric Tie-Backs: The tie-backs for draperies can be cut straight or in a curved shape. Use the fabric of the drapery or a contrasting fabric, and make the tie-back plain or pleated. The tie-back for a heavy drapery should be interlined with buckram. For a plain tie-back, cut the buckram and bind the edge to prevent it from cutting the fabric. Then lay canton flannel over the buckram and cover it smoothly with the fabric. For a straight tie-back, cut the

fabric double, seam it, and turn it to the right side. If you like, it can be pleated. Shape the ends in a curve.

Whatever kind of tie-back you make, finish the ends with rings which slip over a hook in the woodwork. Place the hook carefully and try the effect with the curtain draped at different angles, so you can find the draping line which best suits your draperies and your room.

Cord Tie-Backs: When you make tie-backs of cording, buy them in white and have them dyed to match your draperies. Use a double cord which is knotted. It can hang in tassels or be weighted with covered balls.

LENGTHENING DRAPERIES

The first thought should be, "Is the fabric worth remaking?" A beautiful rich fabric can be remade at very little expense; but a shoddy or worn fabric is not worth the time and money. It would be better to spend the money for new draperies in a cheaper fabric.

The trimming band which lengthens a drapery of napped fabric, such as velours or velvet, should be a matching satin or brocade. If you cannot find the right color, consider buying white and dyeing it. This is not very expensive, and if your local community does not offer such service, you can send your draperies to a city cleaner who specializes in dyeing to match.

For a drapery in brocade or a rich ribbed fabric in one or several colors, the trimming band can be velvet or velveteen.

Both drapery and lining must be lengthened, and the joining should be corded. Duplicate on the trimming band the finish of the drapery. If there is no valance you can piece the top of the drapery and add a contrasting valance to cover the piecing.

Measuring And Estimating

*T**he** amount of yardage in the curtains and draperies can make all the difference, decorators say, between a really lovely room and a drab, undistinguished one. For this reason it is better to use cheaper fabrics lavishly than expensive ones sparingly.*

If you make curtains at home, for the same cost you can expect better material, more fullness, and longer wear than in those you buy. When you buy fabrics for curtains, look in the dress-fabric department as well as for drapery textiles.

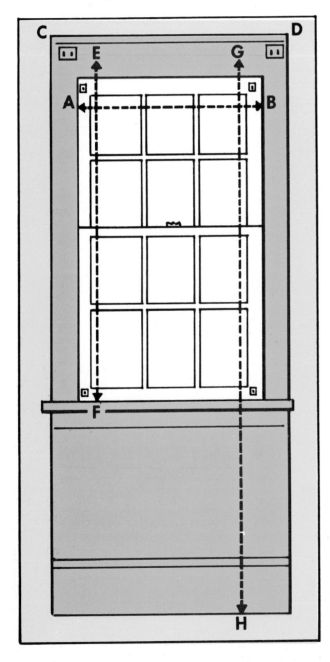

Very often you can find a dress fabric which costs less than the drapery fabric and gives the same effect.

You will, of course, have considered carefully the type of window, the matter of draperies and valances, and the outlook from the window. If you have a lovely view, you will want to give freedom to the windows which overlook it with transparent tie-backs or draw curtains, or side curtains which fall away from the window. If the outlook is poor, use glass curtains and side draperies that hide the view. If the room needs cheer and sunlight use bright yellow ninon.

Curtains hung close to the glass are ½ inch shorter than the window sill. Those hung outside the window frame can be of any length. A few summer curtains, attached to the outside of the window frame, end in a line with a radiator cover or at the lower end of the window sill. Tie-back curtains must allow for the draping.

The size of the window, the style of curtain, and the width of fabric vary so much that the method used by professionals should be adopted. They decide on the style and test all details before estimating yardage. Most large windows need two full widths of 50-inch material. When the fabric is narrow, full or half lengths must be joined, and don't forget to count this as extra yardage.

ESTIMATING YARDAGE FOR CURTAINS AND DRAPERIES

Use these directions for measuring for glass curtains, one-curtain draperies, group-window curtains, draperies, and valances.

Window Measurements: Measure *all* the windows. They may look alike, but sometimes you will find that not all of them have been set true, or the settling of the house may have thrown one out.

Length of Curtain Rod: For glass curtains, measure from jamb to jamb—A to B in the diagram. For an outside curtain pole, measure between the extreme outside edges of the woodwork—C to D in the diagram. For a wider window treatment, set the widening blocks in place and measure for pole or valance which extends beyond the frame.

Basic Length of Curtain or Drapery: To find a working basis for the finished length of your curtain, measure from the rod to the window sill (E to F in diagram), or from the rod to the floor (G to H). Which measurement you use depends upon whether you are making sill-length or floor-length curtains. Once you have this basic or finished curtain measurement, you can add to or subtract from it as needed—for instance, you may want the drapery to sweep

Left: Diagram for measuring windows.
Opposite: The window treatment must be considered an integral part of the decor, as shown here.

over the floor from 10 to 12 inches, or fall an inch above the floor, or at radiator height. The rod should be hung and the length measurement verified before a curtain is cut. Always measure from the bottom of the rod.

Number of Curtains: Make a list of everything you will need—right overdrapery, left overdrapery, right glass curtain, left glass curtain, ruffle, valance, tie-back, trimming—everything down to the last detail. With this list before you, make another, this time of the exact allowances for turns and hems at top, bottom, and sides, plus shrinkage allowances.

Allowance for Lower Hem: The first turn in any hem should be ¼ inch. This means, for example, that the allowance for a hem 2 inches deep is 2¼ inches. The hem at the lower edge of glass curtains may be from 1 to 3 inches deep; in formal draperies, from 2½ to 3½ inches. A double hem is used in transparent fabrics, so in this case you must allow twice the measurement of the hem.

Allowance for Casing and Heading: The allowance for casing and heading at the top should be added to the lower-hem measurement. The casing should be deep enough to allow the rod to slide easily. A 4-inch allowance (plus ¼ inch for the first turn) makes a 1-inch casing and a 2½-inch heading. Yours should be at least that. In pleated curtains the top hem is twice the width of the stiffening bands.

Shrinkage Allowance: To the total length so far, add shrinkage of 1 inch to the yard for rayon fabrics, 2 inches to the yard for cottons. If the material is preshrunk, no shrinkage allowance is necessary.

Example of Computing Length: Here is an example of how to find the necessary length of fabric for a curtain. The curtain in this case is a glass curtain 69 inches from rod to sill.

Finished length.....................................69 inches
Lower-hem allowance (1¾-inch
    hem plus ¼ inch for turn).........................2 inches
Casing and heading allowance
    (4-inch plus ¼ inch for turn)...................4¼ inches
Shrinkage allowance (1 inch per
    yard)...2 inches
        Cutting length...........................77¼ inches

If this curtain were made of transparent material, another 2 inches for the double hem would make a total cutting length of 79¼ inches.

Make a diagram showing the length measurements you will use in your curtain.

Width Measurements: The width of the curtain depends upon the fullness desired. Make the allowance for side hems and estimate fullness as described below.

Allowance for Side Hems: The side hem is measured without selvages but with ¼ inch for the first turn. On some curtains both side hems have the same allowance; on others they are different, because (1) the hem at the center of the window is wider for emphasis, (2) a ruffle is joined (allow ¾ inch for joining a ruffle) or (3) the pole or valance board curves, and an allowance for the return to the wall must be added to the outside hem. The same size hem is repeated in a valance or ruffle.

Estimating Fullness: To estimate fullness, either for gathers or for pleats, you can follow simple rules. Allow the finished width of the curtain as it will hang on the pole and double this figure; or take the same measurement and add one-half to it. The fuller the curtain, the better the finished effect. For the average window, two 50-inch widths of fabric are skimpy; three 50-inch widths is the best rule. Transparent fabrics must be fuller than opaque ones.

In making your estimate for gathered or pleated curtains, you can use the professional method of carefully working out a plan and adjusting the width of the fabric by adding a piece to make it wide enough to carry out the sweeping effect of the plan—or, like most home sewers, decide to use the set yardage of the fabric and adjust it as best you can to your window.

ESTIMATING YARDAGE FOR RUFFLES

The measurement for ruffles on curtains, as well as slipcover skirts, bedspreads, and dressing-table skirts, is based on the measurement of the edge to which the ruffle will be attached. In furniture, measure all around the chair, sofa, or bed, or across one part.

Take the exact measurement of the edge. To add fullness, depending upon the effect you wish, allow double this measure or add one-half to it for the cutting length of the ruffle.

For example, if the edge measures 48 inches, the cutting length of your ruffle would be either 96 inches or 72 inches, depending upon how much fullness you wanted.

Next, set down the width of your fabric—36, 40, or 50 inches—and also the depth of the ruffle, including hem allowance at top and bottom. Divide the cutting length of the ruffle by the fabric width; the answer gives the number of widths of fabric you need to join for ruffles. Multiply this figure by the depth of the ruffle (including hems); the answer gives you the total yardage for one length of ruffle. Multiply this by the number of curtains, and you have the total yardage needed for all the ruffles.

Ruffles for curtains can be from 3 to 5 inches deep; the depth of ruffles for slipcovers and bedspreads is the length from the joining to the floor. The hem is from ½ to 1 inch.

ESTIMATING PLEATS

The following instructions for estimating pleats in curtains, draperies and valances can also be applied to pleated skirts for slipcovers, bedspreads or dressing-tables.

Set down the finished width the curtain will occupy on the pole when hung. Add to this the width of the finished hem, plus the additional measurement required for turning the corner when the curtain is hung on a curved rod or a valance board.

Next, estimate the amount of extra fullness you will use. Divide this extra fullness by the number of pleats you will use; the answer gives the size of each pleat. Always use an odd number of pleats—five or seven, say—never six or eight. Bear in mind that the size of the pleats should be related to the depth of the stiffening band or skirt. The deeper the band, the wider each pleat should be. In simple curtains with a 3-inch stiffening band, use a French pleat 2½ or 3 inches wide, spaced 2 to 2½ inches apart. If the band is 5 inches deep, the pleat should be 4 inches wide.

Box Pleats: For box pleats the space between the pleats should be the same as the width of the pleats. Allow 2½ to 3 inches.

Cartridge Pleats: The pleats should be 2 to 2½ inches wide, and spaced 3 to 3½ inches apart.

Pipe Organ Pleats: These longer and larger versions of cartridge pleats require a deeper stiffening band. The pleats are 6 to 9 inches, with a 5-inch spacing. This space must always be smooth and equal. Remember that in curtains which will be hung on pulleys, the space must be wide enough to let the folded fullness fall into place between each pleat.

Making a Diagram: The next step is to make an accurate diagram representing the width of one curtain. At the ends, note the amount you will need for the center hem, including the outside return only if the pole is far from the wall. At these two points put marks indicating a pleat. At the exact center between these two pleats, place a third one; then fill in the space between the central pleats and each side one.

Example of Estimating Pleats: In the case of a curtain with a finished width of 45 inches, estimate pleats as follows:

To the 45 inches, add 3 inches for the return and 2 inches for a hem. This makes 50 inches. Allowing one-half the measure for extra fullness, you have a width of 75 inches. Suppose that you have decided upon five pleats: 5 into 25 (the measure of the excess fullness) gives you 5 inches as the width for each pleat.

The next step is a diagram representing a 50-inch width. On the left side 3 inches for the return is marked off at A; on the right side, 2 inches for the hem is marked off at B. At A

and B a pleat is marked; then midway between A and B (half of 45 inches) a center pleat is marked at C. That leaves two pleats still to place. The first goes midway between A and C, at D; the other midway between C and B, at E.

Gathered or Pleated Valance: The yardage for gathered or pleated valances should be estimated when you figure the extra fullness for the curtain ruffles and other details. The valance is measured the same way, and it will help if you make a separate chart for the valance, setting down the details for the hems.

Straight Valance: It does not matter whether a plain straight valance is shaped on buckram or cut double and hung on a pole. Take the measurements carefully, allowing 3 extra inches of length and 3 extra inches of width. At the same time measure for the crinoline or buckram, if it is to be used.

The yardage for tie-backs, and any ruffles or stiffening used with them, should be noted when you estimate your curtain yardage. In some widths of fabric, they can be cut from the waste ends from other pieces; other times it will be necessary to buy extra for the tie-backs.

In ordering curtain poles, explain that the length you order is the final length, not the length to which the pole is cut. This means that the fixture which holds the pole is included in the length, and the pole is cut long enough to fit the fixtures, so that the total length of pole and fixtures equals your measure. Making this fact clear at the outset will save disappointments in measuring for curtain poles. Be sure also to say that you have used a yardstick.

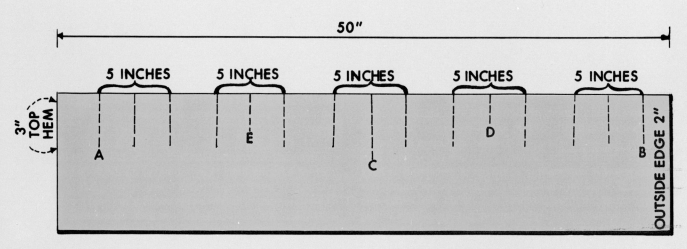

DIAGRAM FOR MEASURING PLEATS IN 50-INCH FABRIC

Making Curtains

Nothing improves a room as dramatically as fresh new curtains. Making your own can be your most satisfying sew-for-your-home project— it's simple, quick, and shows immediate results!

CUTTING CURTAINS

Work on the floor to have space for laying out the fabric. It is not necessary to spread papers over the floor; vacuum-clean the rug or wipe a wooden floor with a damp cloth before you begin. A rug holds transparent fabrics in line so it is easier to cut straight edges and join true seams.

Cutting Straight Edges: If the fabric does not tear, draw a thread and cut on the thread line. If this is not possible, draw a chalkline on a smooth fabric with a yardstick. Use a yardstick when measuring for length, and a tape measure when working on details. Watch the grains of the fabric in all the cutting, folding, and stitching so the curtain will hang straight.

Remove All Selvages: Very often the selvage is woven more tightly than the rest of the fabric. This will not show up in the new fabric as much as it will after the curtain is washed. It is safer to remove all selvages, because if you don't you may find yourself with a baggy curtain which cannot be ironed smooth.

Press Hem Edges: The side hems are turned first. The hem edge is 1 or 2 inches finished. You can save time in making it by putting an ironing board on the floor and pressing in both the first ¼-inch turn and the second 1-inch turn; then you can pin the hem from the outside edge and stitch it without basting. If the curtain has a ruffle, hem only the wall edge.

Top Curtain Finish or Hem: The top hem is basted so that you can hang the curtain to test its length, width, and the way it drapes. When you have decided upon the correct length, join the ruffle, allowing ½ inch for seams. This hanging test is important in all tie-backs, because a tie-back curtain or drape must be longer than the window length. It is important in straight curtains, too, when the window is uneven, because all straight-hanging hem lines must follow the edge of the woodwork.

The finish at the top of the curtain is a matter of style. If you make a casing, the hem is turned deep enough to let the curtain pole pass easily. If you have a casing with heading, turn the hem deep enough for both casing and heading and stitch it twice, once at the edge and once to mark the top edge of the casing. This leaves a ruffle of double fabric, called a heading, above the casing. It is narrow on glass and kitchen curtains, although wider for others. When the top of the curtain is pleated, the top hem is 3 inches deep or more, depending upon the style and spacing of the pleats. In transparent fabrics all hems are cut double, no matter whether the finish has a casing, heading, or pleats.

Shrinkage Tuck: An allowance for shrinking should be considered in the top of any curtain. In addition to the heading and casing, make a small shrinkage tuck which hangs behind the heading and so does not show. The allowance for shrinking differs with the fabric, but the usual tuck is 2 inches, which permits a 4-inch addition to the length of the curtain in case of need. When a ruffled curtain is turned, set your mark for the heading and casing; but before you turn it, make the shrinkage tuck, which extends the full width of the curtain and should be basted to the outside edge of the ruffle. When the tuck has been basted, turn the edge for the casing and stitch it just above the basted seam. Then stitch the heading and casing seams.

Seaming Long Joinings: Smooth the fabric carefully and insert pins without slipping your finger under the fabric. Baste the seam with the fabric still on the floor; pick it up only when you take it to the machine to stitch. Long seams in curtains are joined with an upholsterers' or a flat felled seam.

Pressing Curtains: Curtains can be pressed on the floor before hanging them. Lay a blanket on the floor under the curtain, or use a small ironing board, moving it from spot to spot as needed. This method is used for the final touching up of ruffles, which muss if you iron them on a standing board in the usual way.

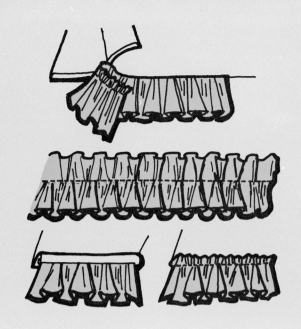

RUFFLED WHITE
TIE-BACK CURTAINS

A favorite curtain is the ruffled white tie-back. When they are used for luxury living rooms, they are very ruffled indeed and sweep the floor. They often have a ruffle on all edges and seams, and double ruffles in the draped heading. In other living rooms they are crossed, sometimes floor-length but usually short. Some have valances, some are finished with double ruffles across the top, some are headed with a double hem, and some are finished with a heading and casing.

Ruffled tie-back curtains are used alone or with print or checked window shades. In the city a glass curtain is often necessary. Hang the glass curtain close to the window and the ruffled curtain on the outside of the window frame.

Fabrics: The fabrics for ruffled curtains should have a permanent starchless finish. Ask for it in organdy or paper muslin for a really grand ruffled curtain. Ask for it also in lawn, dimity, dotted swiss, dotted scrim, net, and marquisette.

Making the Curtain: Spread the fabric smoothly and measure it carefully. First straighten the edge, then measure and mark the edges. The seams for extra fullness are joined first, then the side hems. If you stitch without basting, use pins lavishly. It will help if you press the turned hem on all the edges.

Ruffles: It will save time to cut and join the seams in all the ruffle lengths at the same time. Fabrics cut across the grain usually require 1¾ or 2 yards of ruffling for each yard of curtain length. For bias ruffles you need only 1½ yards of ruffling for each yard of curtain.

The ruffles should be from 3 to 5 inches wide. In some fabrics you can tear instead of cutting straight-grain ruffles. Test your fabric to make sure it will tear. Marquisette, ninon, and voile should be torn crosswise of the goods, never cut bias. Crisp fabrics like lawn, organdy, and taffeta tear lengthwise, but the ruffles show to better advantage if they are cut on the bias. Use a small French seam for joining the pieces of a straight ruffle. Bias ruffles must be seamed crosswise and the seam pressed flat. Snip off the end of the seam if you hem the ruffle by machine so the machine hemmer will work smoothly and not stop at the bulk of the seam.

Before you gather the ruffle, decide upon the type of joining to the curtain. You can use a heading, overcasting, or a flat fell, or a French fold or an upholsterer's seam. Use the gathering attachment of the machine and set your work in the machine so that the gathers come as close as possible to the edge. If you find that this gathered edge is too short when you come to join it, clip the machine stitching every few inches and stretch out the fabric. Ruffles can be gathered by hand. If you do this, make three rows of gathers and mark them so the spacing is even.

Joining Ruffle to Curtain: Work on the floor. Lay the edge of the curtain flat and smooth. Lay the ruffle along the edge, and full around the corners. Pin the edges together and baste them.

Turning Corners: When you apply a ruffle to a curve or corner, allow twice the length of the curve to make the ruffle lie flat and show equal fullness.

French Fold: This joining is used for ruffles when no stitching is to show. Work so the seam is on the wrong side of curtain and ruffle. Place the gathered edge a little back of the curtain edge. Pin and baste the seam, then stitch it. Turn the long edge over the gathered edge and stitch again.

Ruffles Set into Curtains: These ruffles can be seamed in the joining or gathered with a turned edge and applied to the curtain near a marked line.

Double-Ruffle Edge: Cut your ruffle twice the width desired and finish both edges. The center can be finished with machine gathers and the joining stitched through these gathers. To do this, turn the curtain edge up ½ inch on the right side and baste the ruffle over this turn. The ruffle can be gathered by hand if preferred.

Tiered Ruffles: When ruffles are applied in tiers, mark the line where each ruffle is to come. Use pins, a basting thread, a creased line, or a tracing wheel. The ruffle which goes on the edge is joined with a French fold seam. The applied ruffles are basted along each straight line, with the ruffle placed above the line so that when it is basted and stitched it will fall over and conceal the seam.

Small Heading: Turn the top edge of the ruffle over 1 inch before gathering, and gather it ½ to ¾ inch from the edge. Turn the edge of the curtain over ¼ inch on the right side and cover it with the ruffle edge.

Top Finish: A hem at the top, a casing, or a casing and heading finish—whatever the finish, it is stitched when the curtain is finished and extends all the way across the ruffled edge so that the curtain rod will slide the full width from end to end of the curtain.

Tiered ruffles can be joined with a stitching under the ruffle as shown at left or across the gathers.
Ruffled tie-backs can be single ruffled (1), double ruffled (2), all-around ruffle (3), or triangular ruffle (4).

Ruffled Valance: In informal windows the valance can be from 5 to 10 inches wide, and the ruffle can be placed on the edge or tiered ruffles arranged. Try out the ruffles for the valance to determine (1) the length of the valance, (2) the width of the ruffle, and (3) the spacing of the ruffles. Cut the valance in the length and width desired, allowing for a heading and a casing. Add one or two ruffles to the edge. This valance is set on a separate pole or incorporated in the curtain and extends across the top of the window. When a valance is tacked to a board, cut it double and add a gathered ruffle which should duplicate the type used on the curtain in depth, in fullness, in finish, in type of joining and in heading.

Ruffled Tie-Backs: Tie-backs are an important part of ruffled curtains. They are made of the curtain material and can be developed in many interesting ways. The length depends upon the amount of fullness to be held in. Usually tie-backs are from 14 to 18 inches or longer. The ends are finished with rings or loops which are caught on a hook screwed into the window frame. Most ruffled tie-backs are made on a double band of self-fabric 1 to 2 inches wide. The ruffle should match the ruffle on the curtain in width, finish, and fullness. Attach the ruffle to one or both edges of the tie-backs, or attach two or more ruffles to one edge.

Triangle Tie-Backs: Cut a piece of buckram. It should be 7½ inches across the widest part and about 9 inches deep. Try it on the window for size—you may want to make it a little larger or smaller. Cover the buckram with the fabric and attach it to a band of self-fabric 2 inches wide and 9 inches long. Cover the triangle with rows of ruffles and join the tie-back to the window by placing a ring at the point and at the end of the band.

FRENCH-PLEATED CURTAINS

Transparent Rayon Curtains: First decide whether you will finish your curtains with rings, upholstery pins, or an added casing. You will need two lengths of 50-inch transparent material for the average window. If the window is small, use the dress-weight ninons 40 inches wide. The beauty of these curtains is their simplicity. Cut off the selvage and turn the side hems of the curtains so that they are finished with double hems 1 inch wide. These hems should extend the full length into the tucked section at the top of the curtain.

Stiffening the Hem: Transparent curtains need a stiffening 3 or more inches wide in the heading, of firm crinoline or a light-weight buckram. In measuring the turning necessary for the heading, first decide on the depth of the pleat, then turn the top edge in 2 inches more than this measure. Allow a double turn so the buckram will not show through.

In measuring the length of the buckram, measure in 2 inches from the edge, because top stiffening should not extend into the outside hem of the French-pleated curtain.

Now use the chart which you made when you took your measurements. You can turn the heading at the top of the curtain. First baste the edge of the fabric to the buckram. Turn it twice and stitch the hem or baste it. In some curtains the pleats hold the hem and no hemline shows.

French Pleats: Lay box pleats across the top of your curtain and make a stitched line the length of the pleat on the grain of the fabric. Press the fabric in this pleat into three small folds and stitch across the end of the pleats.

With a matching thread make a few stitches across the base of the pleats to hold them on the right side of the material. Work over and over stitches as these hold the pleats.

Finish the back of the curtain with an applied casing basted across the back of the pleats. The casing must be joined securely by hand so that the stitches do not show through on the right side. Or, instead of a casing, use an upholstery pin which is slipped into each group of pleats. The pins hook into the curtain rod. When these curtains are made into draw curtains, sew a ring behind each pleat.

Heavier Fabrics: These heavier curtains are used alone, or with Venetian blinds, or with glass curtains in homes, offices, meeting halls, and play rooms. You can make them of any opaque curtain fabric—cretonne, chintz, monk's cloth, linen, or any of the fabrics used for "summer drapes." They can be tied back or straight and should be abundantly full. The top of the curtain is finished with a stiff French-pleated heading which gives the curtain a professional look. Like the transparent curtains, they can be hung on a rod with a casing, on rings, or on upholstery pins. When a curtain is made for a set space, there should be no fullness between the pleats; for a draw curtain the pleats are spaced wider apart to permit fullness between them.

Fabrics which will stand alone, such as glazed chintz or linen, can be pleated without a buckram or crinoline interlining; other fabrics require the stiffening. If you are making washable curtains, remember that buckram and crinoline lose their stiffening with washing, unless you use a kind especially made to be washed. For washable curtains you can also use a washable stiffening with slits cut as eyelets for the curtain pole. This relieves you of the labor of setting in rings.

Estimate your curtain width and the spacing of the pleats and cut the curtain, allowing a turn-down to form the pleated section 2 inches longer than the pleats. Divide the pleats and mark them, creasing the fabric firmly at each mark. Pin the box pleats and stitch the length. Divide the box pleat and crease it with your fingers, then stitch across.

When you use a patented washable pleater, buy it wide enough so that the eyelets for the rod can be placed exactly on the pole line of the curtain. Then turn the top of the curtain in and stitch the fabric at both edges of the stiffened band. Make another row of stitching on each side of the eyelets to hold the fabric firm. Next make a row of stitching between the eyelets where the pleat creases. Run the pole through the eyelets and press the pleats into shape. You can group them in clusters of three, held by a small stitch; you can space them evenly in close clusters or space them widely. Hang the pole before you finish the lower edge of the curtain.

EASY VALANCES

Pleated and ruffled valances can be added to casual unlined draperies or used as a heading for ruffled or glass curtains. Cut this kind of valance 14 to 16 inches wide and at least twice the length of the window, measuring around the pole at each end. If you want it really full, add still another length.

Gathered Valance: Turn a 6-inch hem at the top and seam it twice for the casing and the heading. Stitch these lines and hem the lower edge. A flat curtain pole is run through the casing, and you can space the gathers on the pole. This type of valance is sometimes run on the same

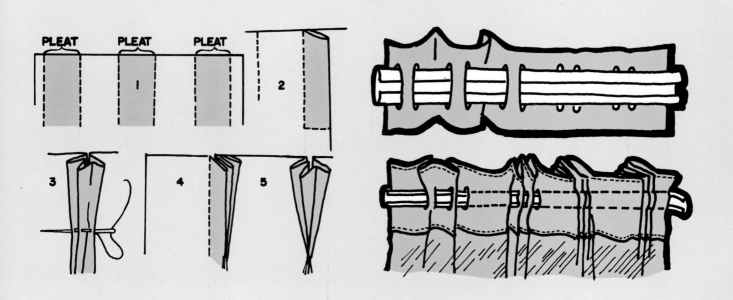

STRETCH GLASS CURTAINS BETWEEN TOP AND
BOTTOM ROD; ROD AT LEFT NOT YET IN PLACE.

LOOSELY STRETCHED CURTAIN TIED IN CENTER.

LOOSELY STRETCHED CURTAIN TIED TO SIDES.

pole with the side curtains to fill in the space between the
draperies. Again, it extends over the top of the draperies in
addition to crossing the window. This requires a separate
pole for the valance.

Pleated Valance: Turn a 4-inch hem and line it with
crinoline or buckram, depending upon the weight of the
material. Stitch the hem and finish the edge of the valance as
directed for French pleats earlier in this chapter.

GLASS CURTAINS

Curtains hung close to the glass on a rod attached inside
the window frame are called glass curtains. They are made
of net, marquisette, scrim, or other sheer fabric. They can
be used alone or combined with a formal or informal
drapery. They are usually neutral in color and hang straight
from a casing. They are sill-length and have soft, full
gathers, which should never be skimpy. Most glass curtains
are finished with a narrow hem.

All glass curtains which can be seen from the street
should be uniform. Inside there can be plenty of variation.

Allow twice the width of the window to a pair of curtains.
Cut these curtains carefully, spreading them on the floor so
they are smooth and the edges straight and true. Turn the
top edge in a casing; if you like, make a narrow heading
above the casing. Put in a shrinkage tuck. Hang the curtains
and measure the hem. When the hem is turned over a
second rod at the bottom of the window, the hem must be
stretched and pinned to the rod. When your window frames
are true and straight you can do this with measurements; if
they are crooked or the pole sags, each curtain must be
individually fitted.

KITCHEN CURTAINS

A cheerful breakfast nook is an American tradition, and
the theme of the breakfast-nook windows should be carried
into the kitchen. In older houses, the kitchen-living-room
can be modernized or developed traditionally. In other
houses the kitchen is simply the kitchen, and the curtains
are correlated to the decorative scheme of the room.

Kitchen curtains must be washed frequently, and so they
are made of marquisette, scrim, dotted swiss, gingham,
chambray, or muslin. They can be gaily colored, white
trimmed with color, or all white.

The traditional white tie-backs are standard in kitchen-
living-rooms; second choice is a straight-hanging white
curtain, simple and plain.

The curtains in dinette windows can hang straight and be finished with a drawstring, or they can be ruffled and tied back. They are usually edged with fringe or trimming stitched all around or at the front, and hemmed.

When the kitchen curtains are edged with a banding, you can insert bands or face the curtain with a band. These bandings are often scalloped at either the lower edge of the curtain or the top of the hem. They can be banded and scalloped all around or only at the lower edge. They can hang straight or be tied back. The valance is run across a pole on a casing, and it can be cut to allow a small heading.

Double Dutch Curtains are attractive for some kitchens which have only one window. The curtains are finished with a casing and a short heading. They can be banded, bound, or scalloped. A rod is placed at the top of each half of the window sash. Use small glass curtain rods and screw them to the sash frame so they go up and down with the window.

LENGTHENING CURTAINS

Straight Curtains: When the possibilities of letting out tucks, letting down the hem, the casing, and the heading are exhausted, we must resort to facings and bandings. In this case the textile interest of the added band is as important as its color. Some kind of false hem which will make the curtain look like new can be found for any straight curtain. Once you have selected a fabric in matching or contrasting color which complements your curtain in texture interest, the trimming band or false hem can be shaped to conform with simplicity or formality of line.

Curtains with French-Pleated Tops: Rich curtains with French-pleated tops can use an added band of lightweight velvet, satin, or velveteen in matching color. It should be lined and joined with a cording. It will make the curtains look like new.

Cotton Curtains: Cotton curtains for bedrooms and informal rooms can be lengthened with a trimming band in self-color or contrasting color. The top of the trimming band is usually scalloped, and when it's well done the curtain looks like new. All-white dotted swiss curtains with colored dotted swiss bands joined with matching rickrack are very effective.

Lengthening with Ruffles: When curtains are narrow as well as short, they can often be adjusted by adding a ruffle.

Decide exactly how wide the ruffle should be and what fabric suitable for ruffles would harmonize with your curtain material and your room. Contrasting ruffles like those used on new curtains should be the basis for rejuvenating curtains. The possibilities include: (1) a ruffle of the same material in a contrasting color, (2) a chintz ruffle on a white curtain, (3) a white organdy ruffle on a chintz curtain; (4) plain-colored chintz ruffles on transparent rayons.

Ruffled Curtains: When you can match the fabric, add a straight band to the end of the curtain and finish it with a ruffle exactly the fullness and finish of the ruffle already on the curtain. When it is not possible to match the fabric, consider the possibility of a contrasting band that looks like a valance.

Another way of lengthening, if the curtain has a ruffled valance, is to use the valance to lengthen the curtain at the top, then replace it with a valance in a contrasting fabric and color. Cut the original valance in half. Rip the heading and casing at the top of the curtain. Sew the end of the curtain to the old valance under the ruffle and use its casing for the top of the curtain.

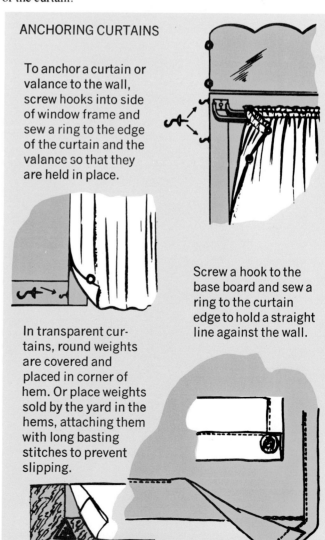

ANCHORING CURTAINS

To anchor a curtain or valance to the wall, screw hooks into side of window frame and sew a ring to the edge of the curtain and the valance so that they are held in place.

In transparent curtains, round weights are covered and placed in corner of hem. Or place weights sold by the yard in the hems, attaching them with long basting stitches to prevent slipping.

Screw a hook to the base board and sew a ring to the curtain edge to hold a straight line against the wall.

Spreads And Covers

T *he* *covering of a bed or couch should harmonize with the furniture and decoration of a room and protect the bedding as well. When twin beds are placed close together, one large cover is often used for both. When they are separated by a small space, the two covers must match; but if they are in different parts of the room a color or textile contrast can be developed.*

Several types of bedspreads are described here so you can choose the one best suited to your room plan and the type of bed. You can also use for beds the suggestions on day beds. Consider the pillows in your choice. Pillows must be comfortable and suited to the individual needs and preferences of each member of the family.

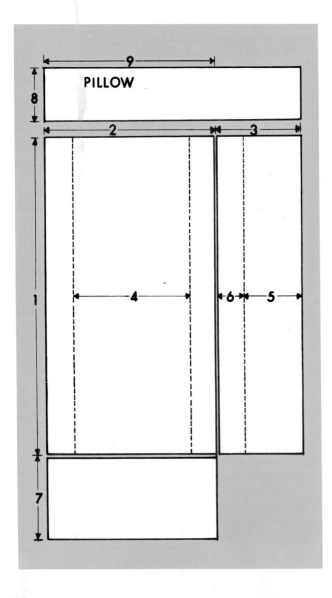

Decide upon the style of spread and make a list of your needs for that style, listing the side pieces separately so you know where a band or ruffle comes, how wide each will be, and how much you will need for hems and joinings. Decide upon the treatment of the top—whether one piece of fabric will cover the whole top or a strip through the center.

Measurements for Bedspreads: (1) Length of bed from headboard to footboard; (2) width of bed from edge to edge; (3) length from top of mattress to floor; (4) width of fabric; (5) length of ruffle from floor to heading; (6) length of band above ruffle; (7) width of tuck-in at foot; (8) length of pillow cover; (9) width of pillow cover.

Count the complete length, including width of pillow cover and tuck-in at the footboard (line X), for the fabric length. To estimate how many lengths of fabric, check the width measures with the width of your fabric. Add hem measurements and all measurements for ruffles or pleated skirts.

CUTTING A BEDSPREAD

Upholstery fabrics are usually 50 inches wide and require no piecing. When narrower fabrics are used, one length is used for the center and the other length split and pieced to each side of the center length. The joining of the pieces is decorated.

Decide whether you want a spread banded around the edge before it turns, banded after it turns, or with a deeper band or ruffle that touches the floor. Decide on the size of the ruffle and band before you start to cut.

Bedspreads are cut as shown in the diagram. The spread can extend to the top of the mattress at the headboard, or it can be 18 inches longer so that it folds over the pillow, or it can be finished with reversed seams at the end so you can turn it back on top of the pillow. Or you can make a separate straight cover for the pillow.

PLAIN BEDSPREADS

There are four types of plain bedspreads to choose from: (1) an unshaped spread which hangs free on all sides, (2) a spread with boxed seams at the foot, (3) a boxed spread with cord or welt seams, and (4) a spread with decorative bands of contrasting fabric.

Left: Diagram for taking basic measurements for estimating materials necessary to make bedspread.

Opposite: Quaint Victorian patterned fabrics complement the turn-of-the-century brass bed.

Opposite: Opulent fabrics in a luxurious bedroom. To keep attention focused on the canopied bed, the window treatment is minimal. Below: Especially effective repetition of a pattern that you can stitch up for your own home. Note the space-making result of pattern against pattern here.

Plain Unshaped Bedspread: Unshaped spreads are often made of unbleached muslin, appliqued, decorated with candlewicking, or finished with a contrasting band of scallops. They can also be made from any cretonne or chintz.

Plain Bedspread with Boxed End: This spread is boxed only at the foot and can be cut long enough to cover the pillows at the other end. It is particularly suitable for a bed with an open footboard. Turn the spread to the wrong side and join the fabric seams so that the edges of the spread hang straight to the length desired. Box the corner at the footboard. You can also mark the edge line of the mattress if you wish. First stitch a seam along the mattress line, then turn the spread to the right side and stitch the seam again. This seam must be reversed at the top of the spread when it is long enough to turn back and cover the pillows.

Corded Edges On Bedspreads: The lower edges of the spread can be corded and a double band corded on both sides of the mattress, extending over the pillows. In other corded spreads, the joinings of the seams are finished with a welting.

Corded spreads are made of monk's-cloth, velveteen and other heavy fabrics, and the cording should be heavy.

When you join the seams, overlap the seam ¾ inch and pin it smoothly. Make the first basting ½ inch back from the edge and insert the cord in the seam. Then baste the seam close to the cord and stitch it with a cording foot. In heavy material it is wise to rip the basting as you stitch, letting the machine push the material ahead of the foot. This avoids puckering.

To make a rounded corner, tie a pencil to a string so you can draw an edge equal to the side skirt of the spread. Hold the string at the seam and swing the pencil in a true line. Cut your corners on the true curve; turn the edge in and stitch it over a covered cord. This makes a more finished edge than turning the hem over a cord.

Plain Spread with Decorative Bands: Sometimes a spread is trimmed with a banding which extends across the pillow bolster and outlines the edge of the mattress. This band can be repeated at the hem of the spread. Bands are pleated, shirred, contrasted, or ruffled. They usually cover a seam joining.

Above: Make a simple quilted unshaped coverlet for a high fashion look at a low budget price.
Below: A variety of ways to finish fitted bedspreads, fitted or not, as described on page 243.

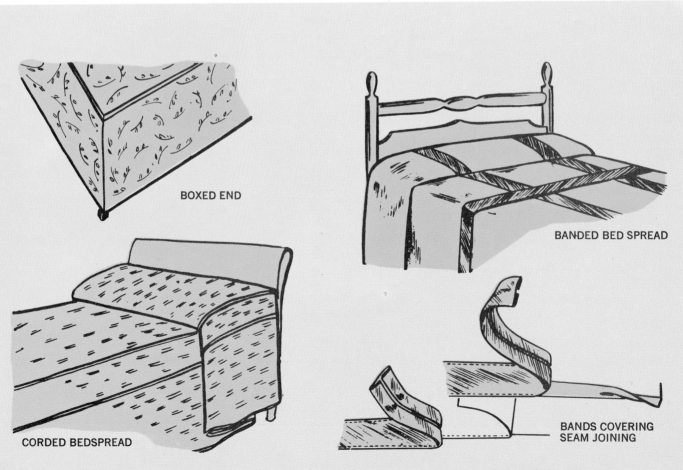

BOXED END

BANDED BED SPREAD

CORDED BEDSPREAD

BANDS COVERING
SEAM JOINING

Quilted spread made with boxed end and finished with self cording repeats the pattern of the drapery fabric. Remember too that a multi-color pattern will hide more stains and wrinkles than solid color.

Below: Another example of an unshaped bedspread that drapes ever so dramatically. The secret is in the cutting of the corners at the foot of the bed and the additional body of the self-bound edges.

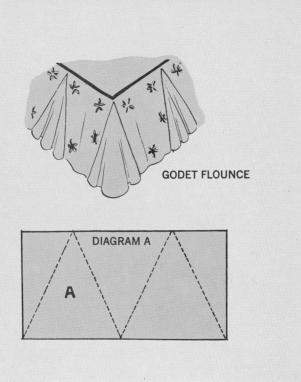

GODET FLOUNCE

DIAGRAM A

A

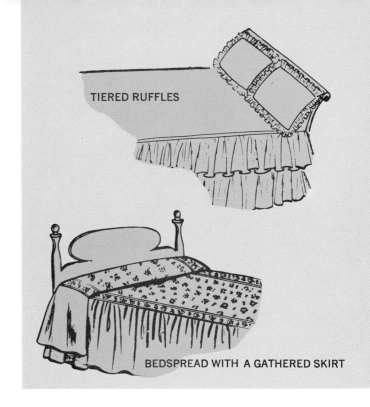

TIERED RUFFLES

BEDSPREAD WITH A GATHERED SKIRT

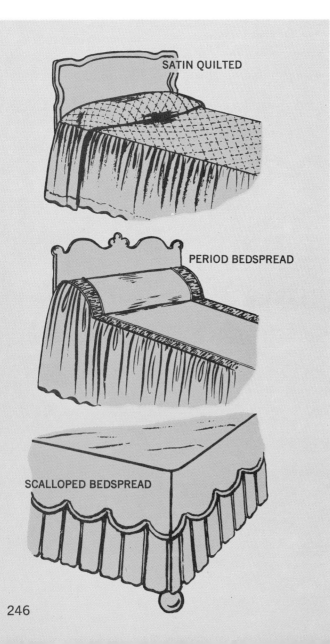

SATIN QUILTED

PERIOD BEDSPREAD

SCALLOPED BEDSPREAD

BEDSPREADS FOR BEDS WITH FOOTBOARDS

Bedspread with Gathered or Pleated Skirt: Cut a panel for the center of the spread. It should be 90 inches long and wide enough to cover the mattress, including the side bands. Cut these bands and join them to the center strip with piping or welt seams. Mark off 18 inches at one end for the turn-in at the foot of the bed. Finish these edges with a hem.

Cut the skirt section 26 inches deep, or the size desired. It can be pleated or gathered. Finish the skirt edge in a hem, gather or pleat it, and join it to the side of the spread. The bolster is finished with corresponding bands. The ends can be hemmed or ruffled to match the edge of the spread.

Godet Flounce Spread: Cut the spread large enough to cover the top of the mattress. Shape one end so that it tucks in at the footboard. Fit the sides of the spread in a straight boxed line. Divide the side length into even spaces and cut a slash in each space. Insert a godet—a triangular piece of self-fabric—into each slash. Diagram A shows the most economical way to cut a godet. These spreads are finished with a very narrow hem.

Circular Flounce Spreads: This spread requires a great deal of yardage and so is very expensive. To cut a circular flounce, fold the material so that the lengthwise grain parallels the crosswise grain. Put a pin in one corner. Tie a pencil to a string, hold the string at the corner, and draw the circular cutting lines for the flounce across the wider width of the fabric. The radius of the curve depends upon the depth of your ruffle. Hem the edge or bind it with ribbon. Join the circular flounces in seams that are hemstitched when the fabric is transparent. In satin or velvet make welted seams. The edges of the spread are finished with piping or ribbon, and placed above the top edge of the flounce. When elaborate spreads like this are used, the pillows are rolled and covered with a plain fabric.

246

Satin Quilted Bedspreads: These are often cut in a size to fit the mattress and finished with a circular or gathered self-fabric ruffle which is not quilted, or a transparent rayon.

Spreads for Period Beds: When a spread is made of velvet, velveteen, or a rich brocade for a period bed, the fabric covering the mattress is cut long enough to extend over the pillows and be tucked down. In spreads of this type the corded seam outlines the mattress and the pillows, and the gathered skirt is cut long enough at the pillow end so that it can follow the curved line and keep an even line at the floor.

Scalloped Bedspread: When combinations of chintz and taffeta, or candlewicking and chintz, are used in a bedspread, the gathered or pleated flounce should be mounted on a separate lining placed over the bed spring. Then you can make a tailored bedspread with scalloped or fringed edges which extends over the ruffle and looks as though it is joined. This is very practical when one fabric is washable and the other is not. Candlewick spreads can be used with a chintz or organdy ruffle if the spreads are tucked in around the mattress and the ruffle falls below and in back of the wooden sideboard of the bed.

Organdy Bedspreads: Use embroidered organdy, eyelet embroidery, or plain organdy. They can have one ruffle, two ruffles, or a ruffle finished with a ruffle. The covering for the mattress can be outlined with ribbon beading or a double organdy ruching. The ruffles can be joined in a piped seam or a gathered heading.

In making this kind of spread, remember that every additional ruffle means extra ironing. Be sure the organdy has a washable finish which requires no starch. You can cover the mattress with the organdy and stitch a ruffle into the seam joining; you can place a double ruffle over the seam joining; or you can use a ribbon beading in the seam joining.

A double ruffle is easy to make. Have your fabric hemstitched and run a machine stitching through the center. Cut the edges in a picot. Turn the lower edge of the flounce to the right side and apply the double ruffle on the turned edge, stitching it through the center. The ruffles for the spread over the mattress are done the same way. Fit a plain boxed cover in white muslin or colored sateen over the bed to form a background for all transparent spreads.

Spreads for Double Post Beds: Double post beds are often covered with candlewick or quilting. The underflounce and canopies are made of fine muslin or organdy, but some people like linen, silk, or any fabric suitable for a spread. The most popular canopies are gathered on both edges and joined to a ruffle with a heading. The canopy ruffle is usually half the width of the skirt ruffle. Join it just as you would the ruffle of a spread.

Pillow Bolsters: Bolsters are cut in one with the spread or cut separately. They can be finished with a hem, a scalloped facing, a contrasting band, a fringe, or a cording. When the curtains in the bedroom are ruffled or a ruffle is used on the edge of the bedspread, the bolster can be finished with a ruffle.

One-Piece Covers: Any day-bed, couch, or cot without arms and back can be suitably decorated with a one-piece cover.

Informal Couch Covers: Take a piece of material long enough to cover the couch and touch the floor at both ends. This material should be placed on the couch so that the material not only touches the floor at the ends, but also at the front. If it is not wide enough to extend fully across the couch to the back, seam another piece of cloth to it. If the fabric has a pattern be sure to match the design at the joining. The corners are curved by cutting off the pointed ends which touch the floor. Make a narrow hem on all the edges. This casual cover can hang free on all sides; but if the couch is placed against the wall, the cover will stay neater if it is tucked under the mattress on the wall side.

Tailored Couch Covers: There are two ways of cutting a tailored couch cover: (1) One piece of fabric is cut to fit the top exactly, and a long contrasting band is cut to extend all around the couch on the sides. (2) Two full lengths of fabric can be cut and joined together and fitted at the corners.

For the first type, lay the fabric that fits the top in place, right side down. Begin at one corner and pin the long band of fabric around this top section—it, too, must face away from you. At the corner pin a seam through the band, then continue to pin the strip along the long edge of the couch cover, and so on all around the cover. If you pin carefully and are an expert stitcher, you can stitch these seams without basting. Turn the cover to the right side and stitch the seam close to the seamed edge, making an upholsterers' seam. Then hem the lower edge, and your couch cover is completed.

For the second type, lay the fabric on the couch, wrong side out, and fit all four corners so the cover is smooth but not too tight. To do this, hold the corner points out and pin a seam line straight down the fabric, close to the couch. Stitch these seam lines and hem the cover. You will have a smooth unseamed edge except at the corners.

Upholsterers' Couch Covers: These covers are boxed and tailored, and the seams are finished with a cording or piping. Cut your fabric as directed for the first type of Tailored Couch Covers above. Before joining the seam, outline the top piece of fabric with a cording by turning the edge over a thick cord and basting it. Be sure the corners are sharp. Lay this piece wrong side out on the top of the couch and pin a long strip of fabric to the corded seam, so that when the seam is stitched the cord will extend around the edge.

Piping is applied the same way, basting it all around the edge of the large center piece so that the seam edge of the piping matches the edge of the cover. Piping is basted to the right side of the fabric. Be sure to turn the corners sharply.

Turn the piece to the wrong side, lay it in place on the top of the couch, and pin the band in place. When the seam is stitched the piping will outline the edge. The lower edge can be hemmed, it can be corded, or the piping color can be continued around the lower edge, or a contrasting band can be stitched to the edge in a faced hem.

247

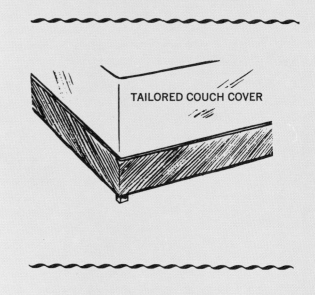

TAILORED COUCH COVER

A quilted spread in a luxury fabric for a formal bedroom, below. The headboard has been covered with the same parallel-quilted fabric—the most elegant example of decor coordination imagineable!

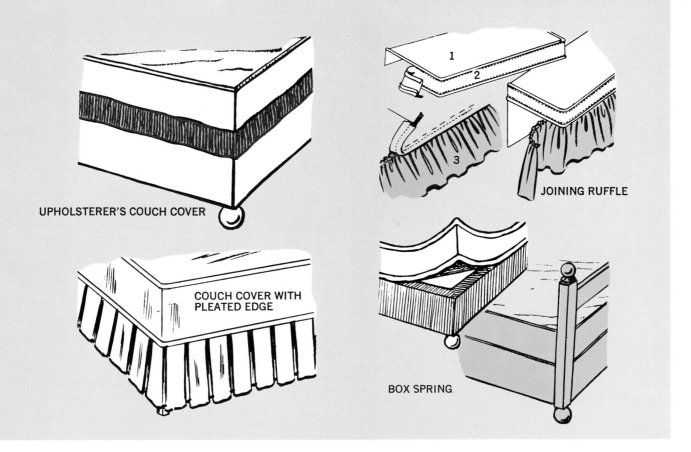

UPHOLSTERER'S COUCH COVER

COUCH COVER WITH PLEATED EDGE

JOINING RUFFLE

BOX SPRING

Couch Cover with Pleated Edge: This couch cover is cut in three pieces. (1) Cut a large piece of fabric the size of the top of the couch. (2) Cut a band, 1 inch wider than the depth of the mattress and long enough to go all the way around the couch. (3) Cut the pleated extension. It should be wide enough to reach from the band to the floor, allowing for a hem, and twice as long as the band.

Turn the edge of the top section around a cord and baste it. Put it upside down on the couch and pin the band to it all the way around. Stitch this seam—the cord will finish the seamline. Turn the lower edge of the band over a cord and baste it. Hem the pleated extension and baste it in box pleats, which can be spaced close together or 4 inches apart. The pleats can be deep, with the fabric meeting in back, or shallow, turned under ¾ inch. Join the pleated extension to the corded edge of the band in a seam, so that when it is stitched, the corded edge heads the pleats. Sometimes a cording is run down each corner.

Ruffled Couch Cover: A ruffled couch cover is cut in three pieces. (1) Cut a piece large enough to fit the top of the couch. (2) Cut a band as wide as the depth of the mattress or more, and long enough to go around the couch. (3) Cut a ruffle 2½ times as long as the band and as wide as you desire.

Decide upon the finish. You can hem the ruffle and stitch the other seams; you can bind the ruffle and pipe the seams, using a color contrast; you can face the ruffle with a contrasting band and make the top of the couch cover in the same contrasting color.

Put the top piece right side down on the couch. Pin the band in place all around it—first basting the piping if it is used. Stitch the band to the top piece. Finish the lower edge of the ruffle with hem or binding and gather the ruffle at the top edge. Seam the ruffle to the lower edge of the band,

spacing the gathers carefully. If the cover is finished with piping, it must be basted to the edge of the band before the ruffle is joined.

Two-Piece Couch Covers: This type of cover can be used only on day-beds or couches with box springs.

Upholstered Box Springs: Cut the band which covers the side of the spring 5 inches wider than the width of the spring and long enough to go around all four sides. (Piecings must not be made at the corners.) Turn the springs on end and apply this band with catch stitches on both edges so that it is smooth and secure. If you wish, the edges of the springs can be traced with a cording applied where the band passes over both edges. The cover for the mattress can be made in two ways: Either cut the cover long enough to tuck in at top and bottom—a long tuck so it will not pull out—or fit the cover as directed for a tailored couch cover and finish the edge to hang over the covered spring. This second method is used when ball fringe and braiding are introduced.

BOXED PILLOWS AND COVERINGS

A boxed pillow covering is sometimes used in a man's room to tuck the pillows into during the day. Boxed pillows are a must when you arrange a day-bed or a studio couch.

The Pillow: Cut out two pieces of unbleached muslin of the size of the pillow. Join the two pieces with a 3- or 4-inch band stitched to the edges. Turn this lining to the wrong side and stuff it. When feathers or down are transferred from one pillow to another, overcast the closure and cover with piped or corded seams.

249

Quilts And Quilting

Two very old and honored needle arts have recently been newly popularized—those of making quilt tops and of quilting itself.

Quilt tops are usually made in one of two techniques, or a combination of them. The favorite of early English and American quiltmakers—and of fashionwise needlewomen today—is "piecing" or "patchwork", the stitching together of comparatively small pieces of fabric into blocks to be joined, or into one large geometric design. A second technique is that of "laid work", which we also know as applique, and which has been described elsewhere (see Index).

PATCHWORK POINTERS

Using a pattern you have adapted from a book or obtained from a commercial source, cut actual-size patterns from sturdy cardboard or fine sandpaper. (Sandpaper patterns can be laid sand-side down on the fabric and will not slip.) Working on the wrong side of the fabric, with a soft pencil outline around the pieces, allowing for ¼ inch seams all around. Right sides together, join the pieces by hand or machine, pressing the seams open as you work. In machine-stitched piecing, you may notice a slight pucker at the corner joinings. If it is really slight, the final quilting will make it invisible; if it is not so "slight", check your marking lines and be sure you are joining correctly. Also check your machine tension.

Below: A curtained sleeping alcove can be opened to display its charming "Daddy Hex" coverlet, or closed to hide the sleeping area entirely behind a draped "wall" of fabric.

Appliqued and then quilted, "Sail Ho" is a quilt for a sea struck young adventurer.

CHOOSING THE DESIGN

If you want to use a traditional design, look in your library for books showing old quilts—you will find a many beautiful books have been written on the subject. Keep in mind the style, period, and color range of the room in which it will be used, and choose your design and fabrics accordingly. Size is also to be considered; mattresses are about 39 inches wide (twin), 47 inches (three-quarter), or 54 inches (full), while 75 inches is the standard length. Thus, a quilt in the standard 81 inches by 96 inches will allow a deep overhang on the smaller beds and also sufficient overhang to cover the top of a dust ruffle on a full size. On a very low bed, you may wish to omit one row of blocks or the border; on a larger one, the reverse would be wise.

MATERIALS AND EQUIPMENT

Top Fabric: The choice of the fabric for the top is a question of appearance—that is, which will best give the effect you are striving for in your design. All fabrics can be quilted, although some more effectively than others. Just be sure they are pre-shrunk and colorfast.

Cotton percales make lovely quilts. Chintz, calico, and other printed fabrics are effective too. Luxury quilts of satin, taffeta, velvet, velveteen, and sateen are best suited to some homes; in others, chiffon, china silk, and transparent cottons are used for luxury details.

Backings: Backings are made of percale, tissue gingham, or in luxury quilts, velveteen. The lining for Italian quilting is waxed cheesecloth, and is often covered with a china silk, chiffon, or other transparent cover.

Filling: The interlining, or padding in the English tradition, is usually batting spread smoothly over the lining. An old blanket may also be used. In wool-growing communities, teased wool is often used in both quilts and tufted spreads.

Thread and Needles: Quilting is usually done with fine polished or waxed thread, using as fine a thread and needle as possible. There are times, however, when a blunt embroidery needle is preferred. Sometimes a colored thread or a heavy thread is used to emphasize a contrast in the design; sometimes the whole spread is quilted in a contrasting color. Decide on the effect desired and secure enough buttonhole-twist cotton, twisted embroidery floss, or sewing cotton or silk, to finish the work. Be sure the thread is as sunfast as the fabric.

Chalk, Pins, Basting Thread: Secure also a box of long pins, some chalk for tracing the design, and basting thread for tacking.

Quilting Frame: For bed quilts or large covers a quilting frame is essential. Small articles can be quilted with or without an embroidery frame. You can buy a quilting frame or make one at home. If you buy one, be sure of these things: (1) The clamps are adjustable. (2) The muslin to which you pin the quilt is firm and will wear. (3) The frame can be adjusted for a narrow width as well as wide. (4) The folding crossbar that holds the frame is strong and set at the correct height. Don't be afraid of the size of the frame. Most experienced quilters who work alone roll the quilt on one side bar of the frame and set the working section in a narrow strip which fits easily into the room.

Above: "Turkey Tracks" is an Early American pieced quilt pattern which has proven to be equally attractive in the most modern room.

Left, above: Appliqued "Apple Blossoms" can be made by hand or on your machine. Note that the quilting motif repeats the applique design.

Left, below: "Friendship Plume" is made in the Hawaiian manner—large applique pieces cut from new fabric in feathery geometrics.

Right: Made with delicate, pastel appliques, "Old Fashioned Rose" is a perfect quilt for the most feminine young girl's bedroom.

When pieced with pastels, "Dresden Plate" is a beautiful classic; made with bright solid colors, it becomes a contemporary masterpiece.

QUILTING BLOCKS

As each block is complete, mark the quilting design on the top. Place filling (cut ¼ inch smaller all around the block) between top and backing. Baste the three pieces together, then stitch by hand or by machine (10 to 12 stitches to the inch) to within ⅜ inch of the edge. When all blocks are complete, fold top and backing edges over each other so filling edges meet. Stitch together, keeping seams straight. (If desired, these seams may be covered with strips of contrasting color to coordinate with the dominant color of the room.)

QUILTING LARGE AREAS

- The purpose of quilting is twofold: first, to hold together the top, the batting, and the backing; and second, to decorate those areas not pieced or laid. A pieced quilt needs less quilting than an appliqued one.
- Straight lines may be marked using a yard stick and pencil, curves and circles with a string and pencil, more elaborate patterns with perforated paper or dressmaker's carbon paper.
- Baste together the top, filling, and backing across one short end; from this end, baste the full length at 6-inch intervals. Pin or baste the first edge to the muslin strip on one rod of the frame, roll the quilt to this side until about the middle. Smooth remainder over the other side of the frame, drop it between the rods, and baste end to muslin strip at far side of the frame. In rolling the quilt, be sure to keep it perfectly straight. Roll the entire quilt on the second rod.

- Quilt from one end to the other, using fine running stitches. Do not knot the ends of threads, but leave a ¾ inch end and quilt over it.
- You will not be able to avoid some slippage. Your basting may have to be loosened, but if the slippage is small, simply trim the edges when quilting is completed.
- Machine quilting can be done with great speed. The quilt top, filling and backing are prepared exactly as above. Loosen the tension of the machine if needed. The work goes faster if you use a quilting attachment which marks the rows. When you do this, the quilt must be tacked more closely to prevent slipping, and the tension must be opened wide. The best designs for a machine-made quilt have continuous lines which do not turn abruptly.

Many home sewers use machine quilting as a background for hand quilting. Others use it to tack the quilt. To do this, you stitch the design all over with a very loose tension in self-matching thread. You can then cover these lines and additional ones with hand quilting.

TUFTED QUILTS

Tufted quilts are easy and quick to make. People who live in wool-raising districts can use teased wool; those who live on farms can save down from plucked chickens; and those in cities can use cotton batting interlinings or an old blanket.

Make the cover of cotton, sateen, rayon taffeta, or a synthetic fabric.

Cut the fabric a little larger than the finished size of the quilt. Should you use wool or feathers, first enclose them in a cover the size of the finished quilt. Lay the three layers out smoothly. Before inserting the work in the quilting frame, tie strings to the frame, running both ways, in a squared or lattice effect. This string design will make the work faster and easier by showing where to spot each tie in the quilt. Pin the quilt to the muslin at the edge of the frame and stretch it. Using a double thread, pass a needle up and down through all the fabrics from one side to the other, bringing the needle out a short distance away from its original insertions. Tie the knot double before you clip the ends, and be sure not to clip them too close. The thread for tying can be yarn or embroidery thread, or even with fine ribbon.

When you take the quilt out of the frame, turn the edges all around with a hot iron so the edges of the seam face each other. Baste the edges carefully and stitch as close to the outside edge as possible.

FINISHING THE EDGES

Turn the edges of lining and outside fabric so they face each other. The edge can be stitched, slip-stitched, finished with piping or cording or bound. When the quilt is planned, consider the edge decoration as well as its finish. On pillows and decorative bedspreads, the edge is often scalloped, and sometimes the scallops are bound. The quilting at the edge can follow a scalloped outline or a straight banded effect. Stitching several rows, equally spaced, and running a soft cord through them makes a lovely edge.

254

Decor Accessories

S **pecial** *touches that are comparatively simple to make can transform a merely "pleasant" room into one which will make you and your* family truly proud. These include pillows, lampshades, and dressing tables for your bedrooms.

Floor length table cover and thick pads for the captain's chairs create a colorful dining area in a wood-paneled room. Suspended lamp spotlights the charming basket of flowers centerpiece.

Pillows! Pillows! Pillows! For every room in the house, and spilling over to the patio, too! Make them of fabric coordinated or contrasted to spreads and upholstery, piece or applique them for unusual color effect—or for the ultimate luxury, quilt the tops by hand or on your machine.

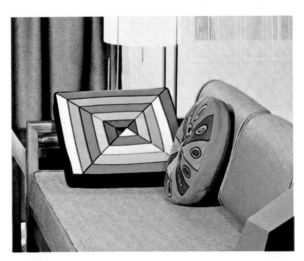

256

PILLOWS

In earlier chapters, bolster pillows and boxed pillows were discussed. (See Index.) By far the most popular—and easiest—decorative pillow is the "knife-edge" type. It is simply two pieces of material sewn together with whatever finish you prefer. Top and back can be the same—cut from leftover drapery or slipcover fabric used in the room, for example. Or you can make as simple or elaborate a top as you wish and use a solid color backing. These tops can be appliqued with a motif from leftover fabric on solid harmonizing fabric, or be a beautiful showcase for a piece of fine crewel or needlepoint.

Pillow Forms: Determine the size and shape—circular, triangular, square, or rectangular—you wish the finished pillow to be. From muslin, cut two pieces ½ inch larger all around. Sew together with ½-inch seams, leaving a 3 inch opening. Stuff with shredded foam rubber or kapok, then stitch the opening closed.

Cover: Cut and join the top and back as for the pillow form, but leave an opening large enough to insert the form. Any inserted trim—cording, ruffling, et cetera—would be sewn in during this step. Applied trim—fringing, twisted cord, or tassels, for example—would be added after the raw edges have been turned in and slip-stitched closed.

Zippers can be set into the opening, to facilitate removing the cover when it becomes soiled, but it is usually simpler to rip the opening and re-stitch it after the cover has been cleaned.

LAMPSHADES

Lampshades are made of paper or fabric stretched over a frame. The type of frame will to a large extent limit your choice of covering, so an analysis of the kinds of frames is given before the descriptions of lampshades you can make at home.

Wire Frames: For a lampshade made of fabric, a wire frame is the most secure foundation. There are several qualities of wire frame, and the strength of the frame should be considered. When you are planning to stretch a plain fabric over the frame, it should be a strong one. A weaker frame is permissible for a gathered covering; and "petticoat" coverings can be put on any kind of frame.

Wire frames come in all sizes and shapes, and the unskilled eye finds it difficult to measure the proportions of an uncovered frame. For this reason many people find it more satisfactory to buy a frame covered with a cheap fabric and replace it with the desired fabric.

Parchment Frames: Many old frames are parchment, and they can be used for the lining of a fabric shade even if the shade is torn on one side; or it can be used as the foundation for a skirt covering.

PAPER LAMPSHADES

Paper shades can be smoothly fitted or pleated. Use any heavy wrapping paper or wallpaper—all types of paper can be shellacked on both sides; use coated paper, which means the surface is coated with a quick-drying enamel; or use old maps.

Smooth Shades: To make a pattern for a smooth paper shade, put a large newspaper on the floor and paint the edges of the frame with white or a color. While the paint is *still wet*, roll the frame across the newspaper (if the shade is not round, turn it evenly). The wet paint will leave the marks of a perfect pattern on the paper.

Cut out this pattern as soon as the paint dries, leaving enough extra at the edge for a joining. Cut your map or shellacked paper by this pattern and join the ends. With coarse thread overcast the shade to the frame at top and bottom. Cover the overcasting with braid which sews on, or decorative self-adhering tape.

Pleated Shades: Pleated paper shades are usually cut circular before they are pleated, and it is very important to test both the shape and the size of the pleat before you start to work on the shade. Cut a piece of newspaper and shape it to your frame, making the pleats the size desired. Pin this paper pattern to the frame between each pleat. When you have finished, remove the paper and use it for a pattern.

Shellacked and lacquered paper must be carefully creased *before* the shellac or lacquer is applied. The top can be overcast to the top of the frame, between each pleat. This is easier than punching holes through which a cord is run. Fasten the joining with white glue.

FABRIC LAMPSHADES

Shades made of taffeta can be gathered or stretched tight on a frame. The taffeta used for lampshades is sheer and comes in a wide assortment of lovely colors. The beige rose tones give good light. If your color scheme requires a still wider assortment of colors, you can also use dress-weight taffeta.

Before you make the shade, decide whether all edges will be finished with a double fold of self-fabric, a decorative ribbon or braid, or a ruffle. Assemble everything you will need for the trimming before you start to work. All wire frames must be wound with seam binding or a bias of self-fabric before they are covered.

Some gathered shades made of dress-weight taffeta are unlined, others are lined; a stretched shade is always lined. Select the color of the lining carefully. No matter what the color of the outside fabric, the lining usually gives a rose-colored glow. Look at the lining fabric over a light when you test its color.

Unlined Gathered Shade: Cut the fabric the width of the frame, allowing 2 inches for seam allowance. It should be 1½ times the length of the largest circumference of the frame. Turn in the top edge and gather it. Space the gathers carefully around the top of the frame, pinning them to the binding. Then overcast the gathers to the top of the frame with strong thread. Pull the lower edge of the fabric over the lower wire and sew it to the wire, stretching the gathers in place as you do so, so they are straight up and down. This makes a tighter, more professional gathered frame than the method in which you gather the lower edge and try to hold it firmly in place.

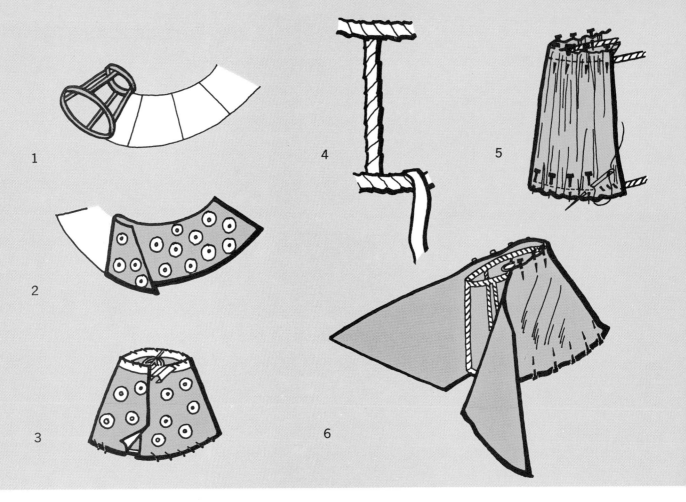

To cover a lampshade frame, paint the frame and roll it over a piece of paper while it is wet to get a "pattern" of the frame (1); using the paper pattern, cut the fabric cover (2); sew to frame (3). Wind bias binding or self fabric over frame (4); gather and pin cover (5); stretched cover pinned (6).

Lined Gathered Shades: When the fabric is very sheer, the glare of the light through it often ruins the effect. This is corrected by making a lining of the sheer taffeta used for lampshades. Cut the lining the size of the largest circumference of the frame, with seam allowances, and 3 inches wider than the depth of the frame. Seam the joining; turn in the top edge and gather it. Space these gathers at the top of the frame. The lining is placed on the inside of the frame with the seams facing out. When the top edge has been securely sewed to the frame, pull the lower edge over the wire at the bottom of the frame and overcast it securely to the frame. Cut away the extra fabric, not too close.

Then cut the outside gathered section as directed above for Unlined Gathered Shade and apply it. When you stretch the lower edge, proceed as though the lining were not there; this edge is overcast over the lining.

Finishing Edges for Shades: The top edge of a gathered shade can be bound with a decorative ribbon. It must bind the inside as well as the outside, so that anyone looking down on the shade sees a finished edge on both sides. Many shades are finished at the lower edge with scalloped-edge, French or straight ribbon.

Shades can also be finished at top and bottom with tailored folds of self-fabric. Cut a true bias twice the width of the finished fold. Stitch and turn it. Apply the fold so that the seam is slip-stitched to the top of the frame, and the fold

extends a little above the frame. The lower edge can be finished with the same kind of fold, or a wide fold can extend below the frame—to cover the light or the base of an ugly fixture. In some lamps this type of fold is headed with a narrow ribbon; in others with a trimming braid.

Stretched Shade: This kind of shade is not hard to make if you work with a true bias. Before you cut the material, stretch it around the lamp so that: (1) the ends securely meet, (2) the fabric really stretches, and (3) the lower edge is securely covered. Trim the material away only a little, then start to pin the fabric around the lower edge of the frame. Before you overcast it in place, press the pinned end against you and pull the fabric over the top edge of the frame, placing pins in the edge as you work. When the fabric is stretched smoothly in all but two or three places, turn the frame again and continue to stretch the fabric at the lower edge, replacing pins as necessary. You often have to loosen a pin at the opposite edge and pull the fabric into a different position to remove a stubborn wrinkle. When the cover looks smooth, join the ends by slip-stitching them together with matching thread and small stitches. With strong thread and big stitches, overcast the fabric to the frame, pulling it as you release each pin.

A stretched shade must be lined. In very costly shades the lining fabric is stretched first and then the top covering. In less expensive ones, only the covering is stretched. The lining is then cut on a true bias and overcast to the lower edge, then stretched to the top of the frame, fitting out all the wrinkles possible. This latter way is successful only in a straight frame. When the frame slopes, both lining and covering must be stretched. The edges of a stretched frame are finished as described in Finishing Edges for Shades.

Heavier Fabric Shades: To make lampshades of the same material as the draperies or other room furnishings, you can use a wire frame and make a stretched shade as described here, or you can use the top and lower band of an old shade, by first using your old shade as a pattern to cut cardboard and then pasting the fabric to the edges of the cardboard.

The edges of the shade can be finished with ball fringe or a folded bias strip. Overcast them in place with soft yarn which will not tear the cardboard.

Petticoat Lampshades: A petticoat shade can be used to cover an old shade, or a new wire frame, for a bedroom lamp. If the frame is wire, with no lining, you can make an unlined shade of glazed chintz, cretonne, sateen, or taffeta. If you want a transparent shade of dotted swiss, organdy, or a sheer rayon, you must either make a lined shade or use the old shade for lining. Test the shade with a light. If the bulb glares through, you need a lining. If the shade gives a pleasant light in the test, you can make the petticoat effect.

Cut the ruffle three times as long as the largest circumference of the shade and 5 inches deeper than the shade. Finish one edge with a hem or binding and turn in the other edge 3 inches for a heading. Pleat or gather the fabric and join the ends. Set this petticoat on the shade and adjust the gathers or pleats so that the top is finished with the heading. This joining can be finished with a ribbon bow, or a plain band of ribbon or trimming can be placed below the heading as a finish.

DRESSING TABLES

A dressing table can be simple or elaborate, large or small. Decide where you have space in your room for it and plan accordingly. It can be set into a corner, or it can be a table. Dressing tables made of unpainted wood, with drawer space and a bar on either side which opens, are sold in the stores.

A small table or a sewing machine can be transformed into a dressing table. To be really comfortable and serviceable, a dressing table should have drawers or shelves and a washable top, either a sheet of glass, an old mirror, or self-adhering plastic-coated paper.

Dressing-table skirts are usually gathered, but you can make them in ruffled or pleated effects, as tailored or as feminine as you wish. There is no rule to control the dressing table—no matter how tailored the room as a whole, a feminine dressing table is in order. Because the skirt must be removed and washed, it is often applied with snapper tape nailed to the edge of the table.

When you space the material for the skirt, split it so that the section which covers the drawer is made separately. When it is attached, it looks like part of the skirt. When the drawer is pulled out, that section of the skirt comes with it.

Dressing-table skirts can be made of taffeta, organdy,

net, chintz, satin, or any sheer cotton fabric used in the decoration of the room. Mount one on a stiffened band or make the heading or shirring with ruffles of very narrow edgings, so that the powder won't accumulate in the edge. For this reason a smooth edge is preferable.

Making a Dressing-Table Skirt: First estimate the yardage, measuring from the floor and allowing for a hem. Measure the outside of your table and allow twice this width for making a gathered skirt. For the foundation of tiered skirts, fit the fabric smoothly to the table.

When the hem is finished, gather the skirt or ruffle. Finish it with a 1-inch binding, which can be a contrasting color. When you attach the skirt to the table with thumbtacks, this banding is pulled down over the tacks. You can put a large or small bow in the center of the binding. If the skirt has tiered ruffles, each ruffle can be bound and tied with a bow, or each succeeding ruffle can be attached underneath the previous one.

You can finish the edge of the skirt with a binding and match it in the turned-down binding at the top. You can applique little bows to the fabric of the skirt to match this color.

Many dressing-table skirts are finished at the top with a scalloped band. Others are finished with shirred bands emphasized by applied trimming. When your dressing table needs a stiff heading under a shirred band, cut a strip of buckram the desired width and length, and cover it with fabric. Stitch this band to the inside edge of the skirt under the shirring.

Shown below: Gathered dressing table skirt set on a band, and a tiered, bow-trimmed ruffled skirt.

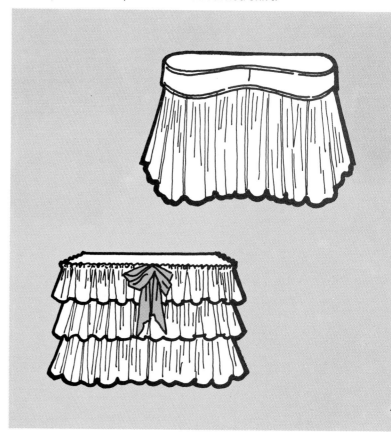

Family Fun Rooms

Camps, *vacation homes, and play rooms are only a few of the rooms which must take hard wear and still be attractive and comfortable. The seashore home presents similar problems. This chapter is given over to suggestions for the decoration of these less formal rooms which include rooms for children of all ages, as well as* suggestions for individual touches in transitory *rooms. In all of them, remember that fabrics must be strong and easily cleaned. They must be practical first and decorative afterward. The same type of decoration described here is appropriate to children's play rooms, adult game rooms, and any home with craft furnishings.*

Below: Repeat a favorite motif for a room to delight a very young child. Note the clever storage drawers, too.

Above: A dream room for a romantic young girl. A difficult corner becomes a draped bed fit for a princess!

CAMPS AND VACATION HOMES

The most suitable fabrics for these interiors are colorful homespuns, often the homecraft of the locality. The Indian country, the Spanish country, the North and the deep South—each has its own characteristic homecraft. Novelty fabrics of this kind are made in the simplest type of straight-hanging curtain with a hem and casing.

In casual interiors, coverings of couches and sofas or the tie-on cushions for chairs in heavier and darker fabrics are made without boxing and are often trimmed with fringe. When the decor is more formal, the same homespuns are tailored and fitted in beautifully boxed couch and bed covers. Cushions are plentiful and planned for use, not for decoration, unless the fabric itself makes a decorative note. People in these homes like comfort without frills, and they insist upon fabrics which can stand wear.

More homes of this type should use draw-string attachments and long simple draperies which can be drawn. This kind of curtain can be pushed aside from the window with a view. These draw curtains are easy to make because the solid fabrics suitable to these interiors need no lining. They should be finished with box pleats, but the heading should be interlined with stiffening as directed for French pleats. (See Index).

Easy-care fabrics are used here for the "double dutch" curtains, the carefully tailored spread, and as a wall covering.

PLAY ROOMS AND GAME ROOMS

Play rooms for children and game rooms for adults must be cheerful, simple, and tidy. They will never function smoothly unless all the paraphernalia of play have a place. The first consideration, therefore, is a large closet and proper shelves. After you have attended to places to put things is time enough to think of color. The walls and floor are the largest color areas, and they should be considered first. Paint is easy to apply, and any homemaker can paint this kind of room. When a rug is not available, paint the floor as well as the walls. Use a washable paint for both.

Be sure there are several lamps, and that the room has ample working space for the hobby of every member of the family. One end of an adult game room can be given over to a carpenter's workbench, amateur photographer's equipment, a sewing corner, or a shop for the budding electrical engineer or a screen for home movies. Bring into this room all the trophies and diplomas—all the treasures so dear and so undecorative in other rooms.

The fabrics used in playrooms must be able to stand wear, be washable, and need no ironing.

SEASHORE HOMES

Cotton and linen are the best fabrics to withstand dampness, especially if they are treated with finishes which repel moisture. This is a big step in the conquest of mildew, and modern science has developed textiles costing very little which are treated to repel water. Fabrics of plastic are adaptable, and the new trend is toward using them for curtains in kitchens, dinettes, bedrooms, and living rooms. These print fabrics, which look tailored and decorative, can be cleaned by wiping with a damp cloth.

For slipcovers use hard-finish denim and drill in dark or gay colors. It will pay you to make boxed cushions for couches and sofas to make them comfortable. Remember that soft cushions merely add a note of luxury. They do not support a relaxed body seeking comfort—for that you need boxed cushions.

Porch and outdoor furnishings and beach cushions can be made of drill or smooth-surface heavy fabrics, or from plain glazed chintz. You can also make them of lightweight oilcloth or from old canvas awnings painted.

CHILDREN'S ROOMS

Mothers know that the child who has a place all his own, which he knows is his own, can be more easily taught consideration for others.

Infants' Nurseries: Every mother has a vision of a lovely frilly bassinette and a beautiful nursery for her baby, and there is no reason why that dream picture cannot be realized in proportion to the space and income of any home. If there is a room available for a nursery, by all means decorate it. Otherwise find some spare part of the house which can be turned into baby's corner, and there assemble all the things you need for his care. This will save you many steps in a day.

Showcase for your children's hobbies in a charming room designed around them. Encourage him to work with you —choosing colors and fabrics as well as general room plans. You'll be pleased with his interest and abilities.

There should be a small chest of drawers and a small closet close to the bathinette. After you have arranged everything needed, think of the decoration. Frilly white curtains which tie back with ribbon fit into the scheme; and if there is no bassinette to decorate with frilly white ruffles, you can pad and line an ordinary clothes basket.

To do this, fit a small hair mattress exactly into the basket, then smooth pink or blue sateen across the sides of the basket, pinning it to the top edge and gathering it to fit the lower edge. Cut a piece of paper the exact size of the bottom of the basket and use it as a pattern for cutting the fabric, allowing seams. Seam this piece to the fabric on the sides of the basket at the lower edge. Then cut a strip of sateen as wide as the outside of the basket and long enough to extend around it. Seam this strip to the top edge of the

lining, leaving an opening for the handle of the basket. Finish the lower edge of the outside covering with a narrow hem and run a cord or string through it. In this way you can pull the lower edge to fit the basket and hold tight. The mattress will hold the inside covering in place. This cover can easily be removed and washed. Then make an outer cover of white, shaping and joining it like the inside one. It should be full and gathered. Cut a ruffle twice as wide as the basket edge and deep enough to allow a hem and a heading. Gather the ruffle and join it to the top edge of the lining. You can trim this cover with bows of ribbon, and wind the handles of the basket with ribbon to match.

Toddlers' Rooms: Be sure there are low shelves within reach of a toddling child. If you stencil decorations on the wall or have panels or pictures, be sure to place them low. Even a baby's eye is attracted to bright decoration when it is low enough for him to see. Be sure the room has a comfortable chair for mother. It should be covered with a slipcover which will add color interest to the room and be easily laundered too. The child's crib can be in this room and a day-bed as well, with a matching cover that is boxed so it does not trip up unsteady little feet. Clear the room of everything unnecessary and everything a child might trip over. Provide low, steady furniture he can hang on to, such as a day-bed or couch. As the child grows, you can add small furniture; but while he is learning to walk, substantial furniture which will steady his footsteps is an asset.

Rooms for School Children: Besides the bed, the two most essential pieces of furniture are a desk or table for homework, equipped with a functional lamp, and low shelves for toys. Psychologists say that a feeling for having "everything in its place" can be cultivated very early by providing a place for the child's own things, and making sure this place is low enough to be handy. Bedspreads, slipcovers, and curtains should be made of washable fabrics which resist wear. Colorful homespuns make covers which need no ironing, and washable fabrics which do need ironing are no more decorative. Somewhere on the wall should be a bulletin board to display the changing hobbies of the child. It is a mistake to decorate the room of a child at this stage, because his interests change so frequently. It is better to use maps and bulletin boards, which can be kept up to date.

A child usually has at least one hobby, perhaps several; and each hobby should be given room, for both equipment and display. Have nothing superfluous in a child's room, and it will be easier to establish practical rules for neatness.

When the girl begins to take an interest in decoration and expresses a desire to "pretty up" her room, make this a mother-and-daughter program. Exchange ideas with her, but insofar as possible follow out hers. This will help her to develop her own talent and to learn the difference between practical and impractical ideas. One eleven-year-old girl wanted frilly bedspreads and curtains in her room. There was no one to do the extra ironing, so her mother gave her her wish on the understanding that she would iron the ruffles herself. The child took pride in doing the ironing herself and continually changed sets of tie-backs for the curtains. She matched these trimming notes in petticoat lampshades for her room, and as she grew older she learned to make sofa cushions which tied into these decorative effects. The child should be allowed to express herself freely in her own room. It is only natural that she should continually be wanting to change everything. That is part of growth. In many homes the girls are given a small allowance for this on condition that they make up their ideas themselves. It is amazing how quickly they get to work, once the small budget is established.

Rooms for Teenagers: Many children in this age group yearn to express their artistic talents. Expect them to be modernists. These youthful ideas need not be welcomed into the family living room or adult bedrooms; but the youth can and should express his own ideas, as far as practicable, in his own room, and he might also be permitted to use them in the family play room.

When sisters share a room and disagree on decoration, face the situation squarely. One mother divided the room in half and assigned one half to each girl. The girls were asked to outline their ideas on decoration, and a time was set to compare them. When the girls presented their plans, each with samples of textiles, it developed that they agreed on the types of construction of curtains, bedspread, and slipcovers; but they had unalterable color preferences. These colors were selected so that they harmonized, and by rearranging the furniture a little, each girl could develop her own color scheme and still have the room as a whole harmonious.

Adolescents love to paint furniture; this is not as destructive as it sounds. One mother let her son paint his mahogany bureau. Three years later the same son came to appreciate the mahogany furniture in the rest of the house, and his bureau disturbed him. Then his mother let him remove the paint and refinish the wood, and he did an excellent job of it. Imaginative children are not really destructive, they are simply avid to express themselves; and one of a mother's greatest interests is to watch this talent develop.

TRANSITORY HOMES

Women who have to live for a time in hotels or furnished rooms are often disturbed by their unhomelike surroundings. They want to freshen the place up with as little expense and labor as possible. If the migration is a long one, slipcovers and curtains of inexpensive fabric can be made quickly, and they will work wonders with a drab room. If you travel and change your home frequently, take with you a plain cover, not boxed, which can be thrown over any bed or couch. A washable cotton spread can be sent to the laundry wherever you are. Plan pillow covers to match, made for a standard bed pillow. Add to this, two lengths of matching or contrasting fabric for side drapes, and take a table cover which you like. This little kit is easily packed and adapted to any room.

DICTIONARY OF EMBROIDERY STITCHES

*T***he** *fine art of embroidery and the luxury effect of hand sewing can add immeasurably to the elegance of your wardrobe or home decor. In this chapter, a variety of stitches and techniques are pictured and explained. Let them inspire you when next you wish to make something really special.*

EMBROIDERY

A fascinating way to have beautifully embroidered fabrics is to accent a basic print. Start with a fabric with a linen-like weave, then emphasize areas of the fabric design with crewel embroidery. You'll need crewel wool and needle, an embroidery hoop, and a bit of imagination.

Let the fabric be your guide—you may wish to outline areas or perhaps fill in flowers or leaves. The stitching can be as elaborate or simple as you choose.

Another method of embroidering without a pattern is to work from charts, counting threads on even-weave fabric. Cross stitch on gingham is beginner-easy and very effective, especially for kitchen decor.

TRANSFERRING DESIGNS

The design can be stamped on the fabric with a transfer pattern that is used with a warm iron, it can be drawn on the fabric with chalk or transferred with dressmaker's carbon paper, or it can be traced onto tissue paper which is placed over the fabric, then torn away when the embroidery has been completed.

On the pages that follow are drawings of a number of embroidery stitches in work, and step-by-step directions for doing them. It is not necessary for you to learn a great variety of stitches to embellish your sewing, but they are included here for your ready reference. When you want to add an extra-dazzling bit of color or personalized touch to a garment or gift, play it simple! A small monogram in satin stitch or a cross stitch or crewel bib trim in the peasant manner are charming.

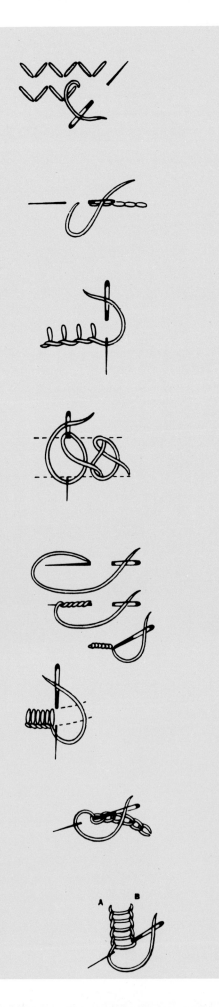

Arrowhead Stitch: Used for medium weight lines and light filling. Bring needle through to right side at top left corner, insert it below and to the right, bring it through to the right at the top line; then insert needle back to lower left next to first stitch.

Backstitch: A basic stitch used for lines, outlines, and foundation for other stitches. Working from right to left, bring needle through to right side the same distance ahead as width of stitch, then insert needle back into point where preceding stitch ended; keep stitches evenly spaced.

Blanket Stitch: Used originally to hold a turned edge or a raw edge, as on a blanket. Can also be a decorative outline stitch, or make a flower when worked in a circle. Working from left to right, bring needle to right side on lower line, hold thread down with left thumb, insert needle to the right and above and bring it out directly below on the lower line over the thread.

Braid Stitch: Worked along a hem or turned edge, from right to left. Bring needle to right side just below edge, loop thread as shown, insert needle through loop and in back of fabric. Bring out a short distance below edge, over thread. Pull thread through and away from you.

Bullion Stitch: Usually worked with heavy metallic threads for a luxuriant encrusted effect. Bring thread to right side, insert needle to the right the distance of stitch desired and bring point of needle back to right side as first step; do not pull needle through. Wind thread 6 or 7 times around point of needle, hold twists down with left thumb, draw needle and thread through fabric and twists. Pull needle and thread to the right and tighten, then insert needle again to the back as shown.

Buttonhole Stitch: Used to cover raw or turned edges, or to outline. Worked the same as blanket stitch, but each stitch is worked adjacent to the preceding one, not spaced.

Chain Stitch: Used primarily for outlining, it can also be used for filling when a number of close rows are worked. Working from the top down, bring needle to the right side, hold thread down with left thumb, insert needle back where thread emerged and bring to right side a short distance down; draw needle out over loop.

Chain Stitch, Open: Especially useful as a garment trim, it can even be used for casings through which a ribbon may be drawn. Working from the top down, it is worked similarly to chain stitch, except that the thread is inserted into the fabric to the right of the first step; see illustration.

Coral Stitch: A simple but effective stitch used for outlining. Working from right to left, bring needle to right side, hold thread in place with left thumb, make a tiny diagonal stitch under and over thread as shown, draw needle through.

Couching: Another outline stitch, this can be worked with two different threads if desired. Place one thread along line to be covered and stitch in place with tiny stitches evenly spaced across. Draw all ends to wrong side when completed.

Cross Stitch: Starting at lower left corner, make a diagonal stitch to upper right corner; continue across, then turn and stitch from lower right to upper left over each stitch. You may work them singly or in groups; just be sure all crosses are worked in the same direction.

Eyelets: Using a stiletto, punch round holes into fabric held in an embroidery hoop. With fine stitches, outline hole, then finish with buttonhole stitch or close overcast stitches.

Feather Stitch: A decorative stitch, worked from top down. Bring needle to right side to left of line to be covered, hold thread down with left thumb, make a slanting stitch to the right and a little below with needle pointing to the left; draw needle through over thread. Carry thread to left side of line and make a similar stitch with needle pointing to right; see diagram.

French Knot: Bring needle to right side where dot is to be made, wind thread 2 or 3 times around needle point, insert in fabric close to where thread emerged and pull to wrong side, holding twists in place. Use double or triple threads for larger dots.

Holbein Stitch: A simple, effective outline stitch. Work running stitch along line to be covered, keeping stitches and spaces equal size, then work running stitch back over the same line, filling in the empty spaces. For fancier effects, another thread can be woven in and out of these stitches.

Lazy Daisy Stitch: A perennial favorite for flowers and light filling. Bring thread to right side in center of flower, hold thread down, insert needle close to or where thread emerged, then bring up at bottom of "petal" over the thread. Fasten down with tiny stitch as shown. Repeat around as needed.

Long and Short Stitch: Used for filling and for shading. It is similar to satin stitch, except that long and short stitches are alternated to give a textured effect; if closely related colors are used, it gives a subtled shaded effect. As in satin stitch, this can be worked solid or "surface".

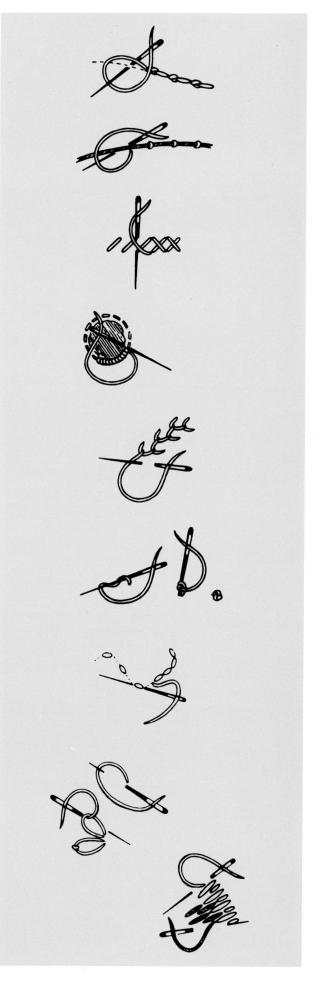

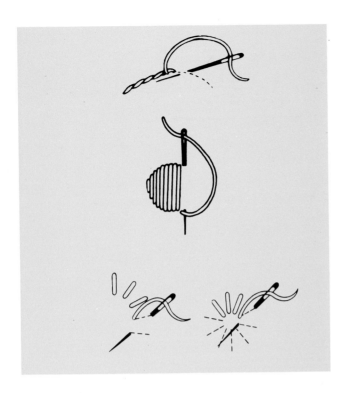

Outline Stitch: Bring needle to right side at left end of line; insert needle a short distance to the right slightly above the line and bring back to the left slightly below; keep thread above the needle.

Satin Stitch: Used to cover an area solidly. Bring needle up at one edge of area, down into opposite edge; carry under the fabric and bring it up next to the original stitch. To save thread, work it only on the "surface"; that is, instead of carrying the thread across the area on the wrong side, bring it to right side next to point of insertion. In either method, stitches may be vertical, horizontal, or diagonal —just be sure they are parallel.

Stem Stitch: Worked in same manner as outline stitch, but the thread is held below the needle.

Straight Stitch: Used as an occasional single stitch in a design or grouped to form a flower; each stitch is always separate from the next one.

SMOCKING

For simple smocking stitches, get an embroidery transfer pattern that stamps on your fabric, and carry out the smocking design planned. For more complex or decorative smocking, professionals first gather the material with row after row of even basting and work the smocking across the bastings, taking care that the lines are even. The smocking stitches include honeycomb stitch, diamond stitch, and cable stitch done single or double.

Honeycomb (or Seed) Smocking: Bring the needle through the first dot, or gathered fold, take a stitch through the second dot or fold, and draw the thread together. Take a second stitch across both previous stitches to secure the fullness and emphasize the color of the smocking. Pass the needle under the fabric to the next dot on the line below and draw two dots together just as you did above. Alternate back and forth between the two rows to the end of your marking. Always pass the thread on the wrong side. Then do another two rows the same way.

Diamond Smocking: This smocking is worked like honeycomb except that the thread is passed on the outside instead of the inside of the fabric. To complete the diamond effect, you work the next row of dots and pass the needle again through the last row of work.

Cable Smocking: This is an outline stitch worked on one row of dots and can be developed in three ways: (1) Bring the needle up at the first dot and take a little stitch at the next dot with the thread above the needle. Continue in this way all along the row. *The thread is always above the needle, and the line of stitches is straight and even.* To vary this stitch, (2) take the stitches the same way, but in the first stitch pass the thread above the needle, in the next stitch pass it below the needle, next above it, and so on, alternating all the way across. (3) Double cable stitch is worked on another row of dots placed very close, and the stitches are worked by alternating the thread and placed so they meet the threads of the last row.

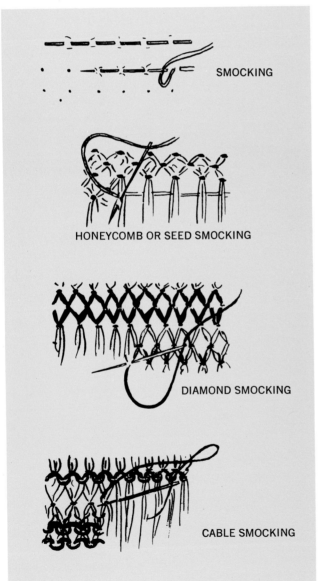

SMOCKING

HONEYCOMB OR SEED SMOCKING

DIAMOND SMOCKING

CABLE SMOCKING

FAGOTING

This can be worked by hand in bar effect or in a crisscross design. Fagoting can be done by machine, and fine ribbon can be used for it. Fagoting fills the space between two finished edges, and professionals baste their work right side down on heavy wrapping paper. The space between the finished edges can be ¼ or ½ inch, or finer if desired.

Bar Fagoting: Use twisted embroidery thread or buttonhole twist. Take a stitch on one side and secure the thread; then take a stitch directly across the space, catching the opposite edge, and bring your needle back, catching the first edge. This forms the cross thread or foundation bar. Cover it with over-and-over stitches, and make the next fagoting stitch about ⅛ inch away.

French Fagoting: This is done like bar fagoting, except that the thread is twisted around the needle several times—enough times to extend across the bar.

Crisscross Fagoting: Use a heavier thread and take a buttonhole stitch in one edge of the fabric; on the opposite edge take another buttonhole stitch, spacing it so the thread slants across the space to be filled. Be sure your buttonhole stitch holds the thread securely so it will not pull in wear.

Ribbon Fagoting: Baste the finished edges to a piece of paper with the wrong side of the fabric up. Pin the ribbon, which should be very narrow, on each edge, crossing it from side to side. Now make a row of stitching through the fabric, catching the folded edges of the ribbon as you stitch.

Machine Fagoting: Purchase machine-made fagoting which is sold by the yard like braid. Baste this fagoting strip to paper and baste the fabric edges over it so that the turned edges of the fabric are face down and the edge covers the side thread of the fagoted braid. Now stitch close to the fabric edge, catching the braid underneath.

HEMSTITCHING

Hand Hemstitching: Hand hemstitching is most successful on linen, cotton, or any loosely woven fabric where threads pull easily. Hemstitching can be placed across a fabric or at the top of a hem. First draw the threads in the desired width across the length of the article to be hemstitched. With fine matching sewing thread fasten the end securely and pass the needle behind three or four or more bars of the fabric thread as desired. The sewing thread should pass under the point of the needle. Pull the sewing thread tight so that the bars of the fabric are drawn together. Now take a tiny stitch in the edge of the fabric and pass the needle behind the next three or more bars of the fabric. Continue in this way across the length of the material.

Hemstitched Hems: Hold the hem toward you and work as directed above, except that the little stitch in the fabric between the drawn threads is caught in the hem.

Double Hemstitch: Hemstitch both sides of the drawn threads. When the hemstitching must end before an edge decide on the width of the hemstitching and slash the fabric at the point where the hemstitching is to end. Now draw the threads.

Hemstitched Corners: There are two ways to work corners: (1) Hemstitch in the usual way, except that in the hem more threads are drawn together. (2) In luncheon cloths, collars, et cetera, the corner of the hem can be mitered.

Starting below is a collection of floral designs in a variety of sizes for you to use in making up your own embroideries. Use only a part of a motif if you wish, work it in outline stitch or satin stitch, make it big or little. Stitch as you wish!

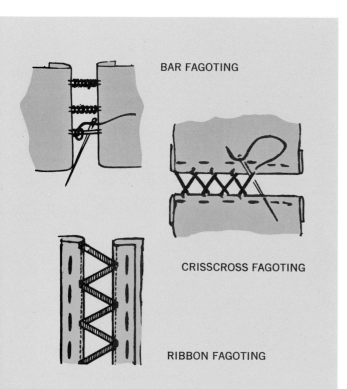

BAR FAGOTING

CRISSCROSS FAGOTING

RIBBON FAGOTING

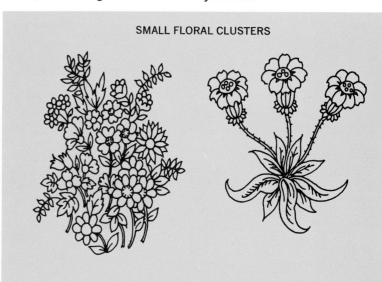

SMALL FLORAL CLUSTERS

MONOGRAMS

When designing a monogram containing more than one letter, if they are all the same size use the first, the middle (or maiden name), then the last initial. If you wish one large and two small, the order be-comes first, last, and middle (or maiden). Use satin stitch, outline stitch, or any others that are suitable, such as chain or Holbein. Cross-stitch monograms are worked from special designs.

Two-Color Cross-Stitch Alphabet

FOR USE WITH PEASANT EMBROIDERY

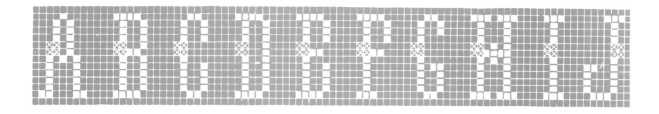

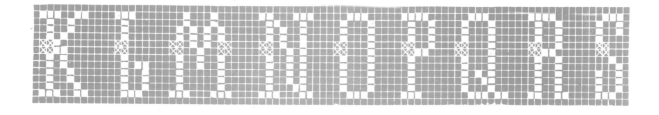

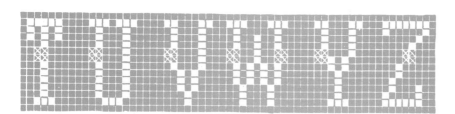

Large Cross-Stitch Alphabet

ABCDEF
GHIJKLM
NOPQR
STUVW
XYZ1234
567890

aBCDEFG

hijklmn

opqrstu

vwxyz12

34567890

GLOSSARY OF TEXTILE TERMS

Adapted from A DICTIONARY OF TEXTILE TERMS BY DAN RIVER, copyright 1971 by Dan River Inc.

A

ABRADED YARN—A manmade filament yarn the outer fibers of which are abraded, leaving a central core of long filaments. The yarn is usually plied with one or more yarns that are not abraded.

ABRASION RESISTANCE—The degree to which a fabric is able to withstand surface wear and other friction such as rubbing, chafing, etc.

ACETATE—A manufactured fiber in which the fiber-forming substance is cellulose acetate. Where not less than 92% of the hydroxyl groups are acetylated, the term triacetate may be used as a generic description. Reg. T.M.'s include Acetate* (Celanese); Acele* (DuPont); Chromspun*, Estron* (Eastman); Avisco* Avicolor* (FMC). See Triacetate.

ACRILAN*—Reg. T.M. of Monsanto. See acrylic.

ACRYLIC—A manufactured fiber. Reg. T.M.'s include Acrilan* (Monsanto); Creslan* (American Cyanamid); Orlon* (DuPont); Zefran* (Dow-Badische Co.).

ACTION STRETCH—Fabrics and garments with stretch and recovery in them in the warp and filling directions, two-way stretch. Popular in ski clothes, pants, and other tight-fitting garments where free body movement is essential.

AIRPLANE FABRIC—Plain weave, mercerized, water repellent fabric which comes in widths of 37, 42 and 60 inches. Textures range around 80-square. Treated with "dope" which is a solution made from a cellulose acetate base and used to cover wings, fuselage and tail of airplanes. Also used in bleached condition, for shirting, collars and cuffs; in dyed state, for boys' suits, ski wear and uniform fabrics.

ALPACA—Cloth of fine, silken nature, soft in feel, light in weight. The fiber is obtained from the animal of that name. The yarn is often used as filling in some cotton warp cloths. Alpaca resembles mohair and is imitated in cheaper cloths or those in combination with the genuine. The cloth has much luster and is boardy in some instances. Much alpaca is now made from wool-and-rayon blends. It is used for women's spring or fall coats, suits, sportswear.

ALPACA WOOL—Fine long-staple wooly hair of the alpaca, a South American goatlike animal.

ANGORA WOOLS—Soft, long, hairlike wool from the Angora goat, native in Anatolia, the homeland of the Turks; now raised extensively in Texas with Kerrville as the center. Used in combination with wool, mohair, and mixture-fabrics.

ARTIFICIAL WOOL—Broad term for any fibrous material made to simulate natural wool.

ART LINEN—Plain weave, cylindrical yarn, very soft finish. Bleached or unbleached sheeting may be used for this well-known needlework base fabric from which it is easy "to draw the yarns."

ASBESTOS—A non-metallic mineral fiber which is not flammable. The fiber is woven into fabrics and used for theater curtains and other industrial work where flame-proof protection is needed. Ironing board covers and dish towels are frequently made of cotton and asbestos.

ASTRAKHAN CLOTH—Rather thick knit or woven fabric with curls or loops on the face to simulate the pelt of the astrakhan lamb. The yarns used as the base are usually cotton, woolen or worsted, while the loops are made with fibers such as luster wool, mohair, worsted yarn, and certain manmade fibers. This fabric is a popular staple in women's wear coating as well as in some sweaters.

ATMOSPHERIC CONDITIONS, STANDARD—Since the temperature and the relative humidity have an appreciable effect on the physical properties of textiles, it is necessary that the conditions under which the samples are tested be rigidly controlled. In standard atmospheric conditions for textiles the moisture equilibrium should be maintained at a standard atmospheric having a relative humidity of 65 per cent at 70° F.

AVLIN*—Reg. T.M. of FMC. See polyester.

AVRIL*—Reg. T.M. of FMC. See rayon.

AWNING STRIPE—Heavy firm-woven cotton duck or canvas with either yarn-dyed, printed or painted stripes. Used for awnings, beach umbrellas, etc. Drills are used for inexpensive painted awning stripe fabrics.

B

BACKED CLOTH—Single texture material with addition of an extra warp or filling that is added for weight and warmth. The extra warp or filling may be of wool, worsted or cotton. This type of construction is found in French-backs, vestings, worsteds, dress goods, suitings, and skirtings. Satin weave construction, as well as twill weaves, may be used in the designing of the cloth.

Balloon fabric—A fine-combed yarn, plain weave cloth with the same breaking strength in each direction. This government-specification cloth, when vulcanized, is used for air cells in planes and barrage balloons. Other uses include artificial flowers, cambric, printed glazed chintz, fine shirting and shorts, oil-treated tent fabrics, etc.

BANDLE—A narrow, coarse, homespun linen made on hand looms in Ireland.

BARATHEA—Closely woven fabric with a characteristic pebbly weave. Either silk or rayon, or these fibers combined with cotton, worsted, nylon or polyester. Used for neckwear, dress goods, lightweight suitings.

BARRE—A bar effect produced by bars or stripes extending crosswise in woven and knitted goods; classed as a blemish on fabric.

BASIC FINISH—One that alters or improves in some manner the texture or surface appearance or effect of a fabric. Examples include mercerizing, calendering, friction calendering, glazing, moire or water-marking, napping, shearing, cropping, embossing, chasing, beetling.

BASKET WEAVE—Two or more warp ends and filling picks which are woven as one in a plain weave formation which resembles a plaited basket. Provides a flat effect, has some porosity, and is a rather loose type of goods. Hopsacking and monk's cloth are examples. Uses include oxford shirtings, decorative materials, and curtains. Fabrics in this sphere do not withstand chafing, friction, abrasion, and wear; hence, they have a limited use in apparel circles.

BATHROBE OR BATHROBE BLANKETING—Double-faced cotton blanketing that is thick and warm. Woven with a tightly twisted warp and two sets of soft filling yarns which can be napped to produce a soft surface. Used for bathrobes, crib blankets, bunting.

BATIK DYEING—See Dyeing of Textiles.

BATISTE—Named for Jean Baptiste, a French linen weaver. 1. In cotton, it is a sheer, fine, combed, mercerized muslin characterized by wide streaks. Woven of combed yarns, given a mercerized finish. Used for blouses, summer shirts, dresses, lingerie, infants' dresses, bonnets, and handkerchiefs. 2. Also made of rayon and polyester and cotton blends. 3. Also made of wool or worsted in a smooth, fine fabric that is lighter than challis, very similar to fine nun's veiling. Used for dresses, negligees. 4. Also a sheer silk fabric, either plain or figured, very similar to silk mull. Often called Batiste de Soie. Used for summer dresses. 5. Also made of spun rayon.

BAYARDERE—Plain or fancy stripes, woven or knitted, which run crosswise in a fabric; a very broad term.

BEADED OR CUT VELVET—Velvet with a cut-out pattern or velvet pile effect. Often done on chiffon velvet. Brilliant designs and effects noted. Made on Jacquard loom. Principal use is for evening wear. Other uses are for hangings, decorative material, salon furnishings. Most difficult to handle and manipulate. Drapes well, will dryclean, crushes. Wear depends on quality and type of design.

BEAVER—Has softer body and longer nap when compared with kersey. Somewhat resembles the animal of that name. Fulled the least when compared with kersey and melton. Heavy in weight. This glossy face finish cloth has to be well handled for good results.

BEDFORD CORD—Strong rib-weave fabric with raised lengthwise lines or cords produced by warpwise "stuffing

threads." In inexpensive grades "stuffer" yarns are not used. May be all wool, silk, cotton or rayon, or combination fibers. It wears extremely well and is used for upholstery, suits, riding habits. Warp Pique is a lighter weight Bedford cord fabric used for dress goods. First made in America in New Bedford, Mass.

BENGALINE—A sturdy, warp-faced fabric with pronounced crosswise ribs formed by bulky, coarse, plied yarn or rubber threads. Filling is not discernible on face or back of goods. Originating in Bengal, India, it is used in coating, swimsuits, mourning material, ensembles, and women's headgear. Grosgrain is "bengaline cut to ribbon width."

BILLIARD CLOTH—The highest grade of material made from the best stock—Saxony, Silesia, or Australia merino wool. Cloth must have body, substance, evenness, and smoothness. Dyed green, its use is obvious.

BIRDSEYE—Cotton or linen cloth with a small geometric pattern that has a center dot resembling a bird's eye.

BLANKET FABRIC—1. Broad term for some woolen overcoating fabrics which have a soft hand and a well-napped finish; interchangeable with the term fleece. 2. Heavyweight reversible cotton blanketing often woven on a Jacquard loom. Low-twist filling yarn used to afford a good napped effect.

BLEACHING—Bleaching removes natural and other types of impurities and blemishes of various types from the goods, takes out coloring matter that might be present, and makes the cloth white, or very nearly white. It also provides for better and clearer dyeing or printing of the material. It aids in the affinity of the dyestuff in the dye bath to give better or improved color effect. It is possible to bleach practically any of the major textile fabrics seen today.

BLEEDING—1. The running of color from wet dyed material onto a material next to it. 2. When colors run together during certain finishing operations such as washing, scouring, fulling, milling. 3. The dissolving of color during washing.

BLEND, BLENDING—1. Combining of fibers of different colors, such as heather-mixture, or of different types of fibers, such as cotton and wool, or Kodel and cotton before spinning. Blends are very popular today and their number is limitless. 2. Mixing of small amounts of the same fiber type from several lots to produce a uniform fabric. 3. Term for the dyeing of pale furs to make them more attractive.

BOTANY WOOL—The finest merino wool in the world, raised in the Botany Bay area in Australia. Used to make billiard cloth and only the best quality woolens and worsteds.

BOUCLE—From "boucle" (French for "buckled" or "ringed"). Staple suiting fabric on the order of worsted cheviot with drawn-out, looped yarn in construction which provides a ring appearance to the face of the goods. Also made in cotton and manmade fiber fabrics. Popular as well in the knitting field, several types of yarn may be used—slub, bug, Knickerbocker, flake, frise, curled, onde, et al.

BLEACH—A substance which whitens. Common bleaches are chlorine bleach, peroxide, and reducing agents such as sulphites.

BONDED FACE FABRIC—That side of a bonded fabric used as the face of the goods in a finished garment or other textile product.

BONDING—Usually refers to fabric-to-fabric bonding in contradistinction to fabric-to-foam bonding or laminating.

BOOK CLOTH—Plain or embossed pyroxylin-treated or "starched-and-clay" cotton cloth used in book binding. Printcloth is the base fabric. Pyroxylin-treated fabric is made washable or waterproof and there is not any blistering, chipping or peeling.

BRAID—Any material made from textile fibers used for binding or trimming in widths up to three or four inches. Braid may be woven round or tubular, or plaited flat.

BRAIDING, PLAITING—To interweave or intertwine, such as plaiting or braiding of one's hair, or narrow strips of material, as in the case of a braided rug or shoe lace.

BROADCLOTH—1. Originally a silk shirting fabric, so named because it was woven in widths exceeding the usual 29 inches. 2. A tightly and plain-woven lustrous cotton cloth with a crosswise rib, resembling poplin, but ribs are finer, and broadcloth has more picks than poplin. Finest qualities are made of combed Pima or Egyptian cotton. Used for men's shirts, women's tailored dresses, and blouses. 3. Smooth rich-looking woolen with napped face and twill back. Better grades have a glossy and velvety feel. Used for dresses, skirts. 4. Also made of a blend of cotton and polyester and/or other manmade fibers.

BROADLOOM—Carpet woven wider than the 3/4 (27 inches) and 4/4 (36 inches); widths usually 6, 9, 12, 15 and 18 feet.

BROCADE—Rich Jacquard-woven fabric with allover interwoven design of raised figures or flowers. Name derived from the French word meaning to "ornament." Pattern is emphasized by contrasting surfaces or colors. Often has gold or silver threads running through it. Background may be either satin or twill weave. Used for dresses, wraps, draperies, and upholstery, depending on the weight.

BROCATELLE—Supposed to be an imitation of the Italian Tooled Leather where the background is pressed and the figures embossed. Both background and figures are tightly woven with generally a warp effect in the figure and a filling effect in the background. Used generally in the decorative trades for upholstery and draperies.

BUCKRAM—1. Ply yarn scrim fabric with a stiff finish. 2. Also made by glueing two open weave, sized cotton fabrics together. Used as interlining in cloth and leather garments. Also in millinery, because it can be moistened and shaped. Name for Bokhara, southern U.S.S.R., where it was first made.

BULKING PROCESS—Any of the several methods or procedures used to crimp, curl or loop textile yarns so that these yarns take on a bulked appearance. The bulked yarn occupies a greater area than non-bulked yarn. High-bulk yarns are spun yarns made by blending high-shrinkage staple fibers with staple fibers of low shrinkage. By definition, bulked process yarns are not textured yarns since bulked processed yarns are made from staple stock and not from continuous filament. Bulked yarns provide a soft, fluff-like effect or an opaque effect on certain woven and knit fabrics.

BUNTING—The name derived from the German *bunt*, meaning bright. Cotton or worsted yarn is used to make this soft, flimsy, plainwoven cloth. Some of the cloth is made from cotton warp and worsted filling. Cotton bunting is made from heavy cheesecloth and comes in the white or is piece-dyed. Ply yarn may be used in this plain-woven, fairly loose-textured cloth which has a texture ranging from 24 x 36 to 24 x 32. All-worsted bunting is used in making flags.

BURLAP—Coarse, canvas-like fabric made of jute, hemp or cotton. Also called gunny. Used primarily for bale covering and sacks (potato), and in furniture manufacture.

BURLING—Removal of loose threads and knots from woolens and worsteds by means of burling irons, a type of tweezer. Many knots are pulled or worked into the back of the fabric if the cutting of them would cause a small hole in the goods.

BUTCHER'S LINEN—Plain-weave, strong, stiff, substantial fabric. Term often used incorrectly in many types of cloths, and unless this material is marked Pure Linen, one may be sure that it does not contain any linen. Sheds the dirt, launders well, is durable, and gives splendid wear. Linen-textured rayon, a popular dress goods fabric, does not contain linen fibers.

BYRD CLOTH*—Registered trademark of Reeves Brothers, Inc., for their light or medium-weight fabric made from combed cotton yarns. The two-up and two-down twill construction shows on both sides of the material which is very high in pick count, about 300 threads per square inch—warp and filling added together. The fabric is very strong but light and supple. Used for rainwear, shirting, and sportswear, it is made wind-resistant and is also water-repellent. Named for the late Admiral Richard E. Byrd.

C

CALICO—Originated in Calcutta, India, it is one of the oldest cotton staples on the market. This plain and closely woven, inexpensive cloth is made in solid colors on a white or contrasting background. Very often, one, two, or three colors are seen on the face of the goods, which are printed.

Calico is not always fast in color. Medium yarn is used in the cloth, and the designs are often geometric in shape. Uses are for aprons, dresses, crazy quilts. Interchangeable with Percale.

CAMBRIC—Soft, white, closely woven cotton fabric with slight gloss on right side. Used for underwear, aprons, shirts, handkerchiefs. Originally made in Cambrai, France, of linen, and used for church embroidery and table linen. Costume cambric is a lightweight cambric in very low count; may be heavily sized and glazed. Washable, with care. Used for fancy dress costumes.

CAMEL HAIR, CAMEL'S HAIR—Hair obtained from camels. Rather wool-like in texture, its natural color varies from light tan to brownish black. This underhair of the camel is lustrous and extremely soft, and used, either by itself or combined with wool, for coats, suits, sweaters, some blankets, and oriental rugs.

CANDLEWICK FABRIC—1. Unbleached muslin bed sheeting (also called Kraft muslin) used as a base fabric on which a chenille effect is formed by application of candlewick (heavy-piled yarn) loops, which are then cut to give the fuzzy effect and cut-yarn appearance of the true chenille yarn. Used for bedspreads, drapes, robes, and so on. 2. A soft woolen dress material made in imitation of the candlewick bedspread, with tufted patterns similarly applied.

CANTON FLANNEL—Heavy, warm cotton material that is strong and absorbent, with a twilled surface and a long soft nap on the back. Later produced by napping of the heavy, soft-twisted yarn. Used for interlinings and sleeping garments. Named for Canton, China, where it was first made.

CANVAS—1. Cotton or linen fabric with an even weave that is heavy and firm. 2. Ada or Java canvas is a stiff open-weave fabric used for yarn needlework. 3. Awning stripe canvas has painted or woven stripes on cotton duck. 4. Cross-stitch or Penelope canvas is used for fine cross-stitch patterns; has stiff, open mesh. 5. Unbleached linen canvas used for coat fronts, lapels, men's suits.

CARDING—A process of opening and cleaning textile fibers which separates fibers from each other, lays them parallel, makes them into a thin web, and condenses them into a continuous, untwisted strand of fibers called a "sliver." This process removes most of the impurities.

CARPET—A floor covering woven from a variety of fibers, including wool, mohair, cotton, acrylic, rayon, nylon, saran, grass, straw, jute, polypropylene fiber, and mixtures. Sold by the yard. Type of carpets include Axminster, chenille, tufted, velvet, Wilton and rag. See Broadloom, Rug.

CASHMERE—The best cashmere goat is found in Thibet, the Kashmir province north of India, Iran, Iraq, and southwest of China. Resembles wool closer than any other fiber. Hair is cylindrical, soft, strong, and silken-like. True cashmere is brownish in shade. Uses include expensive coatings, sport-coating, sweaters, shawls, etc. The word Cashmere has been spelled in at least seventeen different ways since it is a word that seems to signify individuality.

CASSIMERE—Often confused with and sometimes sold as cashmere. Little resemblance between the two. Cassimere is a two-up and two-down right hand twill weave worsted suiting of ordinary stock. Holds crease well. Harsh feeling in either material, worsted or wool. Worsted is far more popular. Easy to tailor, will shine with wear. Finish is somewhat lustrous. Average quality cloth. Known as "a serge with stripes."

CAVALRY TWILL—A strong, rugged cloth made with a pronounced raised cord on a 63-degree twill weave; woolen or worsted yarn is used. The weaves used for cavalry twill and elastique are the same and there is no set weave for either fabric. Cavalry twill is the original name. It has the coarser rib-effect when compared with elastique, which has a smoother effect and feel. Also known as Tricotine.

CELLULOSE—A white, naturally occurring carbohydrate polymer found in many plants. About 96 per cent of cotton is cellulose; it is the substance that forms the cell walls of plant life, as cotton, flax, kapok, etc.

CHALLIS OR CHALLIE—One of the softest fabrics made, and named from the Anglo-Indian term *shalee* meaning soft. Very lightweight and usually printed with a delicate floral pattern. Originally made of wool or worsted, but now made of spun rayon and also combined with cotton. Used for scarves, dresses, blouses, infants' wear, and bed jackets.

CHAMBRAY—1. A plain woven fabric almost square count (i.e. 80 x 76), with colored warp and white filling that gives a mottled colored surface. Used for shirts, children's clothes, dresses. Named for Cambrai, France, where it was first made for sunbonnets. 2. A similar but heavier carded yarn fabric used for work and children's play clothes.

CHEESECLOTH—Plain woven, soft, low-count cotton similar to tobacco cloth and known also as gauze. Coarse grades find use in dust cloths, cheese wrapping, etc. Better grades are used for fancy dress costumes, experimental drapings and cheap flag bunting. Cheesecloth ranges in width from 25 inches to 55 inches; when made 36 inches wide it is called tobacco cloth. May be bleached and given firm starching and in this state is known as scrim.

CHENILLE—1. A fuzzy yarn whose pile resembles a caterpillar. This yarn is used for filling in cloth, for embroidery, tassels, rugs and draperies. Named for the French word meaning "caterpillar." 2. Also name of the fabric woven from chenille yarns.

CHEVIOT—1. Popular staple sports-coating, actually a lightweight cheviot tweed. 2. Named for the Cheviot sheep of the Cheviot Hills of Scotland, a popular tweed named for the wool from these sheep. It is rugged, rather harsh in hand; uneven yarns are used. The wool used is stock-dyed prior to carding and spinning of the yarn, and the single color or shade is the same in both warp and filling yarns.

CHEVRON—Term applied to herringbone weaves or prints in zigzag stripes.

CHIFFON—This term implies thinness, diaphanous or

gauze-like, and softness, as well as strength in a flimsy fabric. Uses include dress goods, even wear, lampshades, millinery, trimming, underwear, etc.

CHINCHILLA CLOTH—A heavy conventional, twill-weave coating, made from pure wool or cotton and wool. It has a napped surface that is rolled into little tufts or nubs. Often the fabric is double faced with a woven plaid or knitted back. It was originally woven to resemble chinchilla fur, but the weave is now varied. Used for coats, jackets and children's clothes.

CHINO—A particular type of all-cotton "Army twill," made of combed, two-ply yarn. It is a vat-dyed Khaki shade, mercerized, and Sanforized. Used by all major armed-service units throughout the world, the summer uniform fabric for all enlisted personnel.

CHINTZ—Glazed cotton fabric often printed with gay figures and large flower designs. Named from Hindu word meaning spotted. Some glazes will wash out in laundering. The only durable glaze is a resin finish which will withstand washing or dry cleaning. Unglazed chintz is called cretonne. Used for draperies, slipcovers, summer dresses and skirts.

CIRCULAR KNIT—Weft knit fabric made on a circular needle-bed knitting machine which presents the material in tubular form. See Flat Knit.

CIRE—Fabric, lace, and ribbon receive this type of wax finish which gives a sort of leather-like surface to the goods. Pressure and heat aid in the proper waxing of the goods. From the French verb *cire*, to wax and polish.

COATED FABRICS—As the name indicates, they are fabrics coated with some substance to make them impervious to water or other liquids. The uses are numerous, and the coating substances or materials include oil, pyroxylin, rubber, resins, melamines, plastics. Coated fabrics include oilcloth, Koroseal, Fabrikoid, imitation leathers.

COLOR ABRASION—Color changes in localized areas of a garment because of the differential wear of two unlike fibers in the goods. This is often evident in cross-dye shades of cotton/polyester blends which have been given durable press finishes. Color abrasion is often known as "frosting."

COLORFAST—A term used to describe fabrics of sufficient color retention so that no noticeable change in shade takes place during the normal life of the garment. Strictly speaking, no fabric is absolutely "colorfast." In buying fabrics make sure that they are fast to the particular color hazard they will encounter.

COLOR SCHEMES—These are: A. Monochromatic, or One-Color Harmony: The use of one color in varying degrees of intensity and value: light blue, medium blue, dark blue. B. Harmony: An agreeable combination of colors, all related to one another. C. Complementary Harmony: A pleasing combination of complementary colors. One of the two could be used in larger areas than the other, the colors might show a difference in value and intensity, and there should be no clashing.

COMBED YARN—A cotton yarn spun from cotton which in addition to having been carded has been combed in order to remove all short fibers (those less than 1⅛") and remaining impurities. Compared to carded yarns they are more even, compact and have fewer projecting fibers. The combing process follows carding. Used for hosiery, underwear, sewing thread and fine fabrics. See Carding.

COMMERCIAL STANDARDS—The U. S. Bureau of Standards issues Commercial Standards which are not laws, but they are important as "recorded voluntary standards of the trade." These standards are usually referred to by number.

COMPATIBLE SHRINKAGE—A bonded fabric term which refers to the need for the face fabric and the liner to have the same or closely similar shrinkage ratios so that there will not be any puckering in the bond.

CONTINUOUS CURE—A method of curing durable press garments by the use of a conveyor system to carry garments into and out of the oven; also known as a continuous oven.

CONTINUOUS FILAMENT—Regenerated, cellulose derivative or synthetic filament manufactured in a continuous filament form as distinguished from all natural fibers except raw silk which have a short staple or length.

CONVERTER—A person or a concern handling gray goods from the loom. The converter gives instructions for the type of finish desired, as well as all other pertinent data, from the time the goods leave the loom until sent to consignee.

CORD FABRIC—In reality, this is not a fabric but merely an interlacing of about 26 ends of cable yarn with two to six single-ply yarn fillings picks per inch. This loose netlike construction is run into the rubber solution in the manufacture of automobile tires. Incidentally, the number of layers of cord fabric determines the ply of the tire.

CORDED FABRIC—One in which there is a discernible filling-rib in the goods as in bengaline, grosgrain, heavy faille, Ottoman, poplin, rep, taffeta, etc. Warp cords are noted in Bedford cord and pique.

CORDUROY—A cut filling-pile cloth with narrow to wide wales which run in the warp direction of the goods and made possible by the use of an extra set of filling yarns in the construction. The back is of plain or twill weave, the latter affording the better construction. Washable types are available and stretch and durable press garments of corduroy are very popular. Usually an all-cotton cloth, some of the goods are now made with nylon or rayon pile effect on a cotton backing fabric or with polyester-cotton blends.

CORE YARN—One in which one type of fiber is twisted around a previously spun or filament yarn, usually another type of fiber. The previously spun or continuous filament yarn serves as the core and is concealed by the outer layer of the wrapped fiber. There are many core yarns being produced currently, and they vary greatly in price and quality. Core yarn can be made with low-quality base yarn since it cannot be seen by the naked eye, or it can be made with a man-made filament yarn and covered with high quality cotton as in the case of core-spun sewing thread to give a very strong thread with the surface friction properties of cotton.

Recently core yarns have come into favor with the rise of textured yarns and those used in stretch fabrics. For example, in core yarn for stretch fabrics, spandex yarns or rubber yarns would serve as the core, while cotton, wool, silk, nylon, acrylic, modacrylic, acetate rayon, triacetate or polyester fibers would form the shell.

COTTON LINTERS—Short-fiber stock that is used to make absorbent cotton, guncotton, rayon, celluloid, and other products from cotton or its seed. Linters are not used to make cotton yarn. The fibers are obtained from second-time ginning of the cotton. First-time ginning is done in the plantation areas at the community gins.

COTTON, LONG STAPLE—Cotton fiber of not less than 1⅛ inches in actual staple length.

COTTON, TYPES OF—

1. ACALA—Mexican variety introduced into U. S. Medium staple cotton grown in the southwestern states, and now in Israel.

2. AMERICAN—Upland cotton grown in this country. It forms bulk of world's crop. Fiber runs from ½ inch to ¾ inch.

3. AMERICAN PEELER—A variety of cotton grown in the Mississippi Delta. Fibers range from 1⅛ to 1¼ inches in length. Used in combined yarns and in fabrics, i. e., lawns, dimities, broadcloths.

4. AMERICAN PIMA COTTON—A cross between Sea Island and Egyptian. Grown in Arizona. Brownish color. Fine strong cotton. Averages 1⅜ inches to 1⅝ inches. Used for sheer woven fabrics and fine knitted goods.

5. CHINA—Harsh, wiry, very short staple. Can be mixed with wool for blankets. Limited uses.

6. EGYPTIAN—Fine lustrous long staple cotton. Several varieties—usually brown in color. 1.4 inch average. Used in U. S. for thread and fine fabrics.

7. INDIAN—Cotton grown in India, for many years the consistent second largest cotton producing country. The Indian cottons imported are generally of the harsh, short staple type (.8 inch to .9 inch) for such uses as blanket filling.

8. PERUVIAN—A variety of cotton whose fibers average 1¼ inches in length and which comes from Brazil, Central America, and the West Indies.

9. SEA ISLAND—Finest of all cotton, very white and silk-like with staple of 1.5-inches or better. Can be spun easily to 100s or better for exceptionally fine cloths. Before the War Between the States was raised on the islands of the Carolinas and Georgia. None of it raised in the United States today, but this type is now raised in Mexico and Central America and it goes into fine, expensive dress goods and men's shirtings.

10. SUPIMA—See SuPima.

COUNT OF CLOTH—The number of ends and picks per inch in a woven fabric as counted by an individual. If a cloth is 64 x 60, it means that there are 64 ends and 60 picks per inch in the fabric. A cloth that has the same number of ends and picks per inch in woven goods is called a square cloth, 64 x 64. Pick count is the term that is synonymous with texture or number of filling picks per inch.

COURSE—The row of stitches across a knitted fabric. Corresponds to the weft or filling in woven goods.

COVERT—Medium to heavy woolen or worsted cloth made with a steep twill, 63-degrees in angle. Two or more shades of stock-dyed wool are used to give the mottled or melange effect observed in the goods. Now made from other major fibers. This compactly-woven cloth is used in coatings of many types, rainwear, riding habits, sportswear and in some suitings.

CRASH—A coarse fabric having a rough irregular surface obtained by weaving thick uneven yarns. Usually cotton or linen, sometimes spun rayon or blends. Made in various weights and used for dresses, draperies, table linens. Softer weave woolen crash used widely for men's and women's suitings, draperies.

CREASE-RESISTANT-FINISH—Also referred to as the CRF Finish, it is chiefly applied to blends which contain a small amount of resin to produce an appealing hand to the goods and a moderate degree of wrinkle shedding. In rayon blends, a higher amount of resin is used to give a desirable hand and proper wrinkle shedding qualities.

CREASE-RETENTION—The ability of a cloth to retain a fold or pleat that has been created purposely, usually by a heat treatment. The heating of the thermoplastic fibers used in textiles will cause creases to become permanently set.

CREASE VERSUS WRINKLE—A crease is a line or mark produced in anything by folding; a fold, or furrow. A wrinkle is a ridge furrow on a surface caused by contraction, folding, rumpling, etc. A crease is a deformation in a fabric intentionally formed by pressing. A wrinkle is formed unintentionally by washing and wearing, and it can usually be removed by pressing. In Permanent Press, however, the crease is not removable and there is an absence of wrinkles.

CREPE—Lightweight fabric of silk, rayon, cotton, wool, synthetic or a combination of fibers. Characterized by a crinkly surface obtained either by use of 1. hard twist yarns, 2. chemical treatment, 3. weave, 4. embossing.

ALPACA CREPE—A heavy dull-finished rayon, acetate, or silk crepe made to resemble wool crepe.

BARK CREPE—Crepe finished with a rough-textured surface that suggests the bark of a tree.

CANTON CREPE—Filling crepe with pebbly surface heavier than crepe de chine. It drapes beautifully and is widely used for dresses; originally was made of silk in Canton, China.

CREPE SATIN or SATIN CREPE—Fabric that may be

used on either satin or crepe side. Crepe back is obtained by alternating hard twisted yarns which give the fabric a dull finish. A silk or synthetic fabric or mixture.

CREPE DE CHINE—A very sheer silk crepe. 1. A fabric or medium luster, woven from raw silk; crepiness is obtained by degumming the fabric. 2. A more lustrous fabric made in Japan with a spun silk warp and a thrown silk filling. 3. As now made, a sheer flat crepe in silk or manmade fibers. Used for lingerie, blouses, and dresses.

CREPE GEORGETTE—A sheer, dull-textured fabric, with a crepy surface, obtained by alternating left and right-handed yarns.

CREPE MAROCAIN—Heavier dress weight crepe similar to Canton crepe in texture.

CRINKLE CREPE (PLISSE)—Thin cotton fabric with puckered stripes or patterns or all-over blistery effect. Obtained by printing part of surface with a resisting agent and then passing fabric through caustic soda, causing untreated portion to shrink. Used for kimonos, nightgowns, lingerie, summer dresses.

FAILLE CREPE—A dress fabric made of either silk or synthetic fibers or mixtures. It has a decided wavy crepe cord filling-wise. Used for dresses, handbags, and trimmings.

FLAT CREPE—A firm silk or synthetic fibered fabric with a soft, almost imperceptible crinkled texture. Used for blouses, lingerie, dresses and linings.

LINGERIE CREPE—Formerly called French Crepe. Originally creped by embossing (pressing over fleece blanket). No longer embossed, so not a crepe texture. Silk, rayon or nylon. Used for lingerie and inexpensive dresses.

MATELLASSE CREPE—A soft, double or compound fabric with a quilted appearance which looks like two separate fabrics held together with creped threads on both sides. Named from the French verb meaning to pad or stud. Used for suits, coats, wraps, trimmings, dresses.

MOSSY CREPE—Fabric woven with a surface that gives a fine moss-like effect. Sometimes called Sand Crepe or Moss Crepe.

MOURNING CREPE—Has dull black finished surface, pressed with hot engraved rollers.

ONE HUNDRED DENIER CREPE—Crepe made of 100 denier viscose rayon yarn in similar construction to a flat crepe.

ROMAINE CREPE—Heavier semi-sheer crepe similar to Alpaca crepe.

ROUGH CREPE—Heavy creped texture fabric made with alternately twisted filling yarns, two right and two left.

WOOL CREPE—Soft fabric made of wool with irregular surface due to slack warp yarns.

CREPES—BALANCED, BOX, WARP, FILLING, MATELASSE—Lightweight dress goods with crinkled, crepe, granite or pebble effect. Crepe yarn and crepe weave used. Comes in white or is printed or dyed. Wide range in price, quality, texture, and finish. This cloth is generally washable without the effect of crepiness being lost. Does not have to be ironed repeatedly.

CRESLAN*—Reg. T.M. of American Cyanamid. See acrylic.

CRETONNE—A drapery and slip cover fabric first made by a Frenchman of that name. Usually printed. Similar to unglazed chintz, usually with larger designs. Can be cotton, linen or rayon. Osnaburg is the base fabric for cretonne.

CRIMP—The waves, seen or unseen, in textile fibers; noted especially in wool fibers in which there are "waves within waves," known as serrations, chiefly not observed by the naked eye.

CRINOLINE—A heavily sized, stiff fabric used as a foundation to support the edge of a hem or puffed sleeve. Also used as interlining, in the millinery and bookbinding trades, and to give fullness to skirts. First made of linen and horsehair and used to support hoop skirts. Usually comes in black, white or brown.

CROCHETING—Separate loops are thrown off and finished by hand successively. In knitting, the entire series of loops that go to form one length, round, or circumference are retained on one or more needles while a new series is being formed by a separate needle. Crocheting may be done by hand or by machine.

CROCKING—The tendency of excess dye to rub off. Napped and pile fabrics in deep colors are most likely to crock.

CROPPED—A staple finish given to woolen fabrics such as melton, kersey, beaver, and some broadcloth. Actually it is a closely-sheared fabric in which the nap effect is quite subdued.

CURE, CURING—The application of heat to a fabric or manfactured garment to cause reaction in the finishing agents in the article.

D

DACRON*—Reg. T.M. of DuPont. See polyester.

DAMASK—Firm, glossy Jacquard-patterned fabric first brought to the Western world by Marco Polo in the 13th century. Damascus was the center of fabric trade between the East and West; hence the name. Damask is similar to brocade but flatter and reversible. It may be linen, cotton, rayon or silk, or a combination of fibers. Used for tablecloths, napkins, draperies, upholstery.

DEEP PILE CLOTH—Refers to wide range of pile and printed pile cloths which simulate pelts and furs of various animals; actually comes under the caption of the so-called fake-fur fabrics. The FTC has decreed that the names of fur-bearing animals cannot be used in advertising and labeling of the product must be absolutely correct in all instances.

DENIM—This staple cotton cloth is rugged and serviceable, and is recognized by a left-hand twill on the face. Coarse single yarns are used most, but some of the cloth used for dress goods may be better quality stock. A two-up and one-down or a three-up and one-down twill may be used in the weave formation. Standard denim is made with indigo-blue-dyed warp yarn and a gray or mottled-white filling. It is the most important fabric in the work-clothes group and it is used for overalls, coats, jumpers, caps. Denim is also popular in dress goods in the women's wear field and has even been used as evening wear. Popular also in the upholstery and furniture trades.

DETERGENT—A cleansing agent. Soap or synthetic material used to emulsify or suspend insoluble foreign matter to aid its removal from textiles, garments, or other substrates.

DIAPER CLOTH—A soft absorbent cotton fabric bleached white. There are four different types: 1. Birdseye diaper cloth in a dobby weave. 2. Soft plain weave cotton flannel. Used for babies' diapers primarily. 3. Twill-weave cotton diaper flannel. 4. Plain-knit diaper cloth. In the Middle Ages diaper meant a rich silk fabric that was made in Ypres, Belgium.

DIMENSIONAL RESTORABILITY—Refers to the ability of some fabrics which shrink in washing to return to their original dimensions by ordinary ironing. A 2% restorability means that while a fabric may shrink more than 2% in washing, it will return to within 2% of its original dimensions when ironed at home.

DIMENSIONAL STABILITY—Ability of a fabric to retain its shape and size after being subjected to wear, washing, and dry cleaning. This stability may be brought about by the kinds of fiber used in the fabric, by chemical treatments, or by mechanical means.

DIMITY—Thin, sheer cotton cloth in which cords or stripes may or may not be in the pattern. A smart fabric, easy to manipulate, launders easily and well. Made of combed yarn, it is finished at 36 inches wide. Used for aprons, pinafores, art needlework, bedspreads, and in many types of dress goods for women and children.

DOBBY LOOM—A type of loom on which small, geometric figures can be woven in as a regular pattern. Originally this type of loom needed a "dobby boy" who sat on the top of the loom and drew up warp threads to form a pattern. Now the weaving is done entirely by machine. This loom differs from a plain loom in that it may have up to thirty-two harnesses and a pattern chain. Is expensive weaving.

DOESKIN—Properly a leather made from the skin of the doe. Also used to describe: 1. A heavy five- or eight-shaft satin-weave cotton fabric napped on one side, or 2. A heavy short-napped woolen fabric used for men's wear. The term Doeskin Finish should be used.

DOMESTICS—1. Ordinary cotton goods such as unbleached muslin sheeting or print cloth. 2. General term to cover household fabrics such as blankets, sheeting and pillowcasing, towels, washcloths. 3. American-made carpets and rugs as distinguished from those made in other countries, especially those known as Oriental rugs. 4. Fabrics made in this country from the major textile fibers as distinguished from those made in the British Isles or on the Continent—covert, serge, cassimere, melton, kersey, beaver, broadcloth, organdy, voile, dimity, and others.

DONEGAL—Originally a thick woolen homespun tweed handwoven by Irish peasants. Now a tweed with colorful thick spots or slubs woven into the fabric. Used for suits, coats.

DOPE DYEING—See Dyeing of Textiles.

DOTTED SWISS—Sheer cotton fabric embellished with small dot motifs. The dots may vary in color and can be applied to the goods by swivel weaving, clipspotting, flock-dotting, lappet weaving, etc. Originated in Saint Gallen, Switzerland about 1750. Uses include dress goods, curtainings, evening wear, wedding apparel, baby clothes, etc. See Swiss.

DOUBLE-CLOTH CONSTRUCTION—It can be made on a plain or a twill weave or in combinations of weaves. Two cloths are woven in the loom at the same time; one fabric is actually on top of the other. Binder threads hold the two fabrics together, one cloth forming the face of the double fabric, and the other the back of the goods. The binder yarns may be made to weave according to a plain, twill, or satin arrangement. A cloth of this type may have a plain-weave face, a twill-weave back, and a satin-weave stitching arrangement. When a double cloth is separated, the face from the back, the binder threads which have held the two fabrics together may be seen. Without the use of binder threads there would not be a true double cloth made; hence, their importance in fabrics of this type.

DOUBLE DAMASK—Table damask made with an 8-shaft satin weave. Single damask is made with a 5-end satin.

DOUBLE KNIT—A fabric knitted with a double stitch on a double needle frame to provide a double thickness and is the same on both sides. It has excellent body and stability.

DOUPPIONI OR DOUPION—Silk thread made from two cocoons that have nested together. In spinning, the double thread is not separated. The yarn is uneven, irregular, and diameter is large. It is used in cloth of this name as well as in pongee, nankeen, shantung and other cloths where this type of yarn is desirable.

DRAPERY—Decorative fabrics for the home. Made of cotton, silk, rayon, nylon, spun glass, acrylic, polyester, wool, mohair and mixtures. Used 1. as hangings at the side of windows and doors for artistic effects, 2. as inner curtains of sheer materials to hang next to the window pane, 3. as draw curtains to insure privacy, or to shut out light as sash curtains.

DRILL—A strong cotton material similar to denim which has a diagonal 2 x 1 weave running upward to the left selvage. Called Khaki when dyed that color. Used for uniforms, shirts, work clothes, ticking.

DROP STITCH—Knit fabrics under this caption are constructed to control the degree of unlooping of certain stitches and to provide for opening needle latches when necessary. The drop stitch construction is generally limited to jersey and rib fabrics for either fabric design or for the separation of rib fabric pieces. Used in knit shirts and dress fabrics.

DUCK—The name duck covers a wide range of fabrics. It is the most durable fabric made. A closely woven, heavy material. The most important fabrics in this group are known as number duck, army duck, and flat or ounce duck. Number and army ducks are always of plain weave with medium or heavy ply yarns; army ducks are the lighter. Ounce ducks always have single warp yarns woven in pairs and single or ply-filling yarns. Generally of ply yarns in warp and yarns of various sizes and weights in filling.

DUNGAREE—Work overall fabric of coarse cotton denim, usually blue. Originally used for sailors' work clothes.

DURABLE CREASE—More or less interchangeable with the term "Permanent Press," it is really limited since it refers only to the property of crease retention. Permanent Press, on the other hand, points to the shape-retaining properties of the whole garment.

DURABLE PRESS—See Permanent Press.

DUVETYNE, SUEDE, FELTED—In a finish in this category, the cloth is napped on one or both sides, and it is then sheared and brushed carefully in order to obtain the necessary closely-cropped nap that is characteristic of the finish.

E

EDGE ROLL—The usual curl or roll that develops at the edges of a single knit fabric, making it rather difficult to handle since it does not lie completely flat.

ELASTIC—A rubber band, cord, fabric or thread which has springiness, flexibility, and resiliency. There are several types used in the textile trade today: lastex, cut-rubber yarn, extruded latex, filatex, rolled latex, and laton. These yarns are used in belts, garters, girdles, gloves, shoes, sportswear, suspenders, etc.

ELASTICITY—The ability of textile fibers to "bounce back" when released from tension or stretch, as noted in woolen yarns.

ELONGATION—The ability of fibers in yarns or in fabrics "to go in the direction of the weave." Also means the increase in length from a tensile force: an example of this, the fibers in yarns as they appear in "baggy trousers" on a rainy day, or the sagginess or some woolen fabrics of low texture or pick count.

EMBOSSING—A popular effect made on cloth by passing it between a series of rollers, each set having one smooth and one embossed roller. These metallic rollers are heated so as to give better results. The embossed rollers have been engraved with suitable patterns, which will be reproduced on the fabric and give the appearance of a raised or embossed surface to the goods. Motifs may be birds, "tear drops," foliage, scrollwork, figures, pastoral scenes, etc.

END-AND-END SHIRTING—Broadcloth, chambray, and madras shirting with the warp, layout arranged as follows: one end of color followed by one end of white in alternate order. The term also covers fabric laid out with two colors alternating. A fine pincheck effect results from the plan.

EYELET—A small hole or perforation made in series formation to receive a string or tape. It is worked around with a buttonhole stitch. Applied especially to garments made of broadcloth, dimity, organdy, pique, etc.

F

FABRIC—A woven, knitted, plaited, braided, or felt material such as cloth, lace, hosiery, etc. Includes materials used in the manufacture. Fabric is also known as cloth, material, goods, or stuff. Garments are made from fabrics. There are three general classes of fabrics—apparel, decorative, and industrial.

FACE-FINISHED FABRIC—Cloths finished only on the face. Much resorted to on meltons, kerseys and on other overcoatings. The weaves used permit the type of finish, notwithstanding the fact that the texture is high and the interlacings tight. Plain, twill and satin weaves are all used jointly in proper construction of the various face-finish cloths. Other face-finish cloths are bolivia, boucle, chinchilla, montagnac, treebark cloths, Saxony overcoating, and Whitney finishes.

FACONNE—French for a fancy type of weave. Small designs appear in the cloth which is made on a Jacquard loom, although some of the goods can be made on dobbies. This rather broad term used in fabrics is popular at times; materials wear and drape well, as a rule.

FAILLE—A ribbed silk or rayon cloth with crosswise rib effect. It is soft in feel and belongs to the grosgrain family of cross-rib materials. Used for coats, dress goods, handbags. Faille is rather difficult to launder well, has good draping effects, and will give good service if handled carefully. Finished at 36 to 40 inches wide.

FAILLE CREPE—Has a smooth, dull, and richer face effect than crepe de chine. Fiber content must be declared if not made of all silk.

FAILLE TAFFETA—Made on plain-weave, occasionally on twill construction, it is crisp and stiff and has a very fine cross-rib filling effect. Made in silk, rayon, or acetate, it is used for coats and dresses.

FAKE FURS—Cotton and manmade fibers are used in these woven or knitted fabrics which have periodic waves of popularity. Their effects may be conservative or bizarre. Simulations of the fur of animals such as broadtail, chinchilla, ermine, French poodle, giraffe, krimmer, mole and pony are all well done; bizarre effects are sometimes used in exaggerated markings and fanciful colorings. Of course, fabrics and garments made of fake fur do not have the actual warmth, generally speaking, of genuine fur but the articles may be dry cleaned and made flameproof. Fake furs find use in lounging apparel, dress and sports clothes, slippers, coats, jackets, etc.

FELT—The cloth is a matted, compact woolen material, of which melton might be cited as an example. There are two types of felt cloth—woven and unwoven. Many types of overcoatings are correctly and incorrectly alluded to as being "felt."

FIBER—The fundamental unit comprising a textile raw material such as cotton, wool, etc. Fibers may be elongated single celled seed hairs like cotton; elongated multicellular structures such as wool; an aggregation of elongated cells like flax; or man-made filaments like nylon, polyester, rayon. Fiber originally meant spinnable material including the natural fibers and short sections of man-made filaments. Such fibers have a length which is many times as great as their diameter. In order to be spun into a yarn, a fiber must possess sufficient length, strength, pliability, and cohesiveness. Fiber is now used in a broad sense to include filament yarns, monofilaments, and tow.

FIBERGLAS*—Reg. T.M. of Owens-Corning. See glass fiber.

FIBER LENGTH—A synonym for staple in spun yarns. Fiber lengths vary widely in natural fibers so that in cotton the fiber length or staple is an intermediate length exceeded by 25% to 35% of the fibers. Man-made fibers are ordinarily spun in continuous filaments of indeterminate length which may be cut to a uniform length for spinning.

FIBRIL—Pronounced "fybril," it refers to a fine or very fine fiber.

FILAMENT—1. A fiber of indefinite length, such as filament acetate, rayon, nylon. May be miles long. 2. A single strand of rayon spinning solution as it is exuded from a spinneret orifice and coagulated in an acid bath or other medium; also true of other manmade filaments. 3. The single unit which is extruded by a silkworm in spinning its cocoon. Actually the silkworm makes two filaments at the one time, and they are cemented or glued together by the sericin, or silkgum, exuded by the silkworm in the action. Filaments are then spun into yarn.

FILLING—1. An individual yarn which interlaces with warp yarn at right angles in weaving fabric. Also known as pick or filling pick. Filling usually has less twist when compared with warp yarn. 2. Weft, the English term for filling, is used in this country in the hand-weaving and the carpet trades. The term, at times, is rather misleading and is often confused with woof, the English term for warp.

FILLING PILE FABRIC—This cloth is formed by floating extra picks on the surface of the goods. These floats are cut in or out of the loom to form the tufts of pile. Corduroy is an example. The filling-pile yarn, appearing on the surface of a cloth, does not always have to be cut since some of the material is used as an uncut pile fabric.

FINDINGS—Refers to pocketings, linings, zippers and other sundry and supplementary fabrics used in the manufacture of all types of garments.

FINISH, FINISHING—A general term which covers treatment of a fabric to give a desired surface effect such as calendered, embossed, lacquered, napped, mercerized, Sanforized, Rigmel, etc. Some finishes add luster, others give a muted dull effect. Special finishes can be applied to make a fabric crease-resistant, crease retentive, waterproof, etc. A finish often contributes much to the "feel" or "hand" of a fabric. It may be said that "cloth is made in the finishing," and that "finishing is an art and a science." It is the application of a pleasing or appealing effect to the fabric, comparable with the application of cosmetics to improve the facial effect of those who use them.

FIREPROOFING—A fabric to be fireproof must be 100 per cent fireproof according to the Federal Trade Commission, Washington, D.C. If treated to prevent the spread of flame, the fabric is then called fire-resistant.

FIRE-RETARDANT—Fabrics treated with special chemical agents to make them retardant or resistant to fire.

FIRE RETARDANT TREATMENT—Any method or process to which a textile material has been exposed which decreases its flammability. Fire retardant treatments may be durable or non-durable to laundering and drycleaning, and may be designed to meet a variety of specifications by a variety of tests depending upon the end-use of the fabric.

FISHEYE—Large diamond-effect linen cloth that is similar in shape to the eye of a fish. Comparable with the smaller pattern noted in birdseye, and used for the same purposes. Durable, has good absorptive properties, is reversible.

FLANNEL—Usually a cotton or rayon fabric slightly napped on both sides to resemble woolen fabric used for some dress goods, blanketing, coating, etc. Woolen and worsted flannels are also popular.

FLAT KNIT—Weft knit fabric made on a flat-bed knitting frame as distinguished from tubular fabric made on a circular frame. Needles are in a straight line. Ideal for manufacture of beltings, collars, trims, and scarves. See Circular Knit.

FLAX—See Linen.

FLEECE—The wool shorn from any sheep, or from any animal in the wool category. Fleece wool means clipped wool, as contrasted with pulled wool. Also the name of a fabric that has a deep fleece-like napped surface that may be wool, cotton, acrylic, nylon or other manmade fibers. Used for heavy coats. (See Pulled Wool.)

FLEECE LINED—A double-knit fabric which has floats on either one or both sides. These floats are napped, which makes the fabric warmer than an ordinary fabric. Used in eiderdown and cotton "sweat-shirts." Term also applied to sheep-lined coats.

FLEXIBILITY—The ability of fibers to bend or flex easily; highly desirable property in many instances.

FLOAT—The portion of a warp or filling yarn that extends over two or more adjacent warp ends or filling picks in weaving in order to form certain motif effects. Some floats are rather "long" from the interlacing points with the opposite system of yarn.

FLOCK, FLOCKING, FLOCK-DOTTING—The application of very short, fibrous stock to a fabric. The motif is usually printed in or onto the cloth with the aid of an adhesive, dusted and then finished as per instructions. The electrostatic methods of application are ideal in this type of work. Usually washable and drycleanable; lacquered motifs, however, may not be durable. Practically any textile may be flock-dotted. Uses include college pennants, signs or sign cloth, floorcovering, decorative materials, etc.

FLUORESCENT FABRICS—Made from dyestuffs that impart brightness to fabrics in daylight and under so-called "black-light conditions." This iridescent effect is used on apparel worn at night such as by firemen, policemen, airport workers, etc. Also effective for road signs.

FOAMBACK—Term used in Great Britain to denote that a fabric has been laminated to a backing of polyurethane foam.

FOULARD—A lightweight silk or rayon cloth noted for its soft finish and feel. Made with plain or twill weaves, it is usually printed with small figures on dark and light backgrounds. Suitable for dresses, robes, and scarves, foulard is always a popular staple for summer-neckwear fabric.

FRENCHBACK—A cloth with a corded twill backing of different weave than the face of the cloth, which is clear finish in appearance. It is a staple worsted cloth. Back weave is of inferior yarn, often cotton, when compared with the face stock. The backing gives added weight, warmth, more texture and stability to the cloth.

FRISE—Sometimes known as Cotton Frieze, the material is used in the upholstery trade. It is usually made with uncut loops and is sometimes styled by shearing the loops at varying heights. Some cloth of this name has appeared on the market with a rayon content in fiber construction. Gives excellent service.

FROSTING—See Color Abrasion.

FULL-FASHIONED HOSIERY—This is knitted flat and it is shaped during the knitting by the inward transfer of the selvage stitches, usually two at a time, on each side in order to provide the correct shape to properly fit the leg.

The narrowings are always located at the calf, heel, and toe, and generally above the knee just below the shadow welt.

In stockings made by the single-unit method the fabric is also widened at the instep to form a heel pocket. This widening is usually over one needle at a time and may be made at the selvages when it is invisible or some wales away from the selvages, in which case a gore line is visible in the heel. The latter method provides a better-fitting stocking. The selvage edges are then joined by a seam.

FUNCTIONAL FINISH—One that alters or improves the wearability or performance of a fabric or garment to afford protection or a longer life to the article and thereby enhance consumer demand. Examples include absorbency, crease-resistance, crease-retention, fire-resistance, laundryproof, mildew resistance, durability, shower-repellency.

FUSED RIBBON—Acetate fabric in wide widths may be cut into narrow ones by the application of heat. A hot knife blade applied to the cloth cuts and causes the edges to sear and bead thereby doing away with selvages on the edges of the goods.

G

GALATEA—Strong, sturdy, warp-effect, 5-shaft left-hand twill cotton fabric used for children's middies and playclothes. Named for the Greek sea nymph. White, dyed or printed.

GARBARDINE—Firm, durable, compactly woven cloth, which shows a decided diagonal line on the face of the goods; made on a 45-degree or 63-degree, right-hand twill. Named for a Hebrew cloak or mantle popular during the Middle Ages. Made from most major fibers, alone or in blends, garbardine is a piece-dyed fabric much used in men's and women's outer apparel. Some fabric may be skein or yarn dyed, or stock dyed. Weight runs from eight to fourteen ounces per yard and cotton yarn is used as the warp in the lower quality goods.

GARNETTING—The reduction of wool or cotton yarn or fabric to fiber so that the fiber may be used again.

GASSING—The process of burning off protruding fibers from yarns and cloths by passing them over a gas flame or heated copper plates. This gives the fabric a smooth surface which is very necessary for fabrics to be printed, and for those where a very smooth, inviting hand is desired. Also called singeing. See Singeing and Desizing.

GAUZE—Thin, sheer-woven cotton, wool, silk or synthetic fabric, similar to cheesecloth, used primarily for surgical dressings. Also used for dress trimming and curtains. First made in Gaza, Palestine.

GINGHAM—This fabric has dyed yarns introduced at given intervals in both warp and filling to achieve block or check effects. The warp and filling may often be the same, even-sided, and balanced. Color schemes range from conservative to gaudy, wild effects. Made from cotton, wool, worsted, nylon, etc.

GLASS FIBER—A manufactured fiber in which the fiber-forming substance is glass. Specially prepared glass marbles are melted in an electric furnace. Melted glass is then extruded through orifices to form continuous filaments and then drawn to the desired size. Registered trademark names include Fiberglas* (Owens-Corning-Fiberglas Corporation); Garan* (Johns-Manville Company); PPG* (Pittsburgh Plate Glass Company).

GLASS TOWELING—Plain weave, cotton or linen cloth with highly-twisted yarns in which red or blue stripes, blocks or checks are used. Other color combinations can also be used. Has no fuzziness or protruding fibers, launders well and gives good service.

GLAZING—The finish provides luster, sheen, shine or polish to some fabrics. It is done by friction calendering and the depth and the life of the finish depends on ingredients used and the settings on the machine. Some fabrics have durable finish while others will not withstand laundering. Chintz is an example of glazed fabric.

GRAY (GREY, GREIGE, GRIEGE) GOODS—Cloths, irrespective of color, that have been woven in a loom, but have received no dry- or wet-finishing operations. Gray goods are taken to the perch for the chalk-marking of all defects, no matter how small. These blemishes must be remedied in finishing of the cloth. Material is converted from the gray goods condition to the finished state.

GRENADINE—1. Cotton curtain grenadine. Fine, loosely woven fabric in leno weave similar to marquisette. Made with dyed filling yarns of all cotton, cotton and silk, silk and wool, and in a clipped dobby design. Used for dresses and blouses. Often made with a swivel dot or figure and used for curtains. 2. Silk cord made by twisting together several twisted strands. 3. A tie fabric of an open, lace-like construction. Frequently made of manmade fibers.

GROSGRAIN—A heavy, rather prominent ribbed fabric made from plain or rib weaves according to various combinations. The ribs will vary from a small number per inch to as high as 30 or 40 ribs to the inch. Made with silk or rayon warp and cotton filling, the fabric is rugged, durable, and of the formal type; it is dressy and in place at formal gatherings. It finds much use in ribbons, vestments, and ceremonial cloths.

GUN CLUB CHECKS—Men's and women's wear dress goods used for street and sports wear. Three colors of yarn are used in making the cloth. The warp and filling make a natty combination in the cloth. Men's wear cloth may have a smaller check than women's wear cloth.

GOODS—Merchandise of all types sold in textile markets, department stores, neighborhood stores. Synonymous with cloth, fabric, material, stock, stuff. Dry goods implies textile goods only.

H

HAND, HANDLE—The reaction of the sense of touch, when fabrics are held in the hand. There are many factors which give "character or individuality" to a material observed through handling. A correct judgment may thus be made concerning its capabilities in content, working properties, drapability, feel, elasticity, fineness and softness, launderability, etc.

HAND SPUN—Yarns which are spun by hand, or fabrics made from such yarns. They are more interesting and more unusual than the absolutely even, smooth machine spinning.

HAND WOVEN or HAND LOOMED—Fabrics which are woven on either the hand or hand-and-foot power loom.

They are admired because they express the individuality of the wearer.

HARNESS—The frame upon which the heddles used in weaving fabric are placed. Warp threads are drawn through their respective heddle eyes. Harnesses, which form the shed of the loom so that the shuttle with the filling yarn wound on it may pass through this shed, are raised and lowered in accordance with the pattern set up by the designer. There must always be at least one harness, raised and at least one lowered to make a shed. Generally speaking, "all ends that weave alike should go on the same harness."

HARRIS TWEED*—A trademark for an imported tweed made of virgin wool from the Highlands of Scotland, spun, dyed and handwoven by islanders in Harris and other islands of the Hebrides. Must be properly labeled. The Harris Tweed certification mark is owned and administered by The Harris Tweed Association, Ltd., London, England. Its exclusive trademark is the long familiar (since 1912) "orb mark," a ball-shaped figure surmounted by a cross.

HEADEND, HEAD END—The beginning of a new piece or run of fabric in the loom, usually showing identification marks of some sort. The term is comparable with the British term, Heading. In the American meaning and usage the term is used to describe a large sample of cloth. Basically, it implies a sample of fabric folded in the same way as is done with a full-length cut or bolt of cloth showing the position of and also one of the labels which appear on a regular piece or cut. Actually, it is a reference sample. Some head ends, of course, are "miniature" or of less-than-fold size; these must be stamped or pintagged for reference.

HEATHER MIXTURE OR BLEND—Combinations of colors, stockdyed, to provide a mottled or melange type of yarn in woolens such as homespun, tweed, cheviot, shetland, etc., for use in coatings, cap cloth, sport coating, jackets, ensembles, suitings, etc. The mixtures suggest the color of the well-known Scottish heather.

HEAT SET FINISH—Heat finishing treatment that will stabilize many manmade fiber fabrics so that there will not be any subsequent change in shape or size.

HEDDLES—The series of wires held by the harness on heddle bars at the top and bottom of the harness frame. Heddles have a top and bottom loop for each of the harness bars so that they can be slipped onto the correct harness. The middle hole has the respective warp end or ends drawn through it. Heddles keep the warp ends under control at all times. They are made of pressed steel wire, string cord, and iron as used in the weaving of fabrics such as carpets, rugs, heavy webbings.

HELANCA*—Product of the Heberlein Patent Corporation, New York City, the company that produced the first commercial stretch yarn in 1947. Helanca is a registered trademark of the company for a nylon or a polyester yarn made under license grant. Continuous filaments are specially engineered to create millions of microsopic curls, obtained through a torque (or tension) technique. The filament is first coiled like a spring and then is heat-set and twisted counter to the coil. The curls formed by this reverse plan open and close to give the stretch; the finer or lighter the denier, the greater will be the stretch.

Not all "stretch yarns" are Helanca. In order to bear the name of Helanca, the yarn must first be approved and then undergo continual tests in the Heberlein Testing Station, High Point, North Carolina. Thus, Helanca is the only torque yarn with universal quality standards because the specifications are kept uniform and constant among the licensees. Quality control is also exercised over fabrics and finished products bearing the Helanca trademark and made by the licensees.

HERRINGBONE TWILL—A broken twill weave giving a zigzag effect produced by alternating the direction of the twill. Same as the chevron weave. Structural design resembles backbone of herring. A true herringbone should have the same number of yarns in each direction, right and left, and be evenly balanced. Thus, all herringbones are broken twills but all broken twills are not true herringbones.

HIGH PILE—A pile in a fabric which is more than one eighth of an inch in height. When the pile is one eighth of an inch or less, the fabric is called a low-pile cloth. See Plush.

HOLLAND—Also known as shade cloth, this plain woven cotton or linen fabric is heavily sized or starched and is often given an oil treatment to make it opaque. Used for curtains and shades. Gives good service.

HONEYCOMB WAFFLE—A raised effect is seen in this material which gives the effect of the cellular comb of the honeybee. The high point on the one side of the material is the low point of the reverse side. Care has been used in manipulation. Used for draperies, jackets, skirts, women's and children's coats and dresses. Belongs in pique family of fabrics.

HOPSACKING—Popular woolen or worsted suiting fabric made from a 2-and-2 or a 3-and-3 basket weave. The weave effect is like that used for sacking to gather hops in the fields. Now made from other major fibers, hopsacking is used also for dress goods, jackets, skirts, and blouses.

HOUNDS'S TOOTH—A medium-sized and broken-check effect, often used in checks, clear-finish worsteds, woolen dress goods, etc. The weave used is a four-end twill based on a herringbone weave with four ends to the right, followed by four ends to the left. The color is completely surrounded by white yarn, and the check is a four-pointed star; this two-up and two-down basic construction fabric is a staple in the fabric trade.

HUCKABACK, HUCK—Cloth has a honeycomb effect; the filling yarns are slackly twisted to aid absorption. Material is heavy. This toweling often has the name of a hotel, school, etc., woven through the center for recognition and to establish ownership. In white or colors. Very absorbent, durable, serviceable for towels and will withstand rough use. Made of linen or cotton.

HIGH-BULK YARNS—Spun yarns made by blending high-shrinkage staple fibers with staple fibers of low shrinkage. Strictly speaking, they are not textured yarns since they are made from staple stock and not from continuous filament. Bulk yarns provide a soft, fluff-like effect or an opaque effect on certain woven and knitted cloths.

HYDROPHILIC FIBERS—Those which absorb water quickly such as cotton, linen, and rayon.

HYDROPHOBIC FIBERS—Those which are non-absorptive since they have "a phobia or fear of" water. Nylon is an example.

I

INTAGLIO—Covers a group of lustrous, brocade-like patterns knitted into nylon tricot fabric. Munsingwear, Inc., was the first company to use this type of motif and coloring on nylon tricot made with a monotone pattern.

INTARSIA—Knitting term in which solid color or intarsia designs or motifs show the same colored yarn on both face and back of the color area. Horizontal striping areas will always be solid; vertical stripes or geometrical designs will have a clear joining on the face in the case of rib or one or two wale overlap of color-joining in Jersey, Purl, and Rib only on the back of fabric.

INTENSITY—Refers to the brightness or the dullness of a color; corresponds to saturation or the purity of hue that a surface can reflect. When red is all red it is said to be in full intensity. When black, white, or gray is used in the color there is a neutralization or a reduction in the intensity.

INTERLINING FABRIC—1. A lightweight, napped, cotton, wool, or other fabric used in tailoring for extra weight or warmth. 2. Firm stiff linen canvas for men's coats.

INTERLOCK KNIT FABRIC—A special kind or type of eight-lock knit cloth, but it is generally described as a double 1x1 rib with crossed sinker wales. The fabric has a smooth surface on both sides, possesses good wearing qualities, and has less elasticity than ribs and does not develop prominent ribs when stretched in the horizontal direction. Fancy fabrics in this category are made with color arrangements, needle set-out, tucking, missing, and combinations of the foregoing. Used in sweaters and underwear.

IRIDESCENT FABRICS—Changeable effects noted in some cloths because of the color arrangement in the warp and filling yarns used to provide contrast and interest. Examples include taffeta and comparable cloths which show these varying tints and hues as the rays of light "strike the goods."

J

JACQUARD—Intricate method of weaving invented by Joseph J. M. Jacquard in the years 1801–1804, in which a headmotion at the top of the loom holds and operates a set of punched cards, according to the motif desired. The perforations in the cards, in connection with the rods and cords, regulate the raising of the stationary warp thread mechanisms. Jacquard knitting is a development of the Jacquard loom and its principles. Jacquard fabrics, simple or elaborate in design, include brocade, brocatelle, damask, neckwear, evening wear, formal attire, some shirting, tapestries, etc.

JASPE—Drapery, suiting or upholstery fabric which has a series of faint stripes formed by light, medium and dark yarn of a particular color.

JERSEY—A plain stitch knitted cloth in contrast to rib-knitted fabric. Material may be made circular, flat or warp knitted; the latter type jersey is sometimes known as tricot. Used in dressgoods, sportswear, underwear. Gives good service and launders very well. A very popular staple. Some fabric of this name is woven.

JUTE—A coarse, brown fiber from the stalk of a bast plant grown in India. Used mainly for burlap, cordage and as a backing for carpets and rugs.

K

KERSEY—Originated in Kersey, near Hadleigh, Suffolk County, England. The present kersey cloth is heavily fulled or milled and made of woolen yarn, has a high lustrous nap and a "grain" face. In Southern districts of this country there is a cheap type of cloth that is a "Union" but is sold as kersey. Kersey when compared with beaver is fulled more, has a shorter nap and a higher luster. Cloth gives good wear and is the dressy, conventional type. Found in blues, browns, blacks and other popular shades.

KHAKI—A pure Persian (Iranian) word in which means literally "of dust." Made of cotton, wool, worsted or linen, as well as from combinations of these fibers and the manmade fibers in blended materials. First used by the British armies as the official color for uniforms at the time of the Crimean War 1853–56. This ideal shade for field service finds only limited use in civilian dress—trousering, riding breeches, work clothes, children's playclothes, etc.

KNIT FABRICS, BASIC TYPES OF—1. Circular Knitting: Made on a circular machine to produce tubular fabric such as jersey, sweaters, seamless hosiery, neckwear. 2. Ribbed Fabric: Made with two sets of needles to give a ribbed or corrugated surface to the fabric. This type of goods is found in bathing suits, underwear, sweaters, scarves, and knitted caps. 3. Flat Outerwear Fabric: This is made by having the needles arranged in a straight line; as distinguished from fabric made on a circular machine. Used in the manufacture of blouses, ensembles, scarves, skirtings, and sweaters. 4. Flat Underwear Fabric: This is made on a machine with only one set of needles; to be distinguished from ribbed fabric which requires two sets of needles. Also see **DOUBLE KNIT**.

KNITTING—The art and science of constructing fabric by interlooping of yarn loops by the use of needles, a "loop within a loop." The most essential unit in a knit fabric is the loop or stitch. A vertical row of stitches is called a WALE; the horizontal or crosswise row of stitches is known as a COURSE. The number of wales per inch, measured across the fabric, depends on the count or size of the yarn used, and the number of needles per inch in the machine. The

knitted fabric should have a ratio between the courses and the wales that is equal to up to 50 per cent more courses than wales. This ratio depends upon the type of fiber stock used, the yarn, the fabric structure, and the type or method to be used to finish the product.

KNITTING GAUGE—This means the actual number of needles in 1½ inches in a knitting machine. Each needle knits one wale in a vertical row of stitches, while a course is a row of horizontal stitches or loops that extend crosswise in the fabric. The higher the gauge, the finer will be the fabric, but this does not necessarily mean that the stocking will be sheerer. For example, a 72 gauge with 15-denier yarn would be heavier or less sheer than a 45 gauge with 15-denier yarn because of the greater number of stitches in the former per square inch of fabric.

L

LACE—The term comes from the old French, las, by way of Latin, laquens, which means a noose, or to ensnare—rather well adapted to lace. A single yarn can produce a plaited or braided fabric or article since it will interlace, entwine, and twist in several directions to produce a porous material or lace. It should be kept in mind that one yarn may be used to make a lace, and that the action is like that of several yarns entering the machine; this action is used in knitting as well.

LACE GOODS—

ALLOVER EMBROIDERY—This is 36 inches or more in width, and the motif is embroidered over the full width of the fabric. Cotton, linen, nylon, rayon, and silk serve as the yarns, while the fabric base may be organdy, plain dimity, cambric, longcloth, pique, etc. The product is without scallops on each side, and is made in white and pastel shades and colors suitable for everyday wear. This type of embroidery is used for blouses, dress fabrics, pillow covers.

ALLOVER LACE—A lace one yard or more wide, devoid of scallops, and with the design spread over the entire width. Many types of design motifs and color shades are used for the fabric, which is made into day and evening dresses.

BEADING EDGES—Refers to embroidery or lace in which the edges are perforated or open so that ribbon may be drawn through and pulled up to give a ruffled effect.

BEADING GALLOON—A band used on some embroidery and lace, having both edges scalloped, it comes in varying widths, with openings in the center for ribbon to pass through, as shoulder straps in underwear, or to adorn dresses.

BEADING INSERTION—A straight edge applied to both sides of embroidery and lace with openings in the center to permit ribbon to be pulled through and gathered or ruffled. Used on baby clothes, children's dresses, carriage covers, shoulder straps.

BOBBIN FINE—Machine-made lace, on the order of shadow lace, in which heavy threads outline the motif.

BRIDE—A small strip or connection which links the details of ornamentation in lace. It may consist of threads overcast with buttonhole stitches, or of twisted or plaited threads. The English equivalent of this French term is "pearl-tie."

LACE CLOTH—Sheer, lightweight material made with a doup or a mock leno weave. Used for summer dress goods, it is always very popular when in fashion. Comes in the white or is dyed usually in pastel shades. Gives good service and withstands rather rugged wear but is not true lace.

LACE SPRIG—A piece of lace fabric appliqued to a net foundation.

LACE TIES—The connecting threads used in lace manufacture.

LACE TYPES—These follow:

ALENCON LACE—Delicate and durable lace with a solid design outlined with cord on sheer net ground. Best machine-made imitations have cord run by hand.

ANTIQUE LACE—Hand-made bobbin lace of heavy thread with large, often irregular, square knotted net on which designs are darned. Imitation antique lace used in draperies.

BATTENBURG LACE—A coarser form of Renaissance lace, made by hand or machine, of linen braid or tape and linen thread brought together to form various designs. Used for collars, cuffs. Machine-made for draperies.

BINCHE LACE—Flemish bobbin lace having a scroll floral pattern and a six pointed star ground sprinkled with figures like snowflakes. Used for dresses, blouses, lingerie.

BRETON LACE—Net which has designs embroidered with heavy, often colored, thread.

CHANTILLY LACE—Bobbin lace with fine ground and designs outlined by cordonnet of thick, silky threads, used for trimmings on bridal veils. Originally made in silk, now made of rayon, nylon or mercerized cotton.

CLUNY LACE—A rather heavy bobbin lace identified by a paddle wheel and/or a bat wing design. May also have a poinsettia. Used for doilies, scarfs, collars.

CROCHETED LACE—Real lace with heavy design made with specially twisted cotton thread and a crochet hook.

DRESEDEN POINT LACE—Type of drawnwork with ground of fine linen with some threads drawn and others embroidered and interlaced to form square mesh.

FRENCH VAL—French Val originated in Valenciennes, France. Real Valenciennes lace is made of linen, the imitation of cotton, and commonly called Val. The imitation must be so described.

IRISH CROCHET—Is typified by a raised rose or shamrock design.

HARDANGER LACE—This city on the Hardanger Fiord in southwestern Norway is famous for this lace which is made by the women folks. In its original form the lace is very old since it was worked with colored silks on a fine gauze netting in Persia and other Asiatic countries for many centuries. This lace, based on the principle of the square, is geometric in formation. The material necessary to make Hardanger includes scrim or loose textured linen, a pair of very sharp, pointed scissors, a tapestry needle and pearl cotton. The stitches used include kloster stitch, Swedish weaving stitch, woven bars with picots, festoon stitch, lace stitch, Holbein technique, feather stitch, kloster blocks, diagonal kloster blocks and fagoting stitch.

IRISH LACE—A variety of laces made in Ireland. The best known are crochet, net embroideries of Limerick and Carrickmacross.

LILLE LACE—Fine bobbin lace with patterns outlined with flat cordonnet. Sometimes dotted.

MALINES—One of the oldest and best known of lace, net and silk fabrics; diaphanous in nature and named for the Belgian city.

MILAN LACE—Originally made in Milan. Tape lace with needlepoint mesh and picot edging. Easily imitated by machine, but machine-made must be so described.

NEEDLE-POINT LACE—Lace made entirely with a sewing needle rather than with a bobbin. Worked with buttonhole and blanket stitches on paper patterns.

NOTTINGHAM LACE—Flat lace originally made in Nottingham, England. Now used as name for lace made anywhere on Nottingham-type machine.

RATINE LACE—Machine-made lace with groundwork of heavy loops similar to turkish toweling.

RENAISSANCE LACE—Woven tape motifs joined by a variety of flat stitches.

ROSE POINT LACE—Venetian needle-point lace which has a delicate and full design of flowers, foliage and scrolls connected by string cordonnet.

SPANISH LACE—Any lace made in Spain. The most common is of silk with heavy flat floral designs held together with varying meshes.

TATTING LACE—Knotted lace worked with the fingers and a shuttle. Made in various designs, the most popular being the clover leaf and wheel.

TORCHON LACE—Sometimes called beggar's lace. Characterized by a shell design. Used on children's dresses, scarfs, doilies.

VAL LACE—See Valenciennes Lace below.

VALENCIENNES LACE—Flat bobbin lace worked in one piece with the same thread forming both the ground and the design. Ground is 1. Round (lozenge shaped) called round mesh Val, once called German Val; 2. Diamond shaped often called French Val.

VENICE LACE—A needle point lace decorated with floral motifs and designs connected with irregularly placed picot edges called brides.

LAMB'S WOOL—Elastic, soft, resilient wool fibers obtained from lambs when they are seven or eight months old—the first or virgin clipping from the animal. This lofty stock is used in better grades of fabrics.

LAME—Brocade, brocatelle or damask in which metallic (laminated) threads or yarns are interspersed throughout the fabric or one in which these threads have been used in the base construction. Most popular threads are those of copper, gold, silver; untarnished aluminum laminated with plastic is also used to provide rather brilliant colorings to simulate true metallic threads. Lame is also the trademark term of the Standard Yarn Mills, Woodside, New York, for its non-tarnishable metallic yarn.

LAMINATION—The joining of two or more layers of material by the use of an adhesive, a binding agent, or heat; joining a face fabric to a foam back in bonded fabrics.

LATEX—The viscid, milky, complex emulsion of proteins, alkaloids, starches, resins, and other substances secreted by the cells of certain plants such as the milkweed, rubber tree, and poppy. The liquid extruded from the rubber tree, when the bark is cut, may be coagulated with lactic acid and compressed into sheets, or solidified into rubber.

LAWN—Made of carded or combed cotton yarn this light, thin cloth was first made in Laon, France. Comes in the white, solid color or in prints. Satin stripes are often used for effect in this plain weave goods. Has a crisp and crease-resistant finish and is usually pre-shrunk prior to manipulating. It is sometimes crinkled to simulate plisse fabric. Crisper than voile but not as crisp as organdy in this family of cotton fabrics.

LENO OR DOUP—An open-effect weave in which every other yarn of warp is crossed, wholly or partially, with its companion yarn. The yarns work in pairs; one is the standard warp yarn, the other is the skeleton or doup yarn. The warp yarns cross each other between the picks in the actual weaving of the material. This plan affords much greater strength to the goods and curbs possible yarn slippage or distortion. Used in marquisette, nettings of many types, containers for citrus fruits, dress goods, and shirting fabrics.

LINEN—Flax is the plant, linen is the product from flax. The term, linen, cannot be used except for natural fiber flax. Among the properties of linen are rapid moisture absorption, fiber length of few inches to one yard, no fuzziness, does not soil quickly, a natural luster and stiffness. Uses of linen include tablecloths, toweling, crease-resistant linens, dress linens, doilies, runners, huckaback toweling, summer dress goods, sportswear, etc.

LINEN CAMBRIC—Cloth may be sheer or coarse; of plain weave. Known also as handkerchief linen. Used also for dress goods. If fairly good quality is used, fabric will give excellent wear and service. Material is sized and gives neat appearance after laundering. Cotton cambric is made from printcloth or lightweight sheeting construction. It is given special sizing treatment and a calender finish.

LINEN CANVAS—There are several fabrics in this category: 1. Open-mesh canvas is used for embroidery; made of hard-twisted yarn, the cloth is very durable, and the most popular type is known as Java canvas. 2. Close-woven canvas is made from hard-twisted yarn in plain-weave construction; comes in various weights, and finishes range from the heavily sized varieties to soft effects.

LINEN DAMASK—A single damask is made on a five-shaft satin weave; double damask is made on an eight-end satin construction. All damask is made on Jacquard looms. This reversible fabric is very durable; the higher the texture the better will be the quality. Damask will launder well, retain luster and may be all linen, all cotton, or a union material—say cotton warp and linen filling. The smaller motifs give the greater strength to the goods because of shorter flat yarns. More luster is possible on the double type because of longer yarn floats, but the single type damask usually gives longer wear. Used for coverings, doilies, curtains, guest towels, napkins, runners, and tablecloths.

LINEN STRAW—Any closely braided or woven straw,

fine in texture, which is given a finish to simulate finished linen fabric.

LINEN-TEXTURED RAYON—A large and important category of rayon fabrics having the distinctive textures of linens. These range from sheer handkerchief-linen texture to heavier, rougher "butcher-linen" texture. Usually plain-weave. Used in lighter weights for handkerchiefs, women's and children's dresses, tablecloths, towels, sheets, pillowcases; heavier weights for summer coats, suits, sportswear.

LINET—An unbleached linen lining fabric made in France.

LINON A JOUR—French for a gauze-like linen fabric used as dress goods.

LONGCLOTH—Fine, plain weave cotton cloth made from high quality yarn. High in texture and has genuine whiteness in finished fabric. Medium-twist yarn is used in the cloth which finds use in children's wear, dress goods, lingerie, and underwear. Comparable with some muslin sheeting.

LUREX—A metallic yarn of plastic-coated aluminum for use in lame fabrics. Yarn is made of an aluminum-base fiber sandwiched between two plies of specially formulated plastic film. Yarn is impervious to tarnish and much lighter than ordinary metallic yarns. Product of Dobeckmun Company, a Division of the Dow Badische Company, Inc.

M

MACKINAC, SKI CLOTH, SNOW CLOTH, WIND-BREAKER FABRIC—These cloths are in the same group. Heavy coating material, usually low in price and fair in quality. Plaid effects are feature of material. 15 to 25 ounces in weight. Napped, and face is often different from back. Double cloth in construction. Strong and durable, difficult to tailor. Used much for every day wear. Keeps shape quite well and does not shine. Good warmth.

MADRAS—One of the oldest staples in the cotton trade, it is made on plain-weave background which is usually white; stripes, cords, or minute checks may be used to form the pattern. Fancy effects are often of satin or basket weave, or small twill repeat.

MANMADE FIBERS—Formerly called synthetic fibers, the term is used, at times rather loosely, to imply all manmade textile fibers, cellulosic and non-cellulosic.

MARQUISETTE—Lightweight, open-mesh cloth made on a leno or doup weave. Made of cotton, silk, and some of the manmade fibers such as glass fibers which are very popular in curtains, the material also finds use in women's and children's apparel. Polyester, acrylic, and nylon are much used in the manufacture of marquisette.

MATELASSE—A rather soft, double cloth or compound fabric which has a quilted surface effect. Made on Jacquard looms, the heavier constructions are used for coverlets, draperies, and upholstery. Lighter weight fabric finds use in dress goods, evening wear, and trimming. Matelasse gives effects such as blistered, puckered, quilted or wadded depending on the cloth construction used.

MELANGE—1. Handmade pillow lace of silk which shows a combination (melange) of conventional Chantilly lace with Spanish effects in the design. 2. French term (melange) for mixture effects in fabrics.

MELTON—A heavily felted, hard, plain face-finished cloth used for overcoatings, uniform fabrics, hunting cloth, and riding habits. Light melton is the fabric used as "under-collar cloth" in coatings. Originated in the famous Melton Mowbray fox-hunting area in Leicestershire, England. Compared with its sister fabrics—kersey, beaver and woolen broadcloth—it is fulled the most, has the shortest nap which is not of the so-called laid nap, and it is dull in appearance and non-lustrous. Given double shearing in finishing to provide the close-cropped face-effect. Qualities vary considerably depending on the types of stocks used.

MERCERIZING—A finishing process used extensively on cotton yarn and cloth consisting essentially of impregnating the material with a cold, strong, sodium hydroxide (caustic soda) solution. The treatment increases the strength and affinity for dyes and, if done under tension, the luster is greatly increased. This latter phase is now considered to be the heart of the process although not a part of John Mercer's original patents, discovered by accident in 1844. Mercerization is done in skein form, on the warp, or in the piece, either entirely or in printed effects. Best results are noted in combed yarns.

MERINO—1. The highest, finest and best wool obtained anywhere in the world. This fiber is used only in the best of woolen and worsted fabrics, billiard cloth, etc. 2. In knitting underwear fabrics the term implies garments made from yarns spun with a mixture of wool, not necessarily merino in type, and cotton, all in varying blend percentages.

MESH—Any fabric, knitted or woven, with an open texture, fine or coarse.

METALLIC—A manufactured fiber composed of metal, plastic-coated metal, metal-coated plastic, or a core completely covered by metal. Metallic yarns are now made with Mylar polyester film as well as with acetate film. Mylar metallic yarns withstand higher temperatures and more rugged finishing and laundering than the acetate-type yarns.

METALLIC CLOTH—Any fabric, usually silk, that has gold, silver, tinsel, or other metal threads interspersed throughout the design in the cloth. Lame is a metallic fabric. Cloths of this type have a cross-rib or rep effect, are rather stiff, harsh, stately, formal, prone to tarnish, and quite durable. Ideal for evening wear, these fabrics come in many grades and qualities.

MOHAIR—Comes from the Angora goat, one of the oldest animals known to man. It is two-and-one-half times as strong as wool and outwears it. Comes from South Africa, Western Asia, Turkey, and California, Oregon, and Texas in this country with Kerrville, Texas, the center of the industry in America. Foreign mohair is nine to twelve inches long and allowed a full year's growth before shearing. California and Texas mohair are shorn twice a year since the fibers would fall out if allowed a one year growth. Uses include fancy dress goods, felt hats, linings, plushes, and in blended yarns for use in men's and women's suiting fabrics.

MOIRE, WATERMARKED—A finish given cotton, silk, acetate, rayon, nylon, etc. where bright-and-dim effects are observed. This popular finish is achieved by passing the fabric between engraved rollers which press the particular motif into the goods causing the crushed and the uncrushed parts to reflect light differently.

MOLESKIN—1. Heavy sateen weave fabric made on a 5-end or an 8-end satin construction with the use of heavy, soft-spun filling in order to provide for a good napped surface effect. Supposed to simulate the fur of a mole. Carded cotton yarn is used and the fabric is napped and sheared to provide what is actually a suede-effect. 2. A type of cotton goods "fleece-lined" and having a soft, thick nap. Used as underwear in cold climates and in lining for the so-called sheep-skin-lined coats.

MONK'S CLOTH—Made of very coarse yarn. A 4-and-4 basket or some similar basket construction is used. Hangings, couch covers, and furniture material are uses of the cloth. Not easy to sew or manipulate; yarns have a tendency to slide. Cloth may sag. It is a rough, substantial, rather bulky fabric.

MULTIFILAMENT—A term applied to manmade yarns having many fine filaments. For example, 150-denier yarn with 40 filaments would be considered a standard filament count yarn in that denier size, but 150-denier yarn, with say 90 filaments, would be considered a multi-filament yarn.

MUSLIN—1. Generic term for a wide variety of cotton fabrics, includes cloths ranging from lightweight sheers to the heavier weight; firmly woven goods such as sheeting. 2. A white-goods finish on print cloth or sheeting which has been given a pure starched or back-filled finish to provide a dull, "clothy" effect and hand. Muslin gray goods, for example, are finished in fabrics such as batiste, cambric, chintz, cretonne, lawn, longcloth, mercerized goods, plain muslin, nainsook, organdy.

N

NAINSOOK—A fine, soft cotton fabric, with a plain weave. Better grades have a polished finish on one side. When well-polished, it may be sold as polished cotton. In low priced white goods, cambric, longcloth and nainsook often are identical fabrics before converting. The finishing process gives its characteristic texture. Nainsook is heavier and coarser than lawn. Usually found in white, pastel colors and prints, and used chiefly for infant's wear, lingerie and blouses.

NAPPING—The raising of the fibers on the face of the goods by means of teasels or rollers covered with card clothing (steel wires) that are about one inch in height. Action by either method raises the protruding fibers and causes the finished fabric to provide greater warmth to the wearer, makes the cloth more compact, causes the fabric to become softer in hand or smoother in feel; increases durability and covers the minute areas between the interlacings of the warp and the filling. Napped fabrics include blankets, flannel, unfinished worsted, and several types of coatings and some dress goods.

NET—A mesh fabric of rayon, nylon, cotton, or silk; made in a variety of geometric-shaped meshes of different sizes and weights. Used for evening dresses, curtains, veils and trimming.

NETTING—The knotting of threads into meshes that will not ravel. Chinese-type lace and fish net have a knot at every intersection. Knitted fabric may ravel or disentangle and the yarn may be used over again to make another fabric. Netting is done by hand or by machine.

NEW WOOL—One interpretation is that it is wool obtained in the fleece after sheep shearing. It also implies that wool fibers, obtained from various sources, have never been utilized in the manufacture of a wool material. This loosely-applied term does not designate as to the fibers being from live sheep, dead or slaughter-house wool, etc. In this meaning the term is rather provincial.

NINON—A smooth, transparent, high textured type of voile fabric. Made in plain or small novelty weaves, the warp ends work in pairs. It finds use in lingerie when made with cotton, silk, acetate or rayon, as well as in dress goods. Glass fibers are used when the fabric is to serve as curtaining.

NONWOVEN FABRIC—A textile structure produced by bonding and/or interlocking of fibers, accomplished by mechanical, chemical, thermal or solvent means, and combinations thereof. The term does not include paper or fabrics which are woven, knitted, tufted, or those made by wool or other felting processes.

NOVELTY-WEAVE—Any small weave made from a combination of the staple basic weaves such as plain, twill, satin, basket, and rib. Novelty-weave effects are used in counterpanes, dress goods, shirtings, linens, and stripe effects.

NOVELTY YARNS—Irregular, uneven-in-diameter yarns made for special textured and textural effects. Examples include boucle, bug, chenille, Knickerbocker, loop, nub, slub, thick-and-thin and so on.

NUB YARNS—A type of novelty yarn where bloated or enlarged portions or segments are effected by twisting one end of a yarn several times around another in a comparatively short space span. A binder or core yarn is often resorted to and around which the fancy or nub yarn is wound, spirally or in some comparable formation. Uses include fancy yarn effects in heavy coatings, some dress goods, sweaters, decorative and upholstery fabrics.

NUN'S VEILING—Plain weave, soft to the touch, lightweight cloth that comes usually in black or white. Rather flimsy fabric but always of good quality. Resembles worsted challis. Made of worsted, fine woolen yarn, nylon, acrylic, polyester, and comparable fibers. Care must be used in manipulating the fabric which washes and launders easily and well, has excellent draping qualities, and gives good wear.

O

OATMEAL CLOTH—Soft, heavy linen cloth with a crepe or pebbled effect that resembles oatmeal paper. Strong, durable, launders well.

OILCLOTH—Fabric which is treated with linseed-oil varnish to give a patent-leather effect. When used for table covers or shelf covering, it may be given a satiny sheen and finish. It comes in plain colors or printed designs. Other uses include waterproof garments for outerwear, book bags, covers, belts, bibs, pencil cases, and other containers, surgical supplies, bags, and luggage.

OILED SILK—A thin, transparent silk fabric which has been soaked in boiled linseed oil and dried. Waterproof and fairly pliable. Used mostly for shower curtains.

OMBRE—A gradated or shaded effect of color used in a striped motif. Usually ranges from light to dark tones of the one color, such as from light blue to dark blue; can give, usually, three or four different casts or tones of the one color in the effect. Used in upholstery, some dress goods, decorative fabrics.

ORGANDIE, ORGANDY—Very light and thin, transparent, stiff and wiry cotton cloth used in dress goods, bedspreads, blouses, waists, curtains, baby bonnets, doll cloth, millinery, neckwear, artificial flowers, etc. Because of chemical treatment, organdy withstands repeated launderings and still retains its crispness. May crush or muss but is readily ironed back into stiff state. Shadow organdy has a fine motif in self-color. Organdy is a true, durable finish cloth.

ORGANZA—A very thin, but stiff plain woven silk, nylon, acrylic, or polyester fabric used in evening wear, wedding attire for women, neckwear, and trimming. Actually is a type of organdy which is made of cotton.

OSNABURG—Coarse cotton cloth often made with part waste in it, plain weave, medium to heavy in weight and resembling crash. Named for town of this name in Germany, it serves as the base fabric for some chintz, and cretonne. Also used in unbleached condition for cement, grain and comparable types of containers. Also has some call for slacks, sportswear, and curtaining and upholstery.

OTTOMAN—Silk or manmade-fiber yarn fabric characterized by a heavy, large, rounded cord effect in the filling direction of the goods. The filling rib yarn is often cotton, wool or waste yarn and none of these show on the face or the back of the goods since the warp covers the filling in entirety. Used for dress goods, coatings, hangings, etc.

OUTING FLANNEL—A soft, lightweight, plain or twill weave cotton fabric usually napped on both sides. Most outing flannels have colored yarn stripes. Soils easily and the nap washes and wears off. Used chiefly for sleeping garments, children's underwear, interlinings, diapers.

OVERPLAID—Actually a double plaid in which the weave, or oftener, the color-effect is arranged in blocks of the same or different sizes, one over the other. Observed in British mufti, golf togs, neat business woolens and worsted for morning, lounge and semiformal wear.

OXFORD—Soft, somewhat porous, and rather stout cotton shirting given a silk-like luster finish. Made on small repeat basket weaves, the fabric soils easily because of the soft, bulky filling used in the goods. The cloth comes in all white or may have stripes with small geometric designs between these stripes. Now is made from spun rayon, acetate, and a few other manmade fibers. Oxford also means a woolen or worsted fabric which has a grayish cast made possible from a combination of black and white yarns or by the use of dyed gray yarn.

P

PALM BEACH CLOTH*—Registered trademark name originated with Goodall-Sanford Company, Inc., Sanford, Maine, but now owned by the Palm Beach Company, Inc., Cincinnati, Ohio. Palm Beach was the first cloth to appear on the market as a tropical fabric, a lightweight summer suiting for men's and women's wear, more than fifty years ago. It was made with cotton warp and mohair filling; since its origin fiber variations and blends of many types have superseded the original fabric.

PANNE—A satin-faced, velvet or silk material named from the French for "plush," which has a high luster made possible by the tremendous roller-pressure treatment given the material in finishing. Panne velvet is often referred to as panne and is a staple silk fabric.

PARACHUTE FABRIC—A compactly woven, lightweight fabric comparable with airplane cloth. It is made of silk, nylon, rayon, or cotton. If the cloth is to be used for personnel, it is made of silk or nylon; rayon or cotton is the fabric used as a carrier for bombs, cargoes, etc.

PEBBLE EFFECT—Fabric with a rough, granite-like, irregular or pebble effect on the face of the goods. Most of the cloth is some type of crepe fabric.

PERCALE—1. Dress percale is a medium-weight, printed cotton cloth with a firm, smooth finish. Made from plain weave the texture is around 80-square. Used for women's and children's dresses, aprons, blouses. Used interchangeably with the word, calico. 2. Sheet percale is fine, smooth, lustrous, and highly textured with a count of 90 to 100 yarns each way for a total of 180 or 200 threads in the goods; a very high grade sheeting.

PERMANENT FINISH—A comparatively much-used term given a number of materials for which some particular claim is made. Examples could include moire or water-marked effect on faille, taffeta, organdy and dimity: the smoothness on broadcloth; embossed fabrics, some crepe effects, glazed fabrics, etc. The term, as well, implies cloths are crease-resistant, shrinkage-resistant, and wear resistant. In reality, however, the safer term to use is "Durable Finish." Actually, very few finishes truly qualify as being permanent for the life of the fabric or garment.

PERMANENT PRESS, DURABLE PRESS—Terms used to describe a garment which will retain its shape-retaining. properties throughout its career. Features include sharp creases, flat seams, smooth surface texture and appearance on the goods, and seams which are free from puckering. (See Permanent Finish, above.)

PILE FABRIC—One in which certain yarns project from a foundation texture and form a pile on the surface. Pile yarns may be cut or uncut in the fabric. Corduroy and velveteen are examples of cut filling pile fabrics; velvet is an example of a cut warp pile fabric while Turkish toweling or Terry cloth is an uncut pile material.

PILLING—Formation of little balls of fibers· called "pills" on the surface of a cloth. Caused by abrasion in wear.

PILLOWCASE LINEN—Plain weave, high count, good texture, bleached. Yarn is very smooth and has high count of turns of twist per inch. Launders easily and well, sheds dirt, has cool feel and appearance, is strong and durable. Very desirable cloth.

PINWALE—A very narrow ridge or rib in a fabric (from 16 to 23 wales to the inch).

PIQUE—Medium weight or heavy fabric with raised cords that run in the warp direction. This substantial cloth is made on dobby, Jacquard, drop–box and other types of looms.

PLAID—1. A pattern consisting of colored bars or stripes which cross each other at right angles, comparable with a Scottish tartan. Plaid infers a multi-colored motif of rather large pattern repeat; the word check refers to similar motifs on a smaller scale and with fewer colors. 2. A rectangular piece of fabric or a garment having a plaid or tartan design, worn by both sexes in Scotland in lieu of a cloak. 3. A woolen cloth with a tartan motif in which plaids, two of them, are woven into the goods; also called overplaid. 4. A woven or printed pattern in a tartan with some appealing cross-barred effect.

PLAIN WEAVE—The most common of the fundamental weaves. Each filling yarn passes successively over and under each warp yarn, alternating each row. Sometimes called the one-up and one-down weave. Used for muslin, print cloth, taffeta, voile, sheeting, etc. (See Satin Weave, Twin Weave.)

PLAITED FABRIC—It is made with a single yarn interlacing freely to make lace or some porous material. More than one yarn may be run into the machine, but the action is that of a single yarn entering the braiding or lace frame. Plaited or lace fabrics can also be made on the idea of plaiting threads according to some plan or motif. Designs are often balanced geometrically, and in some instances are symmetrical. Some plaited fabrics are shoelaces, lace, curtains, gauze, doilies, bedspreads, counterpanes, runners, and veiling.

PLISSE—Cotton, acetate, or rayon fabric treated in a striped motif, or in spot formation, with a caustic-soda solution which shrinks parts of the goods to provide the crinkled or pleated effect (plisse). The effect may or may not be removed after washing; this depends on the quality of the fabric or garment. Ironing, if done, should take place after the fabric is thoroughly dry in order to smooth out double thicknesses such as hems.

PLUSH—A warp-pile cloth covered with a surface of cut pile yarns. The pile is longer than that in velvet but it is not as densely woven. The ground yarn is usually cotton while the pile may be of wool, cotton, mohair, acetate, rayon, and other manmade fibers. Plush is derived from the French term, "peluche," by way of Latin, "pilus," which means hair.

PLY, PLY YARN—Two or more yarns that have been twisted together. Ply-yarn such as automobile tire fabric yarn, may have 9, 10, or 11 ply.

POINT—1. The fine quality of handmade lace without regard to the particular make. 2. French for the many stitches used in making real lace. 3. Formerly used in France to imply imitation stitches made to represent genuine tapestry and embroidery stitches. 4. The ornamental stitching used on the back of gloves.

POINTED TWILL—A weave in which the threads of the right-hand twill and those of the left-hand twill come to a point at the break line in the cloth where they come together. The weave gives cloth a sort of zigzag effect. Uses of fabric made this way are the same as for homespun and tweed, since the weaves are used chiefly for woolen cloths.

PONGEE—1. Thin, natural, tan-colored silk fabric. Originally made of wild Chinese silk with a knotty rough weave, and named from the Chinese, pun-ki, meaning "woven at home on one's own loom." Used primarily for summer suits and dresses, also for decorative purposes in both plain and prints. 2. Staple fine combed cotton fabric finished with a high luster used for underwear. 3. Today pongee is being simulated in manmade fibers.

POODLE CLOTH—A looped boucle or knotted fancy yarn fabric brought here several years ago by Lesur of Paris, France. Resembling the coat or fleece of a French poodle it was first made of wool and mohair yarn, the latter providing the effect. Now made from other fibers, knit-goods of poodle cloth are of the staple variety in the women's coating trade.

POPLIN—A broad term to imply several fabrics made from various types of yarn. Identified by a fine rib effect in the filling direction from selvage to selvage.

POROSITY OR CAPILLARITY—The capacity of fibers to absorb moisture; varies with the several types of fibers in use today.

PRE-SHRUNK—Fabrics or garments which have received a pre-shrinking treatment. Often done on cottons to remove the tendency for cloth to shrink when washed or laundered. Worsted and woolens are also shrunk before cutting the fabric for use in a garment to prevent further shrinkage. The percent of residual shrinkage must be indicated on the label of the goods or garments thus treated.

PRESS CLOTH—Fiber cloth made of camel's hair, cotton, and wool, depending on use. Hair fiber is found in varying percentages in all press cloths.

PRIMARY COLORS—Red, yellow, and blue, from which pigments of these colors may be mixed to make many other colors.

PROGRESSIVE SHRINKAGE—Shrinkage which results from repeated washing, laundering, or dry cleaning; shrinks more after each successive treatment.

PUCKERING—A rippled appearance noted in garments, especially at the seams; irksome and difficult to remove.

PULLED WOOL—Wool obtained from pelts of dead animals by chemical means. Inferior in all respects to sheared wool, it may be used alone or in blends and mixtures for use in low quality fabrics.

Q

QUALITY CONTROL—Continuous testing, checking and inspecting of textile plant operations from raw material to finished fabric to make certain that raw materials, yarns and fabrics meet the quality standards as determined by the particular mill and/or by government agencies or textile associations such as the American Society for Textiles and Materials, Philadelphia, Pennsylvania.

R

RABBIT HAIR—This hair is used in combination with other fibers. It is soft and lustrous and in the better quality fabrics enough hair may be present to justify the use of the term. Much used in varying percentages in wool and blend fabrics.

RATINE—Also spelled ratine. From the French, meaning "frizzy or fuzzy." An overcoating cloth on the order of chinchilla. Used in women's wear coatings in woolen trade. Cotton ratine is a loose, plain-woven cloth with a rough, nubby surface finish; one heavy and two fine yarns twisted together at various tensions form the curly and knotty ply yarn.

RECOVERY—A basic property of stretch yarn and refers to the degree to which a yarn returns to its relaxed position after stretching. Rapid and complete recovery prevents bagging or sagging and is very important in many types of articles, especially in stretch pants.

REGIMENTAL STRIPES—Stripes ranging from one half to one inch in width, which find favor in the better grade of neckwear and hatbands. The colors of the better-known British regiments, as well as the colors of leading universities in this country, provide the color combinations:

REP, REPP—Resembles poplin but has a more discernible, distinctive crossrib cord. Made from a number of the major fibers it finds use in neckwear, beachwear and other sportsclothes, shirting, and upholstery.

REPEAT—An entire completed pattern for design and texture. Repeats vary in size considerably, depending on the weave, type of material, texture, and the use of the cloth.

REPELLENT TREATMENTS—Any one of a great number of treatments that may be applied to fabrics and garments to make them repellent to moths, water, mildew moisture, perspiration, etc. They may or may not be durable in nature. Some disappear after the first washing and laundering, others will give good service, at times almost to the point of permanency. A very few may be classed as permanent.

RESIN—The name commonly applied to chemical compounds used to impart wash-and-wear and durable press properties to fabrics which contain cellulosic fibers.

REVERSIBLE BONDED FABRIC—This means that two face fabrics have been bonded together so that the two sides may be used interchangeably. There are, however, some limitations in this area. It is not advisable, for example, to bond to stiff fabrics such as a nylon taffeta since stiffness would be increased in the bonding; the same holds true in the case of two hard-faced or hard-twisted-yarn worsteds.

RIB—Usually a straight raised cord, formed in a weave by threads which are heavier than the others, lengthwise, crosswise or diagonal. Many knitted fabrics are ribbed lengthwise.

ROMAN STRIPES—Brilliant contrasting stripes that are usually in the warp direction.

RUBBERIZED FABRIC—Any fabric with a rubberized coating on one or both sides making it waterproof and resistant to most stains.

RUBBER SHEETING—A plain cotton fabric with heavy coating of cured rubber on one or both sides. Used in various weights in hospitals and for baby cribs.

RUG—A thick, heavy fabric usually with pile and commonly made of wool, mohair, synthetic, nylon or mixtures. Kinds of rugs:

AMERICAN ORIENTAL—A machine-made domestic rug with Oriental design and colors to resemble a hand-tied Oriental. Designs may be woven through to the back. Moderately priced compared with hand-tied Oriental.

ANTIQUE ORIENTAL RUG—A hand-tied rug from the Orient. It is at least one hundred years old.

AXMINSTER—A floor covering with V-shaped pile yarns which are held in the fabric by binder yarns. Pile made of wool, manmade fibers or blends; back usually jute.

DRUGGET—A rug of 100% wool or wool and cow's hair (pile), and jute ground. India is country of origin. Used for beach cottages and summer porches.

FIBER RUG—A floor covering made of tightly twisted strips of paper often coated with vinyl to resist friction and moisture.

ORIENTAL RUG—Hand-tied rug made in India, the Near East, or China.

PERSIAN RUG—A hand-tied Oriental rug made in Iran. Examples: Kirman, Kashan, Shiraz, Tabriz.

TUFTED RUG—See Tufting.

TURKISH RUG—A hand-tied Oriental rug made in Turkey. Examples: Bergama, Ladik, Ghiordes.

TURKOMAN RUG—A hand-tied Oriental rug from Turkestan. Examples: Bokhara, Beshire and Samarkand.

VELVET RUG—A floor covering woven on a plain harness loom. Pile cut. When pile is uncut, rug is called "velvet twist."

S

SAILCLOTH—Any fabric used for sails; usually a heavy and strongly made canvas of cotton, linen, jute, polyester or nylon. Polyester now accounts for about seventy-five per cent of the annual production.

SATIN—The name originated in Zaytun (Tzu-t'ing Zaitun) China. Satin cloths were originally of silk and simulations are now made from acetate, rayon, and some of the other manmade fibers. The fabric has a very smooth, lustrous face-effect while the back of the material is dull. The satin weave and finishing of the goods provide and enhance the lustrous surface texture. Some fabric is made with a cotton-backing such as cotton-back satin or crepe satin. Satin fabrics may be light or heavy in weight, soft, crepe-like, semi-stiff in finish and hand. Acetate and rayon satins are popular in the lower price range. The major types of satin follow:

1. SATIN CREPE—It is a soft, drapy, lustrous fabric used in dress goods, formal wear, negligees, underwear, bedspreads, and draperies.

2. PANNE SATIN—Often known as "Slipper Satin," the fabric is rather stiff in hand and it finds much use in evening wear, cloaks, and bridal wear.

3. LINING SATIN—Made of panne or crepe satin fabric it is lighter in weight when compared with the so-called dress satin. Much used in coat lining, some formal wear, dress goods.

4. WASH SATIN—Can be either panne or crepe in type and is finished for laundering purposes. Chief uses are for blouses, lingerie and some dress goods.

5. UPHOLSTERY SATIN—This is the "heavyweight satin fabric" and is made with cotton back construction. Used in upholstery, drapes, curtains, and to some degree in formal evening wear.

6. SLIPPER SATIN—Interchangeable with Panne Satin, but not always correctly, this type of goods is a richly embellished material interspersed with metallic threads to enhance the motif. Jacquard motifs are used in the construction and the goods run from the conservative to the bizarre.

SATIN DAMASK—1. A heavy, rich silk cloth made on the Jacquard loom, with fancy weaves and embellishments, or in a pile construction. Used for hangings and curtains. 2. The best quality of linen damask, used for table linen.

SATIN WEAVE—One of the three basic weaves, the others being plain weave and the twill weave. All other constructions, plain or fancy, must be made from these weaves in variations, either alone or in combination. There has not been any new weave conceived since 1747 when a book of weaves was published in Berlin, Germany. The surface of satin weave cloth is almost made up entirely of warp or filling floats since the repeat of the weave each yarn of the one system passes or floats over or under all but one yarn of the opposite yarn system. Intersection points do not fall in a straight line as in twills but are separated from one another in a regular or irregular formation. Satin weaves have a host of uses—brocade, brocatelle, damask, other decorative materials, many types of dress goods, formal and evening wear apparel, etc. (See Plain Weave, Twill Weave.)

SAXONY—1. Originally a high grade coating fabric made from Saxony merino wool raised in Germany. Given a distinctive face-finish this fabric has been a favorite staple overcoating for many years, especially in the United States. 2. Name for a soft woolen cloth with fancy yarn effects and used in sports coating. 3. A highly-twisted worsted yarn used for knitting purposes.

SCHIFFLI EMBROIDERY—Originated in Switzerland and the word, Schiffli, means "boat," identifiable with the boat-shaped shuttle used in the frame. The lace effect is made by embroidering the motifs on a net ground.

SCOTTISH PLAID OR TARTAN—A coarse, durable, rugged twill woven fabric made of native wool in Scotland in color effects of the many clans in Scotland. Also obtainable in worsted and cotton fabrics, the materials come in many weights and widths.

SCRIM—1. An open mesh, plain-weave cotton cloth made from carded or combed yarns in several constructions and weights for use as bunting, buckram, curtains, etc. 2. Cheesecloth, when bleached and firmly sized, is known as Scrim. 3. A lightweight cotton sheer cloth made in doup or in plain weave with single-ply yarns. It is often made with colored checks or stripes and serves as curtaining.

SEAMLESS HOSIERY—Also known as circular-knit or fashioned hosiery; knitted circular or tubular, it is recognized by the absence of the fashion marks. The use of stretch yarns in hosiery has been the cause for the increase in demand of seamless stockings. It should be borne in mind that stretch yarns are also used in full-fashioned hosiery as well.

SECONDARY COLORS—Green, orange, and violet, each of which is obtained by the mixing of two primaries.

SEERSUCKER—Lightweight cloth made of cotton, nylon, silk, and in blends of these fibers. Two warps are used—a base warp which lies flat in goods and a warp that becomes crinkled in the goods because of chemical treatment provided for the purpose. One warp weaves "tight," while the other one weaves "slack." Much used in dress goods, bedspreads, curtains, etc. Does not need ironing after laundering. Plisse is a simulated seersucker; seersucker is durable, plisse is not.

SELVAGE—Each side edge of a woven fabric and an actual part of the warp in the goods. Usually easily distinguishable from the body of the material, other names for it are listing, self-edge, raw edge, and the British spelling is selvedge.

SERGE—One of the oldest basic terms in textiles, it now implies any smooth face cloth made with a two-up and two-down twill weave, especially pertinent to worsted serge. Made in many weights and textures, serge is made from cotton, acetate, rayon, silk, wool and in blended fabrics. The cloth is usually piece dyed. Worsted serge gives excellent service, holds the crease very well but will shine with wear because of the high twist in the yarn and compactness of the goods.

SHANTUNG—1. A silk fabric very similar to but heavier than pongee. Originally woven of wild silk in Shantung, China, now often made with synthetics or mixtures. Very popular for summer dresses and suits. 2. A cotton fabric with an elongated slub filling yarn.

SHARKSKIN—1. Worsted fabric made from a small twill color-effect weave. Very durable, it is often made with two different colored yarns to produce a sort of neutral effect. Resembling the skin of a shark, patterns include stripes, plaids, window panes, nail heads, bird's eyes, etc. 2. Summer fabric for women's wear made from acetate, nylon, rayon, etc. Has a smooth, compact surface and also used in sportswear.

SHAPE RETENTION—The ability of a durable press garment to be washed and still retain the original shape of a new garment.

SHEARING—Cutting of the fleece from a sheep with hand shears or by machine power shears, now widely used. All wool throughout the world, except California and Texas wools which are shorn twice a year, is clipped annually. The fleece should come off the animal in a solid sheet which is then wrapped into a compact bundle with the flesh side outside.

SHEPHERD'S CHECK—Also called Shepherd's Plaid, it is a small check or plaid pattern, often in black and white and fabric is made on a two-up and two-down twill, right or left hand in diagonal line effect. Made from all the major fibers, these fabrics are staples in the men's wear, women's wear, and children's wear.

SHETLAND—1. Suiting or coating cloth made wholly or partially from Shetland wool of Scotland. Known for its raised finish and appealing, soft hand, it is a favored sportswear fabric. 2. A soft knitgoods made of Shetland wool and used in outer apparel. 3. A loosely applied term for various woven or knitted fabrics, soft in hand, that do not contain Shetland wool. 4. A fabric in the family of homespun, twill, cheviot, and shetland with the latter two cloths being closely allied. Shetland has about the same properties and characteristics as cheviot but is softer in hand and more ideally suited for women's wear where it has great demand as a staple outerwear fabric.

SHETLAND WOOL—Rugged wool, ideal for cheviots, homespuns, shetlands, and tweeds, raised chiefly in Scotland and the adjacent islands.

SHOWERPROOF—Some fabrics are treated chemically and by the addition of a wax coating may be made to repel water. Cloth thus treated is more hygenic than nonporous rubber fabric since air cannot circulate through the latter.

SHOWER REPELLENCY—Sometimes referred to as a splash-resistant, the term implies fabric which is resistant to light rains or showers. The treatment is such that washing or drycleaning will gradually remove the finish-coating, thereby diminishing its effectiveness.

SHRINKAGE—The reduction in width and length, or both, that takes place in a fabric when it is washed or drycleaned. Residual shrinkage is the term used to indicate the percentage of shrinkage that occurs in the fabric at the time of its first washing. Shrinkage that may occur on each subsequent washing is the progressive shrinkage.

SHUTTLE—The boat-like device which carries the filling yarn wound on the bobbin which sets in the shuttle from a shuttle box on one side of the raceplate of the loom, through the shed, and into a shuttle box at the other side of the loom. Filling interlaces with the warp yarns to make weaving possible.

SILK—The only natural fiber that comes in a filament

form; from 300 to 1,600 yards in length as reeled from the cocoon, cultivated or wild. Some foreign names for silk include Soie (French); Seide (German); Seta (Italian); Seda (Spanish); Sholk (Russian).

SINGLE KNIT—A fabric knitted on a single needle machine. This fabric has less body, substance, and stability when compared with double knit.

SIZING—1. Application of a size mixture to warp yarn, the purpose of which is to make the yarn smoother and stronger to withstand the strain of weaving, to provide an acceptable hand in the woven gray goods, and to increase fabric weight. 2. Application of starch or other stiffeners to fabrics, garments, etc. 3. The process of determining the count or number of roving or yarn.

SKIN-SIDE COMFORT—A decided advantage of bonded fabrics in that the lining side of the fabric can be made appealing, comfortable, and pleasing when worn next to the skin irrespective of how rough, scratchy or uneven the face may happen to be.

SOIL RELEASE FINISH—Refers to one of several finishes used on durable press blends which provides for greater ease in cleaning the article. Some soil release finishes also provide resistance to soiling as well as ease of soil removal.

SOIL RETARDANTS—Various chemical compounds which are applied to fabrics, especially carpets, to enable them to resist soiling.

SPACE DYED YARN—Yarn dyed in single color or multi-color spaces along a given lineal length or yarn in either repeat type or random type patterns.

SPINNING—This final operation in yarn manufacture consists of the drawing, twisting, and the winding of the newly spun yarn onto a device such as a bobbin, spindle, tube, etc.

STRAW—Fabric made by braiding, plaiting, or weaving natural plant fibers such as stems, stalks, leaves, bark and grass. Used for making hats, bags and shoe uppers.

BAKU—Fine, lightweight, expensive straw with a dull finish. Made from fibers of buri palm along the Ceylon and Malabar coast.

BALIBUNTAL—Fine, lightweight, glossy straw obtained from unopened palm leaf stems.

LEGHORN—Finely plaited straw made from a kind of wheat grown in Tuscany, cut green and bleached, woven by hand in Italy.

MILAN—Fine, closely woven straw used in fine quality women's hats, made in Milan, Italy. Imitations must be clearly described as such.

PANAMA—Fine hand-plaited, creamy colored Toquilla straw used for men's and women's hats, made, curiously enough, primarily in Equador.

TOQUILLA—Strong, flexible fiber obtained from Jippi-Jappa leaves. Used in weaving Panama hats. No other hat should be called ''Panama'' or ''Genuine Panama.''

TUSCAN—Fine, yellow straw woven from the tops of bleached wheat stalks grown in Tuscany. Often woven in lace-like designs.

STRETCH AND RECOVERY—A very important property of knit fabric when bonded to tricot knit. It develops the ability to return quickly to its original position after stretching and being released from tension.

STRETCH WOVEN FABRICS—Originated in Austria and Germany, this type of fabric, first used in ski pants, was found to afford greater movement of the body with no loss in comfort. Stretch nylon yarns are used to provide the action and ''give'' or ''stretch'' needed at the hips, knees and in the seat area for increased comfort to the wearer. Stretch yarn is used in the warp of a warp stretch fabric while the filling may be worsted, nylon, spun rayon or cotton. Stretch yarns can be used in the filling in fabrics, as well as to provide stretch and comfort in pajamas, shirtings, sportswear, undergarments, etc., essential for the elbow and shoulder areas. Stretch woven fabrics present very good surface texture, afford comfort, are durable, and moisture absorptive. A garment made of stretch yarns will return to its original state on release from tension.

STRETCH YARNS—Made of continuous filaments, they are modifications of these filaments in that the filaments do not lie parallel to one another. Fabrics made of these yarns have greater covering power and are softer than materials made from untreated filament yarns.

STRIE—Said of a cloth which has irregular stripes or streaks of practically the same color in the background.

SUEDE FABRIC—1. Woven or knitted cloth made from the major textile fibers and finished to resemble suede leather. Used for cleaning cloths, gloves, linings, sport coats, etc. 2. Some sheeting may be napped on the one side to simulate suede leather.

SUPIMA*—Certification mark which is registered property of the SuPima Association of America. Usage of the mark is controlled by means of a licensing agreement with the Association, and the mark can be applied only to wearing apparel and textile products made entirely of Southwestern extra long staple cotton fiber grown by members of the Association. About 4,000 members grow this irrigated cotton fiber from controlled seed in Arizona, New Mexico, Texas, and California. The certification mark is written ''SuPima.''

SURAH—A soft, twill-woven silk or rayon, often made in plaid effects. Surah prints are popular at times. If made of some fiber other than silk, the fiber content must be declared. Uses include neckwear, mufflers, blouses, and dress goods. Named for Surah, India.

SWANSDOWN—Cotton material made with a modified five-end satin weave, white or cream shades and is given a heavy napped finish.

SWATCH—In the trade, any small sample of material is often referred to by this name. Swatches are used for inspection, comparison, construction, color, finish and sales purposes.

SWISS—A fine, sheer cotton fabric which may be plain, dotted, or figured. This crisp, stiff cloth is often called dotted swiss. Used for dress goods, wedding apparel, curtains, etc. The term ''SWISS'' in textiles as applied to a

303

fabric logically and properly identifies fabrics made in Switzerland. The domestic fabric is known as domestic dotted swiss, etc.

SWISS BATISTE—A sheer, opaque fabric noted for its high luster which is accompanied by special finishing and the use of special grades of long-staple cotton and Swiss mercerization.

T

TAFFETA—A fine plain-weave fabric smooth on both sides, usually with a sheen on its surface. Named for Persian fabric taftan. May be solid colored or printed, or woven in such a way that the colors seem "changeable." Used for dresses, blouses, suits. Originally of silk, now often made of synthetic fibers. There are several taffeta classifications, such as: .

ANTIQUE TAFFETA—A plain-weave, stiff finished fabric of douppioni silk or synthetic fibers made to resemble the beautiful fabrics of the 18th century. When yarn dyed with two colors, an iridescent effect is produced.

FAILLE TAFFETA—Taffeta woven with a pronounced cross-wise rib.

MOIRE TAFFETA—Rayon or silk taffeta fabric with moire pattern. In acetate, moire can be fused so it is permanent.

PAPER TAFFETA—Lightweight taffeta treated to have a crisp paper–like finish.

TISSUE TAFFETA—Very light-weight transparent taffeta.

TAMBOUR—1. A term which signifies work done on the embroidery machine in which the tambour stitch has been used. This stitch produces a pattern of straight ridges which cross each other in every direction at right or acute angles. 2. Tambour is also a variety of Limerick lace that is made in Ireland. 3. Embroidery frame, round.

TAPESTRY—Originally ornamental Oriental embroideries in which colored threads of wool, gold, silk or silver were interspersed for adornment. At present tapestry, for the most part, is power-loomed on dobby looms and Jacquard looms. Hand woven tapestry is still made, of course, and in centers which were founded centuries ago. Some distinctive tapestry designs or motifs are linked with names such as Arras, Aubusson, Beauvais, Brussels, Gobelin, Gothic, Lille, Savonnerie and Verdures.

TARLATAN—Thick or thin scrim or muslin that is heavily starched. Net-like in appearance, this coarse, low-texture fabric finds use in coat lining, dresses, fruit packing, millinery, waist–banding, etc.

TARTAN—Wool, worsted or cotton cloth made in plain weave or in a two-up and two-down twill weave. Associated with Scottish clans, the fabric originated in Spain and was called tiritana. This multi-colored fabric may be conventional or bizarre when made in variations of color effects. The Scottish kilt is known to everyone. Other uses include blankets, cap cloth, dress goods, neckwear, ribbon, shirting, sportscoats, trews or trousers.

TATTERSAL—A heavy, fancy woolen vesting of "loud appearance." Checks, bold effects and gaudy color combinations are used in the material which is often used for some suiting and overcoating, as well. Named for the famous mart for thoroughbred and racing stock in London.

TEAR STRENGTH—The force necessary to tear a fabric, usually expressed in pounds or in grams.

TEBELIZED*—A crush-resistant finish applied to many fabrics, including pile fabrics, and giving material the power to resist creasing, mussing and crushing as well as to recover from wrinkling during wear. The fabric remains the same after washing. The finish is a registered trademark product of Tootal, Broadhurst & Lee Company, Ltd.

TENACITY—The breaking strength of a fiber, filament, yarn, cord, etc., expressed in force per unit yarn number.

TERRY CLOTH—This cloth has uncut loops on both sides of the fabric. Woven on a dobby loom with Terry arrangement, various sizes of yarns are used in the construction. Terry is also made on a Jacquard loom to form interesting motifs. It may be yarn-dyed in different colors to form attractive patterns. It is bleached, piece-dyed, and even printed for beachwear and bathrobes, etc. Also called Turkish toweling.

TERTIARY COLORS—Olive, citron, russet, each of which is obtained by the mixing of two secondary colors.

THREAD—Thread is made from yarn but yarn is not made from thread. It is a highly specialized type of yarn used for some definite purpose such as sewing, basting, embroidery work. Thread is plied to give it added strength when it is being manipulated. Three-ply and six-ply thread are two of the common threads in use today.

THREAD COUNT—1. The actual number of warp ends and filling picks per inch in a woven cloth. Texture is another name for this term. 2. In knitted fabric, thread count implies the number of wales or ribs, and the courses per inch.

TICKING—Compactly woven cotton cloth used for containers, covers for mattresses and pillows, sportswear (hickory stripes), institution fabric, and work clothes. It is a striped cloth, usually white background with blue or brown stripes in the motif.

TISSER—French term which means "to weave." "Tisseur" is a weaver of cloth. "Tissu" is the French word for fabric.

TISSUE—The lightweight versions of fabrics such as batiste, chambray, crepe, dimity, faille, gingham, organdy, taffeta, voile, etc., are known by this term. 2. Curtains with clipspot motifs are also called tissue. 3. Damask, brocade, brocatelle, and some other Jacquard cloths in which metallic threads are interspersed for enhancement of the goods use this term.

TOILE—1. General term used in France to designate vegetable fiber cloths made on plain or twill weaves, especially hemp and linen materials. 2. Name given to tissue goods in which metallic threads are used to enhance the pattern-cloth, of gold, silver, copper, etc. 3. A type of handmade lace in which the body part of the pattern simulates woven cloth. 4. The warp ends which form the ground in pile fabrics. 5. Fine cretonne with scenic designs printed in one color. 6. Some sheer cotton and linen materials are called toile.

TOWELING—General term for bird's eye, crash, damask, glass, honey-comb, huck, huckabank, twill, Turkish or terry, fancy, novelty, and guest towelings. Many of these cloths have colored or fancy borders or edges; some of them are often union fabrics. All toweling has property of good absorption.

TRANSPARENT VELVET—A clear-cut warp pile fabric which comes in several grades and types; good qualities are expensive. Fabric drapes well, is durable, drycleans neatly, but has tendency to crush. Crush resistants, however, are now applied. Ideal for evening wear.

TREE BARK—A rippled or wavy effect which sometimes appears on a bonded fabric only when it is stretched in the horizontal direction or width-wise. It is caused by bias tensions which happen when two distorted or "skewed" fabrics are bonded.

TRIACETATE—The base for this fiber is cellulose acetate. The term "triacetate" may be used to serve as a generic description of the fiber.

TRICOT—A type of warp knitted fabric which has a thin texture since it is made from very fine yarn. The French verb tricoter, means "to knit."

TRIPLE SHEER—A tightly woven, flat surface-effect cloth which gives the impression of being near sheer but is practically opaque.

TROPICAL CLOTHS—Lightweight fabrics used for warm weather wear. They have a clear finish, and high-twist yarns are used to make up for the lack of weight and to provide good service to the consumer. Fibers used include cotton, worsted, acetate, rayon, cotton and mohair, cotton and worsted; and blended fabrics of worsted with nylon or polyester fibers are very popular in the trade. See Palm Beach.

TUFTED FABRIC—A fabric decorated with fluffy tufts of soft twist, multiple-ply cotton yarns. Some are loom-woven but the majority have the tufts inserted and cut by machine in a previously woven fabric, such as muslin sheeting, lightweight duck, etc. The tufts may be intermittently spaced giving the type called candlewick, or arranged closely in continuous lines giving the type called chenille. The patterns vary from simple line effects to elaborate designs. Used for bedspreads, robes, bathmats, stuffed toys, etc.

TUFTED RUG—A rug of scatter or room size, in which yarn is drawn from the face through backing (hemp, jute, etc.) and then through to the face again with long loops left on the face which may be cut or uncut. A shrinkage treatment then contracts the backing so that the rug yarn is held in place. Sometimes a rubber compound is applied to the under side of the backing to help to hold the yarn and to keep the rug from sliding on the floor. Tufted rugs are in no sense woven rugs where the pile is interlocked, the cost of manufacture is higher, and the result provides a very durable rug.

TULLE—Fine, very lightweight, machine-made net in which small mesh effects, usually hexagonal in shape, are seen. Uses include ballet costumes, bridal veils, dress goods, formal gowns, overdraping effects. This cool, dressy, delicate fabric is difficult to launder.

TUSSAH—Name for wild silk raised anywhere in the world. Compared with cultivated or true silk, it is more uneven, coarser and stronger and comes in shades of ecru through brown. Many fabrics of this fiber are known merely as Tussah. Difficult to dye or bleach, it finds much use in pongee and shantung.

TWEED—A rough, irregular, soft and flexible, unfinished shaggy woolen named for the Tweed River which separates England from Scotland. One of the oldest and most popular outerwear fabrics used today, it is made of a two-and-two twill weave, right-hand or left-hand in structure. The term is now rather loosely given to several types of town-and-country fabrics. Outstanding tweeds include Bannockburn, English, Harris, Irish, Linton, Manx, Scotch. Donegal, often called tweed, is actually a homespun cloth since it is made from the plain weave, a one-up and one-down structure. Uses of tweed include cap cloth, all types of coatings and ensembles, sportswear, suitings, etc.

TWILL WEAVE—Identified by the diagonal lines in the goods. It is one of the three basic weaves, the others being plain and satin. All weaves, either simple, elaborate or complex, are derived from these three weaves.

U

UMBRELLA CLOTH—Also known as Gloria Goods, the original fabric was made of cotton warp and silk filling. It is somewhat on the order of taffeta but is more rugged, stiffer, and firmer in body. The fabric today is made also with rayon and/or nylon; a water repellent material.

UNBLEACHED—Many fabrics, especially cottons, in the trade come in an unbleached or natural condition. Materials of this type have a sort of "creamy" or somewhat "dirty" white color cast and much foreign matter is often seen in them—burrs, nubs, specks, et al. These fabrics are stronger than full-bleached fabrics. Examples of unbleached goods include canvas, duck, unbleached muslin, Osnaburg, cretonne, sheeting, some toweling (cotton and linen), and some moleskin and comparable fabric used for pocket lining.

UNCUT PILE FABRICS—Fabrics produced by weaving the yarn that is intended to be the pile stock over wires that have no cutting edge. The result of this is that when the wires are withdrawn, a looped effect appears on the surface of the cloth. Uncut velvet is made in this manner.

UNIFORM CLOTH—A family of serviceable woolen cloth on the general order of kerseys and flannels as the most important. Colors are blue, gray, khaki, brown and mixed effects. The cloth is used as uniform material for military, naval, police, fire, postal, railway, bus, public service, chauffeurs, regal livery and other public and

305

private groups. As most of these cloths are furnished under certain approved and decreed specifications, according to contract, a very exact demand is made on the goods to meet requirements.

UNION CLOTH—1. English material of cotton warp and reused, remanufactured or shoddy-type filling. The cloth is given much napping to improve its looks. Used in overcoating trade. 2. Woolens and worsteds which have textile fibers from other fiber kingdoms in them, e.g., a fabric with a cotton warp and a worsted filling is classed as a union. 3. Name for some fabrics in which manmade fibers are used in the content, in varying percentages. The union method of dyeing is resorted to in coloring the materials. Union cloths are used in dress goods, general decorative fabrics, towelings, sportswear, etc.

UNION DAMASK—Drapery fabric made with cotton or linen warp and woolen or worsted fillings. Satin weave figures are used over a satin background. The material is used extensively for draperies, hangings, and upholstery.

UPHOLSTERY VELVET—A widecut or uncut heavy-weight velvet which appears in plain or pattern effects. Used in draperies and upholstery.

V

VELOUR—1. A term loosely applied to cut pile cloths in general; also to fabrics with a fine raised finish. 2. A cut pile cotton fabric comparable with cotton velvet but with a greater and denser pile. 3. A staple, high grade woolen fabric which has a close, fine, dense, erect, and even nap which provides a soft, pleasing hand. 4. A popular knit fabric similar to woven velour in properties, especially in hand. Ideal for men's, women's and children's wear. Registered Tradenames include Lucerne (Dan River Inc.).

VELVET—A warp pile cloth in which a succession of rows of short cut pile stand so close together as to give an even, uniform surface; appealing in look and with soft hand. First made of all silk, many major fibers are now used in the constructions. When the pile is more than one-eighth of an inch in height the cloth is then called plush.

  BAGHEERA—Fine, uncut-pile piece-dyed velvet with a roughish surface that makes it crush-resistant. Used for gowns and evening wraps.

  CHIFFON VELVET—Lightweight, soft, silk velvet with cut pile. Closer woven than transparent velvet. Used for dresses, suits, evening clothes.

  CISELE VELVET—A velvet with a pattern formed by contrast in cut and uncut loops.

  LYONS VELVET—A stiff, erect, thick piled velvet; made of silk pile and cotton or rayon back. When made of 100% synthetic fibers, the fabric is called Lyons-type velvet.

  PANNE VELVET—Silk or synthetic velvet with a finish in which the pile is flattened and laid in one direction. Lustrous and lightweight. From the French word for plush.

  TRANSPARENT VELVET—Lightweight, soft, draping velvet made of silk or rayon back with a rayon pile.

VELVETEEN—A filling pile cloth in which the pile is made by cutting an extra set of filling yarns. This low-pile

fabric is known as a "cotton-velvet." Comes in all colors, is mercerized and has a durable texture. This strong fabric can be laundered, will provide warmth and tailors rather well. Used in children's wear, coats, dresses, hangings, suitings, etc.

VOILE—Combed yarn, high-twist cotton staple fabric also made from some other fibers at present. There are five types of voile—pique, seed, shadow, stripe, and splash.

W

WAFFLE CLOTH—Fabric with a characteristic honeycomb weave. When made in cotton, it is called waffle pique. Used for coatings, draperies, dresses, toweling. Same as honeycomb cloth.

WALE—1. Chain loops that run lengthwise in knit fabric; course in knit cloth runs in horizontal direction. 2. Ribs in knit fabric. 3. Ribs or "cords" observed in corduroy fabric; these may be wide or when fine in the fabric they are called pinwales.

WARP—The yarns which run vertically or lengthwise in woven goods.

WASHABLE—Materials that will not fade or shrink during washing or laundering. Labels should be read by the consumer to assure proper results. Do not confuse with "wash-and-wear"

WASH-AND-WEAR—Applied to a garment it is one that can be washed by hand or in a washing machine at the warm water setting. In common usage, drip-dried garments do not normally retain creases or pleats but do recover sufficiently from wrinkles to need little, if any ironing. Durable press, however, does retain creases and pleats. Washing and drying conditions should always be specified on the so-called wash-and-wear garments.

WASH-FAST—A term that seems to cause considerable confusion, especially among consumers. The term is applied, rather loosely at times, to fabrics or garments which can be washed and laundered. Much depends on the properties of the article before the term should be applied. All labels or tags should be carefully read and directions for washing followed as given.

WATER-REPELLENT—Ability of a fabric to resist penetration by water, under certain conditions. Various types of tests are used and these are conducted on samples before and after subjection to standard washing and drycleaning tests. Immersion, spray, spot, and hydrostatic methods may be used. Shower-resistant, rain-resistant, and waterproof factors are interpreted from the results of the testing.

WATER RESISTANT—Fabric treated chemically to resist water or it may be given a "wax-coating treatment" to make it repellent. Not to be confused with water-repellent; the terms, however, are often used interchangeably.

WEAR TESTING—Testing fabrics for abrasion, flexibility, resiliency, washing, crushing, crease-retention, crease-resistance by observation of the garment through actual wear.

WEAVE, WEAVING—The process of forming a fabric on a loom by interlacing the warp (lengthwise yarns) and the filling (crosswise yarns) with each other. Filling is fed into the goods from cones, filling bobbins or quills which carry the filling picks through the shed of the loom. Filling may also be inserted into the material without the use of a shuttle, as in the case of a shuttleless loom. The three basic weaves are Plain, Twill, and Satin. All other weaves, no matter how intricate, employ one or more of these basic weaves in their composition. There are many variations on the basic principles which make different types of fabric surfaces and fabric strengths.

WEFT—The crosswise or filling pick yarns in a woven cloth; popular in British Isles and only in hand weaving circles in the United States.

WEIGHTED SILK—Sometimes metallic salts are used in the dyeing and finishing of silk to increase the weight and draping quality—and thus to make it look more expensive. Over-weighting causes deterioration of the fabric. In the United States only a ten per cent weighting is permitted by the Federal Trade Commission for a silk fabric to qualify as a "pure dyed silk." In the case of black a fifteen per cent weighting is allowed for qualification.

WELT—1. A strip of material seamed to a pocket opening as a finishing as well as a strengthening device. 2. A raised or swelled lap or seam. 3. A covered cord or ornamental strip sewed on a border or along a seam. 4. In knitting, it is flat-knitted separately and then joined to the fabric by looping or hand knitting, as the heel to the stocking. 5. A ribbed piece of knit goods used in forming the end of a sleeve or sock to prevent rolling or raveling.

WHIPCORD—A steep twill fabric of the gabardine-cavalry twill group which has a very pronounced twill or diagonal on the face of the goods. Of compact texture, the fabric finds use in dress woolens and worsteds, cotton uniform cloth, bathing trunks, livery cloth, public utility uniforms, suitings, topcoats, and many types of uniforms used in many areas.

WHITE GOODS—A very broad term which implies any goods bleached and finished in the white condition. Some of the cotton white goods are muslin, cambric, dimity, lawn, longcloth, organdy, voile, and so on. Tub or washable silks are sometimes classed as white goods, as well as some of the lightweight crepe or sheer woolen or worsted dress goods materials.

"WHITE-ON-WHITE"—Some fabrics, such as men's shirtings of broadcloth, poplin, madras, etc., are made on a dobby or Jacquard loom so that white motifs will appear on a white background. The madras shirting in this category would have the usual stripe effect with the "two-tone" white pattern set between these colored stripes. Some dress goods for summer wear also have the effect.

WOOF—Comes from the Anglo-Saxon "owef." It is another name for warp or warp yarn but sometimes, chiefly in advertising textiles, the word has been used to imply filling yarn and made to interchange with the other term, weft. It is apparently much safer to use the terms warp and

filling in this country; in the carpet trade and in hand weaving, however, weft is used instead of the American term, filling.

WOOLENS—Cloth made from woolen yarn but not always 100 per cent wool in content. The average woolen has a rather fuzzy surface, does not shine with wear, may hold the crease well, has nap and in the majority of cases, is dyed. Woolen finish is rather easily recognized on fabrics to determine the difference between this cloth and a worsted material.

WOOL PRODUCTS LABELING ACT OF 1939, DEFINITIONS USED IN THE—This Act, effective July 15, 1941, stipulates the following definitions under Section 2, page 21, of this Act:
1. The term "wool" means the fiber from the fleeces of the sheep or lamb, or hair of the Angora or Cashmere goat (and may include the so-called specialty fibers from the hair of the camel, alpaca, llama, and vicuna) which has never been reclaimed from any woven or felted wool product.
2. The term "reprocessed wool" means the resulting fiber when wool has been woven or felted into a wool product which, without ever having been utilized in any way by the ultimate consumer, subsequently has been made into a fibrous state.
3. The term "reused wool" means the resulting fiber when wool or reprocessed wool has been spun, woven, knitted, or felted into a wool product which, after having been used in any way by the ultimate consumer, subsequently has been made into a fibrous state.

WORSTEDS—A wide range of fabrics are made from worsted yarn and are compactly made from smooth, uniform, well-twisted yarns. Little finishing is necessary in these clear surface materials. Plain or fancy weaves are used and the cloth is usually yarn-dyed but piece-dyed fabrics are also popular. Worsted blends are much the vogue today since the major fibers used, nylon and polyester, provide very good service to the consumer. Ideal for summer wear by men and women, some of the fabrics in this fabric family include plain weave worsted, dress goods, gabardine, crepe, serge, tropical, etc. See Tropical Cloths.

WRINKLE RECOVERY—Some fabrics are able to eliminate wrinkles because of their own resilience. Wool is the best in this group of cloths in wrinkle recovery and thermoplastic manmade fibers and some chemically-treated cottons will recover well. Laboratory tests are now made to determine the amount of degree a fabric will recover from wrinkling.

Z

ZIBELINE—Used for cloakings, coats, and capes in women's wear. The cloth is made from cross-bred yarns and the fabric is strongly colored. Stripings, sometimes noted in the cloth, work in very well with the construction and appearance of the finished garment. The finish is a highly raised type, lustrous and the nap is long and lies in the one direction. The cloth may or may not be given a soft finish and feel.

INDEX